Antonio Gramsci
and the Origins of Italian Communism

Antonio Gramsci
and the Origins of Italian Communism

JOHN M. CAMMETT

1967
Stanford University Press
Stanford, California

Stanford University Press
Stanford, California
© 1967 by the Board of Trustees of the
Leland Stanford Junior University
Printed in the United States of America
L.C. 66-22983

To Dee and Lisa

Preface

This work was begun at Columbia University as a doctoral dissertation under the guidance of Professor Shepard B. Clough. I am deeply grateful to him for his helpful criticism, his encouragement, and his warmth and humanity, qualities that are perhaps not so prevalent in the academic community as they ought to be. At the dissertation stage, much useful criticism was also provided by Professors René Albrecht-Carrié, Michael Florinsky, Peter Gay, and the late Garrett Mattingly. The generosity of the Institute of Italian Culture, with its award of an Italian Government Fellowship, allowed me to complete the first cycle of my research in Italy. In 1960, my dissertation was honored by the Society for Italian Historical Studies as the best unpublished manuscript of that year in Italian history. I should like to thank the Society for the encouragement that this award gave me as a younger scholar only recently embarked on an academic career.

In the 1950's, too little research had been done, and too little documentation was available, to make an informative book on Gramsci possible; that time did not come until the 1960's. I am therefore profoundly grateful to the Research Council of Rutgers University, which, by awarding me a Summer Fellowship in 1964, made it possible for me to return to Italy, become acquainted with some of the scholars most active in Gramsci, and purchase the books, articles, and microfilm necessary to bring my own work on Gramsci up to date. While in Rome, I was able to use the facilities of the Istituto Gramsci, and I am most grateful for the help and encouragement of its sincere and dedicated staff—especially Signor Franco Ferri, the Istituto's director, and Signora Elsa Fubini, the editor of the Einaudi edition of Gramsci's *Opere*.

As a result of my further research, I have greatly expanded and almost entirely rewritten the original manuscript. Whatever success I have had in this process would not have been possible without the aid and encouragement of many people. I am especially grateful to four of my friends and colleagues in the Rutgers University Department of History: Professors Eugene D. Genovese, Herbert H. Rowen, Traian Stoianovich, and Warren I. Susman. Their friendly encouragement and sometimes relentless criticism were essential stimuli for me.

I also extend thanks for the helpful suggestions, stimulating discussions, and positive criticism of Professors Julius Briller of the Juilliard School of Music, Norman Dain of Rutgers University in Newark, A. William Salomone of the University of Rochester, Richard A. Webster of the University of California at Berkeley, and John Weiss of Wayne State University. My debt to Professor William J. Bossenbrook of Wayne State University goes deeper; it was his superbly effective teaching that first drew me to the study of history. Generous help with other problems in the manuscript was unstintingly given by Dr. Doris Miller. The support and spirited criticism of my wife, Doris de Podestà Cammett, was also indispensable to the completion of this work.

Finally, I must add the traditional disclaimer freeing anyone else of responsibility for the shortcomings of this work and accepting them as my own. In my case, the responsibility extends to all translations from the Italian in the text.

J.M.C.

Contents

Abbreviations

ACT   Alleanza Cooperativa Torinese (Turin Cooperative Alliance). Formed in 1899 by merging the Railway Workers' Cooperative and the AGO.

AGO   Associazione Generale degli Operai di Torino (Turin Workers' General Association). A cooperative and mutual-aid society founded in 1850.

CGL   Confederazione Generale del Lavoro (General Confederation of Labor). A national association of trade unions and workers' cooperatives founded in 1906. There was a close liaison between the CGL and the Italian Socialist Party.

CPSU   Communist Party of the Soviet Union.

ECCI   Executive Committee of the Communist International.

FGS   Federazione Giovanile Socialista (Socialist Youth Federation, or Young Socialists).

Fiom   Federazione Impiegati Operai Metallurgici (Federation of Metallurgical Workers and Employees). Founded in 1901, the Fiom was the most active and progressive labor union in Turin.

PCI   Partito Comunista Italiano (Italian Communist Party).

PPI   Partito Popolare Italiano (Italian Popular Party). The Catholic political party.

PSI   Partito Socialista Italiano (Italian Socialist Party).

Introduction

In 1947, ten years after his death, Antonio Gramsci was awarded the Viareggio Prize in literature for his "Letters from Prison" (Lettere dal Carcere). Between 1948 and 1951, Gramsci's "Prison Notebooks" (Quaderni del Carcere) were also published. These writings convey such humanity and intelligence that the man's relative obscurity up to that time, even in Italy, is surprising—especially since he helped found the Italian Communist Party in 1921, and was its recognized leader at the time of his arrest in November 1926. Since 1947, however, Gramsci's reputation as a political leader, humanist, and thinker has been established. In Italy the literature of Gramsciana is already extensive; in the English-speaking countries, too, there is a growing interest in Gramsci's ideas, though scholars have done little to satisfy this interest.

Only two general works with any scholarly pretensions have appeared in Italy: those by Giuseppe Tamburrano (1963) and Salvatore Francesco Romano (1965). The former is somewhat polemical, and is not successful as a balanced exposition of Gramsci's life and thought; the latter, while adequate and often perceptive concerning the young Gramsci up to 1921, does not even attempt to deal with the "Quaderni del Carcere," and devotes only a few pages to Gramsci's role in the Italian Communist Party. Giansiro Ferrata's enlightening introduction to the latest anthology of Gramsci's work (1964) is surely an indication that Italian scholars—whose recent work has been so admirable in many other fields of contemporary Italian history—will soon present us with more adequate studies of this extraordinary man and his accomplishments. Meanwhile we must agree with the young French scholar Robert Paris that it is "difficult to introduce or 'translate' an author like Gramsci in the absence of solid studies done in his native land."

This work is not intended as a full-scale biography—though it includes biographical data for every phase of Gramsci's life—for even now only the basic spadework has been done to make such a biography possible, and many lacunae remain. It has a more limited goal: to expound and analyze Gramsci's chief ideas in the fields of politics and history during the two periods of his greatest creativity: first, as the leader in 1919–20 of the Ordine Nuovo movement in Turin; second, as the principal figure of Italian Communism, beginning with his rise to leadership in the Italian Communist Party in 1923 and ending with the composition of his "Prison Notebooks," written for the most part from 1929 to 1934.

Even with these limitations, and with the wealth of material now becoming available, a study of this sort poses problems. In Part I, the problem was to discover, so far as possible, the impact of Gramsci's Sardinian boyhood and his youth in Turin, first as a student at the University and later as a Socialist convert and labor organizer, on his mature ideas. In Part II, a major task was selecting and organizing the most important ideas from the more than 200 articles that Gramsci wrote for *Ordine nuovo* in the two years of its publication, material that for all its richness was written *alla giornata* and not intended as a permanent contribution to the history of ideas. In Part III, which traces Gramsci's rise to a dominant position in the Italian Communist Party, the problem was to show how Gramsci worked out a path of his own between Amadeo Bordiga's left-wing extremism and the Moscow-centered admonitions of the Comintern.

Perhaps the most difficult task of all was choosing, in Part IV, a suitable approach to the tremendous amount of material in the "Prison Notebooks," which would require a library of analysis to plumb their depths. In the end it seemed to me best to confine my discussion to Gramsci's ultimate views on two major problems of political theory and modern Italian history that had engaged him from the beginning, namely the nature and tasks of the political party, and the historical role of Italian intellectuals. Much of the other writing in the notebooks is interesting, and some of it is profound; but it is on these two topics above all that Gramsci lavished the hard-won wisdom of his political career.

Part I

The Early Years

1. Prelude in Sardinia

Ho conosciuto quasi sempre solo l'as-
petto piu' brutale della vita e me la
sono sempre cavata, bene o male.

—Gramsci, October 3, 1932

During his long years of imprisonment, Antonio Gramsci often
thought about writing the story of his life. With characteristic modesty, he asked himself what might justify an autobiography. Pride, he
felt, was no justification: the proud man's implicit assumption that
his life is different from other lives may render his autobiography
valueless to the reader. On the other hand, a "political" autobiography might be justified: "We know that any man's life is similar to a
thousand others, but that by 'accident' it has taken a path that the
thousand others could not and in fact did not take." An autobiography can suggest the processes that have led to the "accident" and
determined the direction of the writer's life, and in so doing can
"help other men to develop in certain ways and in certain directions."[1]

Unfortunately, Gramsci never wrote an autobiography, but his emphasis on "accidents" has definite roots in his own experience. His
life was deeply influenced by several accidents or chance events—
some unfortunate, some propitious. Salvatore Francesco Romano has
recently classed Gramsci among the few political leaders whose personal and intellectual experiences have decisively affected the historical relevance of their thought and actions.[2]

Gramsci was born on January 22, 1891, in Ales, a small agricultural center on the island of Sardinia. His father, Francesco, was
descended on his father's side from Albanians who had come to Italy
from Epirus in 1821, during the Greek war for independence,[3] and
on his mother's side from one of the many Italo-Spanish families in

southern Italy. Antonio's mother, Giuseppina Marcias, was of pure Sardinian origin.[4]

Gramsci's grandfather, Gennaro Gramsci, had been a colonel in the Bourbon gendarmerie of the old Kingdom of the Two Sicilies.[5] Francesco, Antonio's father, was born at Gaeta, on the mainland of Italy, in 1860. After completing high school, he was sent to Sardinia as a lower-echelon clerk in the state bureaucracy. Antonio's mother was related to the Corrias family, one of the more respected families in her part of Sardinia. Despite his background, Francesco Gramsci seems to have been a rather ineffectual and unsuccessful man. As Antonio wrote many years later:

My father and my brothers are always busy preparing mountains of projects and hypotheses. But then they forget the essential thing, and all their projects fail. . . . They thought they had great capacities for commercial affairs, and were forever constructing great castles in the air and criticizing other Sardinians for their lack of initiative. Naturally nothing ever came of their ventures, and it was always someone else's fault, as though the someone else had not previously existed and should not have been taken into consideration from the outset.[6]

From 1894 to 1897 the family lived at Sorgono, a town in central Sardinia near the Gennargentu Mountains, where Gramsci and his sisters were sent to a nursery school maintained by a religious order. It was in this period that Antonio's first great "accident" occurred. When he was four years old, he fell from the arms of a servant and down a steep flight of stairs. The family gave him up for dead, and even prepared a little casket and shroud. His aunt, however, took care to anoint his feet with oil from a lamp dedicated to the Madonna, and to this treatment she afterward attributed his recovery.[7] Antonio survived, but at the cost of permanently poor health and a hunched back. Certain psychological effects inevitably followed: one of these was his first awareness of his own "existence as a physical person" (as he delicately put it later).[8]

In 1897, while working as a clerk in the land office at Sorgono, Francesco was arrested for an "administrative irregularity" and condemned to five years' imprisonment.[9] His wife was left with the terrible burden of raising the seven children (Antonio was the fourth child and the second son). Soon afterward, the Gramscis moved to Ghilarza, a somewhat larger town near the railroad between Cagliari and Sassari, the two principal cities of Sardinia. It seems to have been an especially unhealthy place, infested with malaria and having no sewers or municipal water supply.[10] The Gramsci house had no running water, no toilet facilities, and no illumination except a single candle that Gramsci's mother needed for her nightly work as a seamstress.[11] It was a hard life, and Gramsci was always grateful to his mother for pulling them through: "If she had been another woman, who knows what disastrous end we might all have come to as children? Perhaps none of us would be alive today."[12]

Like all Sardinians, wrote Gramsci, his mother felt deeply about family ties and responsibilities,[13] and she was strong-willed—*Corrias, coriazzu* ("A Corrias is tough"), as Gramsci punned in Sardinian.[14] She was also intelligent, witty, and a good storyteller. Antonio appreciated these qualities in his mother, and his later alienation from his origins never prevented him from expressing his gratitude to her.

You can't imagine how many incidents I remember in which you always appear as a beneficent force, full of interest in us. . . . Since all our memories of you are of goodness and strength, that strength that you gave in bringing us up, you have gained the only true paradise, which for a mother, I think, is in the hearts of her children.[15]

The attentions of such a mother were of inestimable value to the Gramsci children when they began to attend school. Indeed, wrote Antonio, "our family had a certain fame in the schools of Ghilarza."[16] Antonio and his younger sister Teresina were especially avid readers. He reminded her in 1930 of how "fanatical we were about reading and writing,"[17] and Teresina later recalled that a lady of the town bequeathed to Antonio a large collection of books, including *Robinson Crusoe* and *Uncle Tom's Cabin*.[18] Perhaps the boy was too confident of his abilities: at the end of his second year in elementary school, at the age of nine, he applied for permission to take the "leaving examinations" (*esami di proscioglimento*), which were normally taken at the end of the third year (and which in those days were the essential determinant of the right to vote). Antonio wanted to skip to the fourth year of elementary school:[19] "I was sure I could do this, but when I appeared before the principal to present my formal request, I was brusquely asked the question: 'But do you know the eighty-four articles of the Statute?' I hadn't even thought of these articles. I had merely studied the explanation of the 'rights and duties of the citizen' in the textbook."[20] Gramsci here passed this episode off as a joke, but we know from an article he wrote in 1915 that it had considerable importance for him: "And the poor boy, crushed by that question, began to tremble. Grief-stricken, he returned home and gave up all thoughts of taking the examination at that time."[21]

In later years Gramsci was frequently angered by the misuse of authority, especially by educators to discourage students' enthusiasm and ambition.

Antonio's early education was not confined to formal schooling. *Robinson Crusoe,* and Salgari's romantic novels about the naval battles of the corsairs, were his favorite reading as a child.[22] In addition, he had a deep love of nature, and especially of animals, which he saw simultaneously as they were in real life and in his imagination. Of such a mixture—direct experience and the fabulous—are the charming stories of animals that he wrote for his children while in prison.[23] There was a shop window in Turin, containing a display of both stuffed and live birds, which was a favorite stopping place for Gramsci. Leonida Répaci, who knew Gramsci in the days of Ordine Nuovo, tells us: "He had a special liking for birds. I can't forget Gramsci's eyes, kindly and filled with a soft reverie, when he looked at those living and dead creatures."[24] "As a boy," Gramsci recalled, "I raised many birds and other animals—falcons, barn owls, cuckoos, magpies, crows, goldfinches, canaries, chaffinches, swallows ... also a little snake, a weasel, and some hedgehogs and turtles."[25]

In view of the mature Gramsci's intellectual tastes and interests, mainly in philosophy, history, literature, and languages, it is surprising that as a young boy he seemed especially drawn to mathematics and the sciences.[26] The results of his esami di proscioglimento, which he finally took on July 24, 1901, show a definite superiority in mathematics. He received the highest possible grade, 10, in "arithmetic, theoretical and practical"; his other grades were 9 in Italian composition, dictation and reading, history, geography, and the "rights and duties of the citizen," and 8 in calligraphy.[27]

This promising beginning was cut short by another bitter "accident." Antonio's father decided that the family could not afford to send the boy to the *ginnasio* (roughly, junior high school) at Santu Lussurgiu, eleven miles away. As the second son, Antonio was responsible by tradition for the well-being of the women of the family; accordingly, the eleven-year-old child was sent to work in his father's land office.[28] He worked ten hours a day, with only half a day off each week, for a salary of nine lire a month (less than $2.00 at the then rate of exchange). His income meant an extra two pounds of bread a day for his family.[29]

Antonio was disappointed and resentful at the loss of what then appeared to be his only chance to overcome his limited prospects and his physical handicap. He later observed, "Adults can no longer remember when they were children; hence they find it hard to understand the way of thinking and reactions that develop in the minds of the children they deal with."[30] On another occasion, and with reference to the same event, Gramsci remarked that he had "almost always known only the most brutal aspect of life."[31]

It is remarkable that in Gramsci's entire correspondence—and nearly a thousand pages of his letters have now been published—he never has a word of praise, or of reproval, for his father, or gives any direct indication of his feelings for the man. Gramsci later remembered relations between adults and children in Sardinia as being generally brutal. One day, as a boy, he accompanied a woman of Ghilarza to a junkyard outside the town. In the corner of this place was a kind of pigsty, about four feet high and without windows. The woman unlocked the door and was greeted by a kind of animal yelping.

Inside was her son, a robust boy of 18, who couldn't stand up and hence scraped along on his seat toward the door, so far as he was permitted to move by a chain linked to his waist and attached to a ring in the wall. He was covered with filth, and his eyes shone red, like those of a nocturnal animal. His mother dumped the contents of her basket—a mixed fodder of household leftovers—into a stone trough. She filled another trough with water, and we left.[32]

Antonio was sickened by the event, but he mentioned it to nobody: "Even when people spoke of the sorrows of that poor mother, I never spoke up to remind them of the misfortune of that poor human derelict, cursed with such a mother." The young were just as cruel to the old. A young woman he knew in Santu Lussurgiu tried to have her perfectly sane, if somewhat senile, mother committed to a madhouse for life.[33]

The cruelty, both to children and to old people, came chiefly from what Gramsci called the "middle generation," the generation between twenty and fifty. Many people of this age emigrated. Those who remained to scratch out a living became bitter and self-centered, and too often vented their bitterness on their children and their unproductive elderly relatives.[34] Gramsci felt that he had been a victim of this treatment: "I was forced to make too many sacrifices. Because my health was so poor, I persuaded myself that I was merely something to be tolerated, an intruder in my own family. Such things are not easily forgotten, and leave much deeper traces than we might think."[35]

Gramsci's interrupted schooling made him resent the rich and privileged of his society. He speaks of developing an "instinct of rebellion against the rich. I could not go to school, I who got tens in all the sub-

jects in elementary school; yet the sons of the butcher, the pharma-
cist, and the draper were going."[36] He saw a direct connection between this childhood experience and his later political identification
with the lower classes.

Fortunately, however, Gramsci was out of school for only two years
before his mother and sisters put together enough money from their
meager earnings as seamstresses to send him to the ginnasio at Santu
Lussurgiu. (He soon began helping out with the finances by working
as a bookkeeper whenever school was not in session.[37]) Since the
school was eleven miles from his home and the only transportation
was a slow stagecoach, Antonio took lodgings in a peasant house near
the school. He paid five lire a month for a room, bed linen, and frugal
meals.[38] Often he spent weekends in Ghilarza, returning home on
Saturday, sometimes on foot, and leaving Monday morning.[39] The
ginnasio was a sorry place, financed by the commune rather than the
State. It had a staff of "three so-called professors," none of them
"worth much more than a dry fig," who were responsible for teaching
all five grades.[40] Gramsci's interest in science and mathematics ended
here.[41]

From 1908 to 1911, Gramsci attended the Liceo Giovanni Maria
Dettori, in the Sardinian capital city of Cagliari, about seventy-five
miles from Ghilarza. He chose the Greek curriculum rather than the
mathematics, in hopes of becoming a professor of literature. He has
told us little of his life in Cagliari, perhaps because of his unpleasant
experiences there. He later wrote to his brother Carlo:

At times you have probably envied me because it was possible for me to go
to school. But you certainly don't know what I had to go through to study.
I will mention only what happened to me in the years from 1910 to 1912.
In '10, because Nannaro [Antonio's older brother, Gennaro] was employed
at Cagliari, I went to stay with him. I received the first month's expenses,
then nothing more. I was completely in Nannaro's charge, and he did not
earn more than 100 lire a month. We changed our boardinghouse. I had a
little room that had lost all its plaster because of the humidity. There was
only one little window, which opened on to a kind of shaft that was more a
latrine than a courtyard. I realized immediately that we couldn't go on that
way because of Nannaro's bad humor. He blamed me for everything. I began by not taking my morning coffee. Then I kept postponing dinner until
later and later, thus avoiding supper. In this way, I ate only once a day for
about eight months; and ended my third year at the liceo in a very serious
state of malnutrition.*

---

* G to Carlo, 12.ix.27, *Lettere* [2], pp. 124–25. At least two letters of this Cagliari
period have survived. In one of them, sent to his father on January 31, 1909, we

Gramsci's future political attitudes began to take conscious shape in Cagliari. In October 1910, in a composition entitled "Oppressed and Oppressors," we find him praising mankind's "incessant struggle" against the tyranny of "one man, one class, or even a whole people."[42] This composition, for all its naïveté, directly anticipated much that he later wrote about politics and the class struggle: "Men, when they feel their strength and are conscious of their responsibility and their value, do not want another man to impose his will on theirs and undertake to control their thoughts and actions." After protesting that all Italy idolized Garibaldi but no one really valued his high ideals, Gramsci ended the essay on a radical note reminiscent of Vico: "The French Revolution abolished many privileges and raised up many of the oppressed; but it only replaced one class in power with another. However, it did teach one great lesson: that *social privileges and differences, being products of society and not of nature, can be overcome.*"[43]

The Greek curriculum at Cagliari seems to have awakened Gramsci's interest in philology, which became the abiding avocation of his life. His passion for languages was intense, perhaps in part because, like every educated Sardinian, he had to learn two languages, Sardinian and Italian. Sardinian was the language of his childhood, and he was later happy that it had been. He came to believe that neglect of the local dialect, a neglect characteristic of many southern Italian bourgeois families, restrained children's creative fantasy and discouraged them from expressing themselves concretely and precisely, even in Italian.[44] In 1927 he wrote his sister Teresa about her son:

What language does he speak? I hope you let him speak Sardinian and don't make things difficult for him in this matter. To me, it was a mistake that Edmea [Gennaro's daughter] was not permitted to speak Sardinian freely as a child. This was harmful to her intellectual development and put a straitjacket on her imagination. You shouldn't make this mistake with your children. . . . Besides, the Italian that you will teach him would be a poor and flat language, made up solely of the few words and phrases of your conversations with him. . . . He will have no contact with the world around him

---

can see the grinding poverty of Antonio's situation in his almost desperate request for four lire to buy textbooks. A facsimile of the letter appears in "Sulla strada di Gramsci," p. 6. It has apparently not been republished elsewhere. Readers may be interested in a vision that frequently assailed Gramsci during this period: "In 1911 while I was seriously ill from cold and malnutrition, I seemed to see an immense spider, which lay in ambush at night to descend and suck my brain while I slept." See G to Giulia, Ferrata and Gallo [12], p. 39. (Bracketed numbers refer to the numbered list of Gramsci's writings in the Bibliography, pp. 274–97; full publication data for all works cited are given in the Bibliography.)

and will end up learning two jargons and no language. . . . I strongly urge you not to commit such an error, but instead to let your children suck in all the Sardinianism they want to and develop spontaneously in the natural environment they were born in.[45]

This request suggests not only a knowledge of child psychology, but a certain Sardinian patriotism. In the same letter, Gramsci also mentions urging his Russian wife to teach their son a Sardinian folk song, although Sardinia was scarcely the boy's "natural environment," since he had never lived there. Gramsci even admitted that he once favored independence for Sardinia: " 'Into the sea with all the continentals!' How many times I repeated these words."[46] Of course, this hostility toward "continental" Italians was no more than a generalization of his earlier "instinct of rebellion against the rich." As a Sardinian, he regarded the Italian State as the island's main oppressor and the prinicpal cause of its backward condition.[47]

Little is known about Antonio's earliest political activities. His sister Teresina does recall that at fourteen he received a subscription, perhaps from Gennaro, to *Avanti!,* the Socialist Party daily, and that he asked the postman "to give him the newspaper directly, because the remarks and reproaches of my father displeased him."[48] Whatever the significance of this episode, it is certain that Antonio was sympathetic to Socialist ideas as early as 1910.* By that year, he was already an assiduous reader of *Il Viandante,* a socialistic publication of Milan whose contributors included Socialists and radicals like Arturo Labriola, Antonio Graziadei, G. M. Serrati, and Cesare Spellanzon. It was not an official Party sheet, but was strongly anti-reformist and opposed to the pro-Giolittian direction of the Party, a consistent attitude in all of Gramsci's thought.[49] Still, Antonio was far from being a committed Socialist in these early years. He himself has testified that his early reading of "things by Marx" was occasioned by no more than intellectual curiosity.[50]

During Gramsci's youth, Sardinia was an incredibly backward area, even by southern Italian standards. A feudal system of land tenure remained in force there until 1835, long after its demise else-

---

* Antonio's older brother, Gennaro, was employed by the labor movement in Cagliari before 1909, and on one occasion his activities there led to a police investigation. Antonio, who was also in Cagliari during this period, wrote to assure his mother that nothing serious would come of the affair. His witty and mordant observations on the role of the police make his political convictions plain. A facsimile of the letter, previously unpublished, appears in "Sulla strada di Gramsci," p. 6. (This letter now appears in Fiori's *Vita di Antonio Gramsci;* Fiori mistakenly asserts that it was previously unpublished.)

where in Europe (except for Russia). The abolition of feudalism changed very little. Elsewhere abolition had given rise to middle-class enterprise and ultimately to "national" revolutionary patriotism; in Sardinia nothing like that happened. The island was isolated geographically, socially, and culturally. Its ruling class, the landed nobility, had little sense of identity with Italy or with Sardinia as such. Perhaps in part because the Spanish suzerainty had been longer and more continuous in Sardinia than in any other part of Italy, the island had no cultural tradition of its own. According to Gramsci, "The Sicilians have a great tradition and are strongly united. In Sardinia, there is nothing of that."[51]

Economically, conditions on the island were comparable to those in the most underdeveloped regions of southern continental Italy. Poverty and crime were endemic. In Gramsci's time, there were more thefts and frauds in Sardinia than in any other region of Italy.[52] Of a total population of 868,181 in 1911, only 34,055 persons were employed in industry, and this figure includes more than 15,000 men who worked in the lead and zinc mines of Iglesias, in the extreme southwestern corner of the island.[53] Local Chambers of Labor[54] had succeeded in organizing only 2,790 workers, so that the Sardinian labor movement was barely in its infancy—and Sardinian Socialism all but nonexistent.[55]

In 1910 the miners of the Iglesias region, led by organizers from the continent, finally succeeded in creating a labor union of some importance; but the union made little headway against the resistance of the local peasants, who suspected the miners of having designs on their property.[56] Small as this movement was, Gramsci always considered it important. In 1918, he asked Angelo Corsi to write a few articles on the "Sardinian proletariat" for *Il Grido del popolo,* the Turin Socialist weekly, to acquaint the paper's readers with "the new Sardinia" and to help "reinforce the class solidarity of the Italian proletariat."[57]

Life in this relatively static society had a profound effect upon Gramsci. He never set foot outside Sardinia before he was twenty . . . indeed he had scarcely been outside his own province of Cagliari. Years later, he recalled his "continual effort to overcome those backward ways of living and thinking characteristic of Sardinians at the beginning of the century." He spoke of his strong need to replace his parochial approach to life with a "national" and "European" approach.[58]

As a boy, he felt unloved, alienated, humiliated. In letters to his wife, written in 1923–26, he refers to "the sewer of my past,"[59] to living like a "bear in a cavern," to hiding his feelings "behind a hard mask or an ironic smile . . . to prevent others from knowing what I really felt."[60] Though he wanted to be sociable, his relations with others were enormously complicated. "That I could be loved" seemed to him "an absolute, almost fatal impossibility," and this feeling still occasionally assailed him in later years.[61] These feelings may help explain his long unwillingness to commit himself to the Socialist movement and his later reluctance to assume his rightful position as a national leader of that movement. "How many times I wondered if a man could bind himself to the masses if he had never loved anyone, not even his parents; if one could love a collectivity when one had not profoundly loved single human creatures."[62]

Gramsci's response to these psychological wounds was neither passivity nor self-pity, but the conviction that he could rely only upon himself. He wrote to his brother Carlo: "Expect nothing from anyone, and you will avoid delusions. We must do only what we know we can do, and go our own way."[63] Or again, "Almost always I've known only the most brutal aspect of life, but I've always managed, for better or worse."[64]

Gramsci's Sardinian heritage also had its positive side, however. For one thing it helped him understand the social and economic problems of the Mezzogiorno (southern Italy) far better than most of his colleagues in the North. Between 1914 and 1926 he made several attempts to cement political relations between the workers' movement in the North and the peasant organizations of the South; and at the end of his active political career, in 1926, he made a major contribution to the literature of the Mezzogiorno problem in his essay "Alcuni temi della quistione meridionale." Many of his writings in the "Quaderni del carcere," his prison notebooks, have to do with peasant problems: the gulf dividing the educated southerner from the peasant; the linguistic differences between peasants and intelligentsia and their class connotations; the problem of the "two Italys," a relatively advanced and industrialized North and a backward and semicolonial South. Even his interest in Machiavelli seems to have come in part from Machiavelli's program for including peasants in a militia created for the defense of Florence.[65]

Sardinia also left its mark on Gramsci's personality and values. What could be more suitable for a future master of dialectics than the petty-bourgeois poverty of his origins? For at a very early age

Gramsci was faced with basic contradictions: between his aspirations and the near-impossibility of realizing them; between his inquiring mind and the age-old immobility of his surroundings. In the end his learning and his achievements were profoundly Italian, but the impulse that had led to them was Sardinian.[66]

After graduating from the liceo at Cagliari in September 1911, Gramsci left Sardinia for the University of Turin. Though Gramsci could not know it, Turin was to become his adopted city, first as a student, afterwards as a leader of the young but rapidly growing Turin labor movement.

2. The Formative Years in Turin

*Partecivamo in tutto o in parte al movimento
di reforma morale e intellettuale promosso in
Italia da Benedetto Croce....*

—*Gramsci, August 17, 1931*

Italian Politics and Culture in 1911

In the early months of 1911, pre-Fascist Italy had in many ways reached its apogee. In its fifty years as an independent kingdom, and especially in the last ten, Italy had made striking progress politically, socially, and economically.[1] The International Industrial Exhibition, held in Turin from April to November of 1911, was a visible symbol of this growth and of the facile optimism that accompanied it. More than 260,000 people attended the Exhibition and left fully convinced of "the progress of progress."[2]

The star of Giovanni Giolitti, arbiter of Italian politics from 1903 to 1914, had never shone brighter. His policy of changing Italian Socialism from a revolutionary movement to one aimed at improving the position of the working class *within* capitalism had apparently proved completely successful. But the basic deficiencies of the Italian economic structure were not to be denied political expression, and the next few years brought to fruition such far-reaching changes in Italian politics as to confound even the old "Piedmontese Fox," for all his extraordinary political understanding. Extremism made dramatic gains on both the Right and the Left. In 1910, Italian nationalist extremists had organized a party. One of its more demagogic slogans pictured a "proletarian Italy" arrayed against the "plutocratic" nations of Europe.[3] As for the Italian Socialist Party, although Giolitti had declared before the Chamber on April 8, 1911, that "Karl Marx has been relegated to the attic"[4] (that is, that the moderate reformist elements had gained complete control), only a year later the revolutionary wing regained command—nor would the moderates ever again achieve a majority in the main body of Italian Socialism.

Ironically enough, the Libyan War of 1911–12, which shattered the quasi-harmony of antebellum Italy, was in great part the work of Giolitti himself.[5] The war pushed most of the Socialist movement toward radical criticism of the whole Giolittian regime, and increased the power of the nationalists; it was also partially responsible for the Italian economic crisis of 1911–13.[6] By 1913, when the first elections based on substantially universal male suffrage were held, Giolitti's position was so weak that he could stay in power only by an agreement with the Catholics. Even so the Socialist vote doubled in this election, and shortly thereafter Giolitti decided to resign. He was replaced by Antonio Salandra, the leading representative of the Right.

Italian culture was also in a state of crisis in 1911, and much more obviously so than Italian politics.[7] Positivism, the attempt to apply the methods of the natural sciences to every aspect of reality, had lost its dominance among Italian intellectuals. Dealing only with abstract "types" or isolated facts, never with concrete reality conceived developmentally, asking such questions as what forms of political and social organization were most "natural" to man, positivism was in touch neither with the Socialist aspirations of the Left nor with the nationalist aspirations of the Right.

As positivism declined, a host of irrational ideologies emerged: the "cult of personality," the exaltation of pure feeling or action as opposed to thought, the glorification of violence. In April 1914, the Futurist leader, Filippo Marinetti, addressing the Dante Alighieri Society in Turin, was applauded for the following remarks: "For us Futurists the word Italy means something above all the parties. It means the genius of the Latin race, and it is even more resplendent than the word freedom. . . . War is a necessary cleansing. It is hygiene. Life is based on struggle."[8] A more characteristically Italian expression of the contemporary lack of philosophical guidance was a profound skepticism. In the field of literature this took the form of melancholia, defeatism, and an aesthetic that saw only the episode or the fleeting image as real and worthy of attention.

There were more comprehensive philosophies current in the Italy of 1911, notably the historical idealism of Benedetto Croce and Giovanni Gentile, and Marxian dialectical materialism. Both philosophies had attacked positivism and were partly responsible for its decline.

The University of Turin

The University of Turin before World War I was somewhat behind other Italian universities in assimilating the new currents of thought. Neither Marxism nor idealism was strongly entrenched there.[9] Achille Loria, professor of political economy at Turin, considered himself a Marxist, but he was a very misguided one if we accept the disdainful judgment of Friedrich Engels.[10] Crocean idealism won its first substantial victory at Turin with the appointment of Umberto Cosmo as professor of Italian literature in 1913.[11] Most of the outstanding professors in Gramsci's time remained faithful to the positivistic method, or at least to the best elements of that method: precision, accuracy, and rigid standards of documentation. Others professed an almost romantic moral code. Witness the following description of Arturo Farinelli, the professor of German literature, by one of his students:

There was something volcanic in his lectures. . . . Every now and then he would turn his head toward the window to the left, and the light that fell on him, together with his laugh and the curly locks on his forehead, gave him a strange look, the look of an angel or a devil who was showing us the way. It was a new morality that he taught us, whose supreme laws were complete sincerity with ourselves, the spurning of convention, and sacrifice for the cause to which we had dedicated our lives.[12]

Politically, however, the University was one of the most active in Italy. During the great "movement toward Socialism" of the 1890's many of the professors and intellectuals of Turin had joined the Socialist Party, and in 1893 a Socialist circle was founded at the University by the writer Edmondo De Amicis.[13] Most of the University's Socialists, it is true, had extremely vague and sentimental ideas about the nature of Socialism, and after 1900 many of them left the Party, but the great majority remained firm democrats and militant liberals. In time these professors, with their high standards of scholarship and their active liberalism, gave the University a reputation for "political intransigence and militant culture."[14]

Among those who attended the University with Gramsci between 1911 and 1915 were the future Communist leaders Palmiro Togliatti, Umberto Terracini, and Angelo Tasca, the future Socialist leaders Umberto Calosso and Giuseppe Romita, and such future militant liberals as Piero Gobetti, Carlo Levi, and Mario Lamberti. The Communists continued to draw many of their most important leaders

—among them Luigi Longo and Felice Platone—from the ranks of the Turin students.[15] Togliatti has said that *L'Ordine nuovo,* the newspaper Gramsci founded after World War I, "was born in the University of Turin."[16]

Gramsci arrived in Turin without financial resources. His salvation was the University's special scholarship fund, established many years earlier, for needy students born in the old provinces of the Kingdom of Sardinia. The competitive examination was difficult, much more so than the pre-graduation examinations required at the Italian lyceums; but successful candidates were rewarded with a relatively handsome stipend—seventy lire a month, nine months a year, for all the years of the University course or as long as the student made good grades and attended lectures regularly.[17] Gramsci placed fifth in the examination and received one of the scholarships.[18] Another successful competitor was Palmiro Togliatti, a dry and serious young Piedmontese who had also attended a liceo in Sardinia. The two soon became fast friends.

At the University Gramsci took courses in Italian, Latin, and Greek literature, linguistics, Romance languages, German, geography, modern history, the history of philosophy, and theoretical philosophy.[19] This curriculum reflected not only the standard Italian emphasis on the classics, but also Gramsci's special interest in languages and linguistics. While still a student, he made several contributions to learned journals in the field.[20] Matteo Bartoli, Gramsci's professor of linguistics, expected great things of him, particularly in combating the "neogrammarians," who reduced linguistics to formal analysis rather than studying language in its social and historical context.[21] Bartoli even chose Gramsci to help him prepare the syllabus and bibliography for his linguistics course of 1912–13.[22] To Bartoli's disappointment, Gramsci ultimately dropped the idea of a career in linguistics, but his linguistic training proved an important asset in his studies of society and culture.

Gramsci's study habits were very thorough. He outlined everything important that he read. He filled notebooks, organized by subject, on his readings, and even kept a card file of newspaper articles that interested him.[23] The many references in the "Quaderni del carcere" to articles that appeared in Gramsci's youth testify to his intellectual organization. As a student, he was quick to recognize the limitations of philological erudition, as we see from a satiric essay he wrote in 1914, a weighty dissertation on the "history" of a certain rusty nail from its earliest days in the main beams of Jason's *Argo* to its present home in Gramsci's pocket.[24] Yet he retained a respect for the best of the philologists, and especially for their distrust of superficiality and subjective judgments: "Today I would strongly defend the old traditional pedantry against a certain superficial or Bohemian shallowness that has brought about, and is still bringing about, so many woes."[25]

Another professor who influenced Gramsci was Umberto Cosmo, whose lectures on Dante introduced his students to the works of the great literary critic Francesco De Sanctis (1817–83) and, through De Sanctis, to the philosophy of Hegel and Croce. Neo-idealism became, as we shall see, so strong an element in Gramsci's thought that he later described his entire intellectual orientation as "more or less Croceian."[26] Gramsci was on close personal terms with Cosmo, and remained so for some years after leaving the University.[27] Cosmo was a political liberal. Two other liberal professors esteemed by Gramsci were Luigi Einaudi and Francesco Ruffini, who lectured respectively on the Italian political economy and on relations between Church and State.[28]

During his university years Gramsci worked hard, and his poor constitution was severely strained. In 1916 he wrote his sister that he could not remember a single day in the preceding three years when he had not suffered from headaches, dizzy spells, or stomach trouble.[29] He was unable to take any of his examinations scheduled for the fall of 1913 until the following spring.[30] Despite these difficulties, Gramsci did very well in the seven university examinations he took between November 1912 and November 1914.[31] In linguistics he received a perfect grade (30 points) with special praise.

Yet he never completed the requirements for his degree. He registered very late (January 30, 1915) for his final year, and showed up for classes looking listless and preoccupied.[32] Annibale Pastore, professor of theoretical philosophy, whose lectures Gramsci attended in 1915, saw him as increasingly disenchanted with mere intellection and eager for practical action. His main concern during his last academic year, according to Professor Pastore, was "how thought brings about action . . . , how thought makes hands move, and how and why we can act with ideas."[33] This concern with action, coupled with his recent activity in the Socialist Youth Organization, had made him wonder if he should continue his University work or enter wholeheartedly into active political life.[34] The dilemma was solved for him when Italy declared war against Austria-Hungary on May 23, 1915.

Turin and Italy

Piedmont is isolated from the Mediterranean by the Maritime Alps and the Apennines, and is far from the historic centers of Italian culture. It is one of the most "provincial," i.e., least Italian, of the Italian regions, and also one of the most "European," for in the past its ties with France have been close.[35] It is also, for excellent economic and historical reasons, an important industrial center.

After about 1900 Piedmont's larger cities, especially Turin, enjoyed an extraordinarily rapid and thorough industrial development, while the smaller towns and the country districts continued in their traditional way of life.[36] A concomitant of this development was a vast movement of population to the larger cities from the small towns and the countryside. While the total population of Piedmont remained almost stationary from 1901 to 1911, that of Turin alone increased by more than 27 per cent, from 338,000 to 430,000.[37]

The population of Turin itself was divided essentially into two classes: an industrial proletariat and a capitalistic bourgeoisie. The city had no artisans to speak of, and very few middle-class wage-earners in such activities as government service and commerce. There were a number of historical reasons for this state of affairs. For one thing, when the capital of Italy was moved from Turin to Florence in 1865, a large proportion of Turin's government functionaries moved with it.[38] For another, the great banking catastrophes of the 1880's and 1890's were particularly disastrous to those Turin middle classes not connected with industry.[39] The most important reason, however, was the character of the Piedmontese economy. Both the artisan tradition and older forms of commerce were less important in backward Piedmont than elsewhere in northern and central Italy.[40] Most industry in Piedmont began as modern industry.

Piedmont's new industries tended to be large; among them were Fiat and Olivetti.[41] Fiat in time became so huge that Piero Gobetti could describe it as "a little absolute state with its own autocrat."[42] These industries came to dominate the social and political life of Turin, and in time won over what remained of the city's middle classes.[43] Unlike their counterparts in Milan or Florence, the Turin middle classes remained conservatives or Giolittian liberals; there were few extremists of either the Right or the Left. Only in the University, where Giolittian and conservative policies came in for articulate criticism, was there any significant middle-class support for the militant Socialism of the lower classes.[44]

The Italian Labor Movement in 1900

In 1901, Italian industry employed some four million persons over nine years old or 23.8 per cent of gainfully employed Italians.[45] The percentage was by far the lowest in Western Europe.[46] Moreover, the 1901 census defined as industry "any activity aimed at the production of goods," and nearly a million and a half of the workers counted were artisans, independent spinners and weavers, and others engaged in activities unrelated to modern industrial capitalism. A 1905 survey, which excluded artisans and construction workers, found a total of 1,412,000 workers employed in 117,000 "industrial plants" (*opifici*).[47] Add the 1901 census figure of 552,000 construction workers, and the total number of modern industrial workers comes to about two million, a relatively small figure. Of this two million, moreover, about forty per cent were women, children, and adolescents.

Workers in Italian industry did not have the sense of class solidarity that was so characteristic of most European proletariats. There was a high rate of migration from country to city, and many of the workers retained their peasant attitudes and worked in part-time agricultural jobs. In addition, most plants were run on a very small scale of production. These factors produced a low general level of skill in Italian *industrial* workers. Italy as a whole did not lack skilled workers, but most of these employed themselves in pre-industrial artisan activities—and the artisan tradition in Italy tenaciously resisted the institution of modern industry. In Italy there was practically no intermediate stage between the unskilled and the highly skilled worker, "between the artisan and the peasant turned worker—the laborer [*manovale*] who has no skills but his youth and the strength of his own arm. The 'common worker,' a characteristic type in more advanced stages of development, the worker with relatively standard schooling and occupational skills, was still little in evidence."[48]

Italian labor in 1900 was organized in two fundamental types of institutions: the trade union (Federazione di Mestiere) and the Chamber of Labor (Camera del Lavoro). The union was open to all workers, or at least to all skilled workers, in a given industry. But the Italian unions—reflecting the deep-rooted artisan and corporative tradition—emphasized the hierarchy of skills and trades within the union to a greater extent than those in other countries.[49] A metalworker thought of himself not as a metalworker, but as a foundryman, a coppersmith, or a shearer.

Nearly all Italian unions were founded as organs of "resistance"; that is, as militant representatives of labor in the class struggle against capital. But weak as they were in these early years, their concern was necessarily less with social revolution than with merely obtaining recognition. The majority of them were formed between 1900 and 1904, and as late as 1911 there were only 219,408 workers enrolled in all the trade unions.[50]

Although the early Italian trade unions were weak, the Italian labor movement as a whole was by no means negligible.* One source of its strength was the Chamber of Labor, a territorial organization designed to include all workers in a given commune or province. Similar organizations existed in other European countries—the Trades Councils in England, the Kartelle in Germany, the Bourses de Travail in France. The last-named in fact provided the model for the first Italian Chambers, which were established in the 1890's, a decade before the major national trade unions. The early Chambers functioned as employment bureaus, and provided facilities for recreation and education; for these purposes, they often received subsidies from local governments.[51] They also protected the interests of workers against capital, mainly through arbitration. Their orientation was almost strictly economic: many of them, including the one at Turin, forbade any meetings of a "political or religious character" on the premises.[52]

Structurally, the Chambers of Labor were less suited to the conditions of modern industry than the trade unions. Their membership was composed of local leagues and unions, whose classifications of workers tended to be more rigorous and more minute than those of the Federations; usually the individual trades within the larger Federations were recognized by the Chambers of Labor. For example, a lathe operator was classified as a metalworker in the Italian Federation of Metalworkers, but only as a lathe operator in the local Chamber of Labor.[53] (Only in the Turin Chamber did the metalworkers form a single section, probably because large industry was more common in Turin and differences in trades were not so strongly felt.) Owing to the Chambers' regional base, their executive committees reflected a considerable diversity of occupations and thus were often too heterogeneous to be effective.

For all these reasons, the trade-union leaders hoped that the Chambers of Labor would eventually be completely replaced by national trade-union federations.[54] This was one reason for the founding of

* Procacci considers it comparable in importance to the powerful labor movement in Wilhelmine Germany. ("La Classe operaia," p. 52.)

the Secretariat of the Resistance in November 1902, and for the
eventual formation of the General Confederation of Labor in October 1906.

But the Chambers of Labor had advantages that the Federations
lacked. In bringing together all the workers of a given area, they
were ultimately forced to consider general political and humanistic
problems, not merely bread-and-butter issues; indeed, they were in
many respects organs of popular self-government. And in general they
reflected the conditions of Italian economic and political history
much better than the Federations. Above all, the Chambers were
reluctant to accept a specifically class orientation:

In a country like Italy, with a still poorly developed modern industry and a
labor movement arising gradually out of the democracy of the Risorgimento,
a class and trade-union orientation threatened to isolate the nuclei of workers from the great mass of the "people," to cut into a revolutionary and
popular solidarity based on the old democratic ideals.[55]

Giuliano Procacci argues that the very backwardness of the Italian
labor movement, especially in the Chambers of Labor, prevented it
from being "trapped," like labor movements elsewhere, in the "trade-
union phase" of economic development. In Italy, clear distinctions
between union and political struggles, between working-class demands and democratic demands, could not be made. The movement's
fundamental problem, according to Procacci, was to "ensure those
general conditions of democracy and civil society in which a [labor]
movement could develop into an organic element of a modern society."[56] One of these "general conditions" was an end to police
brutality, which even under Giolitti often resulted in the senseless
killing of workers and peasants. In eleven such incidents between
1901 and 1904 for which statistics are available, some 32 persons were
killed and 212 wounded.[57]

At all times, the Chambers of Labor had many more members than
the Federations; in 1911, for example, the membership figures were
485,000 and 219,000 respectively. Another difference was geographical. The Federations, except for the railway workers, were confined to
the North, whereas the Chambers also had a firm basis in southern
Italy, especially at Naples, Palermo, and Catania, and hence were
more representative on a national level.[58]

A tactic peculiar—at least in its frequency—to the Italian labor
movement was the urban general strike, which ultimately grew into
the national general strike. These strikes were, as Procacci says, a

combination of the typical working-class strike and "traditional forms of popular protest."[59] Being essentially political, they could only have been led by the Chambers of Labor. The first urban general strike in Italy occurred in Turin in February 1902. As we shall see, the city made an important contribution to this characteristically Italian form of labor protest.

The Labor Movement in Piedmont and Turin

The power of the Turin working class was certainly not great in 1900. Milan and the Emilia-Romagna region were much more advanced in labor organization, and even such Piedmontese towns as Biella and Alessandria had made more important contributions to the labor movement.[60] Although Turin's population was already about 300,000, there were scarcely 60,000 workers in shops and homes; and half of these, mostly women, were employed in the dress industry. Turin did not yet have a modern industrial plant—only six of its firms operated on anything like a large scale.[61] Thus the fundamental shortcomings of the Italian labor movement in 1900 were felt at least as strongly at Turin as elsewhere: a high percentage of women and children in the labor force (because of the importance of the dress industry), and a limited number of "common workers" as compared with artisans and laborers.

Throughout the first decade of the twentieth century, the institutions of the Turin working class reflected this backward state of affairs. The local Socialist weekly, *Il Grido del popolo,* complained that "in no other city are the workers so apathetic to forces making for their welfare. Of the 120 or 130 workers' societies in Turin, no more than three are societies of resistance."[62] Although the Turin Chamber of Labor was founded on May 1, 1891—one of the first in Italy—it remained smaller for some time than those in Milan, Rome, Naples, and other cities.[63] Membership in the Turin Socialist section, founded on November 15, 1892, remained almost incredibly small for many years. At the Provincial Congress of the Party in September 1906, only 1,328 members were represented.[64] And in 1910, after three years of declining militancy among the workers, the number of Socialists in Turin was only 600.[65]

In the areas of cooperation and mutual aid, by contrast, the Turin workers were remarkably progressive. As early as 1885 Piedmont had more mutual-aid societies than any other region in Italy.[66] Indeed, the largest working-class institution in Italy was the Turin Workers' General Association (Associazione Generale degli Operai di Torino—

AGO). Founded in 1850, it adopted that name in 1865, at which time
it had 10,000 members and a capital of 250,000 lire. It provided its
members with medical care, sick pay, and pensions, and became the
first labor organization in Italy to practice retail cooperation.[67] In
1899, the AGO and the Railway Workers' Cooperative, the "real
powers of the labor movement" in Turin, merged into the Turin Cooperative Alliance (Alleanza Cooperativa Torinese—ACT), which
was to play a tremendously important role in Turin's political life.[68]

The Turin Socialists were also quite successful in electioneering.
As early as 1897, Piedmont had the highest Socialist vote in Italy,[69]
and in 1904 it was second only to Emilia-Romagna in percentage of
Socialist votes.[70]

Beginning about 1900, the Turin workers, as distinct from and opposed to their organizations, began to develop a fierce militancy. The
first urban general strike in Italian history occurred in Turin in February 1902.[71] Provoked by the use of soldiers as replacements for
striking gas workers, it was unplanned and spontaneous, receiving
only reluctant support from the Chamber of Labor. Again, in the
first national general strike (September 1904), many Turin workers
were already on the streets before the Chamber of Labor declared its
support. Still another general strike was declared in Turin in October
1907, this time against the explicit advice of the Chamber of Labor.
Finally, on October 12, 1909, the metalworkers called for a general
strike in honor of Francisco Ferrer, the condemned Spanish free-
thinker and revolutionary. This movement, too, was only reluctantly
followed by the leadership of the Chamber of Labor and the Socialist
Party. Giulio Casalini, a reformist Socialist leader, complained that
"the Turin proletariat does not have deep strength. It is exuberant
but immature. The demonstration for Francisco Ferrer was not or-
derly and silent, as it should have been."[72]

These events illustrate one of the most serious difficulties of the
Turin labor movement at this time—the gap between the reformist,
Giolittian temper of its leaders and the violent tendencies of the
masses. A close relationship between the leaders and the rank and file
was not established until the metalworkers' strike of 1912. For years
the Turin section of the Party was concerned mainly with cooperative
and insurance activities. In March 1902, the section even declared
that the Party had nothing to do with the workers' economic struggles![73] Considerable efforts were also made to gain control of the municipal administration, as had been done at Milan.[74] Despite the
heavy Socialist vote, this goal was not achieved, primarily because of

the difficulty of forming political alliances with other social classes in the city.*

In these early years, nearly all the leaders of the Italian Socialist Party were Lombards, Emilians, Romagnoles, or Southerners. The only important Piedmontese was Oddino Morgari, the creator of "integralism," a position that attempted to reconcile reformism and maximalism, the ideologies of the Party's right and left wings, respectively.[75] This call for "unity in variety" was really, as Spriano puts it, an emotional "state of mind" rather than a tactical expedient. Morgari defined integralism as "the synthesis of the present possibilities and future hopes of Socialism, of idealism and practicality, of direct action and representative action, of anti-statism and state legislation, of revolution and legality, of syndicalism and anti-syndicalism, of intransigence and cooperativeness."[76]

The rise of Turin Socialism to a more creative role is directly tied to the vast expansion of metalworking industries in the city, notably the automobile industry, which grew rapidly after 1904. The Fiat Corporation, the first true automobile plant in Italy, was formed on July 11, 1899, by a group of Piedmontese motor pioneers, and produced its first machines in November of that year. The sporting aspect of the industry—automobile races, international competition with France, the novelty of possessing an industrial curiosity—predominated during the early years. At that time automobile workers were usually highly skilled and well paid, and were isolated from the general labor movement; and union membership among them was uncommon.

By 1905, however, the automobile industry had become "the most salient fact . . . of the decade."[77] Italian industry was offered a rare opportunity to compete with the more industrialized countries in producing a commodity for which there was an enormous potential demand.[78] Other industrial nations had no more experience in automobile production than Italy. Turin had special advantages for the new industry: water and hydroelectric power were easily available; foreign capital could be attracted from nearby France and Switzerland; a fair number of capable metalworkers were already in the city. From 1905 to the spring of 1906, Fiat's assets grew from four million to nine mil-

* In the national elections of March 1909, the Turin Socialists received a majority of votes in the city. However, the urban bourgeoisie became alarmed, and an all-out campaign for a solid alliance of liberals and Catholics was undertaken. Thus in the administrative elections of June 20, 1909, the "constitutional" bloc was able to defeat the Socialists by a handy margin. See Spriano, *Socialismo e classe operaia,* pp. 238–41.

lion lire; and the other auto works in Turin showed similar gains.[79]
By 1907 there were 66 auto companies operating in Italy. Twenty of
them, including the largest ones, were located in Turin. The city also
had six of the nineteen body plants and most of the plants that manufactured automobile accessories.[80]

The tremendous labor shortage and higher wages in the automobile industry caused the "most intelligent workers in the city to abandon the old plants and turn to the new industry," the old jobs being
filled by immigrants from the countryside.[81] From then on, and especially in the critical years of 1906–7 and 1912–13, the Turin labor
movement was led by the metalworkers and their union, the Federazione Impiegati Operai Metallurgici (Fiom). The Fiom was founded
at Leghorn in June 1901, but its headquarters were soon established
at Turin, and most of its leading officials were either Turinese or at
least Piedmontese.[82]

The Fiom's first important victory, which was greatly abetted by
the labor shortage, was the Fiat contract of March 2, 1906, recognizing
the ten-hour day as "normal" and accepting the principle of worker
representation in the factory. Disputes would be dealt with by the
management and an ad hoc committee of five workers chosen from
their fellow employees. This "internal committee" (*commissione interna*)—roughly comparable to the shop steward in the United States
—was not regarded as a permanent institution by the industrialists;
the idea was to choose a new committee for each dispute.[83] But the
workers had other ideas, and the effort to make these committees permanent was of major importance in the labor conflicts that followed
World War I.[84]

In the spring of 1906, Turin's textile workers struck for a ten-hour
day, with the support of the city's entire working class. After eight
strikers had been wounded by police fire, the Turin Chamber of Labor
called for a national general strike, and such a strike was in fact carried out in most of the large northern cities.[85] The strike aims of the
Turin textile workers were finally achieved, but only after the city's
industrialists had been aroused to a sense of their unity as a group.
On July 20, 1906, the Turin Industrial League (Lega Industriale
Torinese) was founded. It initially represented more than 200 companies, and its eventual aim was to include all industries in the area.
All the large companies in the fields of chemicals, textiles, electricity,
and automobiles (except Itala) were members. Its elected president
was Louis Craponne, a silk manufacturer of French origin. The
League was the first of its kind in Italy.[86]

Three months later, in October 1906, the General Confederation of Labor (Confederazione Generale del Lavoro—CGL) was established. Turin was chosen as its headquarters, and Rinaldo Rigola, a Piedmontese cabinetmaker, became its first president. In Turin, the first Catholic labor organization in the country (the Lega del Lavoro) was founded. It attracted only 300 members; most Turin workers were far to the left of the social gospel of the Church.[87] In these years, the Chamber of Labor finally became a truly representative force in Turin, moving from 8,800 members in 1906 to 15,600 in May 1907; and the ACT flourished more than ever.[88]

The high point of labor's success in Turin was reached with the signing of the Itala-Fiom contract on October 27, 1906. The contract provided for the establishment of a union shop with a checkoff system and a permanent internal committee in return for a no-strike pledge during the three-year period of the contract. Both the reformist leaders of Turin Socialism and the Giolittian group of the daily newspaper *La Stampa* were strong supporters of the contract, but opposition to it was extremely vociferous. The Turin Industrial League was furious with Itala for coming to terms without the League's consent, and the revolutionary syndicalists regarded the no-strike pledge as a betrayal.[89]

In 1907 the tide turned. In April of that year, workers in the Savigliano metalworking plant in western Piedmont struck for a ten-hour day and an internal committee. When the strike spread to the Savigliano plant in Turin, the Fiom decided to declare a boycott of both establishments (the first ever by an Italian labor organization). The Fiom secretariat was encouraged by foreign examples to hope that Turin's other metalworking firms would tolerate the boycott out of their desire to profit at Savigliano's expense.[90] The hope proved unwarranted. Not only did the Industrial League close ranks and condemn the boycott, but a severe depression, completely unforeseen by Turin's Socialists, hit the economy. Since Italian automobiles were then almost exclusively luxury products, the industry was particularly vulnerable to a depression.[91] The highly watered Fiat stock fell from 445 to 80, and then to 40. The discharge of a thousand auto workers in late September effectively ended the boycott.

Another defeat for Turin's labor movement came in connection with the national general strike proclaimed at Milan on October 11, 1907, in response to the killing and wounding of striking workers by *carabinieri* in that city. Most of the large cities in northern and central Italy quickly responded to the appeal of the Milanese Chamber

of Labor. At Turin, however, a conflict between the reformist and
syndicalist elements in the Chamber of Labor prevented the proclamation of the strike until October 13, when the syndicalists finally
achieved a slight majority. But the timing of the strike—it had already
ended at Milan—and the continued opposition of the reformists en-
sured its complete failure. Only the metalworkers responded. Moreover, the Industrial League chose this moment to go on the offensive
and proclaimed a general lockout in the city for 48 hours. All the
large firms complied, and some 30,000 workers were locked out. The
revolutionary syndicalists replied by proclaiming a 72-hour urban
general strike, against the advice of the Chamber of Labor; the strike
failed ingloriously when only about 5,000 workers responded to the
call.[92]

The industrialists did not hesitate to press their advantage. In
March 1908, under the auspices of the Turin Industrial League, the
Piedmontese Industrial Federation (Federazione Industriale Piedmontese) was established, with Craponne as president. The new federation consisted of 500 important firms, which altogether employed
more than 100,000 workers.[93] In Turin the Industrial League became
even larger in 1908–9, encompassing 291 firms employing some 48,000
workers. The League initiated a series of agreements with firms in
Genoa, Milan, and Terni, whereby the signatory firms agreed not to
hire any strikers during a strike and for three months afterward.[94] In
May 1910, the founding in Turin of an even larger association—the
Italian Confederation of Industry (Confederazione Italiana dell'Industria)—established the prestige of Turin industrial capitalism
throughout Italy. The Confederation's statutes were based on those
of the Turin Industrial League, and Craponne, as usual, was elected
president.[95] By October the Confederation comprised 2,100 firms
with some 250,000 employees.

Meanwhile, the owners of Itala canceled the Fiom contract of October 1906, allegedly because of the participation of Itala workers in the
1907 general strike. Other plants followed suit. Many of the benefits
won by workers in 1906 and 1907 simply disappeared between 1908
and 1911. These were years of "almost absolute silence" in the world
of Turin labor.[96] The Chamber of Labor had lost half its members
by 1909, the Socialist Section was down to 600 members by 1910, and
the Fiom in 1911 represented little more than 1,000 of the 30,000
metalworkers in the city.[97] Clearly, the union and the Party had all
but lost contact with the workers in the shops.

Toward the end of 1911, economic prosperity returned, and the labor movement revived. The 1907 depression had eliminated all but the most efficient companies (Fiat, Spa, Itala, Scat, and Lancia), those that were able to produce cheaper models. In 1911 nearly three times as many autos were produced as in 1907.[98] Workers, particularly the skilled, were once again in great demand, and enjoyed a relatively high wage scale.[99] Yet the long hours (10 to 11 hours a day, six days a week) and the heavy, taxing work were not conducive to industrial peace in the city.

In 1911 the Fiom's main demand was for a shortening of the workweek from 60 to 57 hours without loss of pay by converting to the *sabato inglese,* or a seven-hour day on Saturday.[100] In November 1911, after this goal had been attained by several thousand auto workers, the Turin automobile manufacturers responded by forming the Automobile Factories Association (Consorzio delle Fabbriche d'Automobili), which included the seven main firms, with a labor force of about 6,500.[101] The Consorzio demanded complete obedience of its members, each of whom was required to deposit a blank check as security. With unity of action thus assured, the Consorzio presented the workers with a new contract, applicable to the entire industry. In return for a no-strike pledge and an agreement to dispense with internal committees, the industrialists would grant the sabato inglese (though with a smaller premium for overtime on that day) and a four per cent increase in hourly wages. They also proposed to divide the workers into two wage categories: the skilled workers, who were usually members of the Fiom, would receive forty centesimi or more an hour; the unskilled and unorganized laborers would receive less. As in 1906, the Fiom was chosen as the best guarantor of labor stability, and in December 1911, the Consorzio and the union agreed on the above terms. In addition, the Consorzio agreed to recognize the union and apply a checkoff system; it refused, however, to make union membership compulsory.

The unorganized workers unexpectedly refused to accept the new contract. They pronounced the wage increase unsatisfactory (the four per cent increase did not compensate for the reduction of hours), and the two-categories system unacceptable. On January 10–12, 1912, some 2,000 of these unorganized workers established a new union: the Independent Union of Automobile Workers (Sindacato Autonomo degli Operai Automobilistici). The Consorzio thereupon withdrew its offer to the Fiom on the ground that the workers had demonstrated the Fiom's inability to bargain on their behalf.[102]

The revolutionary syndicalists—practically nonexistent in Turin

after 1907—sent an agent to the new Sindacato from a stronghold in
Emilia, and the organization was soon firmly under their control. On
January 17, the new union proclaimed a strike, to last until the owners agreed to negotiate with it. Although the Fiom at first ignored the
call, the great majority of workers stayed out of the plants. Despite
this support, the Sindacato proved a sorry affair. Its chief, Pulvio
Zocchi (a member of the Bolognese Chamber of Labor), offered only
empty words:

Strikes that win so much a day for the workers are all very well for Germany,
England, and the Nordic countries, where the national temperament is
different from ours and where the masses are organized from the hair of their
heads to the soles of their feet. We are an impulsive and enthusiastic people.
Everyone feels the will to sacrifice. The revolutionary proletariat is watching
us![103]

The industrialists, after organizing a strike-insurance fund, declared
a lockout. The disunited workers were incapable of offering effective
resistance to this tactic, and on March 21 the strike collapsed. The 65-
day effort had resulted only in the loss of the new contract—with its
recognition of the Fiom—and the return of the 60-hour week in most
of the industry.

Several months later, a new militancy appeared in both the national and local Socialist organizations. At the Party's 13th National
Congress (at Reggio Emilia, July 7–12, 1912), the revolutionary faction, with the support of the Turin delegation, achieved a majority,
whereupon it turned on the right-wing reformists, who had supported
the Libyan War, and expelled them from the Party. At Turin, too,
the left wing of the Party won a complete victory. From now on both
the Party and the ACT were firm supporters of the workers in their
industrial disputes. The Fiom took heart and began preparations for
a new strike, this time under the leadership of Bruno Buozzi. Its membership in the city rose to more than 2,000, and in the fall of 1912 the
new Fiom program was approved by the vast majority of the workers.
It called for a reduction of the workweek from 60 to 54 hours with
the same weekly pay, a revision of the piecework schedules, and full
recognition of the union and internal committees. An agitation committee of three workers from each auto plant was elected, including
some members of the all but discredited Sindacato. Thus the stage
was set for the great metalworkers' strike of 1913.[104]

In early March, the Fiom presented its demands to the Consorzio.
They were rejected out of hand, and the strike began on March 19.
The Fiom received food and money from the ACT, the CGL, many

Chambers of Labor, and even the German Metallurgical Federation. On May 20, in an effort to cut off this outside aid, Craponne took the extreme measure of calling for a general lockout in all the metal industries, which would have laid off another 17,000 workers in the city. In making this move, he seriously miscalculated the intentions of the government. Giolitti had moved considerably to the right since 1911, but he was no man to let management resistance to moderate labor demands paralyze the entire economy. Alfredo Frassati, the editor of *La Stampa* and a close associate of Giolitti, rebuked Craponne, arguing that his logic would require lockouts throughout Italian industry to defeat a single strike; and Giolitti personally attacked Craponne as a foreign troublemaker.[105] The prefect of Turin stated that in the event of a general lockout, the police could not be counted upon to protect the industrialists' property. The League was shaken by these signs of official disfavor, and Craponne was forced to resign as president. The lockout did not take place.[106]

Only after the strike had lasted for 75 days and 90 per cent of the workers voted to go on, did the industrialists agree to negotiate. On June 23, after a 93-day strike, the new contract was signed, and the plants reopened. Although the rewards seemed meager enough, the workers regarded the settlement as a victory. The workweek was to be reduced to 59 hours for the remainder of 1913, to 58 hours in 1914, and to 57 hours in 1915, with a yearly increase of 2 centesimi an hour for all categories of workers. Thus the skilled workers, who received from 60 to 70 centesimi an hour, were barely compensated for their loss of one hour's pay per week; whereas the unskilled workers, whose pay was 30 to 40 centesimi an hour, actually gained about two hours' pay per week, despite the shorter workweek. On the part of the skilled workers, then, this settlement can be seen as a triumph of class solidarity over personal greed. As Gramsci put it a few years later: "The skilled workers and technicians of Turin ... do not have the petty-bourgeois mentality of the skilled workers in other countries, for example in England."[107]

Gramsci and the Socialist Youth Federation

Meanwhile the Socialist Youth Federation (Federazione Giovanile Socialista—FGS) was also becoming a political force in Turin. The Federation's first Turin *fascio,* or section, was established in May 1909 by Giuseppe Romita, Gino Castagno, Angelo Tasca, and others.*

---

* See Gramsci, *La Città futura* [22], p. 4; Tasca, p. 3; Zucaro, "Gramsci all'Università," p. 1100. The Youth Federation was first established in Italy in 1898. As

The Central section consisted almost entirely of workers, Tasca and Romita being the only students. Other sections were organized in suburbs and neighboring towns, and the movement soon took on a regional character, divorcing itself from the extreme syndicalistic tendencies of the Federation's sections elsewhere in Italy. The leaders of the Central section did their best to bring some minimal measure of Socialist sophistication to the sections outside the city,[108] and at the same time worked to improve their own intellectual foundations. According to Tasca, the "positivistic" culture of the members was gradually eliminated by assiduous reading of Giuseppe Prezzolini's *La Voce* and Gaetano Salvemini's *L'Unità,* journals established to combat the alleged provincialism of Italian culture in the early years of the century. Salvemini was especially revered by the young Socialists because of his campaign in favor of the southern peasantry, his all-out attack on Giolitti's electioneering methods in the South, and his opposition to the Libyan War. His excellent relations with Mussolini—then the leader of the "Young Turks" of Italian Socialism—also made him popular.[109]

The Young Socialists in Piedmont tended to be puritanical. On one occasion the Federation's Borgo San Paolo section launched a crusade against drunkenness, and when this encountered resistance from local Party leaders (most of whom were heavy drinkers in the best Piedmontese tradition), indignantly set up separate headquarters and proceeded with the campaign.[110] This puritanical streak in Piedmont's younger Socialists was often resented by Party members from other regions.

In 1912–13, university students began to join the Socialist Youth Federation in larger numbers, Antonio Gramsci among them. Gramsci was not active at first; according to Togliatti, he seemed "rather narrow in his concerns, and still full of doubts about what course to pursue."[111] Philosophically, he was probably more a Crocean than a Marxist in these early days, but he was arriving at a Marxist position through his study of idealist philosophers, including Hegel, Croce, and Gentile.[112] The ideas of Croce and Gentile were closely related to those of Marxism in Italy. The connecting link was Antonio

---

early as 1906, a "circle of social studies" had been set up by young workers in Turin. In 1910 this developed into the "scuola moderna Francisco Ferrer," which became a point of contact between young Socialists and anarchists. (See Spriano, *Socialismo e classe operaia,* p. 40.) Romita (d. 1958) later became a member of the Italian Social Democratic Party; Castagno is still a member of the Italian Socialist Party; Tasca (d. 1960) was a member of the Italian Communist Party until his expulsion in 1929.

Labriola, a Marxist who matured in the Hegelian school at Naples.*
Hence, the gap between idealism and Marxism was not a difficult one
to bridge.

Gramsci's complete absorption in the Socialist movement dates
from the parliamentary elections of October 1913, which occurred
while he was in Sardinia awaiting the reopening of the school year.
These elections were the first in Italy based on nearly universal male
suffrage. Although corruption in the elections was widespread in the
southern and insular provinces, Gramsci was deeply impressed by the
sight of large peasant masses participating for the first time in political action. Meditation on the results of the election—the number
of Socialist delegates was doubled—fired him with enthusiasm, and
he began to devote more and more of his time to the Socialist movement.[113]

Gramsci's earliest work in the FGS was teaching the young workers
enrolled in the Central section. Many of these workers were self-
educated, serious, and intelligent; but what pleased Gramsci most
was their "force of character and moral rectitude," qualities he considered essential for building a stronger Socialist movement. He was
an extraordinarily effective teacher: "Those he instructed came out
profoundly and permanently transformed, and always remained
grateful to him."[114] Gramsci later recalled the sense of comradeship
and community of ideas:

We often left Party meetings in a group surrounding our leader. We continued our discussions through the streets of the by now silent city, while
the few late passersby stopped to watch us, amazed at our ferocious assertions, our explosive laughter, our sorties into the realm of dreams and the
impossible.

He especially valued

the feeling of trust that came from being comrades, from having the same
passion, the same dominant ideas.... That intimacy was our strength.
Thanks to this strength we could goad the Party into changing direction;
we could force it to realize that in us, the young men, lay the future. We
saw that future as a perfect alloy of the old Socialism, mistrustful and over-

---

* Labriola (1843–1904), sometimes called the first Italian Marxist, was a professor
of philosophy at the University of Rome. He should not be confused with Arturo
Labriola (1875–1959), the principal Italian theorist of revolutionary syndicalism
and Giolitti's Minister of Labor in 1920–21. In his earlier years, Antonio was a
leading figure in the Italian Hegelian school. Later he made important contributions to Marxist historical and philosophical theory and exerted a great intellectual influence on the young Benedetto Croce. See Labriola's *Essays on the Materi-
alistic Conception of History* (Chicago: Kerr, 1908).

cautious, which was losing contact with the proletarian masses, and the new Socialism, full of moral and revolutionary energy, in which there was not a Party and a proletariat but a single mass moving rapidly toward a goal that we sometimes saw as very near indeed.[115]

In 1914, Gramsci and Togliatti joined the Turin section of the Socialist Party. Their first important action as party members was to support a proposal, made by Tasca and Ottavio Pastore, that the Party nominate Gaetano Salvemini as its candidate for the parliamentary seat left vacant by the recent death of Pilade Gay, a Socialist deputy from Turin. Salvemini was known as a champion of the farm laborers (*braccianti*) of Apulia, his native region. The plan was to make his candidacy the first move in a campaign to gain support for the Socialist Party among the agricultural workers of the South. The executive committee of the Turin section approved the plan, but Salvemini did not accept the offer.[116]

At Salvemini's suggestion, the younger Socialists turned next to Benito Mussolini, at that time editor of *Avanti!,* the Party's central organ, a man whose revolutionary militancy was widely admired by young Party members. The majority of the Turin section, however, supported the candidacy of Mario Bonetto, a Turin worker; and Mussolini, despite his prior acceptance, was unable to stand for the seat. Nevertheless, both Salvemini and Mussolini came to Turin to support Bonetto in the campaign. Gramsci always thought of this episode as an important step in the history of the Italian Socialist movement. The leaders of an important northern section had accepted Salvemini, a representative of the southern peasantry, as the Party candidate in their constituency. This was something new. Even though Salvemini refused the offer, Gramsci felt that Turin's action set it apart—and marked it as one of the most progressive of Italian sections, since it had recognized the Mezzogiorno problem as one that the revolutionary proletariat must solve.

3. The War Years in Turin

Si sente odore di novità nell'aria.
Il mondo è ad una svòlta decisiva.

—*Gramsci, February 11, 1917*

The PSI and World War I

The World War threw European Socialism into the worst crisis of its history. Were Socialists to repudiate their internationalism and fight for their country, or were they to repudiate their country in the name of the international working class? Because of Italy's neutrality, Italian Socialists had a better opportunity to work out a consistent position than Socialists in the belligerent countries, and when Italy did enter the war in May 1915, the Party's official line was established: "Neither support nor sabotage." Trotsky later complained that this position was inspired less by Socialist principles than by humanitarianism or pacifism, but the criticism is unjust.[1] It took courage for Socialists to oppose the war, especially when opposition led to imprisonments and other disciplinary measures by the government. Moreover, the Party's solidarity on this point was impressive: its leaders and most of its members steadily opposed the war from 1915 to 1918, and members with other ideas were immediately recalled to order or expelled.[2] Lenin's praise of the PSI as a "happy exception" among the parties of the Second International was well deserved.[3]

Antiwar sentiments were especially strong among the Turin Socialists. Interventionism was widespread among the workers of Parma and had won over a few of the Milanese, but at Turin "no cracks appeared in the neutralist ranks of the working class."[4] The absence of a strong Radical-Republican tradition in Turin helped, since such groups, where they did exist, were thoroughly interventionist. The city's neutralism also extended to its Giolittian liberals and bourgeoisie in general, since the winter of 1914–15 had brought a boom in the automobile industry.[5] In April 1915, the Turin Chamber of Labor asked the national executive committee of the CGL to hold a referendum to determine if a general strike should follow a mobilization order. Most members of the Confederation responded negatively, but the council of the Turin Chamber voted almost unanimously for the general strike, as did the Socialist section.[6]

On May 16, 1915, while the Party directorate was meeting at Bologna to decide what to do about Italy's imminent participation in the war, the Turin workers declared a general strike. "All the factories were closed, all public services completely paralyzed. The strike was total among all categories of workers."[7] The entire working force of the city gathered before the Chamber of Labor, and then slowly marched—without the urging of speeches—toward the Prefecture to protest the war. At this point, the mounted police intervened, killing one worker and wounding 14 others. The crowd dispersed, but reassembled in the afternoon, whereupon the police attacked the Chamber of Labor itself, sacked the building, and arrested several dozen workers gathered there. Meanwhile, news arrived from Bologna that the Party directorate had decided to let each provincial Federation make its own decisions about antiwar measures. This decision left the Turin workers completely isolated, and they abandoned their general strike the next day. Four days later, on May 23, 1915, Italy entered the war.[8]

This declaration of the Party directorate revealed a certain incoherence in the Party's thinking. Its members genuinely opposed the war, but had no concrete program for making their opposition effective. Perhaps because of the recent formation of the Italian State and the growing pains that still assailed it, many Italian Socialists underestimated the importance of nationalism in the war, and some Socialist leaders denied the very concept of "nationality" in Italy. When workers who had pondered the experience of the French and Belgians asked how Socialists should behave if Italy were attacked, the Party's answers were too theoretical to satisfy them. Moreover, some Party members were actively interventionist on the ground that Italian participation in the war would bring rapid industrialization and a consequent movement of the peasants into the factories.

In October 1914, Benito Mussolini became the spokesman for Socialists dissatisfied with the Party's "absolute" neutrality. In a series of editorials appearing in *Avanti!*, Mussolini called for different Socialist attitudes toward the Central Powers and the Entente. He also argued that a Socialist general strike could not prevent war, and that

Italian Socialists could not ignore the national question, especially in the Trentino.

If the concept of nation is "outdated," if national defense is an absurdity to a proletariat that has nothing to defend, we must have the courage to rebuke the Socialists of Belgium and France, who, faced with the German invasion, united themselves—temporarily, of course!—with the nation; and consequently we must deduce that the only genuine, authentic, and pure Socialism in the world is Italian Socialism. But for many reasons such sanctimoniousness would be unbecoming![9]

Few Italian Socialists were willing to follow Mussolini in repudiating neutralism; but many of the younger Socialists and a few of the older moderates were for a time impressed by his arguments. Leftist democrats like Salvemini were frankly enthusiastic:

Dear Mussolini,

While on the train I read your magnificent article on non-absolute neutrality, and I feel I want to congratulate you on it. Again your healthy and strong instincts have led you to do the right thing. It is no small act of courage, this violating the letter to save the spirit of internationalism in this country of sextons and chatterers.[10]

Shortly afterward, a complex debate on neutrality appeared in the pages of Turin's Socialist weekly, *Il Grido del popolo*. Angelo Tasca published two articles on October 24 and November 7, and Gramsci contributed an article entitled "Active and Operating Neutrality" to the issue of October 31.[11] Tasca felt that opposition to the war was valuable as a "negative myth," helping to separate the working classes from bourgeois authority. Gramsci, by contrast, saw the Party's official neutralism as teaching a "Buddhist renunciation" of action, a passivity (*attesismo*) incompatible with the Party's aspirations to an active role in national life. This was particularly unfortunate at a time when the Italian proletariat was developing a "national consciousness" and a sense of solidarity.[12]

In this hesitant support of Mussolini, Gramsci clearly thought of the Romagnole leader as still a revolutionary Socialist. Gramsci felt —and he assumed Mussolini agreed—that the war itself would bring about a collapse of the bourgeois order: "Nor does Mussolini's position deny (indeed it presupposes) that the proletariat should renounce its antagonistic attitude. After the failure or evident impotence of the ruling class, it can eliminate that class and take over the state—if I have properly interpreted his [Mussolini's] somewhat disorganized declarations."[13] However, this pronouncement is not typi-

cal. The principal element of continuity between the young Gramsci
and the mature thinker is a stress on the creative and active role that
Italian Socialism must play if it is to realize its revolutionary poten-
tialities.

Gramsci's qualified defense of Mussolini was short-lived. After November 15, when Mussolini began publishing his frankly interventionist newspaper, *Il Popolo d'Italia,* Gramsci and all his friends opposed him.* In that same month the neutralist majority of the Turin
section accepted Gramsci as a regular contributor to its weekly organ,
Il Grido del popolo.[14]

Gramsci's first ties in the Party were with its revolutionary "abstentionist" faction, led by Amadeo Bordiga of Naples. Bordiga's
opposition to the war was more thoroughgoing and logical than that
of the Party leadership; he had developed his position in a series of
articles in *Avanti!,* written in 1914–15, which affirmed, as Lenin had,
the imperialist nature of the war.[15] Gramsci's adherence to this faction marks the beginning of his rise in the Party, which was facilitated
by his exemption from military service owing to poor health. At the
beginning of 1916, in addition to his work for *Il Grido del popolo,*
he began to write the local news and theatrical columns for the Turin
edition of *Avanti!*[16]

Zimmerwald and Kienthal

Just as the great metalworkers' strikes of 1912–13 had established
the economic militancy of the Turin labor movement, so the events
of May 1915 established its political militancy. "Public" meetings
were forbidden, and censorship of newspapers and other publications
was applied from the day Italy entered the war; but political debate
did not stop within the Socialist organizations. In Turin, as elsewhere, Socialists took two positions toward the war. The moderate
leaders, while rejecting direct support of the war, insisted that the
Party's task was not to weaken the country but to protect the proletariat against exploitation. This was also the position of the Party
directorate: "Neither support nor sabotage." The left wing, on the

---

* Tasca, "La Storia," p. 4. Aldo Romano contends—correctly in my opinion—that
Tasca is incorrect in attributing an "interventionist" position to Gramsci, even in
October 1914. Gramsci seriously intended a "neutralità attiva e operante" even if
Mussolini did not. Spriano (*Torino operaia,* p. 90) points out that Tasca and Ottavio Pastore wrote to Mussolini in the hope of dissuading him from this final
break with the Socialist movement. Mussolini characteristically answered: "Alea
jacta est. I must speak to the masses every day."

other hand, wanted complete disassociation from the "bourgeois war"; it refused to participate in public bodies constituted to deal with the war effort, even if its participation might have benefited the working class. By late 1916, it had taken an almost insurrectionary position.[17]

In Turin the left wing controlled the section—directly or indirectly—from the beginning of the war until August 1917. This was not as significant as it might have been, since the Socialist deputies from Piedmont, the Socialists on the city council, and many Turin labor leaders were moderates. Moreover, the section had less than a thousand members in 1915. Still, the Left spoke for the majority of the Turin workers throughout the war, as the events of 1917 were to show.

The leaders of the Left called themselves "rigid intransigents." Francesco Barberis, perhaps the best known, had the "ardor of a tribune of the people."[18] His role in the textile workers' strike of 1906 had made him famous, and his fiery plebeian oratory was popular in the city.[19] Pietro Rabezzana had come to Socialism from the Republican Party, and often expressed ideas close to those of revolutionary syndicalism. Other leaders of the Left were Giovanni Boero, a worker who distrusted intellectuals and excessive emphasis on the "cultural" tasks of the party, and Elvira Zocchi, noted for her work in the women's movement and her uncompromising "defeatism," that is, total opposition to the war effort. She probably spoke for many of her fellow intransigents when she said, "I came to Socialism mainly through feeling, through that instinct for rebellion that is common to all members of the working class."[20]

The Turin intransigents were at first unable to organize any effective program of opposition to the war, in part, perhaps, because they disdained cooperation with the neutralist middle classes of the city.[21] They were more successful in the area of proletarian internationalism. By 1915, the Second International had all but disappeared. Efforts to replace it in one way or another were soon made, and the Italian Socialist Party contributed greatly to the success of these efforts. According to Guido Miglioli, "In those years, Italian Socialism wrote the purest and most appealing page of its history.... Once again it was distinguished from the Socialism of almost all other countries."[22]

In July 1915, Oddino Morgari and Angelica Balabanoff met in Bern with Russian, Polish, and Swiss Socialists to plan a conference of all Socialist organizations, from both neutral and belligerent states, that had maintained their opposition to the war. All factions of the PSI declared themselves in favor of such a meeting. On September 5, the Conference opened in the Swiss mountain village of Zimmerwald. About 40 delegates representing 13 countries were present, though the German and French delegations belonged to the minority opposition within their parties. The Italian delegates were Balabanoff, Morgari, G. M. Serrati, Costantino Lazzari, and G. E. Modigliani. The Conference split over Lenin's proposal to transform the capitalist war into a revolutionary war; most delegates favored the Italian position, which emphasized measures aimed only at ending the war. All, however, including Lenin, supported the so-called Zimmerwald Manifesto.[23] This proclamation called the war a product of imperialism, and condemned those Socialist parties that had abandoned the class struggle and accepted the war. It called for mass action to end the war and bring about a peace settlement without annexations or indemnities.

The editor of *Avanti!*, Serrati, published the Manifesto despite the vigilance of the censors.[24] On the evening of October 13 Serrati, as required by law, sent his four-page newspaper to the Milan censor, who approved it. As soon as the copy was returned, Serrati replaced the innocuous second page of the newspaper with a page containing the Zimmerwald Manifesto and other news of the conference. The edition was distributed throughout Italy, except for Milan, and even in France.*

The whole structure of Italian Socialism—the Party directorate, the CGL, and the Socialist local administrations—approved the work of Zimmerwald. In Turin, Bruno Buozzi announced the Fiom's support of the Zimmerwald decisions,[25] and the Young Socialists adopted a pin with the letters FAZ ("Zimmerwald Alpine Federation").[26] Gramsci praised the Conference as evidence that the malfunctioning of the Bureau Socialiste International at Brussels did not mean the end of proletarian internationalism:

For us the International is an act of the spirit. It is the consciousness of unity that the proletarians of the world have (when they have it), . . . a sense of united forces striving by common agreement, though in a variety of national forms, toward one common goal: replacing the bourgeois civilization with Socialism.[27]

---

* No proceedings were instituted against Serrati because the government was afraid that such a move would stir up even greater proletarian resistance to the war.

A second conference, held in Kienthal, Switzerland, in April 1916, was more radical than the first. It condemned the pro-Entente policies of the Brussels Bureau, and, at Lenin's suggestion, discussed abandoning the Second International and founding a Third. Lenin was supported by Serrati and Balabanoff, but the majority rejected a total break with the Bureau.[28] On June 21, Serrati went to Turin to lecture on the lesson of Zimmerwald and Kienthal: in Gramsci's words, this was "that the womb from which all proletarian movements have sprung is not exhausted, that no bourgeois surgery can make it sterile."[29] Years later, Gramsci praised Serrati for his largely successful efforts to maintain Party unity while rejecting the war, and called him "the noblest representative of the old school of Italian revolutionary Socialism."[30]

After Kienthal, the political activities of Turin Socialism increased. Pietro Rabezzana gave a series of lectures on the "union of the workers of the world," which he claimed took precedence over the International; he attacked moderate Socialism and exalted the trade union as the basis of the social revolution. In May 1916, Maria Giudice, a particularly simpleminded intransigent, became editor of *Il Grido del popolo* and began an all-out attack on the moderates. To a complaint that the paper was becoming too simple, she answered: *"Il Grido* is not yet simple enough, easy enough, clear enough. Propaganda is aimed at the humblest of the masses, who are used to reading less in books of theory and more in the book of life. . . . Theories or no theories, when the masses *feel* like Socialists, they will act like Socialists."[31] Gramsci was not one to sympathize with such a policy, and he wrote only four more articles for *Il Grido* until he himself became its editor in August 1917. During this period his journalistic activity was otherwise limited to writing the Turin page of *Avanti!*

Gramsci's Work in 1916

Until the summer of 1917, Gramsci took no direct part in the political debates of the Turin section. From his journalistic work, however, it is plain that he had no sympathy for the methods and ideological baggage of the intransigents, though he certainly shared many of their aims. He was even further from the few reformists in the Turin section. The young Socialists who had been closest to him had been called up by 1916—notably Tasca, Terracini, and Togliatti. Consequently, the young Sardinian devoted himself exclusively to his work for the Socialist press, deriving his only income from this work. In January 1916, he began to write his column "Sotto la Mole" for the Turin page of *Avanti!* Spriano describes the column as a "brilliant daily lesson in a robust journalistic style that was new to the Party press."[32] Years later, Professor Umberto Cosmo suggested that Gramsci collect and publish these articles.[33]

The articles demonstrated a deep concern with the cultural and educational aspects of Socialism. A characteristic one, published in June 1916, is entitled "Socialism and Culture."[34] It attacks the propensity, then common in Turin, to oppose "culture and intellectualism" to "*practice* and the *historical reality* by which the [working] class is preparing the future with its own hands." Gramsci emphasizes the need for a creative dialectic between the daily struggles of the workers and their ideological level. He finds a basis for his position in Vico's assertion that the consciousness of human equality produced the democratic republics of antiquity.

By culture, however, Gramsci does not mean encyclopedic knowledge. Pure learning, he says, results only in a false sense of superiority. Thus any student or lawyer looks down on the "best of skilled workers, whose precise and indispensable performance of his task is worth a hundred times what the others do."[35] Gramsci asserts that self-knowledge and knowledge of one's historical rights and duties do not come spontaneously,

but by intelligent reflection, first by a few and then by the whole class, on why certain conditions exist and how best to convert the facts of vassalage into the signals of rebellion and social reconstruction. In short, every revolution has been preceded by hard critical thinking, the diffusion of culture, and the spread of ideas among men who are at first unwilling to listen, men concerned only with solving their own private economic and political problems, men who feel no solidarity with others in the same condition.[36]

Thus the Enlightenment had given all Europe a "united consciousness, a bourgeois spiritual International, sensitive to the common woes and misfortunes, which was the best possible preparation for the bloody French revolution that followed." And thus the working class must create its own Enlightenment, based on knowledge of "the 'others,' their history, and the successive efforts they have made to become what they are, to create the civilization they have created, which we seek to replace with our own."[37]

In other articles, Gramsci deplored the contemporary emphasis in education on book learning, rather than on what he called the "re-creative spirit."[38] He opposed a purely technical education for workers as playing into the hands of bourgeois industrialists.[39] In an article celebrating the tenth anniversary of the first important textile strike in Turin, Gramsci saw the strike as having been above all an education in class consciousness. The worker has now (1916) become "the warrior of an idea. He is the crusader on his way to the conquest of a promised land. He knows what he wants, has closed ranks and forced others to recognize his values, . . . when only a little while ago he was humble and resigned."[40]

Gramsci's ideal of the Socialist intellectual as educator was best expressed in his praise of Charles Péguy. Gramsci saw Péguy as a man "who wore himself out in a daily struggle for the inner education of others, sacrificing his own artistic personality to give the youth of France a new consciousness." Gramsci fancied that Péguy, like himself, expected the redemption of society from corrupt values to come only "from the depths, from the lowest social classes."[41]

Gramsci's emphasis in "Socialism and Culture" on "solidarity with others in the same condition" undoubtedly reflects his continuing concern with the Mezzogiorno. In another article of 1916, he praises Arturo Labriola as the only deputy courageous enough to raise the question of the effects of the war on the South.[42] Gramsci asserted that the upswing in capital development that the war brought about would increase the economic gap between North and South, since "where the factory already exists, it continues to develop through investment, but where every enterprise is uncertain and flighty, savings . . . are invested where they can immediately be put to use." Although Salandra's government had promised a new postwar plan for the South, Gramsci argued that this plan would be "forgotten, like many others made in the past."

La Città Futura

By far the most important of Gramsci's early writings was *La Città futura,* a short treatise published in newspaper format by the Socialist Youth Federation of Piedmont on February 11, 1917, as part of a campaign to attract recruits. The work may be regarded as a summary and synthesis of Gramsci's University training and his experiences in the Italian Socialist movement. It also offers an interesting indication of his ideas on the eve of the February Revolution in Russia. The theme of *La Città futura* is Gramsci's belief in the power of the will, guided by an intelligent analysis of reality and disciplined by a strong political party, to effect fundamental changes in society and the state. In a word, his concern is with "the Mazzinian tradition in Socialist terms."[43]

The lead article, "Tre principi, tre ordini," maintained that the

Socialist revolution would come sooner in Italy than in the advanced states of Western Europe, precisely because of the backwardness of Italy. This thesis was a frontal attack on the Italian reformists, who insisted that Italy would become Socialist only after Italian capitalism and its liberal state were "mature." Gramsci supported his argument by an analysis of the following problems: will as an agent for effecting change; the English and German States as expressions of mature capitalism; a comparison of them with the Italian State.[44]

According to Gramsci, human activity, to be effective, must have an aim capable of being realized. This is especially true of Socialist activity, since Socialists must overcome the masses' reluctance to risk the chaos that might accompany the transition to a new society. The Utopian Socialists, in attempting to overcome this reluctance, outlined their future society in every particular. But the complexity of events makes it impossible to predict the future so completely; hence it is hard to persuade people to work to bring about utopias of this sort. No such difficulties attend the support of an idea, a juridical principle, or a moral "law," since these can be conceived of apart from the specific nature of the society in which they are embodied. Thus, the French revolutionaries of 1789 did not attempt to establish the capitalist order; their aim was to propagate the "Rights of Man."

To be sure, the bourgeoisie in the end benefited most from the Revolution. Nonetheless, the principles established by the bourgeois revolutions were regarded as rational and universal—therefore, applicable to all men. On the basis of these principles an "ethical state" was created, a state that ideally stood above the interests of specific persons and classes. This state was an ideal, not a reality; however, it was precisely its ideal character that gave it strength and made it a powerful conservative force. In the hope that it might finally be realized in its complete perfection, many could not bring themselves to work for its overthrow.

Contemporary England and Germany were the best examples of this ethical state. In a formal sense they seemed radically different, but both were powerful political organisms that presumed to stand above the interests of their individual citizens. Liberalism was the key principle of the British State, whereas authority with the aid of reason guided the German State.

Liberalism arose in England as a product of the struggle for constitutional freedoms; it contended that truth came from the free competition of ideas, and economic strength from the spontaneous development of productive forces. Thus Lloyd George, commenting on Socialist proposals shortly before the war, said that a Socialist government would come about when and if the Socialists proved in the marketplace of political ideas that they were the strongest and most capable party. Astonishing as this statement appeared to Italians, who thought of their government as unrelated to the vital forces of the country, it "was not empty rhetoric." It referred to a right won by the English people in two hundred years of political struggle.

The German State, by contrast, was authoritarian. It deplored as inefficient the competition of freely operating political forces, and favored a stable program based on reason. The German parliament had no real power. It existed only because one could not rationally assert the infallibility of the executive power, and a parliamentary discussion might bring forth truth. Yet injustice was rare in Germany, and the interests of all classes were protected.

These two "ethical states" were the basic models for the liberal and conservative parties of Italy, England for the liberals, Germany for the conservatives. But Italy had never gone through the period of political and economic development that had created modern England and Germany; hence both models were anticipatory. Worse, their essential import was that the Italian *proletariat* must sacrifice its economic and political interests so that the new Italian State might be created in the shortest possible time. Both the liberals and the conservatives were bent on transforming Italy's present disorder into a new order, but in each case this new order could be achieved only if the power of the Socialists remained limited.

For Gramsci, however, the nonexistence of a political order in Italy was the Socialists' "greatest source of energy and aggressiveness."

In countries where open conflicts do not take place, where fundamental laws of the State are not trampled on, where arbitrary acts of the dominant class are not seen, the class struggle loses its harshness, the revolutionary struggle loses its drive and falters.... Where an order exists, it is more difficult to decide to replace it with a new order.

The Italian Socialists did not have to substitute a new order for the old, but merely to create an order where none existed before. The Italian order would "give every citizen the chance to fulfill himself," and thus would repeal the traditional privileges of the Italian ruling classes. Since "all the principles of the Socialist maximum program are organically related to this one, the program is not utopian...

It can be actuated by will." In the circumstances, Gramsci believed that a Socialist order "will be created in Italy sooner than in any other country."

This article has been summarized in considerable detail because it provides a framework for all the other writings in *La Città futura*, and because it indicates the strength at that time of Gramsci's "idealist" and "voluntaristic" tendencies, for which he was often criticized by his enemies in the Socialist Party.[45] In itself the article "Tre principi" is unimpressive. Many of its ideas are not sufficiently developed, and its conclusion, however interesting, is analytically weak. The remaining articles of *La Città futura* are less grandiose and more down-to-earth.

In the "Indifferenti," Gramsci eloquently attacks those who refuse to involve themselves in the political movements of the time.[46] The article is also a clear statement of his lifelong opposition to historical determinism:

It seems that history is only an enormous natural phenomenon, an eruption, an earthquake that leaves us all victims, both him who wills and him who is indifferent. The latter becomes irritated. He would like to disassociate himself from the consequences, to make it clear that he did not will and is not responsible. . . . But almost nobody asks himself, "If I too had done my duty, if I had sought to make my will and counsel prevail, would this have happened?"

The following article urges young men to join the Socialist Youth Federation. For Gramsci, joining a political party was the most effective way of influencing the development of history:

To join a movement means to assume a part of the responsibility for coming events. . . . A young man who joins the Socialist youth movement performs an act of independence and liberation. To discipline oneself is to make oneself independent and free. Water is pure and free when it runs between the two banks of a stream or river, not when it is dispersed chaotically on the soil.[47]

In the same antideterministic vein, Gramsci attacked the reformist Socialism of Claudio Treves:

Life for them [the reformists] is like an avalanche seen from afar in its irresistible descent. "Can I stop it?" asks the homunculus. "No. Therefore, it obeys no will. Since the human avalanche obeys a logic that may not be mine, and since I as an individual do not have the strength to stop it or divert it, I am convinced that it does not have an inner logic, but obeys natural, unbreakable laws."[48]

This kind of determinism, according to Gramsci, was destroyed by the late-nineteenth-century crisis in scientific thought, which had resulted in the limitation of scientific method to those problems it was competent to solve. True Socialism had survived that crisis: "The tenacious will of man was substituted for natural law and the pseudo-scientific fatal course of things. . . . Socialism is not dead, because men of good will toward it still exist."[49] This strongly "subjectivistic" judgment is a result of Gramsci's training in idealist philosophy.*

The newspaper was completed by several other articles and notes on problems of culture and Italian society, including writings selected from the works of Salvemini, Croce, and Armando Carlini. The *Città futura*, in spite of its immaturity of expression, is an important document in Gramsci's life. It represents his first effort to come to terms with some of the basic values that later made him a leading figure of the Italian Left: a strong antideterminism, a belief in the importance of planning, an emphasis on political discipline, and a commitment to the philosophy of the Italian idealists, particularly Croce, whom Gramsci called "the greatest thinker in Europe at this moment."[50]

The August Insurrection

Soon after the publication of *La Città futura*, Gramsci's participation in the Socialist movement moved beyond mere journalism. On August 21, 1917, the great insurrection for "peace and bread" broke out in Turin. Gramsci described this desperate uprising as "an armed revolutionary struggle on a large scale," and called Turin "the Petrograd of the Italian proletarian revolution."[51] The authorities referred to it in the traditional phrase "i fatti di Torino," the Turin events, thus playing down its political character.[52] The facts of the insurrection have only recently been revealed by the work of Monticone, Avigdor, Spriano, Zucaro, and Ambrosoli.[53] Its origins go back at least to September 1916, when a number of demonstrators were arrested at a meeting held at the AGO to protest the death sentence of the anarchist Carlo Tresca. The report (or "sentence") of the Territorial Military Court on the events of August 1917 refers to this as the "first of a series of meetings, nominally private but really public, that were held in rapid succession."[54] A few days later, Maria Giudice

---

* Years later, in 1931, he remarked (G to Tatiana, 18.iv.31, *Lettere* [1], p. 124) that the West's "almost religious faith in science" had been destroyed by modern philosophy, "and by the disaster of political democracy." Here the "limitation" of science, though still accepted as a historical fact, is clearly seen as regrettable.

and Umberto Terracini were arrested for distributing flyers on the Kienthal meeting. Terracini was immediately conscripted and sent to the front.

The anarchists offered the most violent denunciation of the war. A typical anarchist manifesto (dated September 21, 1916) urged immediate revolt:

Are you not yet convinced that this dynastic war, this bourgeois war, this war that has been destroying the fruits of your labor and killing your children for over two years, can be ended only by opposing proletarian violence to bourgeois violence? . . . Your social emancipation will be obtained only by social revolution. . . . The guns that the bourgeoisie has made to destroy you, carry them into the streets, to the barricades, into battle against the authorities. . . . Proletarians! Up with your axe and pick; the barricades, the social revolution! Your enemy is not at the so-called frontiers, but here! You have no fatherland to defend, but rather the life of the proletariat, a proletariat wounded by the bullets of the bourgeois and the military. Workers, the course the government has set for you is revolt! Ready your arms, take your positions, and let the battle start![55]

The Young Socialists also called for the "hour of action," and the intransigent Socialists began a more intense campaign against the moderates. In a meeting of September 22 at the AGO, Barberis warned his listeners that they "must prefer going to prison to dying in the trenches. . . . Now deeds and not words are needed. We must persist in our efforts to make the Socialists of Italy and Europe understand that only with force can we create peace and destroy imperialism and militarism."[56]

The "rigid intransigents," unable to convince a majority of the section to follow them, lost control of the executive committee by a narrow margin at the end of 1916, but the new leadership, like the old, favored all-out opposition to the war. The Prefect of Turin, in fact, asked permission of the Minister of the Interior to dissolve the Socialist section, the Chamber of Labor, and the Youth Federation, but the request was not granted.[57] Despite the intransigents' minority status in the section, their political line remained influential. Indeed, the Turin delegates to the Socialist convention held at Rome on February 25–27, 1917, were all intransigents (Rabezzana, Barberis, Giudice, and Carlo Chiappo), and they supported extremist motions, notably Bordiga's motion for revolutionary action to end the war.[58] In Turin, the section went so far as to pass a resolution—though by a narrow margin—calling for Socialist members of communal and provincial administrations to prepare to resign from office, a step that would have sacrificed the Socialist administrations of Milan and Bologna. On February 26, *Avanti!* described the Turin Socialists in general as "the fiercest intransigents," and the Director of the State Police warned the Prefect that "moderate Socialist elements have lost all influence" over the working class of the city.[59] This was the political atmosphere within which Gramsci wrote his articles for *La Città futura*.

Economic conditions also influenced the mood of the Turin workers in 1917. On the basis of research by Fossati and others, Spriano has concluded that in Italy as a whole real wages decreased from 1915 to 1918, and that the decrease accelerated from one year to the next.[60] In Turin, the great majority of the workers found their real wages lagging behind prices, although the more skilled and better organized, like the automobile workers, sometimes managed to keep up with prices by working overtime or sending unemployed family members to work. Even Giuseppe Prato, a rather conservative economist, noted the absolute decrease in Turin of meat, butter, and sugar consumption between 1912–14 and 1917–18.[61] But these conclusions all derive from postwar research; during the war, there was much grumbling by the middle classes about the allegedly high wages and reckless spending of the workers. Prato himself, though his judgment evidently changed after the war, inveighed against the "universal display of luxury, as costly as it is vulgar," and the "thoughtless squandering by the masses that has been made possible by their excessive wages."[62] Somewhat later, Gramsci answered such charges with the biting irony that he reserved for academicians he considered pedantic and demagogic:

[Professor Prato] should have explained to us, since we know we are ignorant and always seek to drink at the fountains of knowledge, by what critical process an increase in the sale of wine by the Alleanza Cooperativa becomes a scientific proof of intense alcoholism, and why it cannot be less demagogically explained by the opening of new stores and by the greater number of customers who drink this wine while dining. By what critical process does the fact that the Socialists, like economic liberals, are against forced savings lead to the conclusion that the workers do not save, when the savings-and-loan bank of the ACT shows the contrary with its figures? This critical process is called "ignorance of the document"; and Prato did not know the document because the scholar in him gave way to the partisan, because Prato, in addition to being a scholar, is a demagogue. Demagoguery is not a practice restricted to Socialists, but a general set of mind by which, in order to vanquish one's adversary, one neglects considerations that might support his position.[63]

Prato's polemic reflects the fury of the Turin middle class, which found itself caught between "war profiteers" on the one hand and "privileged" workers on the other. Many of this class found their savings and modest salaries almost obliterated by wartime inflation.

The workers, for their part, resented not only the economic difficulties brought about by wartime inflation, but also wartime working conditions. Rigid military discipline and long hours prevailed in most Turin factories during the war. In each shop, the government had established a "Committee of Industrial Mobilization," which was composed of owners' and workers' representatives and presided over by a government official who held the real power. Although many factories also had an internal committee elected solely by the workers, this organ was not legally recognized and had little power to negotiate.*

Despite all these causes for discontent, the most important reason for the August insurrection was probably the news of events in Russia. Nearly everyone in Italy was at first pleased with the February Revolution—the constitutional parties because it seemed to give the Allied cause a more consistently democratic character, and the Socialists because for them it represented the first stage in the breaking up of the old European order. As the situation in Russia deteriorated, however, opinions soon divided. On April 29, the Turin Socialists indicated their support of Lenin when *Il Grido del popolo* called him "the most Socialist and the most revolutionary of the authoritative leaders of the Russian Socialist parties." Lenin's name and some of his doctrines, it will be remembered, were already well known in Italy because of the Zimmerwald and Kienthal conferences. Gramsci predicted in the same number of the Turin weekly that the revolution "must naturally result in a Socialist regime."[64] And at a meeting in Turin on May 6, Barberis attacked Ugo Mondolfo for his skepticism regarding the possibilities of building Socialism in a backward country like Russia.[65] Throughout the spring, a series of flyers exalting the Russian Revolution were distributed in Turin and the provinces. Spriano reproduces the following example from the reports of the Prefect:

* Montagnana, pp. 56–57; Spriano, *Torino operaia*, p. 170. Ambrosoli (*Nè aderire*, pp. 212–13) points out that although the internal committee was at this time elected solely by the workers, half of its members had to be chosen from a list of names drawn up by the management, at least in factories where the workers were represented by the Fiom.

Comrades, our comrades in Russia, in an admirable example of proletarian force, are carrying out a work of justice. If all other peoples would do likewise, war would cease. Let us imitate them, comrades. Proletarian soldiers, when they tell you that the proletariat hates you, give them the lie. What we are doing is for the common good. Follow the example of your Russian comrades. Don't be parricides. Unite with us in the cause of peace and freedom.[66]

This inflamed atmosphere continued throughout the spring and early summer of 1917. The intransigents led the campaign. On May 27 Rabezzana insisted that the time had come for a general insurrection; the workers were to equip themselves with explosives from the factories where they were made, and use them against anyone who opposed "the movement and the will of the people."[67] Serrati came from Milan, apparently to coordinate the Turin movement with those in other cities;[68] but this show of interest was not enough to allay the dissatisfaction of Barberis and Rabezzana with the "zigzag politics" of the Party's national leadership, from which they forthwith resigned.[69] In Florence, during July and early August, the Turin intransigents helped form a national "intransigent revolutionary faction" of the Party. The new faction, which proved to be especially strong in Turin, Milan, Naples, and Florence, decried nationalism as a bourgeois sentiment and preached violence as "the midwife of all societies pregnant with the revolution."[70] The authorities simply ignored this direct challenge to the war effort, perhaps because they underestimated the potential strength of the new faction.

Among the middle classes of the city, neutralism was becoming more assertive. A police inspector reported that "in Turin public opinion in all classes has always been generally opposed to the war, and remains so. It is therefore natural that in Turin, more than elsewhere, one finds fertile ground for the seeds of peace, however prematurely sown."[71] In June the mayor of Turin, Teofilo Rossi, was forced to resign after he announced that "Giolitti is more than ever in the hearts of Italians."[72] On August 13 Giolitti himself attacked the government for its leadership in the war, and especially for sanctioning "unequal sacrifices" and "social injustice."[73]

On August 13 another event occurred that linked enthusiasm for the Russian Revolution with local discontent and defeatism. In late July, the Kerensky government, with the express consent of the Allies, had sent a delegation of the Petrograd Soviet to visit England, France, and Italy. The delegation, headed by Joseph Goldenberg and com-

posed entirely of Mensheviks, was to present to the workers of Western Europe Kerensky's program for a simultaneous struggle for peace
on the diplomatic level and a continued war effort at the front. For
the first time since the beginning of the war, the Italian government
permitted public meetings of Socialists to greet the delegation. On
August 13 the group arrived at Turin, the culminating point of their
trip,[74] where a crowd of about 25,000 workers gathered to hear them.[75]
To the Russians' surprise, they were greeted with cries of "Viva
Lenin!" (Shortly before the meeting, Gramsci, in *Il Grido,* had exalted the Bolshevik leader—at that time an outlaw in Russia—as the
hope of the Russian Revolution.)[76] Lenin apart, the meeting was a
great success. Goldenberg's speech, in which he praised the peace
movement but did not favor a separate Russian peace with the Central Powers, was "translated" for the crowd by Serrati, who evidently
made it appear that the Russian was calling for an immediate end
to the war.[77] Other speakers were Maria Giudice, Barberis, the anarchist Anselmo Acutis, and the wounded war veteran Giuseppe Pianezza, who assured the crowd that "the soldiers were tired of the war
and ardently desired peace."[78]

Spriano calls this rally the "spark" that ignited the "barrel of
powder."[79] The actual explosion occurred a week later, when an
economic spark was added to the political effect of the Russian mis-
sion. A shortage of grain in Turin had been noted much earlier in
the year, but a true crisis began in August. On the morning of August
21, about eighty bakeries in the city failed to open.[80] A number of
demonstrations occurred—most of the demonstrators were women
and children—and the authorities responded by importing unusually
large supplies of wheat for sale on the 23rd. This move came too late,
however, and the agitation quickly shifted from an economic to a
political base.[81] Mario Montagnana, then a worker in the Diatto-
Fréjus plant, vividly describes this change: "Instead of entering the
factory, we began a demonstration outside the gates, shouting: 'We
haven't eaten. We can't work. We want bread!' " When Pietro Diatto,
the factory owner, assured them that a truckload of bread would soon
arrive and urged them to enter the factory, "The workers were quiet
for a moment. They looked at each other as though they were tacitly
conferring. Then all together they shouted, 'To hell with the bread!
We want peace! Down with the profiteers! Down with the war!' And
they left the factory en masse."[82]

The first clashes between police and workers took place that afternoon. Pitched battles between workers and soldiers followed, most of them in the working-class quarters around the periphery of the city, notably the Borgo San Paolo, the Barriera di Nizza, and Barriera di Milano. The workers protected their quarters in the traditional revolutionary manner by elaborate barricades of trees, railway cars, and trams.[83] Several military barracks were assaulted to obtain arms, and at least two churches were sacked.* For strategic reasons the insurgents tried to reach the center of the city, and on August 24, at the height of the revolt, they nearly succeeded; but they were finally turned back with machine guns and tanks. By August 26, after five days of desperate fighting, the revolt was essentially over. It was one of the bloodiest events in the history of the Italian labor movement.

There were two principal reasons for the failure of the uprising. The first was the inability of the insurgents to win over the soldiers.[84] According to one source, a "whole platoon of Alpini that had received an order to fire handed their rifles to the workers,"[85] but this was evidently an isolated episode. Gino Castagno describes a more typical unit, the Sassari Brigade, "famous for the rigidity of its officers and the ignorance of its soldiers, who were poor peasants and shepherds of Sardinia." According to Castagno, these peasant-soldiers had been stirred up against the workers by being told that their families' poverty was a direct result of the workers' high wages.[86] The use of Sardinian peasants against Turinese workers was of course especially painful to Gramsci. The second and more serious reason for the revolt's failure was the almost complete lack of leadership, either local or national, among the workers—despite long months of fiery revolutionary agitation by the intransigents. Even on the tactical level the anarchists seem to have provided what little direction did exist.[87]

On the 23rd, some thirty political and trade-union leaders (representing both reformists and intransigents) met to provide some direction to the movement. According to Montagnana, who was present, "nobody, neither the reformists nor the 'revolutionaries' (naturally including myself), knew what to do."[88] Castagno, also present, noted that the leaders were attempting to "assume responsibility for a movement that nobody had planned and that was developing spon-

---

* The church of San Bernardino in the Borgo San Paolo was apparently sacked in belated revenge for an incident of the preceding year, when the monks of the church had whipped and beaten several boys whom they had surprised in the garden of the church. According to Gramsci, the monks even cut the sign of the cross on the boys' heads! See "L'Utilità delle dimostrazioni" (9.ix.16), *Scritti giovanili* [9], p. 45.

taneously."[89] The result of the meeting, a joint resolution of the Party
section and the Chamber of Labor, was distributed in a flyer on the
24th; it praised the workers for their resistance to the "stupidity and
provocations of the authorities," asserted that the movement was "in
good hands," and asked the workers to wait for further instructions
and avoid acts of "useless violence."[90] On the 26th, Turin's Socialist
deputies asked the workers to return to their jobs, and by Tuesday,
August 28, complete order was reestablished in the city.[91]

Older memoirists, such as Montagnana and Germanetto, estimated
the number of dead at 400 and the wounded at 2,000.[92] Monticone,
who made a careful study of this question, concludes that there were
probably about 50 dead and 200 wounded, and Spriano is in substantial agreement.[93] In the course of the uprising, the authorities arrested
a total of 822 Socialists and anarchists, including almost the entire
leadership of the local section. Of this number, about 300 were "exempted" workers under military command in the factories, and 177
of them were sent to the front between September 4 and October 6,
1917.[94] The alleged "leaders" of the uprising were tried before the
Military Court of Turin from June 3 to August 2, 1918.[95]

From this brief recapitulation, it should be clear that the uprising
of August 1917 was both spontaneous and of a mass character. Spriano
estimates that thousands of workers took part in it, and at certain moments tens of thousands.[96] Monticone asserts that a minority of intransigents led the masses astray, but this seems unlikely, especially
since there is no evidence of a break between reformists and intransigents during the uprising.[97] Spriano regards the affair, except for
its magnitude, as essentially similar to the clashes of 1904, 1909, and
1915, which had created an "explosive tradition of street demonstrations, strikes, and violence."[98] There were, however, two new elements in 1917, according to Spriano: Socialist agitation for peace and
the stimulus of the Russian Revolution. Unlike earlier insurrections,
the August 1917 uprising took on an international character in the
eyes of the insurrectionists. Indeed, Lenin himself regarded the "explosion of the masses in Turin" as part of the "development of the
world revolution."[99]

The insurrection gave rise to a number of controversies in later
years. In 1927, the Communist newspaper *Lo Stato operaio* asserted
that Mayor Rossi, a Giolittian neutralist, had urged a delegation of
workers to strike in order to "impede the war."[100] Some years later,
Gramsci took up this charge and elaborated on it. He argued that the

Giolittians, fearing anti-neutralist measures by the new Boselli government of June 1916, had deliberately created a food shortage to provoke a riot, which they hoped would bring down the government.[101] Both Monticone and Spriano, however, after examining the documents of the trial and those of several governmental inquiries, conclude that such allegations have no basis in fact.[102]

Another controversy concerns the effect of the uprising on the Italian military debacle at Caporetto. This disastrous battle began on October 24, several weeks after the 177 "exempted" workers who participated in the August rising were sent to the front.[103] According to the American Ambassador at Rome, Thomas Nelson Page, many of these workers were sent to Caporetto, where their defeatism was a factor in the collapse of Italian morale.[104] And the Communist Ruggiero Grieco claimed that "news of the events in Turin reached the front and prepared the way for Caporetto," which Grieco regarded as an "episode of the Italian revolution."[105] By contrast, Piero Pieri, the dean of Italian military historians, insists on the purely military character of the defeat at Caporetto. He asserts, among other things, that instead of the alleged 40,000 deserters there were less than 4,000, most of whom merely overstayed their leaves by a few days.[106]

Gramsci and the "Intransigent Revolutionaries"

The events of August 1917 in Turin had another important effect: Antonio Gramsci was brought to the forefront of the Socialist section. All its leaders, whether reformist or intransigent, were discredited by the failure of the uprising. Gramsci, however, had not held a leading position in the section, and was not identified closely with either of the factions. In *La Città futura* he had criticized both the passivity of the reformists and the demagoguery of the intransigents; moreover, unlike the intransigents, he was convinced that the working class should have a thorough revolutionary education. In September 1917 Gramsci was made solely responsible for the publication of *Il Grido del popolo,* not only as its editor, but as its "only reporter."[107] He inherited a journal devoted to "local news and evangelical propaganda"; he immediately set about converting it into an organ of "Socialist culture developed according to the doctrines and tactics of revolutionary Socialism."[108] For the first time, Gramsci was also given a leading role in the political activities of the Socialist section. On September 30 he became a member of the provisional executive committee that governed the section until the beginning of 1918.[109]

Unfortunately, very little is known about the work of the Turin section until the end of the war, because of the unusually rigid censorship that prevailed after August 1917.

Shortly after he became a member of the Turin directorate, Gramsci consolidated his position—and assured the financial solvency of the section—by winning a political battle for control of the capital of the ACT. The cooperative had been administered for many years by the Socialist section, but its capital was held mainly by the railroad workers of Turin and their families. When wartime inflation and growing confidence in the ACT increased the value of each share of stock from 50 to 700 lire, it was proposed in some quarters that the increment of 650 lire per share be distributed to the stockholders; but the Party persuaded the stockholders to accept dividends based on the original evaluation, since the object of a working-class institution was not to make profits but to further the revolutionary struggle. Not all stockholders were content with this decision, however; the political reaction following the August uprising and the attendant discouragement among the workers gave rise to a new demand for a capital distribution. This time the proposal was supported by the Turin newspapers and also, according to Gramsci, by certain reformist Socialists led by Quirino Nofri. Since wartime censorship prevented the directors of the Socialist section from publicly opposing the distribution, Gramsci organized an informal but carefully controlled educational campaign among the stockholders and other workers. When the question was brought to a vote, the Socialist Party obtained the support of 700 of the 800 stockholders. This was Gramsci's first significant political victory.[110]

Meanwhile, the revolutionary elements of the PSI, with whom Gramsci was loosely identified, were increasing their strength all over Italy, in direct proportion to the increase of defeatism in the country. On August 23, 1917, a "Committee of the Intransigent Revolutionary Faction" had been formally established at Florence. Its manifesto called for an end to opportunism and collaboration with the bourgeoisie, and proclaimed that the hour of revolution was drawing near.[111] The military debacle at Caporetto in October only intensified this spirit, which was further exacerbated by reformist defections to the cause of national unity. Immediately after Caporetto, Filippo Turati, leader of the Party's right wing, delivered an address urging support of the war effort. The intransigents responded by calling a special conference to discuss revolutionary strategy.

The conference met at Florence on November 18, 1917, and was attended by representatives from many of the Party's provincial Federations. Gramsci and Arturo Terrini came as representatives of the Turin revolutionaries.[112] Also present were Bordiga, Bruno Fortichiari, and Giovanni Germanetto, all important leaders of the intransigent faction. Costantino Lazzari, the party Secretary, and Serrati, the editor of *Avanti!*, came as representatives of the majority, or so-called "maximalist," group of the PSI. They did not trust the younger, more virulent leftists, whom they considered irresponsible and extremist, but they were willing to cooperate with them to ensure the defeat of the right wing.

Although the conference had been officially prohibited by the government, the police unaccountably permitted the delegates to meet until midnight, at which time they were to disperse. Bordiga, a national leader of the Left, opened the meeting by calling for an immediate Socialist revolution: "The debacle has occurred. The Italian State is disorganized. The time for action has arrived. The workers of the fields and factories are armed. They're tired of it all; we must act."[113] A realistic appraisal of the situation in the PSI and in the labor unions would have demonstrated the futility of such advice, but in those apocalyptic days, with the electrifying news of the Bolshevik Revolution less than two weeks old, Bordiga's words seemed plausible. Gramsci and all his faction voted with Bordiga. But Lazzari, Serrati, and most of the provincial representatives dissented: they preferred the official Party formula, "Neither support nor sabotage."

At this point the meeting was broken up by the police, but most of the delegates, including Gramsci, reassembled at a private home in Florence, where the manifesto of the conference was drawn up. In its final form this document was no more than a strong statement of the official Party formula. It called for a continuation of "intransigent hostility toward the war" and asserted that "the political attitude of the Socialist Party could not depend on the vicissitudes of military operations." It deplored and condemned the actions of "those comrades and representatives of the party who have been led by recent events to support the war."[114] Each delegate was given a copy of the manifesto to reproduce and distribute in his local district. Gramsci returned to Turin with his copy, and its contents were soon well known in the city.

For Gramsci the most important aspect of the conference, in which he played a very small role, was his meeting with Bordiga. These two

men were later to cooperate in founding the Italian Communist
Party, and, still later, to break completely on the issue of Bordiga's
extremism. Gramsci was by nature cautious and thorough, virtues
that were not Bordiga's; but his youthfulness (he was 26 in 1917) and
the incensed atmosphere of the times made him temporarily receptive
to Bordiga's exuberant personality and superficial brilliance. Moreover, he thought Bordiga was right to insist that the Italian proletariat begin to think about seizing power.[115] Bordiga made a strong
impression on most young Socialists during these years. Giovanni
Germanetto, one of Gramsci's associates who also met Bordiga at the
Florence Conference, has given us his initial impressions of the dynamic Neapolitan:

It was on that evening [November 18, 1917] that I heard Bordiga speak for
the first time. He made a deep impression on me. After his speech Socialism
seemed far more real to me. . . . Bordiga's speech opened up new horizons
before me. It helped me to understand what was happening in Russia. I
understood Gramsci better, but Bordiga was exactly suited to my temperament. It seemed to me that these two comrades supplemented one another.
And I somehow sensed agreement between these two men, physically so
different from one another: [Bordiga] tall and imposing, [Gramsci] thin,
small, and sickly; the first a powerful and impetuous speaker, the second a
thinker.[116]

Even at this time, Gramsci did not completely share the views of
the intransigent faction. Even if he was in no serious sense guilty of
the "Bergsonism" and voluntarism that a fellow delegate at Florence
accused him of,[117] he deplored the "fatalistic and mechanical conception of history" that dominated the conference.[118] At Florence as
later, it was his positive, creative attitude toward the problems of
revolutionary Socialism that distinguished Gramsci from most of his
comrades.

Gramsci and the Russian Revolution, 1917–18

If Gramsci's political position in the PSI was at this time subordinate to Bordiga's, his articles written in the aftermath of the Russian
Revolution showed his vast superiority in the realm of theory. Gramsci's articles of 1917 and 1918 in *Il Grido del popolo* and in the Turin
edition of *Avanti!* were the only perceptive Italian comments on
events in Russia.[119] Whereas writers like Bordiga, Serrati, and Panfilo
Gentile tended to reduce the debate on the Revolution to "scholastic
disquisitions . . . on abstract formulas," Gramsci made a serious at-

tempt to absorb the spirit of Leninism and apply it to a study of conditions in Italy.[120] Gramsci's precocious liberal friend Piero Gobetti described the result:

In 1918, the little propaganda weekly of the Party became a journal of culture and thought. It published the first translations of the Russian revolutionary writings and offered a political interpretation of the Bolsheviks' activities. The animator of this work ... was Gramsci. To him, Lenin stood for a heroic will to liberation. The fundamental ideals of the Bolshevik myth ... were to serve not as the model imposed on the Italian revolution, but as a stimulant for free Italian initiative coming from below.[121]

Knowledge of Lenin and the Russian Revolution was not easy to come by in 1917–18, for wartime censorship was so strict in Italy that very little news from Russia reached the country, especially after the October Revolution. Some recent articles by Lenin and Trotsky were published in *Avanti!*, along with reports by Henri Barbusse, Romain Rolland, and John Reed. Immediately after the war, Gramsci began receiving copies of the *Liberator*, an American pro-Soviet publication edited by Max Eastman; until the founding of the Third International, this was an important source for Gramsci of news from Russia, Hungary, and Germany.[122] Togliatti tells us that "only in 1918 did Lenin begin to be known, translated, published, and widely read in Italy. It was mainly, however, his writings dedicated to the immediate struggles of those years [that were known]." Only a few of his important theoretical works were known in 1918.[123]

To Gramsci, Lenin was no revisionist of Marx, as many Western European Socialists thought him to be. However, Gramsci's conception of Marx himself was very different in 1918 from that of most of his comrades in the PSI. Marx was "not a Messiah who left a string of parables laden with categorical imperatives and absolutely incontrovertible norms outside the categories of time and space. The only categorical imperative, the single norm, is 'Workers of the world, unite!' " Gramsci's Marx was a historian who found history in "the realm of ideas," but not ideas that are mere fictitious abstractions. "Their substance was in the economy, in practical activity, and in the systems and relations of production and exchange." But Gramsci's judgment does not in any way imply economic determinism. Through a knowledge of objective reality, "man knows himself, how much his individual will is worth, and how it may be rendered potent. By obeying necessities and disciplining himself to them, man comes to dominate necessity itself by identifying it with his own ends. Who knows himself? Not man in general, but he who feels the yoke of necessity."[124]

A renewal of his polemic with the reformists—their theoretical journal was *La Critica sociale*—gave Gramsci an opportunity to discuss the voluntarism he was constantly accused of:

It seems that the new generation wishes to return to the genuine doctrine of Marx, in which man and reality, the instrument of labor and the will, are not separated but come together in the *historical act*. Hence they believe that the canons of historical materialism are valid only after the fact, for studying and understanding the events of the past, and ought not to become a mortgage on the present and future.

Gramsci particularly emphasized the importance of the war in "modifying the normal historical environment." The war "did not destroy historical materialism," but it did give an unusual temporary importance to the "collective social will of men." For Gramsci, the creative will in history is of fundamental importance—within certain limits, of course. Even determinism can be creative: "Vico said before Marx that even the belief in divine providence had worked beneficially in history by becoming a stimulus for conscious action. Hence, even the belief in 'determinism' could have the same efficacy, in Russia for Lenin and elsewhere for others."[125]

In these articles of 1917 and 1918, Gramsci gloried in the creative character of the Russian Revolution, which he saw as leading, in Marx's words, from the "realm of necessity to the realm of freedom." He saw all past Russian history as a history of compulsion, necessary, to be sure, but deplorable in its effects:

The Russian Empire was a monstrous necessity of the modern world: to live, to develop, to ensure themselves ways of activity, ten races and 170 million men had to put up with a ferocious political system, had to renounce humanity and become mere instruments of those in power. . . . Individuals lost all autonomy and freedom so that the State could be autonomous and free among other states.[126]

Of course, neither Gramsci nor anyone else could envision how much of that burden the people of Soviet Russia would continue to bear.

Long before most observers, Gramsci identified Lenin and the Bolsheviks with the Russian Revolution itself. Even in July 1917, when Lenin was outlawed and Kerensky had apparently isolated the Bolsheviks from the mainstream of the revolution, Gramsci was predicting their eventual triumph, on the ground that they would not settle for halfway measures or for marking time in deference to the theories of the determinists. The Leninists understood that Socialism had no deterministic timetable. Instead, they were convinced

that it is possible to realize Socialism at any moment. . . . They are revolutionaries, not evolutionists. And revolutionary thought does not see time as a factor of progress. It denies that all intermediate stages between the conception of Socialism and its realization must have an absolute and complete test in time and space. To pass through one stage and advance to another, it is enough that the first stage be realized in thought.[127]

The most interesting and controversial article Gramsci wrote in this period was entitled "The Revolution against *Das Kapital.*" He argued that *Das Kapital,* both in Russia and in Italy, was "the book of the bourgeoisie, not the proletariat." It had been used to foster the deterministic idea that a Western type of civilization must exist in Russia before Socialism could be built. Recent developments, said Gramsci, had discredited this idea. When the Russian Bolsheviks said they were not Marxists, they meant that only the vital elements of Marx interested them, those elements that put man, not raw economic facts, at the center of history.

In the same article, Gramsci advances an idea that has recently become important in the study of economic development: the idea of a penalty for being first. The United States, says Gramsci, is more advanced than England because it began immediately at the stage England had reached only after long evolution. In the same way,

The Russian proletariat, socialistically educated, will begin its history at the maximum stage of production that England has reached today; having to begin, it will begin from what has already been done elsewhere. From this level it will reach the economic maturity that Marx considers a necessary condition of collectivism. The revolutionaries will themselves create the necessary conditions for the full and complete realization of their ideal. They will create them faster than capitalism would.[128]

These passages never mention the need for Western revolutions to support the success of Socialism in "backward Russia." Gramsci's emphasis is always on the creative role of the Russian proletariat and its revolutionary leaders. Years before the Bolsheviks themselves, Gramsci is here anticipating the doctrine of "Socialism in one country."

Gramsci saw in Lenin the qualities of leadership and understanding that he considered essential to the success of an Italian revolution. For Gramsci, Lenin was above all a "cold student of historical reality" and a "revolutionary who builds without frenetic illusions, in obedience to reason and wisdom."[129] When Lenin and Trotsky quarreled over the signing of the Brest-Litovsk treaty, Gramsci sided with Lenin. He reprinted an article by Karl Radek supporting Trotsky's refusal to accept Germany's harsh terms, but only to dismiss Radek's arguments as phrasemaking. Radek spoke of "German imperialism" and "the revolutionary struggle"; Lenin saw things as they were. Germany was strong and Russia weak. "In practical terms, the 'revolutionary struggle' meant war, and to make war the Russian Revolution needed an army. But the Russian army was disintegrating."[130]

These early articles reflect Gramsci's initial enthusiastic response to the Russian Revolution and Leninism. In studying the Revolution further and reflecting on its lessons for Italy, he soon came to focus on the role of the Russian soviets, or revolutionary councils of workers, peasants, and soldiers. Gramsci's life in 1919 and 1920 was mainly devoted to the theoretical justification and actual establishment of revolutionary workers' councils in Italy. It was in these years that he gained a national reputation and made his first original contribution to the Italian labor movement.

Part II

Ordine Nuovo

4. *Ordine Nuovo* and the Italian Soviets

*In Italia l'esistenza del Consiglio
ha incominciato a Torino, nell'industria metallurgica; è un particolare
che nell'avvenire sarà ricordato dagli
eruditi.*

—*Gramsci, November 8, 1919*

Italy and the PSI in 1919

The World War shook the unstable political and economic structure
of Italy severely. Her year of neutrality and the opportunistic circumstances of her entry into the conflict intensified the hostility
between interventionist and neutralist groups, and these groups remained hostile in the postwar period. The war cost Italy half a million lives; another half-million persons were mutilated, and over a
million were wounded.[1] Italy had to import most raw materials for
the war effort, and the budgetary deficit of the Italian government
rose from 214 million lire in 1913 to 23 billion in 1918–19, while the
cost of living climbed from 100 to 624 between 1913 and 1920.[2] Worst
of all, these enormous expenditures had gained very little for Italy,
although the government had expected sweeping annexations of
territory. Government officials and generals at the front had regularly promised the troops rich rewards for their suffering. The peasants were promised land, the workers greater returns for their labor.[3]
Afterwards, nothing was done to fulfill these promises.

These fundamental political and economic tensions were aggra-
vated by the psychological mood of the times. On November 20, 1918,
the Prime Minister, V. E. Orlando, declared that the war was the
greatest politico-social revolution in history. On the same day Antonio Salandra, authoritative leader of Italian conservatism, was
urging youth to assert itself: "No one thinks that the end of the storm
means a peaceful return to the past."[4] In fact, all Europe was charged
with revolution: the Hohenzollerns and Hapsburgs had been

wrenched from their thrones; there were Bolshevik revolutions in Russia, Hungary, and Bavaria; the Spartacist uprising broke out in Berlin. Pietro Nenni wrote, "All the extraordinary and clamorous events at the end of 1918 and the beginning of 1919 fired the imagination, and inspired the hope that the old world was about to collapse and that humanity was on the threshold of a new era and a new social order."[5]

In view of the Italian situation in 1919, it is a wonder that no revolution took place. Most veterans, whether peasants or workers, returned from the war with advanced democratic, if not Socialist, ideas. In June 1919, the National Veterans Association held its first Congress at Rome, and adopted a program calling for a constituent assembly, abolition of the Senate, and a Mazzinian conception of nationalism, related to humanity in general and "distinguished from national egoism."[6] Meanwhile, the peasants had begun to demand a long overdue redistribution of the land, and the number of workers enrolled in the CGL increased from 250,000 in 1918 to 1,000,000 in 1919.[7] By 1919 the PSI, or at least a majority of its leaders, had abjured all halfway measures, such as the demands of the veterans, workers, and peasants. At a meeting of the Party directorate in December 1918, Serrati, the director of *Avanti!*, reversed his earlier position, declaring himself against a constituent assembly and for the institution of a dictatorship of the proletariat. This was adopted as the official Party line.

At the December meeting, however, certain immediate requests were made of the government, such as a return of constitutional liberties and rapid demobilization. These demands, inspired by Turati's reformists, were far from revolutionary.[8] The meeting pointed up one of the fundamental shortcomings of the PSI in the postwar period: the coexistence of revolutionary and gradualist elements in a single body. From September 1918 to the final victory of Fascism, the Party machinery was controlled by the revolutionaries, or "maximalists." But the Socialist parliamentary deputies were consistently gradualist during this period, although rank-and-file opinion often forced them to appear more leftist than they really were. The leaders of the CGL, the trade union organization, were usually reformist in outlook, but often attempted to strike a middle course between the Party directorate and the parliamentary group because of pressure from below.[9]

As Pietro Nenni has demonstrated (in *Storia di quatro anni*), every Socialist party in a capitalist state is both a party of the future, with aims transcending the economic and political realities of the moment, and a party of the present that must come to terms with those realities. Few Socialist parties have resolved this dilemma, but few have so perversely refused to face it as did the Italian Socialist Party at this time. The need for Party unity was realized, but the various factions of the Party drew further and further apart.

Another major deficiency of the PSI was closely related to the first. The Party had no plan for meeting the revolutionary crisis in 1919. The radically different theoretical positions within the Party were one reason for this failure; however, the Party's blindness to the actual Italian situation was even more decisive. The reformists argued that Italian capitalism would fall of its own weight when conditions were ripe. The maximalists depended on the Russian Revolution to solve the problems of the Italian revolution by an overwhelming defeat of enemies inside and outside of Russia; hence, the columns of *Avanti!* were primarily devoted to registering the victories of the international proletariat.[10] Gramsci noted that in Italy it was the masses that guided and "educated" the Party, rather than the reverse.[11]

Those areas where the party was most effective only emphasized its weaknesses as an organ of the Italian proletariat. In most matters of international proletarian solidarity, for example, the PSI was active. On March 18, the party leadership had decided, by a vote of ten to three, to abandon the Second International and join the Comintern, founded at Moscow less than two weeks before.[12] Allied military operations in Russia in 1918–19 brought a massive protest from all the Italian Socialist groups.[13] The International General Strike of July 20–21, 1919, was the high point of this protest. The strike was intended to express solidarity with the Russian and Hungarian Soviets, and was to take place simultaneously in England, France, and Italy. In the end, only the Italians participated, but in Italy participation was nearly complete.[14]

The Party was not always clear about the purposes and results of strikes, the only tactic in which they really led the masses. Many Socialists seemed to regard strikes as the only action needed to produce revolution.[15] Others underestimated the dangerous psychological consequences, in a revolutionary period, of even the most successful strikes. The General Strike of July 1919 is a good example. Though many Socialist leaders were careful to call the performance "demonstrative and not revolutionary," the movement was so grandiose that it dissipated all the energy of the workers without improv-

ing their political position. Somehow, the workers expected a revolution, and the absence of one, as the CGL later reported, "brought,
not discouragement, but a violent disillusionment to the workers;
and it incited previously weak-willed industrialists to begin a struggle to break the power of the unions."[16]

The PSI won 32 per cent of the popular vote in November 1919,
electing 156 national deputies.[17] But this meant that Socialists must
come to a quick agreement on essential policies, and the Party had no
definite program. During October 5–8, a month prior to the elections,
the PSI had held its Sixteenth National Congress at Bologna.[18] The
relative strengths and positions of the several factions were made
clear, and most of the figures responsible for the direction of left-
wing movements throughout the postwar period came into promi-
nence there.

The reformists, led by Filippo Turati and Lodovico d'Aragona
(the General Secretary of the CGL), were undoubtedly the most
homogeneous group. They controlled the majority of the Socialist
parliamentary group, the central offices of the CGL, and most of the
labor unions and Socialist communal governments. The reformists'
long parliamentary and administrative experience inclined them
toward strict adherence to the methods of bourgeois democracy.
Their failure to understand the revolutionary character of the times
limited their political appeal among the masses.

G. M. Serrati's maximalists (or "electionist maximalists," as they
called themselves at this time) constituted an overwhelming majority
of the delegates at Bologna, but they were by no means a unified
group. Their strength lay in control of the Party directorate and
lesser Party offices and in the possession of the Party daily, *Avanti!*
With the growing political and economic crisis in the country, Serrati's position had moved rapidly to the left in the months preceding
Bologna. By then, he wanted revolution, through violence if necessary, but he did not wish to risk party unity by imposing his stand on
everyone. Costantino Lazzari (Party secretary, 1912–19) had similar
aims, but hoped to avoid violence.

The third faction present at Bologna was the abstentionist group
that Amadeo Bordiga had recruited from the "intransigent revolutionaries" of 1917–18. The group took its name from its principle that
the Party must abstain from elections, which it regarded as diversions
from the fundamental task of preparing the revolution. The abstentionists had a network of small groups throughout Italy, but their
center was at Naples, where Bordiga had published *Il Soviet* since

December 1918. Some of the Turin intransigents had joined them, notably Giovanni Boero and Giovanni Parodi. Most of the leaders of the FGS, including its secretary, Luigi Polano, were also abstentionists. These men favored a dictatorship of the proletariat, and demanded the immediate expulsion of the reformists and all others with equivocal attitudes toward the possible use of violence or the program of the Third International.

The Italian liberal state was rapidly disintegrating, there was widespread sedition in the army, and inflation was rampant. Thus the Congress overwhelmingly approved such measures as adherence to the Third International, rejection of its program of 1892 as inadequate,* and the eventual replacement of the bourgeois state by soviets, or workers' councils. In the balloting on the final motions of the various factions, Serrati's maximalists won a resounding victory with 48,000 votes. Lazzari's motion, similar to Serrati's but emphasizing the need to avoid violence if possible, won only 14,000 votes. The reformists, who knew that an openly rightist appeal would have received no support, voted with Lazzari. The Bordigan communists received only 3,000 votes, since few delegates were prepared to oust the reformists and fewer still wished to boycott the elections.

The Congress of Bologna reflected the incendiary character of the times, but its outcome masked equivocations that would soon shatter the unity of the Party. For example, the reformists qualified their adherence to the Third International as an "idealistic" act of solidarity with the revolution, thus leaving themselves free to criticize the specific program of the International.[19]

Gramsci and the PSI in 1919

Gramsci had never been deeply involved in the factional politics of the PSI. His real interests were educating the working class and elaborating a cultural basis for a society of the future. Nevertheless, in the Turin section's frequent changes of leadership, Gramsci was usually included in the directorate. In May 1919, when Gramsci founded *Ordine nuovo,* he was the only intellectual included in the new executive committee of the section. This body was elected on a platform that included participation in the national elections "as a form of revolutionary education for the masses."[20]

---

* The PSI had retained its Genoa Program of 1892 throughout the War, a striking example of its inability to formulate first principles. The Italians were not alone in this: The Social-Democratic Party of Germany followed its Erfurt Program, adopted in 1891, until 1921, when it adopted the reformist Görlitz Program.

Gramsci shared this rejection of the "abstentionist" faction to a considerable extent. He disliked its sectarian tendency to concentrate on the creation of a "truly" communist Party, often ignoring the task of fostering conditions in the masses that would ensure the success of such a Party.[21] He especially objected to its doctrinaire attacks on the Party's participation in elections. Gramsci supported Socialist electioneering because he thought that enough PSI deputies would "make it impossible for any leader of the bourgeoisie to form a stable and strong government."[22] This was a purely negative reason, reflecting the chaotic situation in 1919. He argued more positively that Socialists could use Parliament to draw the masses' attention to the real problems of the country, and point out the solutions to these problems.[23] Nevertheless, the abstentionists impressed Gramsci with their eagerness to expel the reformists and their absolute commitment to the program of the Third International.

Gramsci's attitude toward the reformists remained as contemptuous and antagonistic as it had been during the days of *La Città futura*, but his assessment of the maximalists was not yet openly hostile. He hoped that the Sixteenth Congress would give maximalism a "more concrete" character, that is, impel the maximalists to abandon mere sloganizing and begin organizing the specific conditions for an Italian revolution.[24] Hence, he reserved his judgment on maximalism until the end of 1919.

Gramsci himself was occasionally guilty—in the earlier months of 1919—of some of the tactical errors committed by the Serrati group. On April 15 the Fascists burned the Milan headquarters of *Avanti!* Gramsci applauded the resistance of the Party directors to those members anxious for revenge as "one of the most forceful acts that the party has carried out in this period."[25] His concern lest the masses become aroused too soon is understandable; but the political consequences of inadequate resistance to extralegal violence after 1920 show that Gramsci sometimes viewed the political struggle in Italy with mistaken serenity.[26]

But maximalism committed a number of errors not shared by Gramsci, even in this early period. The maximalists rarely troubled to explain the advantages of Socialism to the middle classes, and often frightened them with a blustering emphasis on violence. Gramsci, however, always stressed the "national" character of the future proletarian revolution. Socialism proposed to better all the underprivileged classes of the nation, including the petty bourgeoisie, and it wished to free the Italian economy from subservience to foreign capital.[27]

Although both Gramsci and the Party majority wanted an alliance of workers and peasants, the Party had never seriously considered the problems of such a coalition. Gramsci resented the lack of information on the southern peasant problem in the Party press, a lack that forced Italian Socialists to turn to foreign reviews.[28] In fact, Socialist influence in the South was still weak—only 10 per cent of the PSI deputies elected in 1919 were southerners.[29] Gramsci attributed this weakness to the reformist tendency to favor working-class "aristocracies" in the North over the southern peasant masses.[30]

Gramsci saw the danger of uttering inflammatory statements about the coming dictatorship of the proletariat, as the maximalists did, while demanding nothing from the workers but passive expectation. As Pietro Nenni has said, the *Ordine nuovo* group under Gramsci's direction represented "the only attempt to face up to the technical side of the revolution" in 1919–20.[31] By mid-1919, Gramsci knew that the only hope of success for the Italian revolution lay in a revival of Socialist institutions and in political and economic education of the workers.

The Foundation and Program of "Ordine nuovo"

After the war, Tasca, Togliatti, Terracini, and Gramsci reassembled the old student group of the FGS, intending to found a collectively managed journal of Marxist theory and culture. Their academic training and considerable Socialist experience qualified them for the task,* and they felt that existing publications in this field were inadequate: *Avanti!* talked revolution, but did nothing about it; *Critica sociale* was a reformist organ; and *Il Soviet,* Bordiga's recently established Neapolitan weekly, was too concerned with abstention from elections. Accordingly, the group convened in Gramsci's office at the Turin headquarters of *Avanti!*; by the end of April 1919, plans had been made for launching a weekly newspaper, *L'Ordine nuovo,* and its first issue appeared on May 1, 1919. This journal is important in the history of the Italian labor movement for two reasons: first, because the men associated with *L'Ordine nuovo* became in time the directing nucleus of the Italian Communist Party; and second, because the newspaper was a vehicle for Gramsci's campaign

---

* All except Gramsci were graduates of the University of Turin. Togliatti had received two degrees, one in law and another in letters and philosophy. Terracini also received a law degree, and is still considered one of the best lawyers in Italy—despite eighteen years in a Fascist prison. Tasca soon developed a reputation for meticulous scholarship: he was responsible for editing Antonio Labriola's letters to Engels (in *Lo Stato operaio,* 1927–30); every page of them reminds one of an annotated edition of the *Divine Comedy.*

to organize Italian soviets (*consigli di fabbrica*), and the soviet was
a crucial issue in the immediate postwar period.

The *Ordine nuovo* group was almost puritanically serious, a quality already noted as characteristic of the younger Piedmontese Socialists. Gramsci warned Party members that they "must be cold and
lucid in every situation, and not permit themselves to be carried away
by exaltation and hasty solutions. Unfortunately, states are not created by generous heroism and passion: the essential qualities are discipline, perseverance, coherence, and scorn for irresponsibility."[32]
Employing these "essential qualities," obtained from serious academic study, Gramsci and the men about him attempted to dispense
with the rhetoric so common among Italian revolutionaries.

Despite their seriousness, none of its founders expected *L'Ordine
nuovo* to change the spiritual outlook of the Italian workers; indeed,
Gramsci asserted that "the only feeling that united us in those [early]
meetings was an uncertain passion for a vague proletarian culture."[33]
Still, he proposed some very definite ideas, which were noted in the
minutes of these meetings.

At this time, Gramsci first suggested the fostering of Italian institutions similar to the Russian soviet. Until recently, the background
for this turn in Gramsci's thought remained obscure. We had been
told only of certain general influences that moved Gramsci to study
the representative institutions of the working masses. Among his interests, besides the soviets, were the English shop-steward movement,
the American magazine *The Liberator,* and the American Socialist
Daniel De Leon.[34] Thanks to a recent article by Emilio Soave, it is
now possible to prove that Gramsci and the young Turin leaders in
general had shown increasing interest in "proletarian organization"
since the beginning of 1918.[35]

Soave found that the section "Organizzazióne proletaria," which
appeared regularly in *Il Grido del popolo,* contained a "surprising
amount of information" on labor's institutions. On April 27, 1918,
the *Grido,* which Gramsci had edited since the previous August,
published an unsigned article on the "Evolution of English Trade
Unions" that anticipated many of Gramsci's criticisms of the traditional union structure. For example, it attacked the old Federations
as "basically corporatist, traditionalist, and conservative"; because
of the bureaucratic centralism of the unions, "the masses only ratify
and passively obey," while "all action is by the executive power."
The anonymous author argued that the vast expansion of modern
methods of production during the war required a further development of institutions for the class struggle. Above all, the unions had

to give the proletariat greater responsibility so that the "initiative, the impulse to action," would originate "in the masses, in the plant."[36] The article ended with a detailed description of the shop-steward movement, the English attempt to overcome the limitations of the trade union by direct representation of the workers in the plants.

Another article in the same section of the *Grido* summarized recent developments in the German Metallurgical Federation, commenting favorably on the strengthening of left elements in the German movement and on the outbreak of spontaneous strikes in Berlin and Leipzig. It castigated the tendency of nearly all European trade unions to collaborate with their governments. The consequent reduction of unions to purely economic and technical functions, said the *Grido*, made "nonsense" of trade-union organizations, whose real task was "complete transformation of the institutions of capitalistic privilege."[37]

The author of this article was certainly aware of the connection between metalworking strikes in Italy, England, Germany, and Russia from 1916 to 1918. For the first time in the history of the European labor movement, the trade unions had become part of the governmental structure of their respective countries through participation in the apparatus of production. Formally, this integration brought a certain amount of power and responsibility to the trade unions, but the ability of the unions to protect the interests of the workers was severely limited. The English example may serve for all: "The Trade-Union leaders . . . , by giving up the right to strike and undertaking to cooperate, on terms, with the government and the employers, . . . had given up their power to conduct a militant policy for raising wages or defending Trade-Union claims."[38] As Soave puts it, the labor movement, to defend itself, "was forced almost everywhere to express itself in new forms, often unorganized and 'spontaneous,' which in areas of more developed capitalism tended to become councils of delegates from shop and factory."[39] In this context, the soviet must be viewed as a general tendency of the European labor movement, as well as the Russian. In 1921 Richard Müller, a founder of the wartime Berlin workers' councils, stated that these institutions "resulted from the economic repercussions of the war, from the repression of all freedom of movement in the working class because of the state of siege and the total incapacity of the unions and political parties." With reference to the Berlin strike of July 1916, Müller observed that councils "functioned just as did the shop committees of the big enterprises of Petrograd in 1905, although [the Berlin workers] knew nothing of [these committees]. . . . The political struggle, in July 1916, could not have been led by either the parties or the trade unions."[40]

As far as is known, Gramsci did not write any articles in 1918 explicitly discussing proletarian institutions in the factory. Nevertheless, in an article of October 1918, he indicated dissatisfaction with the existing organizations of Italian labor: the trade unions "are very far from representing those democratic forces capable of reciprocal control that are necessary for action by a political and economic class." For Gramsci, the greatest weakness of the Italian proletariat was that "a small minority of the members participate in the inner life of the Leagues and Chambers of Labor." Worse, the normally passive majority might still intervene "in decisive moments of the life of the organization, bringing to this suffrage the frivolity and recklessness of those who, having given nothing to the day-to-day activity of the organization and not understanding the possible meaning and consequences of a decision, do not have a sense of responsibility for their acts." Therefore, the trade-union "leaders gain an authority and an importance they ought not to have in view of the egalitarian and essentially democratic spirit of the organizations."[41] In another article of the same period, Gramsci complained that the Socialist Party had not succeeded in creating organisms that could permanently organize the masses; however, at this time Gramsci did not propose new methods of organization, but merely urged the massive recruiting of new members for the PSI and CGL, the "necessary and sufficient organisms for the disciplined and conscious development of the class struggle."[42]

Many Italian revolutionary leaders hoped for the development of soviets in Italy. On March 13, 1919, Giovanni Boero, then the secretary of the Turin section, called for the introduction of soviets in that city. However, he was unable to suggest any practical means of forming them.[43] In the same month Alfonso Leonetti published an important article, entitled "At the Dawn of the New Order," in *Avanguardia,* the journal of the FGS. Leonetti advocated the creation of soviets as "the surest guarantee of the movement toward Socialism" and the best means of imparting a modern character to the Italian labor movement.[44] But it was Gramsci, heading a small group of Socialist intellectuals, who first saw that soviets might be developed in Turin by transforming the "internal committees," institutions that already had a long, though precarious and intermittent, history in the city.

By 1918, a considerable number of internal committees had been established in Turin, especially in the metallurgical plants; however, with few exceptions, they had not been officially recognized by the industrialists or the government.[45] In February 1919, when a Fiom contract with the automobile Consorzio was signed, the internal committees did achieve this official recognition.[46] They were formed in the following way: the Fiom consulted the "best workers" in each plant, and a list of five members was agreed upon and then "presented, discussed, and approved at a meeting [of organized workers] attended by a representative of the Federation." At first, the committeemen were chosen from those acceptable to management, but later they were often selected from members of the Socialist Party.[47] Thus the internal committees were not democratically elected bodies that accurately represented the views of all the workers. They mostly represented the ideas of the trade-union leaders, and unorganized workers were almost entirely neglected. Furthermore, the tasks of the committee were limited to the usual disputes on wages, hours, and working conditions. Problems basic to the soviet—proletarian control of production, the preparation of the proletariat as a ruling class, and so forth—were not even considered.

Gramsci suggested to his comrades that they study the internal committees and find a means to transform them into full-fledged soviets, *workers'* bodies rather than trade-union groups. They would also study the capitalistic factory unit "as the necessary form of the working class, as a political organism, and as the 'national territory' of working-class self-government"; that is, Gramsci thought it necessary to relate the factory to the Socialist worker in the same way that the commune or electoral district was related to the bourgeois "citizen."[48]

Angelo Tasca objected to making this program the object of *Ordine nuovo*; more precisely, he objected to campaigning for the initiation of Italian soviets without prior agreement with the industrial and trade unions. Tasca had participated in the FGS since 1908 and was active in the great metallurgical strikes of 1912–13. He was, therefore, intimately associated with the leaders of the Turin labor movement, and hesitated to undertake a program that might threaten their interests. Moreover, Tasca's conception of a journal of "Socialist culture" was quite different from Gramsci's. For Tasca, the purpose of such a journal was to review Socialist intellectual history; the work of Antonio Labriola, the only significant Italian contributor to Socialist thought, would be the focal point of this study, and its ultimate goal was a revision of Marxism.

Togliatti and Terracini supported Gramsci's plan; but since Tasca was the one able to borrow the 6,000 lire necessary to begin publication, the early numbers of the new journal reflected his influence.* Gramsci described its format up to the issue of June 21 as nothing more than an "anthology" or a "review of abstract culture"—abstract for Gramsci because it contained nothing specifically Turinese, but could as well have been published "at Naples, Caltanissetta, or Brindisi."[49] The journal had no concrete program and no central idea capable of moving the Turinese masses.

The originality of *Ordine nuovo* began with the seventh number, of June 21; for in mid-June, Gramsci and Togliatti carried out a successful "editorial coup d'etat." Gramsci presented the problem of the internal committee and its transformation into the soviet in his first editorial, "Democrazia operaia," with immediate success. He, Togliatti, and Terracini were invited by workmen's circles and many internal committees to discuss the new policy of *Ordine nuovo,* which rapidly gained many adherents. Gramsci's most important speech was probably one given to the entire Socialist section on June 24, 1919. After an appeal to transform the internal committees into soviets of the type developed in Russia and Hungary, "according to the revolutionary experiences of the English and American working masses," Gramsci asserted that soviets would be much easier to create before the revolution than afterward, when "polemics and the clash of tendencies would become fiercer." In an appeal to the abstentionists, who were becoming stronger in Turin, Gramsci argued that establishment of soviets would in itself be a creative and effective criticism of the value of parliamentary activity.[50]

In August 1919, Gramsci's program achieved its first concrete results. At a congress of the FGS held early in the month, the program of *Ordine nuovo* was discussed at length. Mario Montagnana declared that *Ordine nuovo* must become for the Socialists what Prezzolini's *La Voce* had been for the bourgeoisie.[51] More important, the internal committee at Fiat-Centro, the largest plant in Turin, re-

---

* Ferrara and Ferrara, p. 47. Gobetti (pp. 118–19) has described Tasca's work for the journal: "He began with a series of studies on Louis Blanc, work done with the bibliographic care of a staff writer for the *Giornale storico della letteratura italiana.* Beyond his integrity in citation and reference, his interest revolved around the problem of small property and exhibited sentimental attitudes that were almost petty-bourgeois; something patriarchal, of Bakunin and Turati together, remained in his thought." But Gobetti's judgment is certainly too harsh. Tasca later became a courageous anti-Fascist, and still found time to write a standard work on the origins of Fascism (*Nascita e avvento del fascismo*).

signed and called for the election of a council including a "commis-sar" from each industrial division of the plant. By October 26, 1919, more than 50,000 Turinese workers in 30 plants were so organized.[52] This figure grew to 150,000 at the end of that year.[53] On November 1, the Turin section of the Fiom, with 16,000 members, elected a new executive committee that adopted the principles of the factory coun-cils; henceforth, the councils were to represent the union in the shops. In December the Turin section of the PSI also accepted the councils, and appointed a committee of study headed by Togliatti.[54] Finally, in December, the Turin Chamber of Labor passed, by a large ma-jority, a resolution approving the council movement—which it de-scribed as "spontaneously issuing from the factories of Turin"—as a "sign of the maturity of the working class."[55]

The Theoretical Basis for Gramsci's Factory Councils

Gramsci did not spend time and effort in transforming the internal committees into "true" soviets because he thought the Russian Revo-lution should be slavishly imitated, but because of the great respect for "councils" almost everywhere in postwar Europe and because of his general conception of the Socialist theory of revolution. To the Marxist the proletariat is a new class contained within the structure of capitalism, and its very existence hastens the collapse of that struc-ture. As a new class, the proletariat will create a new state, Socialist in character because of the conditions of modern industry and the work-ers' belief that only Socialism can end the exploitation of one class by another.

According to Gramsci, this Socialist state "already exists potentially in the institutions of social life characteristic of the exploited working class."[56] In order to create this new state, however, it was necessary to delineate the essential conditions for effecting a transition to it. The basic condition was certainly that all the workers enter the framework of Socialist institutions, for only so could the whole class become aware of its role in creating the new state. None of the existing insti-tutions of the working class could meet this condition. The Party was hardly in a position to assimilate the entire working class in a short period of time; and even if it could do so, the Party would cease to be the "vanguard" of the proletariat and the beacon of the future. In-stead, it would be dominated by the realities of the moment. The trade unions spoke only for the members of specific trades and, in any case, proposed only limited goals, such as improvements in wages and hours; hence, the future did not lie with them.

It was necessary to create another institution, which could organize the proletariat to "educate itself, gather experience, and acquire
a responsible awareness of the duties incumbent upon classes that
hold the power of the State." The new institution should also contain,
in itself, the model for the proletarian state.[57] The soviet as developed
in Russia met both of these requirements, and Gramsci regarded the
internal committee as a potential soviet; hence, he sought to transform
it into an effective instrument.

One deficiency of the committees was that they represented only
those workers organized in trade unions. The unorganized workers—
unskilled and white-collar for the most part—were not represented.
And, like the unions, the committees limited their activities to questions of wages and hours. Since all the workers were not represented,
"education" of the entire working class was not possible; similarly,
duties confined to the relations of owners and employees would not
prepare the workers for their great responsibility in the coming Socialist state. An effective transformation of the committees into true
soviets, or councils, would entail the elimination of these imperfec-
tions.

The committee's nature enabled the Socialists to create the conditions necessary for revolution directly within the factory, the primary
unit of Socialist society. According to Gramsci, the centers of capitalist power were commercial and financial (banks, exchanges, cartels,
trusts, and chambers of commerce), but the centers of power in a proletarian society would be industrial (the factory and groups of factories).[58] The essence of the Socialist revolution lay in recognizing
this economic truth and in working to make the factory a political institution. Economics precedes politics, but revolution is a political
act; hence, the factory had to be given the necessary "organic form
and systemization" to make it the basis of political revolution.[59]

The backwardness of the Italian economy made this move all the
more necessary. An outbreak of revolution would not ensure the victory of Socialism in Italy, even if the bourgeois state were successfully
overthrown.[60] The majority of the population might agree to the destruction of the present system, but only the factory workers could
guarantee a victory of Socialism. Only they—unlike the peasants and
petty bourgeoisie—were "mathematically" certain of never becoming
owners in a capitalist regime; hence they alone would be totally convinced that Socialism, a new order based on collective ownership, was
necessary.[61] The future of Socialism therefore demanded the political
organization of workers within the factory. And for Gramsci, develop-

ment of factory councils was not a mere wish: the conditions for their formation already existed.

Technological developments in the factory had changed the position of the master craftsmen and technicians in the plants. The worker could proceed without supervision in many technical duties, and thereby achieved greater autonomy. The technician, no longer necessary when self-discipline replaced the martial discipline of the factory, had also been "reduced to the level of a producer" connected to the capitalist by the "naked and crude relations of exploited to exploiter."[62] Consequently, his psychology had become less petty-bourgeois and more proletarian.

The development of finance capitalism, with its attendant physical separation of owner from factory, had rendered the role of the capitalist superfluous. His foresight, initiative, and individual interests were no longer essential to production.

The captain of industry has become the *cavaliere d'industria,* hidden in the banks, salons, bourses, and ministerial and parliamentary corridors. The owner of capital has become a dead branch in the field of production. Since he is no longer indispensable—since his historical functions have atrophied —he has become a mere agent of the police. He puts his interests immediately into the hands of the State, which will ruthlessly defend them.[63]

Factory workers had acquired a high degree of autonomy through the elimination of the legitimate capitalist role in production. And they were prepared to use this autonomy to good advantage because factory life, with its intense and methodical production, had taught them to respect order and precision. Proletarian class solidarity—the strength of the workers—was directly dependent upon these qualities and an attendant division of labor, as seen in the factory. Every worker came to think of himself as inseparable from his comrades in labor. "The more the proletarian is specialized in a job, the more he feels the indispensability of his comrades, and thinks of himself as a cell of an organized body . . . , [then] the more he feels the need for order, method, [and] precision. . . ." The worker began to conceive of society as "one immense factory, organized with the same precision, method, and order that he sees as vital in the factory where he works."[64]

The Program and Organization of the Factory Councils

On October 31, 1919, the first general assembly of the Turin factory commissars discussed and approved a program of general concepts and specific regulations for the organization of factory councils, first in Turin (where the movement already encompassed 50,000 workers), then in Piedmont, and eventually in all Italy.* This program, entirely reproduced in the issue of *Ordine nuovo* for November 8, directly reflected Gramsci's ideas on the purpose of the councils. Even the language of the document, with its Hegelian overtones, is Gramsci's, although he modestly called the program a collective product of the "Committee of Study" appointed by the commissars.[65] The councils were carefully constructed to avoid the shortcomings of the contemporary Italian Socialist organizations.

After a lengthy analysis of the relations between trade unions and councils, the "Programma" stressed the importance of democratic principles in the operation of the councils: those elected as factory commissars must execute the will of the mass. However, this democracy was not based solely on numerical expression of the mass will; in addition, it reflected the functions of labor and the organization that the working class "naturally assumed in the process of professional industrial production and in the factories."[66] Within each division of a given factory, every "labor squad"—a group devoted to a single function or operation—elected one commissar. Ultimately, administrative and directing personnel would also be represented, whether engineers, technicians, or clerks.[67]

To ensure that commissars continually enjoyed the trust and respect of the workers, the mandate of the commissar was revocable by referendum at any moment.[68] In this way the stultifying bureaucratization that the trade unions had allegedly experienced would, it was hoped, be avoided. Only one limitation was placed on the complete equality of all the factory proletariat: every worker had the right to vote, but only those workers organized within the various trade unions might serve as commissars.[69] This proviso was justified by the political immaturity of many of the unorganized workers, by the danger of capitalist subversion in the new institution, and by the need for frequent council intervention in matters concerning the trade unions.[70] It also gave a dual responsibility to the commissars. As representatives of the whole factory proletariat, they represented a social class; and, as organized workers, they were spokesmen for the trade-union categories within each plant.

The regulations of the Programma provided for the nomination of

---

* The first council in Turin had been formed at the Brevetti-Fiat plant in early September 1919. Thirty-two commissars representing seven industrial divisions were elected, with all but three or four of the 2,000 workers employed exercising their right to vote (*L'Ordine nuovo* [10], pp. 456–57).

an executive committee, chosen from the council of commissars and consisting of three to nine members, depending on the size of the factory.[71] This executive committee took the place of the old internal committee, and was to be recognized as doing so by the management of the factory.[72] Actually the council—hence the executive committee—had much broader powers than the internal committee, but it was necessary to secure early recognition of the new institution from the management.

The commissars had many different duties; nonetheless, they were not permitted to leave their own factory jobs except in circumstances requiring their presence outside of their divisions. The Programma contains eleven numbered items under the heading "The Tasks of the Commissars in the Factory." Essentially these may be reduced to three: defense of the rights of labor, preparation for the seizure of power in the factories, and education of the workers.

Education of the workers was viewed in an entirely new way. The commissars were responsible for organizing, within the factory, a school for increasing the workers' skills in their own trades or industrial functions.[73] In addition to these "Labor Schools," *Ordine nuovo* established a "School of Culture and Socialist Propaganda" in December 1919, attended by both university students and workers. Gramsci, Togliatti, Tasca, and Pastore gave frequent lectures there, as did several professors from the University.[74] This school examined the idea of the *Stato dei consigli,* a new state completely replacing the liberal state by a "system of councils."

Ordine nuovo itself attempted to further the workers' education with regular features, like one entitled "The Battle of Ideas," and special contributions, like Aldo Oberdorfer's study of Leonardo da Vinci or Togliatti's translations of Walt Whitman.[75] For Gramsci, the deficiencies of Italian education affected more than the working class, but only that class could organically relate education to life. Only through education could the workers attain the maturity to seize power; hence, Gramsci wanted to convince the working class through the councils "that it is in their interest to submit to a permanent discipline of culture, to develop a conception of the world and the complex and intricate system of human relations, economic and spiritual, that form the social life of the globe."[76]

The educational program was directly related to another task of the commissars in the factory councils, namely, preparation for the seizure of power. This task was primarily one of preparing the workers to become autonomous producers. The commissars were therefore required to study "bourgeois systems of production" and, whenever possible, to suggest ways of accelerating production by eliminating unnecessary work. If technical innovations—even those proposed by management—seemed useful in production, the workers should be urged to accept them, even at the cost of "temporary damage" to their interests, provided that the industrialists were also willing to make sacrifices.[77] In this way, the worker should begin to think of himself not as a wage earner but as a producer, with an awareness of his precise place in the process of production "in all its levels, from the factory, to the nation, to the world."[78] This enlarged vision was thought by Gramsci to be the best guarantee for the total transformation of the existing capitalist system.

The ultimate goal of the councils was stated with great clarity by Togliatti in January 1920:

The constitution of Councils has value only if it is viewed as the conscious beginning of a revolutionary process. Control of production has meaning only if it is an act . . . in this process. . . . The typical counterrevolutionary program regarding the constitution of councils, organs of future society, consists in having them recognized by the State, the supreme organ of present society. . . . Between a bourgeois organization and an organization of the workers, there can be no compromise. There is no power to be divided between them; there is power to be conquered.[79]

Gramsci thought that the councils, if permitted to develop the functions outlined above, would replace the bourgeois state:

The factory council is the model of the proletarian state. All the problems inherent in the organization of the proletarian state are inherent in the organization of the council. In the one and in the other, the concept of the citizen declines and is replaced by the concept of the comrade; collaboration to produce wealth . . . multiplies the bonds of affection and brotherhood. Everyone is indispensable; everyone is at his post; and everyone has a function and a post. Even the most ignorant and backward of the workers, even the most vain and "civil" of engineers eventually convinces himself of this truth in the experience of factory organization. Everyone eventually acquires a communist viewpoint through understanding the great step forward that the communist economy represents over the capitalist economy. The council is the most fitting organ of reciprocal education and development of the new social spirit that the proletariat has succeeded in creating. . . . Working-class solidarity . . . in the council is positive, permanent, and present in even the most negligible moment of industrial production. It is contained in the joyous awareness of being an organic whole, a homogeneous and compact system that, by useful labor and disinterested production of social wealth, asserts its sovereignty, and realizes its power and its freedom as a creator of history.[80]

For these reasons, Gramsci in September 1919 stated that "the formation of a system of councils represents the first concrete assertion of the communist revolution in Italy."[81] Some time was to pass before he realized that the council movement was also the *last* advance made by the "communist revolution in Italy."

Trade Unionism and the Factory Councils

The most important of the many problems raised in forming the factory councils was the relationship of the councils to the trade unions and the PSI. Gramsci pointed out that both Party and unions arose in a historical period dominated by capitalism. The whole proletarian movement was thus not autonomous. It did not obey "laws" implicit in the life and historical experience of the working class but "laws" imposed upon it by the proprietary class, the capitalists. Like any other phenomenon of the period, the proletarian movement was only a development of "capitalist free competition." The unions "competed" economically, and the Party politically. To this fact, Gramsci traced "all the inner conflicts, deviations, hesitations, and compromises that characterize the whole life of the proletarian movement, which culminated in the bankruptcy of the Second International."[82]

In Gramsci's judgment, the grossest error related to the historical origins of the trade-union movement was the tendency of many leaders to regard its economic struggle with capitalism as the essential activity for social revolution. Gramsci viewed this as a *contingent* and not a *permanent* struggle. The trade union itself originated in reaction to hostile historical conditions (*imposto*), rather than as an autonomous formulation of the workers (*proposto*). Dependent as the trade union was upon capitalist laws, it did not have "a constant and predictable line of development"; hence, it was incapable of embodying a positive revolutionary movement.[83]

Because trade unionism was merely a form of capitalist society, it organized the workers as a group within the capitalist regime charged with selling a commodity called "labor." In order to sell this commodity at the highest price, the unions organized the workers on one of two principles, depending upon circumstances: according to the tool of a particular trade, which resulted in craft unionism; or according to the material to be transformed (e.g., iron ore into steel), which resulted in industrial unionism. Both of these principles were imposed upon the unions by the capitalist regime. Since the use of a lathe rather than a loom, for example, or the manufacturing of steel rather than cloth, was dependent on differing levels of capacity and training among the workers, both amounts of effort and amounts of gain were often highly stratified. This led the workers to regard their labor not as a "process of production, but as a pure means of gain."[84]

The factory council, by contrast, led the worker to regard himself as a producer, not a wage earner, because he saw himself "as an inseparable part of a whole system of labor summed up in the manufactured object." The council helped him realize the "unity of the industrial process, which demands the collaboration of the unskilled and skilled worker, the administrative clerk, the engineer, and the technical director."[85] Gramsci emphasized that this conception was essential to the revolutionary process.

Even though the trade union was an instrument of the class struggle (or "class competition"), it had not gained any significant victories over the institutions of private property and profit. An early awareness that the elimination of capitalism was beyond its strength (actually caused by the union's origin and its conception of the worker) soon led the trade union to direct all its efforts to the immediate end of raising workers' standard of living by demanding higher wages, shorter hours, and a body of social legislation. Living standards did improve relatively, but all the victories of trade unionism were obtained within a system of private ownership. Profit was rarely affected. When the rate of profit was successfully lowered by trade-union action, it "found a new stability: by free competition in the case of nations with world economies, like England and Germany, and by protective tariffs for nations with limited economies, like France and Italy." Thus, the increased expenses of industrial production were transferred either to the colonial masses or to large strata of the population in more backward independent nations. In neither case could union action produce a social revolution.[86]

The trade union was limited in freedom of action by its increasing observance of strict legality in relations with the propertied class.[87] Indeed, its legalism was the best guarantee of its ability to perform its proper task, the negotiation of labor contracts. Increasing size and the development of a centralized bureaucracy had gradually detached the trade unions from the masses. But this ostensible weakness was the real strength of the trade-union movement. Its detached bureaucracy was beyond reach of the tumultuous masses; therefore, it was able to contract pacts and assume obligations. The entrepreneur could be sure that the union was a stable organization, capable of obtaining the respect of the working masses for contract obligations. This certainty was the basis of "industrial legality," which certainly improved the condition of the working classes.

Nevertheless, industrial legality was a temporary compromise, justified only in circumstances unfavorable to the working class. Insofar as the unions recognized the temporary nature of the compromise and tried to increase the power of the working class and prepare it for a more positive role in society, they would be a revolutionary instrument in the class struggle. Even if industrial legality were enforced with such ends in mind, it would be justified by the need for revolutionary discipline. Unfortunately, however, the trade-union movement often viewed industrial legality as a *perpetual* compromise. In this event, clashes with the frankly revolutionary institutions of the working class were inevitable.

The factory council negated industrial legality, since its primary purpose was to educate the working class for the seizure of power through control over production; whereas the union, to guarantee continuity of labor and wages to the workers, insisted upon the maintenance of industrial legality. "The council tends, because of its revolutionary spontaneity, to unleash the class war at any moment; the union, because of its bureaucratic form, tends to prevent the class war from ever being unleashed."

In conclusion, Gramsci regarded the specific tasks of union and council as completely opposed in principle, and he asserted the primacy of the council's role. This primacy did not imply that the role of trade unions had come to an end. So long as society was based on the principle of private property, the labor movement would continue to bargain with its employers. Even in a Socialist state, trade unions would control the technical education of all the workers in a given trade or industrial process.

But there was serious danger in attempts by the unions to stifle or attenuate the councils. For the successful development of the proletarian movement, the specific roles of each institution must be realized. Gramsci recommended that union and council cooperate "to create conditions in which the departure from legality (the offensive of the working class) comes at the most opportune moment for the working class."[88]

The Relationship of the Party to the Factory Councils

Gramsci's ideas on the relationship of the Socialist Party to the factory council were based on the same premise used in his analysis of the trade union; namely, that the development of the Party into a revolutionary organ was hindered by its origin in a capitalist society as an organ of competition with the bourgeoisie. Although the restrictions imposed on the Party by the nature of its origin were different from those suffered by the trade union, the two shared one failing: insofar as they were forms of liberal democracy, they would decline with the collapse of capitalism, which was politically expressed by liberal democracy.[89]

This danger was greater for the Party than for the trade union, since the postwar collapse of capitalism would be the demise of a social and political system, not of an economic system based on the factory—and the Socialist Party, unlike the union, was a purely political institution. By relating the postwar crisis in the Italian State and the spectacle of a Socialist Party beset with internal contradictions, Gramsci advanced an idea of great theoretical value, characteristic of his extreme historicism.[90] According to Gramsci, the Party could avoid the dangers inherent in this situation by encouraging the development of a strong council movement. This would root the Party in the economic life of the working class and present it with the continual challenge of winning a friendly majority in each council.

The Party, as the "vanguard of the proletariat," was composed of the most class-conscious and disciplined members of the working class. It stood above the transient interests of that class in order to direct the long-range struggle for the conquest of power. With its superior discipline, knowledge of the "laws" of historical development, close analysis of contemporary events, and intimate awareness of conditions among the laboring masses, it was equipped to delineate the strategy and tactics of the class struggle.[91]

The council, on the other hand, was charged with the economic and political education of the whole laboring mass, to be achieved through control over production. Ultimately, the councils would replace the State as the organ of government. Nevertheless, Gramsci recognized the possibility that many councils would support for a short time the non-Socialist ideologies of the proletariat, particularly syndicalism and anarchism. This was so because the unqualified democracy of the council reflects the momentary interests and tumultuous desires of the masses.[92]

The above distinctions were characteristic of Marxist-Leninist thought in general, but Gramsci went on to relate them to his analysis of the dangers in the Party's origins. He described the Party as a "voluntary" or "private" institution, whereas the council was a "representative" or "public" organism.[93] The party was a "voluntary" organization because the worker adhered to it "by an explicit act of consciousness" or, in the language of traditional political theory, by "express consent." At any moment he could withdraw his consent by denying the "contract" between himself and the party. In contrast, the council was a "representative" organization because it was an organ of government, actual and potential. The structure of the council reflected the position of its members in the world of production; each worker participated in it by virtue of his role in production, and not by his consent as an individual. The Party was "born in the field of political freedom, in the field of bourgeois democracy, as an assertion and development of freedom and democracy in general," but the council was created "in the field of industrial production, in the factory." There, democracy did not exist; it was the business of the council to create it.

The problem of how the Party and council would function in a revolutionary situation remains to be discussed.[94] The Party was the most important agent of the revolutionary process. Insofar as the masses accepted its analysis of events and its predictions of the future, the disintegration of the old order would be hastened.[95] As greater numbers followed the guidance of the Party, its control of the revolution would increase. But the revolutionary process itself was not to be found in the area of freedom and liberal democracy proper to the Party, but in the social relations of the factory, "where freedom does not exist" and "where the relations are those of the oppressor to the oppressed, the exploiter to the exploited."

The Party had no control over the course of events among the masses unless the masses gave their allegiance to the Party. But complete identity of Party and working class was possible only after a long period of education. In the meantime the council, which was capable of organizing the entire working class, could attempt to control the revolutionary process. The council, in turn, could facilitate and discipline the revolution only so long as it was completely responsive to its workers—that is, truly democratic. For this reason the Party was urged not to impose its own judgments and beliefs upon the councils, lest they lose contact with the mood actually prevailing among the masses. According to Gramsci, the German revolutionary movement in 1919 failed because the Social Democrats attempted to impose councils controlled by their own men upon the workers; hence, the revolution was "shackled and domesticated."[96] In such a case the revolutionary movement would certainly continue, but it would no longer be subject to any control, because the council, the only body immediately responsive to the mood of the workers, would no longer truly represent their desires.

Ultimately, Gramsci's view of the relationship between Party and council was the same as the Marxist view of the relationship between politics and economics: "Any form of political power can be conceived and justified historically only as the juridical apparatus of a real economic power."[97] If the Socialist Party were to bring about revolution in Italy, the economic base for a Socialist state would have to be secured. This was precisely what the council was attempting to do by helping the workers to educate themselves as producers. Only through such a process could the revolution pass from a mere insurrection against the bourgeois state to the Socialist reconstruction of Italy. By encouraging the free development of councils, the Party— and the trade union as well—would help create the economic conditions for a victory of this second stage of the revolution:

The Party and the union ought not to consider themselves tutors or ready-made superstructures of this new institution [the council] in which the historical process of the revolution takes controllable historical form. They must consider themselves conscious agents of its liberation from the forces of suppression centered in the bourgeois state. They must organize the general external (political) conditions in which the process of the revolution will develop its greatest speed and in which the liberated productive forces will find their greatest expansion.[98]

Gramsci so emphasized the obligations of the Party and trade union to the council that his words frequently sound as though he believed in the possibility of a "spontaneous" revolution of the working class without the political direction and discipline afforded by the Party. Gramsci's theoretical judgment of political parties as such was not really so negative; however, he had become increasingly aware that the PSI had far too many shortcomings to direct the course of the revolution successfully. In 1919 he believed that the Party could be renewed from below by the construction of the councils, but the catastrophic events of 1920 convinced him that only a reorganization of the Party could ensure the success of the councils.

Gramsci vs. the PSI Directorate on the Factory Councils

Gramsci had never been an enthusiastic supporter of the maximalist directors in the PSI; however, it was only toward the end of 1919 that his hostility overcame his desire for Party unity. Thereafter, the break between *Ordine nuovo* and maximalism widened, eventually contributing heavily to the Socialist schism at Livorno in January 1921.

Along with *Ordine nuovo,* the Turin labor movement as a whole was progressively alienated from the national leadership of the Socialist Party. This was apparent as early as October 1918, when the workers of the city pledged 10,000 lire toward the foundation of a Piedmontese edition of *Avanti!,* to be written in great part at Turin.[99] G. M. Serrati, the maximalist leader and editor of Milan's *Avanti!,* had opposed such a move on the ground that it would tend to split the journal's unity of direction.[100] This was the first event in a long and increasingly violent polemic between Serrati and the Turin labor movement.

In November 1919, Serrati announced his opposition to the inclusion of unorganized workers in the structure of the factory councils. On November 6 a General Assembly of workers, technicians, and clerks at Turin rejected Serrati's position, after a speech by Gramsci and a lively debate.[101] Meanwhile, and for the same reason, *Battaglie sindacali,* organ of the CGL, had also attacked the council movement. Gramsci dismissed its criticism with the remark that, since the paper was a reformist mouthpiece, any discussion between it and *Ordine nuovo* was "organically impossible."[102] For Gramsci, only the opposition of the maximalists was to be taken seriously.

Oddly enough, a laudatory letter from Lenin to Serrati provided material for Gramsci's first attack on the maximalist leader. This incident is a rare example of Gramsci's adopting a critical attitude toward Lenin. The letter was written on October 29, 1919, and was first published in Italy by *Avanti!* on December 6. After congratulating Serrati for the "communist" victory at the Congress of Bologna, Lenin expressed particular satisfaction with the decision of the PSI to participate in elections: "The example of the Italian Socialist Party will have a great influence on the whole world." He warned that "open or disguised opportunists" in the PSI might attempt to annul the decisions of Bologna, but felt that its current leadership would be strengthened by the results of the Congress. Finally, Lenin was convinced that "The excellent work of the Italian communists is a sure guarantee that they will succeed in winning to communism the whole industrial and agricultural proletariat, and also the small proprietors."[103]

Gramsci did not disagree with the political ideas and suggestions contained in the letter. But he felt that Lenin's praise of the Italian "communists" (that is, maximalists) was unmerited, and indeed "sanctioned a situation that is neither happy nor reassuring." According to Lenin's own doctrines, the "skilled" revolutionary must know the revolution's process of development, and not be a mere agitator. The world proletariat and the Third International had recognized that this process was now marked by the rise of councils. But the PSI had done nothing to further the concrete development of councils. Instead of giving power to a system of soviets and struggling to win a communist majority in them, the PSI had retained its "trade-union corporativism and party sectarianism."[104] According to Gramsci, Lenin's own words condemned the policy of the maximalists. The Serrati group had no intention of opening an all-out attack on the reformists, as Lenin wished them to do.[105] Also, as noted earlier, the current policies of the PSI were not calculated to act on Lenin's advice of "winning to communism the whole . . . *agricultural* proletariat."

It is clear that Gramsci's disagreement with Serrati and the maximalists was general, based on an entirely different conception of the revolutionary process. Serrati viewed this process as "essentially the work of a handful of 'technicians' of politics, propaganda, administration, and trade unionism, whose task is to drag along with them the whole undifferentiated mass of workers."[106] Alberto Caracciolo uses the term *blanquismo* to describe this "aristocratic" and "sectarian" view of the party, because of its similarity to the views of Auguste Blanqui, the nineteenth-century French revolutionary. Gramsci abhorred this conception of the Party and the revolution. He believed that the Party was merely the "agent" of the revolution; the workers themselves must be the embodiment of the revolution. Hence, Gramsci emphasized a combination of thoroughgoing democracy in the factories with a program of "communist" education.[107] The break between Gramsci and the maximalists was therefore most distinct on the question of the factory councils.

In accordance with the decision of the Congress of Bologna, a National Council of the PSI, held at Florence in January 1920, approved a plan drawn up by Nicola Bombacci for the establishment of councils. The councils were to be "unique organs of power and supreme direction for the organization of production and distribution, as well as for the regulation of the whole complex of economic, moral, and political relations that derive from it."[108]

It was the purely legalistic approach of Bombacci's plan that disgusted Gramsci. Councils, he felt, could not be established by bureaucratic decree, but only by agitation that would induce the workers themselves to form such bodies. Bombacci ignored the responsibility of the Party in such agitation. Umberto Terracini reflected Gramsci's judgments on the project when he commented, "If approval of the program read at Florence were enough to create the workers' state, the undertaking would indeed come too cheaply."[109]

Support of Bombacci's plan—whatever its worth—was by no means unconditional, even among abstentionists and maximalists like Bordiga and Serrati.[110] Serrati objected to the creation of a system of councils completely independent of the trade unions, calling those who supported such a plan *amburghesi,* because the idea was allegedly derived from the revolutionary syndicalists of Hamburg.[111] Serrati was on surer ground when he expressed a fear that the PSI was treating the question of workers' councils in the same pseudo-revolutionary manner as so many other problems in this period. With irony, he commented: "Today, he who speaks of reflection and study can be only a vile reformist. The greatest revolutionary is the one who promises the masses that they can touch the sky with their fingers if they would only stand on the tips of their toes." Although Gramsci might have agreed with this criticism, Serrati objected not only to the spirit of Bombacci's project, but also to the workers' council itself; for he concluded the article by recommending that such organisms be initially established in one single locality or province, since he doubted their adaptability to Italian conditions.[112]

Bordiga, too, objected to the idea of workers' councils as revolutionary organisms.[113] In a clever, if specious, argument Bordiga asserted that the idea of councils as economic-technical instruments for the control of production was sheer reformism, "the error that the proletariat can emancipate itself by gaining ground in economic relations while capitalism still holds the political power through the state."[114] A few months later, he insisted that "control over production is conceivable only when power has passed into the hands of the proletariat," and went on to accuse the *Ordine nuovo* group of overemphasizing this question, perhaps because the advanced conditions of production in Turin led its working-class leaders to exaggerate the importance of the factory in national life.[115]

Serrati, unlike Bordiga, was not willing to make the fundamental changes in the nature of the Party that Gramsci had begun to recognize as necessary to establish an effective system of councils. Gramsci's open hostility to the leadership of the PSI can be dated from an editorial entitled "First: Renew the Party," published in *Ordine nuovo* in January 1920. He declared that the PSI had succeeded in only the most elementary part of its historical task, that of carrying on agitation among the masses and attracting them to its revolutionary program. But it was not succeeding in its more advanced task, the conquest of political power. Instead, it was being overcome by the rush of events, losing control of its own destiny.

> The necessary and sufficient conditions for the proletarian revolution are present on both the international and national levels. But the Socialist Party is unworthy of itself and its mission. A party of agitators, negators, and intransigents in questions of general tactics, [a party of] apostles of elementary theories, it has not succeeded in organizing and disciplining the great masses in movement.[116]

Gramsci's chief explanation for this incompetence was the continued presence of the reformists in the Party. It was the reformists who were "systematically sabotaging all revolutionary action," and who were "a party within the Party, and the stronger party, because they are the masters of the motor ganglions of the working-class body."[117] Gramsci bitterly pointed out the resulting paralysis of the Socialist Party during the current (January 1920) strikes of the postaltelegraph workers and the railway workers. Those strikes reduced the State to a position of near collapse and, at the same time, pushed the bourgeoisie closer to an offensive against the working class. Yet the workers were given no political direction in this situation, but instead were exposed to the proddings of anarchistic extremist propaganda. Therefore, argued Gramsci, "The Socialist Party must be reinvigorated if it does not wish to be overturned and crushed by the rush of events. It must be reinvigorated because its defeat would mean the defeat of the revolution."[118]

Meanwhile, Gramsci had won over a majority of the Turin section to his point of view. He himself wrote the "Program of Action" of its Electoral Committee, which indicated the criteria for selection of new officers for the section. Essentially, the Program was a denunciation of the PSI for permitting an ever-increasing reformist influence in its directing organs, a situation that reflected the growing confusion and uncertainty of the maximalists.

For Gramsci, the only answer to the problem was to reestablish contact between the Party and the masses by creating a network of workers' councils all over Italy as soon as possible. Because of the number of councils already established in Turin, the Turin section would have primary responsibility for promoting the campaign.[119] To combat the predominance of the reformists in the trade unions,

Gramsci suggested the "formation of permanently organized communist groups" within each trade union. In anticipation of conflicts with the Serratian direction of *Avanti!*, he urged that the Turin edition of the newspaper be managed "in conformance with the ever-growing needs of our region," that is, in a more autonomous way.[120]

An Evaluation of Gramsci's Factory Council Movement

In 1954, Angelo Tasca stated that Gramsci's articles published in *Ordine nuovo* in 1919–20 "constitute the most original and powerful expression of Socialist thought in the last fifty years."[121] Certainly this statement is somewhat exaggerated. In 1919–20 meaningful Socialist ideas had to be formulated in close conjunction with developments in Russia, since a Socialist state was actually being created there. Few Socialists, even the most revisionist, wanted to dissociate themselves completely from the Russian "experiment," and even a casual study of the writings of Lenin and the documents of the Comintern will reveal the source of much of Gramsci's thought.

Yet this thought is fresh and exciting, and is not a mere copy of what had already been said in Russia. There is much originality in Gramsci's work, though this originality is more limited than Lenin's. Gramsci's conceptions of the origins of the Party and the trade unions, and of the tasks of the factory councils, certainly contain many novel insights, as do his essays on the historical roles of anarchism and Christian democracy.[122] Even Gramsci's literary style, with its caustic wit, its occasional traces of his earlier Hegelian training, and its coldly logical form pervaded by a sense of intense urgency, is so personal that his work is immediately recognizable.

Like Lenin—and indeed like the mainstream of Marxian Socialism—Gramsci was no determinist. Marxism for him was a philosophy of praxis, a belief that the goal of proletarian liberation could be achieved through the voluntary political activity of the proletariat itself, or rather by means of a continually progressing dialectic between the proletariat and its class-conscious vanguard. Unlike both the maximalists and the reformists, Gramsci did not think it necessary to wait for the "fullness of time" to bring about the revolution. In his refusal to accept passively the limitations of the contemporary Italian situation, and in his elaboration of a constructive program for going beyond it, Gramsci distinguished himself among Italian Socialists of this period.

Some years later, when Gramsci and all that he had struggled for

were threatened with annihilation by victorious Fascism, his desperate efforts to reconstruct a powerful labor movement led him to
reflect on his experiences of 1919–1920:

We must seek to rebuild an atmosphere like that of '19–'20 with the means
at our disposal. At that time, no project was undertaken unless first tested
by reality and until we had sounded out in many ways the opinions of the
workers. Consequently our projects almost always had an immediate and
broad success and appeared as the interpretation of a widely felt need, never
as the cold application of an intellectual scheme.[123]

There are certainly very few moments in the history of the labor
movement—and not only in Italy—where the opinion of the rank
and file was so eagerly sought and appreciated!

Gramsci examined Italian conditions in the light of Lenin's theses,
and much of his theory of the factory councils was derived from
Lenin; but he adapted his work to his own experience and to specific
conditions at Turin. He found the "germ" of the soviet in the internal
committees and the possibility of achieving a full-fledged soviet in the
militant tradition of the Turin proletariat. To the scene of his activity, the city of Turin, he assigned a special role. Partly through
Gramsci's own efforts, this "proletarian city par excellence" had developed a working class that was "compact, disciplined, and *distinct*
as in few other cities of the world."[124]

The proof of this statement, as well as a proof of Gramsci's creative
energy, is that the factory council movement at Turin succeeded in
enrolling the majority of the city's workingmen. These workers, according to Piero Gobetti, "spoke the language of unconscious Hege-
lians," reflecting the influence of Gramsci's own formulations of
Leninist thought, based on his own education and cultural background.

It is Gramsci's sense of total crisis that gives his work such vigor
and sincerity, and supplies the raison d'être of his whole program in
these years. He regarded the situation in postwar Italy as the collapse
of the whole tradition of the Italian liberal State. The working class
alone was unscathed by this collapse; however, its institutions, such
as the Party and the trade unions, were tainted by their origins in a
capitalist regime, and would have to be reinvigorated. The new institution of the factory council, expressing the values of a new ruling
class of producers, would ensure the autonomy, and hence the survival, of the proletariat.

Gramsci did not perfectly distinguish the immediate role of the
factory council as an instrument of struggle against the bourgeoisie

from its ultimate role as the basic unit of a new proletarian state. Hence, Bordiga and others could criticize Gramsci's emphasis on the function of the councils in technical education—part of its ultimate role—as being merely another version of reformism which would, in effect, help the capitalists. Nonetheless, this emphasis derived directly from Gramsci's desire to prepare the workers completely for their coming hegemony over other social classes. This hegemony could be assured only by a total superiority—economic, technical, political, and cultural—of the workers to the other classes.

The nature of the times stimulated a sense of crisis in many men, but none in Italy responded so fervently to it as Gramsci. The whole energies of the Ordine Nuovo movement were directed toward totally refashioning the culture of the workers as producers by means of the councils. This program and the councils actually created by it were unique in Italy.

5. The Turin Labor Movement in 1920

*Oggi Torino ... è la città industriale
per eccellenza, è la città proletaria
per eccellenza. La classe operaia
torinese è compatta, è disciplinata,
è distinta come in pochissime città
del mondo.*

—Gramsci, *January 17, 1920*

Political Conditions in Early 1920

The political and economic decay of the Italian State had continued
with fearful rapidity in late 1919 and early 1920. D'Annunzio's successful occupation of Fiume in September 1919 excited rather than
assuaged the feelings of Italian superpatriots, who were already
aroused by alleged neglect of Italian interests at Versailles. The adventure also encouraged sedition in the army, and thereby weakened
the forces of law and order in the country. Moreover, the traditional
parties of the Italian liberal State no longer enjoyed a majority in the
Chamber of Deputies; the formation of a stable government, acceptable to all its internal factions, that did not incur the united and
active hostility of the opposition was a very difficult problem.

This political instability was accompanied by economic problems
of great political import. Rapid inflation swept Italy in 1920: the
average weekly expenses of a typical family in Milan increased from
109.24 lire in July 1919 to 124.67 lire in January 1920, and then to
189.76 lire in December 1920.[1] For the salaried middle classes, whose
incomes lagged far behind rising price levels, this inflation proved
ruinous, and helped force their ultimate adherence to Fascism. Nor
was the magnification of prices concurrent with increasing production and rising levels of consumption. On the contrary, production
actually fell in many industries, and unemployment was widespread
in 1920, particularly at the beginning and end of the year.[2] The industrial workers, for their part, found it difficult to maintain their
purchasing power on a level with prices, despite the many strikes for
higher wages held during this period.

The early months of 1920 in fact marked the crest of the postwar strike wave throughout Europe.[3] Most of these strikes had economic rather than political ends, but the specific incidents that caused them were often so trivial that social unrest and political dissatisfaction were plainly behind them.[4] The strikes were certainly not coordinated in a political sense: the postal and telegraph workers settled their strike on January 21, only one day after the railroad workers began another. The only important strike with a basically political objective was the April general strike in Turin, which will be analyzed in this chapter.

The political reticence of the labor organizations, and consequently of the Socialist leaders, was soon noticed by representatives of the State and the industrialists. In the fall of 1919 Francesco Nitti, Premier from June 1919 to June 1920, reorganized the police, whose power was almost nonexistent in the early months of the year. He also established a "Royal Guard" with 377 officers and 25,000 men and raised the number of carabinieri to 160,000.[5] These forces were responsible for the deaths of about 100 workers and peasants between October 1919 and May 1920.[6] Socialist workers—even Socialist deputies—were also subjected to violence by bands of students, Fascists, and other nationalistic groups. By early 1920 opposition to the Socialist movement had revived in strength.

Italian capitalism reacted to the Socialist danger by establishing the General Confederation of Industry (Confindustria) on March 7, 1920.[7] It included all large industries and three-fourths of the medium and small manufacturers—11,000 members in all. The Confindustria adopted a complete and detailed plan of action, which outlined tactical methods for combating strikes and suggested the political rehabilitation of Giovanni Giolitti.[8] Gino Olivetti, the able secretary of the organization, briefed his colleagues on the factory councils, asserting that they must be destroyed.[9] The organizational unity of Italian capitalism was complete on August 18, when the General Confederation of Agriculture was founded on a basis similar to Confindustria. "The future belongs to the organized classes," said Olivetti.

These indications of renewed resistance to Socialism were obvious to Gramsci, although few other leaders of the Italian Left were so perceptive, partly because Socialist electioneering had been so successful —and would continue to be through 1921. In May 1920 Gramsci flatly predicted that either Socialism or open reaction would follow current events: "The present phase of the class struggle in Italy is the phase that precedes either the conquest of political power by the revolu-

tionary proletariat . . . or a tremendous reaction by the capitalists and
the governing caste. Every kind of violence will be used to subjugate
the agricultural and industrial proletariat."[10]

The Turin General Strike of April 1920

The conflicting developments of 1919 and early 1920—the uncertain Socialist advance, the strengthening of repressive bodies like the
carabinieri and Royal Guards, economic chaos, the reactionary measures of the bourgeoisie, and the rapid development of the Turin factory councils despite the opposition of the PSI—all contributed to an
event of monumental importance, the great Piedmont general strike
of April 1920. The strike's outcome was an unmitigated disaster for
the whole of Italian Socialism; hence, it is important to establish the
sequence of events that led to the strike itself.

The first stage of this debacle is often called the "clock-hands strike"
(*sciopero delle lancette*). Daylight saving time had been widely introduced in Italy during the war, and it generally remained in use thereafter. However, some of the workers objected to daylight saving time
as another example of the bourgeois state's meddling with their lives.
It was charged that the profits of electrical companies would be increased by this practice, although why this should be so was not made
clear. Several Socialist municipalities and Chambers of Labor refused
to adopt daylight saving time in the spring of 1920. The Turin strike
was alleged to have begun because the Fiat workers refused to accept
the decision of the management and adopt daylight time.

A number of historians—all of them evidently depending upon
Luigi Einaudi's account—speak of resistance to daylight saving time
as very widespread among the workers. Tasca even declares that the
issue "reveals the state of mind existing in that period in certain industrial centers."[11] But Mario Montagnana, then a Fiat metalworker,
insists that the campaign against "legal time" was carried on by "a
few old maximalists," and had no serious political content.[12] If the
first thesis is correct, then it was the intransigence of the workers and
their leaders over a relatively minor issue that precipitated the strike.
If Montagnana's statement is true, then the main body of the workers
and their leaders took no interest in the question of "clock hands,"
and the real cause of the strike was quite different. In general, Montagnana's thesis seems the more likely, for it best explains the strike's
actual course of development.

According to Montagnana, the episode began on the morning of
March 29, when the clocks in all the Fiat plants of Turin were ad-

vanced one hour. At the Industrie Metallurgiche, a Fiat subsidiary, a worker set the clock at the entrance back one hour without asking anyone's permission. After being identified by the plant guard, he was immediately fired. At that point, the factory council asked the workers to protest with a sit-down strike, to which the management immediately responded with a lockout. The closing of Industrie Metallurgiche led to a sit-down strike in all the Fiat plants; and two days later a lockout was proclaimed in the whole Turin Fiat complex.[13]

This was the first phase of the April strike, when it was still limited to the metalworkers of Turin. There are some important discrepancies between this narrative and the events recounted by historians who depend on Einaudi's account. According to them, the factory council itself turned back the hands of the clock. By way of proof, it was stated that the factory council at Industrie Metallurgiche had been quickly dismissed by the management.[14] However, given the general hostility of the industrialists toward the councils, the dismissal is not in itself a proof of the council's complicity in the clock-hands episode. Moreover, this thesis assumes that the council members were anxious for a showdown with management, or at least were willing to risk a direct encounter. But the facts contradict this assumption.

The leaders of the Turin labor movement had observed with great uneasiness the elaborate preparations of the city's industrialists for a decisive clash with the workers. This counteroffensive had already begun on March 7 with Gino Olivetti's report (later reprinted by Gramsci in *Ordine nuovo*) to the Confindustria on the necessity of crushing the factory council movement. Shortly afterward, large numbers of troops were sent to Turin: the Roman newspaper *Il Giornale d'Italia* found this event important enough to warrant sending a special correspondent to the city.[15] This is why Gramsci declared that the industrialists had seized upon the clock-hands incident as a "Cleopatra's nose," that is, as an event of chance that could change the course of history if properly exploited.[16]

During the first phase of the strike the workers and their leaders demonstrated a far from intransigent attitude. On April 9 the metalworkers voted to accept the proposals of mediation offered by the Prefect of the city.[17] According to Tasca, who follows Einaudi's interpretation of the incident, this vote was sanctioned by the Assembly of Divisional Commissars.* Nevertheless, chances for an early settle-

---

* Tasca, *Nascita*, p. 126, n. 5. Tasca uses the term "Assembly of Divisional Commissars." He probably means the factory council itself, but it is not completely clear that he is not referring to a subdivision of the council.

ment vanished when representatives of the workers and industrialists met on April 11. At that time the owners demanded "clarification" of the role of the factory councils.[18] In fact, they insisted that these bodies should have no more authority than the old internal committees. Acquiescing to such a demand would have completely repudiated the character of the Turin labor movement. As Gramsci remarked, "The Turin working class was drawn into the struggle. It did not have freedom of choice."[19]

Actually, the significance of the April strike does not lie so much in its immediate causes as in what it came to stand for after April 11, a conflict between two irreconcilable principles: absolute control by employers in the factories, and working-class control of production as envisioned by Gramsci and the other proponents of the factory councils. In the serenity of afterthought, Gramsci glorified the strike as "the first time in history [that] a proletariat undertook a struggle for the control of production without having been impelled to action by hunger or unemployment."[20]

On April 13 the Turin Chamber of Labor, in conjunction with the Fiom and the Socialist section, declared a general strike in defense of the factory councils. The proclamation denounced the intention of the Industrial League to destroy the internal committees, "which have shown themselves . . . capable of becoming the instrument of new conquests."[21] After April 15 the Piedmontese edition of *Avanti!* became the "Daily Bulletin of the General Strike," and *Ordine nuovo* temporarily suspended publication. The strike became general, first in the city of Turin, then in the province, and ultimately in most of Piedmont. Riccardo Bachi stated:

In its extension it was certainly the most notable movement of solidarity that one can recall in Italy. All the factories were closed. Only the most important public services continued to function, in a reduced measure. The municipal guards and the customs officers struck, as well as the tram workers, the railroad workers, and the post and telegraph workers.[22]

At its peak, the strike included about half a million industrial and agricultural workers and affected a population of about four million.[23] It was also supported by the railroad workers of Genoa, Pisa, Florence, and Livorno, who successfully impeded the further movement of troops to Turin.[24]

Nevertheless, by April 19 it was clear that the strike could not continue much longer. On April 23 the Socialist section agreed that the battle was over, and accepted the terms of settlement suggested by the

Prefect Taddei. The last bulletin of the strike committee openly admitted that the workers had been defeated: "In view of the failure to extend the movement for workers' control throughout Italy, the divisional commissars recognize that the industrialists, supported by the armed force of the bourgeoisie, have once again imposed their will." This recognition of defeat was not erased by the proclamation's conclusion: "This battle for communism, the first but not the last, shows that in the present hour the passive resistance of the proletariat is vain.... This battle is finished. The war continues."[25]

The Turin labor movement was indeed defeated, and far more seriously than the conditions accepted for the conclusion of the strike would indicate: the factory councils' control over the workers was reduced; but those bodies continued to exist, and no reprisals were to be made against any of the strikers.[26] Still, if it is true—as Togliatti says—that this general strike was "the most impressive movement of the whole postwar period in Italy,"[27] then the failure of the workers to defend their institutions was a serious defeat. The very dimensions of the movement, when compared with its negative results, discouraged the workers. Montagnana considers the April general strike the high point of the workers' movement in Italy; the occupation of the factories in September was merely a dramatic aftermath.[28]

This great action failed for three basic reasons. First, the political efficacy of a strike, however total, is rarely very great.* Secondly, the industrialists were well prepared for a clash and, actually, forced the workers into an all-out struggle. Thirdly, the strike was almost entirely confined to a single region of Italy.[29] Gramsci insisted that the national leadership of the PSI, by its refusal to support the strike, had deliberately isolated Piedmont from the rest of the nation.

The PSI and the General Strike

On April 19–21, at the height of the general strike, the leaders of the Socialist Party met in a National Conference. Originally planned for Turin, the Conference was abruptly shifted to Milan because, as Gramsci sarcastically remarked, "a city in a general strike was not adapted to Socialist discussions."[30] Although Togliatti was sent to the Conference as the representative of the Turin section, not a single bulletin was published supporting the strike; the Milan edition of *Avanti!* refused to publish even the strike manifesto of the Turin sec-

---

* The surprising thing about the strike is not that it failed, but that it lasted eleven days. Montagnana (p. 122) surmises that eleven days was almost a record in the history of general strikes.

tion.[31] Opposition to the Turin group was general, and a majority of the delegates refused to authorize the extension of the strike beyond Piedmont.[32]

The refusal was preceded by a very confused discussion of the general political line of the Party and another debate on the feasibility of establishing workers' councils—as though this had not already been decided upon at Bologna and Florence. Many of the Party's most important leaders did not hesitate to attack the whole council program. Bordiga, although on the extreme left, argued that the soviets, "as the form proper to the victorious proletarian State," could arise only after the political victory of the proletariat.[33] More moderate spokesmen like Vincenzo Vacirca insisted that the soviets might very well be infiltrated by demagogic elements, and Lazzari urged that rather than pursuing an "impractical" idea like the soviet, the Socialist Party would do well to "remember the communal tradition of the Italian people and the affection of the workers for the institutions so far created by our Party."[34]

True, a motion sanctioning a project for the construction of councils was again approved by a large majority; but while the party leaders chattered about theoretical projects at Milan, they were permitting the real thing to be destroyed at Turin. "They decided how to organize conquests not yet achieved, and left the Turin proletariat to its destiny."[35]

On April 29 Serrati attempted to answer this criticism:

We are not bound to accept battle every time that the enemy, feeling himself strong and prepared, provokes it. It seems that the opinion of the leaders of the Turin movement is quite different. After seeing themselves attacked, they let down their defenses rather than parrying the blow. Becoming hard pressed, they ran around at the last minute in search of aid from those less strong and prepared than themselves—after having hurled enough provoking statements to make the enemy believe that their action was no less than the beginning of revolution in a Turin by now ready for Communism. Thus, while negotiating in the Prefecture with Casalini, Frola, and Buozzi, they gave the impression elsewhere that the insurrection was at hand, so that later they might burden the capacious shoulders of the Party directorate with the responsibility for a defeat that did not touch it at all.[36]

Serrati may have been correct in indicting the provocative language of the Turin Socialists, but he was wrong in assuming that they could "parry the blow" of the industrialists.

In its reply to Serrati, Turin's *Avanti!* was at first unwilling to admit the gravity of the defeat: "The general strike of Turin has great significance in the history of the international proletariat. Never before had a working class confronted the problem of control [over industry] except when driven by the pangs of hunger," etc.[37] The defeat was real, however, and Gramsci frankly recognized it in his report on the Turin movement, sent to the Executive Committee of the Comintern in July 1920. He saw the chief cause of the defeat, as shown above, in the deliberate isolation of the Turin proletariat from the rest of Italy by the central organs of the Party, "which did nothing to help it."

Actually, the battle between Serrati and the Ordine Nuovo group had become a battle between the Communists of Turin and the maximalists of Milan. Serrati thought of the possession of power as the culmination of the general elevation of the masses, whereas Gramsci believed that the masses could be elevated only by possessing power.[38] The principal difference between the Second and the Third Internationals is contained in this contrast.

Just before the National Conference, Gramsci wrote one of his most important editorials of this period, "For a Renewal of the Socialist Party."[39] It was presented as a report to the Conference at Milan, and had previously received the unanimous approval of the Socialist section at Turin.[40] The article criticized the PSI for its political and organizational deficiencies in a general Italian situation that could end only in revolution or "tremendous reaction." Gramsci attacked the directing bodies of the Socialist Party: "They understand absolutely nothing about the phase of development that national and international history is going through in the present period." The PSI itself, despite the decisions of the Congress of Bologna, had therefore remained "a mere parliamentary party, which holds itself immobile within the narrow limits of bourgeois democracy."[41]

Gramsci also blamed the Party's incompetence on the many reformists in its ranks, who were tolerated by the maximalist directorate:

The central organs of the Party have done nothing to give the masses a political education in the Communist sense, to induce the masses to eliminate the reformists and the opportunists from the direction of trade-union and cooperative institutions. . . . Thus, while the revolutionary majority of the Party has not had an expression of its thought and will in the directorate and the newspaper, the opportunist elements are strongly organized, exploiting the prestige and authority of the Party to consolidate their positions in the parliament and trade unions. The directorate has permitted them to concentrate, and to vote resolutions contradicting the principles and tactics of the Third International.[42]

Another shortcoming of the PSI, closely related to the strength of reformism within it, was its relative isolation from the activities of the Third International, which had already held two meetings in Western Europe. Unaccountably, the Italian party had not been represented at these meetings. *Avanti!*, said Gramsci's editorial, gave more space to reformist thought than to the political line of the Third International; the Party press continued to publish works representing the positions of the Second International while neglecting important expressions of the Third, like Lenin's *State and Revolution*.

Gramsci's answer to the problem: the Party must become "a homogeneous, cohesive Party, with its own doctrine and tactics and a rigid and implacable discipline; the non-Communist revolutionaries must be eliminated from the Party."[43] By now he was convinced that even the factory councils could not be created without the existence of such a Party. Therefore, he proposed, in the name of the Turin Socialist section, that groups of similarly minded comrades of all sections meet and prepare a congress aimed at eliminating all non-Communists from membership in the Party.

Gramsci's report, brought to Milan by Togliatti, went almost unnoticed at the Party headquarters; however, it was read at Moscow.[44] Lenin praised it at the Second Congress of the Comintern, while deploring the absence of a delegate from the Turin organization.

The Second Congress of the Communist International

The "Italian Question" was a principal topic of debate at all the Congresses of the Third International from 1920 to 1924. All the factions of Italian Socialism had indicated their adherence to the Comintern at the Congress of Bologna. By the Second Congress (Moscow, July–August 1920), however, the reformists were definitely unwelcome at Moscow, so that their representatives in the Italian delegation (D'Aragona, Nofri, and Colombino) made no direct attempts to influence the Congress. The rest of the large delegation included Serrati, Bordiga, Bombacci, Antonio Graziadei, and Luigi Polano.

Throughout the spring of 1920, Lenin had supported Serrati—who at the time represented the majority of the PSI—hoping to bring him over to a more consistently Communist position.[45] Lenin had followed the situation in Italy with particular interest because it "presented marked revolutionary characteristics" and because the Italian was the only important Socialist Party adhering *en bloc* to the Third International. The principal task of the Second Congress, according to Lenin, was to clarify "the conditions of affiliation to the Communist International."[46] With regard to the Italian party, these conditions involved the elimination of two conflicting tendencies: parliamentary abstentionism and reformism.

Bordiga, leader of the abstentionist faction, had by 1920 also become the recognized leader of the various "Communist" groups in the PSI through the agency of his weekly newspaper *Il Soviet,* which was entirely devoted to the organization of the "Communist" faction. Nevertheless, Lenin was greatly disturbed by the extremist elements in Bordiga's position. Bordiga feared that participation in parliament would corrupt the Communist deputies with "social-democratic" values. Even before the Second Congress, Lenin had warned Bordiga that abstentionism was merely a cheap way of avoiding "the difficult problem of combating bourgeois-democratic influences inside the working-class movement."[47] At the Congress itself, Lenin pointed out that in most countries Parliament can be destroyed only by working within it in order to expose its real character, and that, for the moment, Parliament was "an arena of the class struggle."[48] Although Bordiga voted against a Bukharin motion that affirmed the need for continued work in Parliament, he did agree to halt his opposition to such work in the future.[49]

Eliminating reformism in the parties of the International was a more difficult problem. This was the major purpose of the famous "Twenty-one Points," the list of conditions of affiliation to the International. Articles 7, 16, 17, and 21 illustrate the spirit of the Congress, and are particularly applicable to the Italian Party:

7. Parties that wish to join the Communist International are obliged to recognize the necessity for a complete and absolute break with reformism and with the policy of the "Center." ... The Communist International demands unconditionally and categorically that this break be effected as quickly as possible. The Communist International is unable to agree that notorious opportunists, such as Turati, Modigliani, Kautsky, Hilferding, Hillquit, Longuet, MacDonald, etc., shall have the right to appear as members of the Communist International. That could only lead to the Communist International becoming in many respects similar to the Second International, which has gone to pieces.

16. All the decisions of the Congresses of the Communist International, as well as the decisions of its Executive Committee, are binding on all parties belonging to the Communist International. The Communist International, working in conditions of acute civil war, must be far more centralized in its structure than was the Second International. Consideration must of course be given by the Communist International and its Executive Committee in

all their activities to the varying conditions in which the individual parties have to fight and work, and they must make decisions of general validity only when such decisions are possible.

17. In this connection, all parties that wish to join the Communist International must change their names. Every party that wishes to join the Communist International must be called: *Communist* party of such and such a country (section of the Communist International). . . .

21. Those members of the party who reject in principle the conditions and theses put forward by the Communist International are to be expelled from the party.[50]

Nevertheless, Serrati defended Turati at the Congress: "If Turati is useful to us, let us keep him; if he is dangerous to us, let us remove him. I hold no personal feelings against anyone."[51] To this Lenin dryly responded, "No sentimentalisms, please." Lenin was well aware of Serrati's hesitations; in his major address to the Congress he remarked:

With regard to the Socialist Party of Italy, the Second Congress of the Third International considers that the criticism of that party and the practical proposals submitted to the National Council of the Socialist Party of Italy in the name of the Turin section of that party, which were formulated in *L'Ordine nuovo* of May 8, 1920, and which fully correspond to all the fundamental principles of the Third International, are in the main correct.

For this reason the Second Congress of the Third International requests the Socialist Party of Italy to convene a special congress of the Party to discuss these proposals, as well as all the decisions of both Congresses of the Communist International, for the purpose of rectifying the line of the Party and of purging it and its parliamentary group of non-Communist elements.[52]

Thus Lenin clearly indicated his support of Turinese Communism in preference to Milanese maximalism. On July 30, in his "Speech on the Conditions of Affiliation to the Communist International," mainly an attack on Serrati, he was even more forthright: "We must simply tell the Italian comrades that the trend of the Communist International corresponds to the trend of *Ordine nuovo*, and not to that of the present majority of Socialist leaders and their parliamentary group."[53]

The document praised by Lenin was Gramsci's report to the National Council of the PSI entitled "For a Renewal of the Socialist Party," described earlier in this chapter. The members of the PSI directorate had chosen to ignore the report until their attention was forcibly drawn to it at Moscow. "But after it was read at Moscow by the comrades of the Executive Committee of the Third International, the Italian Socialist Party was judged on the basis of its report."[54]

Lenin was surprised by the hostility that his support of the Ordine Nuovo group aroused in the entire Italian delegation—Bordiga's Communists included. Bordiga himself later remarked that "none of the Italian delegates accepted [Lenin's] formulation." Indeed, after the Italians had one by one expressed their disapproval of Ordine Nuovo, Lenin and Bukharin—again according to Bordiga—"declared formally that they had not meant to express a judgment on the orientation of *Ordine nuovo,* on which they were not sufficiently documented." Nevertheless, they insisted that the specific article in question represented a political position that they approved.[55]

Despite these conflicts, Serrati—who was elected to the Executive Committee of the International—promised to call a special congress of the PSI to approve the Twenty-one Points and expel the reformists. Afterwards, however, little was done because of Serrati's own vacillations. By the fall of 1920, it was clear that he would not go through with the expulsions.

Dissension in the Ordine Nuovo Movement

The Ordine Nuovo group had little representation in the national organs of the PSI. There are several reasons for this deficiency. For one, Gramsci was perhaps overly reticent in demanding a place in the Party directorate. "Intellectual seriousness and a repugnance for any kind of demagoguery were combined in Gramsci with a great personal modesty, which prevented him from immediately assuming leadership, as he ought to have done."[56]

An even more serious error also contributed to the political weakness of the Turin movement: *"Ordine nuovo* had not openly faced the problem of creating a national faction in the Socialist Party."[57] Although, as Togliatti has said, the Ordinovisti had developed a great mass movement at Turin, they were limited to personal, unorganized contacts in the rest of the country. In contrast, the reformists controlled the CGL, the trade unions, the cooperatives, much of Socialist local government, and the parliamentary group. The maximalists controlled the central organs of the Party and its daily newspaper. The abstentionists had a national network of factional groups and commanding support in the Socialist Youth Federation. Indeed, the Socialist section of Turin itself was often controlled by an abstentionist majority.[58] Hence, the already existing abstentionist group was

the force that coordinated the various Communist factions in the
Socialist Party during the last months of 1920. In the darkness of
January 1924 Gramsci frankly analyzed the failure of his own group:

> Essentially, we are now paying for the serious errors we made in 1919–20.
> For fear of being thought power-hungry careerists, we didn't try to create a
> definite faction that could be organized throughout Italy. We didn't want
> to give the Turin factory councils an autonomous directing group that might
> have greatly influenced the whole country because we were afraid of a split
> in the unions and a premature expulsion from the Socialist Party.[59]

Gramsci's hands were tied with regard to the abstentionists; he recognized the necessity of supporting them in order to eliminate the
reformists from the Party. At no time did he openly attack the abstentionists, even though Bordiga, at the Second Congress of the International, had seen fit to attack the Ordine Nuovo group.[60] It is
true that Gramsci occasionally criticized what he considered elements
of purism or sectarianism in the abstentionist position.[61] Indeed, at
the National Conference of the "Communist-abstentionist" faction
held at Florence on May 8–9, Gramsci, who was there as an observer,
expressly stated that he did not believe a political party could be
founded on the narrow principle of abstentionism. Broad contact
with the masses was necessary: this could be achieved only through
new forms of organization.[62] These suggestions, however, were never
intended to destroy confidence in the leadership of the Bordigan
group.

Ultimately, the most important reason for Ordine Nuovo's lack
of national political strength was a disunity among the Ordinovisti
themselves, which took several different forms. Above all, there was
a recurrence of the old disagreements between Gramsci and Tasca
concerning the relationship between the trade unions and the councils. On May 30 Tasca delivered an address before a congress of the
Turin Chamber of Labor on the "Political and Trade-union Values
of the Factory Councils."[63] As we have seen, Gramsci thought it essential for the councils to remain independent of the trade unions—
and even of the Party, which would have to conquer the councils
from within rather than mechanically subordinating them to itself.
Tasca, however, believed that political circumstances did not permit
the organization of entirely independent councils, which would inevitably clash with the Party, the Chambers of Labor, the trade
unions, and the State; it was therefore essential to subordinate the
council movement to the trade unions and Chambers of Labor.[64]
His speech met with considerable approval in the Turin Chamber

of Labor, since many of the unions represented there were still directed by reformists hostile to Gramsci's conception of the councils.

Gramsci countered with a furious editorial assault on Tasca. Tasca had not only repudiated *Ordine nuovo's* conception of the councils, but failed to understand it in the first place; he had made numerous factual errors, giving the wrong reasons for recent changes in the Russian soviets and the wrong authorship for the Regolamento of the councils; his intervention had ruined an educational program that had cost the Ordine Nuovo group a year of intense effort.[65] According to Tasca, Gramsci's attack was so violent that a Russian comrade wrote to *Ordine nuovo* deploring the break, especially since a new Party Congress was coming up.[66]

The last executive committee of the Turin section had been elected in February. It was composed of various "Communist" elements in the section, and included Gramsci, Togliatti, and a number of abstentionists (Boero and Parodi are the best known). Although the entire executive committee had agreed on a program emphasizing closer bonds between the section and the working masses of Turin, its efforts had been dissipated in constant quarrels about trivia—abstention, responsibility for the defeat of the April general strike, and relations between Party, trade unions, and councils. The dispute between Tasca and Gramsci was part of this situation. The more moderate Socialists caused further confusion by supporting the Communist faction that favored participating in national elections.[67] In view of this paralyzing confusion and the imminence of communal elections, the executive committee felt compelled to resign on July 10.

Togliatti, among others, called for a full discussion of all the problems of the section. Each faction was to draw up a clear program so that the section could choose a homogeneous group to form the next executive committee. Three groups emerged from the discussions: the "maximalist electionists" (sometimes also called "Communist electionists"), the "Communist abstentionists," and the "Communist education group." The first group included Togliatti, Terracini, and Tasca, and stood for firm opposition to the increasing influence of anarchists and syndicalists in the Turin labor movement. They favored participating in the elections, as well as purging the section of "reformists and opportunists." The "Communist abstentionists" were of course opposed to electoral activities, but also had little faith that the "electionists" would do an effective job in purging the section.

The third group, led by Gramsci and supported by Battista Santhià, Andrea Viglongo, and a few others, refused to present its own

slate of candidates or to vote for any other group. Gramsci objected
to the organization of factions on the basis of "utterly secondary tactical elements" (electionism vs. abstentionism). For him, this meant
that nothing could be expected from the leaders but "sectarian in-
trigue similar to the rancors and quarrels that lacerated the Party
during the war." The whole issue indicated that the level of political
education, even among Party members, was still mediocre. The real
struggle was to be found in the "area of mass action: for Communist
groups in factory and trade union; for workers' councils; and for
proletarian unity, which is threatened by the uncertainties of Socialist
and union leaders." Gramsci hoped to unify all "Communist" elements in the section by ending quarrels over tactical problems and
concentrating on the "fundamental questions of the working class
and the Communist revolution."

In important respects, however, Gramsci's views and the position
set forth in the program of his faction were not as neutral as they
seemed. His refusal to join the other Ordinovisti was in itself a step
toward the abstentionists. He certainly had Tasca in mind when he
referred in his program declaration to certain "irresponsible" persons, "who attach themselves to the established interests of unions
and cooperatives" and who "work in beer halls and union cabals"
rather than among the masses. The electionists had favored a purge
of the section, but had qualified it until it was meaningless: they
felt that the Party was not ready for an immediate schism or numerous expulsions. Gramsci, by contrast, stood with the abstentionists
in his desire to end compromises with the reformists.

On July 24, the maximalists and reformist elements in the section
voted for the electionist slate, which easily won. At that time, Togliatti was elected secretary of the Turin section, an office he retained
until the Congress of Livorno. From this point on, Gramsci believed,
with the abstentionists, that the old Italian Socialist Party was already dead, and that its corpse deserved no special attention. The
culmination of this attitude is in his editorial "The Communist
Party," written in September–October, where the new party is described as "rising from the ashes of the Socialist Parties."[68] Gramsci
blamed the leaders of the PSI for "the colossal historical error of having believed that they could save the old structure of the Party from
its inner dissolution." For Gramsci, the PSI had become "different
in no respect from the English Labour Party. . . . It is a conglomera-
tion of parties."[69]

In 1923–24, at the beginning of his struggle with Bordiga for the leadership of the Italian Communist Party, Gramsci referred to this political situation of July 1920. From letters to Togliatti and Mauro Scoccimarro, we know that Gramsci intended his action of 1920 as a move toward the abstentionists.[70] To Togliatti, he wrote that he "did not wish to enter [Togliatti's] Communist faction, but insisted on greater agreement with the abstentionists."[71] A few months later, Gramsci explained to Scoccimarro that in August 1920 he had separated himself from Togliatti and Terracini. "Then it was I who wished to maintain relations with the Left rather than the Right, while Palmi and Umberto rejoined Tasca, who had detached himself from us since January."[72]

The Occupation of the Factories

Meanwhile, political conditions in Turin remained, if anything, more tense than before the April general strike. Several workers were killed during the May Day celebration, and later conflicts between the workers and the police or army were frequent and bloody.[73] Nevertheless, the next great postwar struggle of Italian labor, the occupation of the factories, did not begin at Turin, but at Milan.

In June 1920 the Fiom directors presented the industrialists with a memorandum requesting certain adjustments in contracts and considerable increases in wages. Although a new contract had been signed as recently as September 1919, inflation had been so great that the gains of the workers were more than obliterated. This situation had caused the labor organizations of the other political groups (Catholics, anarchists, and Republicans) to make similar demands.[74]

On July 15, negotiations were opened. The Fiom demanded substantial wage increases in view of the great rise in the cost of living and also in view of similar concessions recently made in industries far less specialized than metalworking. The AMMA (Associazione Industriale Metallurgici, Meccanici, ed Affini) replied that wages were already on a par with rises in the cost of living, as proved by the statistical bulletins of Milan—a city with a Socialist administration.[75] Moreover, conditions in other industries were irrelevant, since the metalworking industry was passing through a depression.

At the next two bargaining sessions (July 29 and August 10) the Fiom strengthened its arguments by presenting an analysis of conditions in every branch of the industry and a report on the real state of wages among the metalworkers. It then demanded that the industrialists proceed to discuss the original memorandum and the individual requests made in it. To this demand, the AMMA gave a flat refusal based on the alleged industrial crisis, foreign competition, and high taxes. Negotiations were terminated.

The Fiom directors were determined to avoid a strike, which the industrialists would almost have welcomed, considering the depressed state of economic activity at that time. On August 16–17, an alternative plan of action was presented to an emergency Congress of the Fiom: it called for a *sciopero bianco* or slowdown, to be achieved while scrupulously following the regulations and norms prescribed for each industrial operation. If the industrialists responded with a lockout, the workers were to occupy the factories immediately. The Congress unanimously approved this plan and the slowdown commenced on August 21. The Fiom's justification for its use of a slowdown was put in purely bread-and-butter terms:

A slowdown ought to hurt the industrialists, since their general expenses will be unchanged while production falls off. For their part, the workers, though their earnings will be reduced because of the lower production, will still have pocketed sufficient wages to enable them to carry on the struggle for a time.[76]

At first, the industrialists discounted this "obstructionism" as an ineffective substitute for a strike. Within a few days, however, they were greatly alarmed by the precipitate decline of production—down to 60 per cent of its former level in some plants.[77] They also claimed that the workers were engaging in sabotage, and that the lives of some of their personnel had been threatened. On August 30 the directors of the Alfa-Romeo plant in Milan, alleging "the sudden presence in the personnel of foreign provocative elements," declared a lockout.[78] The workers immediately countered by occupying the Alfa-Romeo plant and, by way of protest, at least 280 other factories in the Milan area. The Fiom declared:

No one must leave the factories, and everyone must remain there for the express purpose of working until the lockout is removed from all the plants. The industrialists have the armed forces for their defense. Let us show that our strength is superior. It is the strength of labor and faith in our cause. Remain at your posts. Leave the machines intact. Keep faith in the battle.[79]

Thus the occupation of the factories did not begin as a revolutionary movement; instead, it was a desperate attempt by the Fiom leaders to find a less costly protest than the strike. Their manifesto even declared that the factories would be abandoned as soon as management agreed not to use the lockout as a weapon. Indeed, the Fiom leaders, mainly reformists, would probably never have taken a radical step like occupation of the factories had they not expected rapid government intervention, which would have quickly settled the economic questions originally raised by the union.[80] Then, too, the reformists felt compelled to appear more to the left than they really were. This was caused by pressure from the rank and file in the PSI and by the resolutions and theses of the Comintern. As D'Aragona of the CGL put it, "The moderates were falling into line to avoid excommunication."[81]

On September 1 the metallurgical plants of Turin were occupied, and shortly thereafter nearly all Italian heavy industry was taken over.[82] Such diffusion of the movement was necessary to avert a collapse of the original effort. It must be remembered that the occupation was not a sit-down strike, but an attempt to keep the factories operating—with or without the owners. For this purpose, each plant required raw materials and parts that could be supplied only by other industrial establishments. Naturally, the other industrialists were reluctant to deliver these items to occupied plants; hence, the Fiom was forced to extend the scope of the action. Because the metallurgical industry included extremely complex enterprises like automobile manufacturing, even light industries—textiles, for example—were eventually taken over by the workers.

Although this particular movement had not been initiated in Turin, there is no doubt that the workers of the city participated in it with more enthusiasm than those elsewhere.[83] In contrast to the situation during the general strike of April, Turin no longer seemed isolated from the rest of the Italian labor movement, a point strongly emphasized by the local editors of *Avanti!*:

Today the problem of workers' control has been placed on a national scale for all industries: today, five months after the defeat of the Turin proletariat, workers' control no longer seems a madness of fanatics to anyone, not even to the industrialists. The Turin workers were right in April 1920. The Turin workers were on the threshold of history, that is, on the threshold of the world revolution.[84]

Many of the leaders in Turin, as well as a large part of the rank and file, probably thought that the occupation was itself a seizure of power.[85] One of the most intelligent "bourgeois" observers in Turin, Piero Gobetti, was strongly impressed by the "revolutionary" character of the occupation:

I am following with sympathy the efforts of the workers, who are really building a new order. I do not feel the strength in myself to follow them in their work, at least for now. But it seems to me . . . that the greatest battle of the century is under way. My place would then be on the side that has the greatest dedication and spirit of sacrifice. Today the revolution is being put forth in all its religious character. Certainly the hour is difficult even for the workers. At least at Turin, they have now liquidated the organizers and old leaders, abstract and dishonest in practice, and they are going ahead by themselves. . . . The movement is spontaneous and directed to other than material ends. This is a true and proper attempt to realize not collectivism but a labor organization in which the workers, or at least the best of them, will be what the industrialists are today. . . . We stand before a heroic fact.[86]

Gramsci, according to some, was not optimistic about the possibilities of revolution; yet there is nothing in his writings that betrays doubt about the correctness of the movement.[87] On the contrary, the occupation of the factories meant that the trade-union leaders, despite their reformism and anti-Bolshevism, were forced by the logic of events "to carry on the struggle in a new field, in which, even if violence were not immediately necessary, the study and organization of violence became immediately necessary."[88] This new development was equivalent to a victory of the factory council over the trade union:

Meanwhile a new situation was created by the new method of struggle: when the workers were fighting to better their economic position by means of the strike, the task of the workers in the struggle was limited to having faith in their distant leaders. It was limited to developing the virtues of solidarity and resistance expressly based on this generic faith. But if the workers . . . occupy the factories and wish to continue production, the moral position of the workers immediately assumes a different form and value. The trade-union leaders can no longer direct. [They] disappear in the immensity of the picture. The masses must themselves resolve the problems of the factory, with their own means and men.[89]

Resolving the "problems of the factory" ultimately proved to be immensely difficult, for the occupied factories were deprived of nearly all their engineering personnel. At first, the industrialists seemed to be less successful in keeping the technicians out of the plants. In fact, the Associazione Generale dei Tecnici delle Industrie Metallurgiche ed Affini denounced this attempt on the part of the industrialists as "a maneuver expressly intended to make the technicians depart from their neutral line of conduct and throw themselves into the fight against the workers." In a burst of enthusiasm the association even announced that its members intended to continue work, if only to ensure "the preservation of the means of production," especially since the industrialists were apparently completely uninterested in the fate of the machines and equipment in the invaded plants.[90] These remarks are a measure of how deeply the moral force of the Turin labor movement had affected even the non-proletarian elements of the population. In the end, however, most of the technicians withdrew and left the workers to their own devices.[91]

Other technical problems—the difficulties in procuring raw materials and disposing of the finished products, the impossibility of obtaining credit—made it impossible for the factory councils to meet the workers' payrolls. The problem was partly solved by an agreement between the provincial labor federations and the workers' cooperatives, by which the cooperatives advanced a certain proportion of the wages. Provision was also made for additional payments based on actual work done, after the outcome of the movement had been settled. Meanwhile, scrip in the form of ten- and twenty-lire notes was issued to the workers, but they were ordinarily unable to redeem it for goods.[92]

The actual management of the plants lay in the hands of the factory councils. In Turin, Giovanni Parodi achieved a moment of glory with his intelligent and militant direction of the Fiat industrial complex. Montagnana and Battista Santhià were among the many other leaders, most of whom soon became members of the Italian Communist Party.[93] Since it was impossible for the workers to leave the plants, the strictest discipline had to be maintained. The use of alcoholic beverages was forbidden, and punishments for stealing were severe. Unfortunately, the workers were unable to devote all their working hours to industrial production—indeed, for the first few days, the slowdown policy was deliberately continued in most plants. It was assumed that the factories would eventually be attacked by the armed forces (Turin, for example, was surrounded by troops throughout the occupation). Therefore, some of the workers manufactured arms of various types. Others were enrolled in the "Red Guards," organized at first to protect the plants against assault, later used to maintain discipline among those workers whose enthusiasm began to wane.

The councils did succeed for a time in giving the workers high standards of discipline and seriousness. These qualities are evident in the following description of a visit made by Gramsci and Montagnana to the Fiat-Lingotto plant during the occupation:

While we were quietly talking with the representatives of the factory council, the sirens began to screech. It was the alarm signal. The young Red Guards of the Fiat-Lingotto, who had spent the night circling the plant on their bicycles, had noticed that some strong patrols of soldiers and Royal

Guards were approaching from different directions at the same time. It was necessary to prepare for a possible attack.

In a split second . . . the machines stopped. Workers in every department of the huge plant, still in their work clothes, their faces black with oil and dust, ran to their weapons. Some had revolvers, some hand grenades or rifles, while others had only iron spears that they themselves had forged and sharpened. All were prepared to defend *their* plant, even at the cost of their lives. . . .

After a few minutes, the sirens stopped. The alarm had passed. The workers laid down their arms and returned to their machines as if nothing had happened, without wasting time in idle chatter. The trivial event must not interfere with production.[94]

Such discipline and enthusiasm accounted for whatever successes the workers did achieve during the occupation. At the Fiat-Centro, an average of 37 cars a day were produced, instead of the 67 or 68 made in normal times.[95] At the mechanical works of Savigliano (between Cuneo and Turin), production was greater than usual.[96] Other plants in the Turin area also produced in a similarly impressive manner, so that the Piedmontese edition of *Avanti!* could assert, on September 21, 1920, that "In Turin, work was done in all factories. Little work in the first days, much in the following. In some shops the average production was surpassed."[97] Yet everyone knew that ultimate victory did not depend on the rate of production. After the first wave of euphoria had passed, the factory councils began to realize that the problem of the occupation must be resolved in the political arena. Either the workers must take power or the occupation would die a natural death.

Giovanni Giolitti and the Defeat of the Occupation

Although the Fiom leaders had expected prompt government intervention, the new Giolitti government, after an initial attempt at reconciliation, stood apart from the struggle. Arturo Labriola, the ex-syndicalist Minister of Labor, observed that his government had attempted to maintain neutrality, and that intervention would in effect aid the industrialists.[98] Actually, Giolitti was convinced that an intervention was not a wise solution, even for the manufacturers. During the early days of the occupation he received a delegation of industrialists; one of them, more infuriated than his colleagues, asked Giolitti to have the intransigent workmen bombarded. With his courteous and ironic smile, Giolitti responded: "And will you permit me to begin by bombarding your factories?" The proposal was declined.[99]

Two years later, Giolitti indicated that his refusal to intervene was based on the belief that the occupation would be instructive to the workers if they were given enough time to see that they could not run Italian industry by themselves.[100] In any case, his inaction did force the Fiom leaders to reconsider the purposes of the occupation. The PSI and the CGL would have to be consulted to determine whether the workers should move forward to political power or try to extricate themselves from the situation by reopening economic negotiations.* Although the PSI and the CGL met in a joint session at Milan on September 4–5, they did not extend the scope of the movement beyond the original economic demands of Fiom. Instead, they passed a motion approving unconditional solidarity with the workers and threatening to extend the struggle to all categories of labor if "employer obstinacy" or "the violation of neutrality on the part of the Government" prevented "a satisfactory solution of the conflict."[101] Nonetheless, an awareness of the great danger inherent in the situation is apparent in the strong language of the motion.[102]

Indeed, the country as a whole did seem to be verging on revolution. In certain districts of Sicily and Lucania, the peasantry was beginning its own "occupation" of unexploited lands belonging to large estates.[103] Although there was no connection whatever between the two movements—the peasant leaders seem to have been members of the Catholic Partito Popolare or leaders of veterans' organizations—their simultaneous occurrence did increase the sense of instability in the country. The PSI, though in no sense responsible for the actions of the peasantry, tried to take advantage of them. On September 6, the Party published a manifesto "to the peasants and soldiers." It asked for rural support of the metalworkers' struggle: "If the workers succeed in eliminating the excess profits of the owners, it would be possible to sell you machines at better prices." The manifesto ended in a spirit that Spriano calls "pre-insurrectional":

If tomorrow the decisive hour of the battle against all the owners and exploiters is sounded, you too will come to its aid. Take over the municipal governments and lands. Disarm the carabinieri. Form your battalions together with the workers. March toward the big cities to help the people who are fighting the police paid by the bourgeoisie. Perhaps the day of freedom and justice is near.[104]

---

* One discovery during the occupation tempted the workers to begin outright revolution: in the safes of several Turin plants they found documents that proved the existence of a blacklist of militant workers, as well as an espionage service directed against the labor movement. See Nenni, p. 100, and Spriano, *L'Occupazione*, pp. 95–96.

Actually, however, the Party did nothing to hasten the "hour of decision," whether among the workers or the peasants. With regard to the question of armaments, which received much attention in the conservative press of the time, the Party's approach was almost exclusively defensive. "At Turin, where the vanguard was bolder and better armed than elsewhere," wrote Angelo Tasca, "the Communist leaders showed no initiative in this direction, and even curbed the Fiat groups that had prepared trucks for a sortie."[105]

This diffidence of Turin's Communists is at first surprising in view of their past attitudes, but it was really nothing more than fear that the movement in the city would be isolated, as it had been in April. On September 9 Togliatti, as secretary of the Turin Socialist section, was present in Milan at a meeting of the directing council of the CGL. When asked if the Turin workers would be ready to move first in an armed insurrection, Togliatti replied: "You cannot count on action being taken by Turin alone. . . . The revolution, if it comes, must be Italian, otherwise the two most advanced cities, Turin and Milan, will be overcome. Preparation is lacking." A year later an editorial in *Ordine nuovo* explained that the Turin labor leaders "could not assume the responsibility of an armed struggle without assurance that the rest of Italy would also fight, without assurance that the Confederation, in its usual way, would not let all the military forces of the State concentrate on Turin as in April."[106]

A second joint meeting of the National Council of the CGL and the Socialist directorate on September 10–11 at Milan compelled the Party to explicitly define the scope of the strike for the first time. None of the groups concerned were willing to assume this responsibility. Bruno Buozzi, the Fiom secretary, began by refusing to sign any agreement without the consent of the CGL. Ludovico D'Aragona, speaking for the CGL, then declared that there were only three possible courses of action: restrict the occupation to the metalworkers, broaden it to other categories and demand control of industry by the workers, or begin open insurrection. The CGL preferred the second course, since the first had already proved inadequate and the third implied action outside the scope of a labor union. Nonetheless, the CGL council offered to turn the whole movement over to the Party, if it wished to assume command.

Egidio Gennari, secretary of the PSI, who had previously insisted on revolutionary action, now demanded that the CGL first poll all the representatives of its members. Two motions were offered, one representing the CGL point of view, the other calling for immediate socialization of industry (that is, a revolution). The CGL prevailed by 591,245 to 409,569, mainly because of the unanimous support of the more conservative agricultural workers, who were very numerous, and the abstention of the Fiom with its 93,623 votes.[107] Gennari hastened to accept this vote, with its implication that the occupation should remain no more than an economic movement. He declared:

The pact of alliance [between the CGL and the PSI] states that for all questions of a political character the Party directorate may assume the responsibility for the direction of the movement.... At this moment, the Party directorate does not intend to avail itself of this privilege.[108]

Another reason for this hesitation by the Party leaders may have been, as Spriano says, their sense of isolation from the Comintern. News of the occupation was very slow in reaching Moscow, so that the Executive Committee could not deal with the problem until September 21. On September 22, the ECCI declared to the Italian workers that to avoid defeat the occupation must become a general seizure of power by the working class, which would organize a proletarian dictatorship. This was to be achieved by "cover[ing] the whole of Italy with councils of workers', peasants', soldiers', and sailors' deputies," and by driving out the reformists.[109] However, by September 22, the occupation was already in its last stages; hence, *Avanti!* did not even publish the appeal. Nonetheless, Spriano asserts that the "failure of coordination is not the least of the factors that contributed to the weakness of the PSI."[110] This judgment seems implausible, since it is impossible to see how Russian advice would have repaired the weaknesses of the PSI. In any case, on August 27, just before the occupation, Zinoviev, Bukharin, and Lenin had sent a letter to the PSI asserting that "in Italy there are at hand all the most important conditions for a *genuinely popular, great proletarian revolution.*" The Russian leaders denied that the Entente would be able to "send its troops against the Italian working class"—a gloomy prediction often used by the reformists to temper the ardor of Italian revolutionaries. Warning against "artificially provoked 'putsches,' " the letter went on to state that the Comintern was "equally opposed to the proletarian party turning itself into a fire brigade that puts out the flame of revolution when that flame is breaking through every crevice in capitalist society."[111] The conviction of the Russian leaders that the Italian situation was revolutionary had been clearly communicated. What more could they be expected to say? Yet this was small consolation to Italian revolutionaries of September 1920.

Meanwhile the decision of the joint meeting of September 10–11 did clear the way for a reopening of negotiations, which began on September 15 at Turin and were completed on the 19th at Rome. Present were Giolitti himself, the Prefects of Milan and Turin, and representatives of the industrialists, the CGL, and the Fiom. The bread-and-butter aspects of the contract were quickly agreed on, for the industrialists were anxious to regain control of their plants. All workers received an additional four lire per day, which amounted to a 10–20 per cent increase, improvements in overtime rates, and pay for work done during the occupation (however, the industrialists were to determine the value of that production). Six paid holidays per year were guaranteed, in addition to periodical cost-of-living adjustments. The management agreed not to dismiss any worker with more than three years' seniority, or take reprisals against the leaders of the occupation.[112]

Agreement on workers' control of industry proved more difficult. At first the industrialists were unwilling to even consider it, whereupon Giolitti threatened to present the Chamber with a bill embodying such a principle.* The owners accepted the "principle" of workers' control, leaving its definition to a tripartite commission of industrialists, labor leaders, and government officials.

The whole contract was ratified by a National Congress of the Fiom held on September 21–22, although the delegates from the Turin section voted against it.[113] A referendum of the workers participating in the occupation was held on September 24, and the contract was overwhelmingly endorsed. Even the Turin workers supported the referendum, since a failure to do so would have meant more complete isolation than in the days of the April general strike.[114] From the 25th to the 30th, the plants were returned to the owners.

The terms of the contract were certainly very generous. In fact, most Italians imagined that the Fiom had won a great victory. Yet within a year most of these gains were obliterated. As for the principle of "workers' control," the bill finally presented to the Chamber— though soon shelved—essentially contained nothing more than a project for establishing a committee of industrialists and workers charged with collecting economic data. By the end of 1921, it was no

---

* In explanation, he later said with "his usual kindly and astonished ingenuousness" that there was no reason to be afraid of the word "control." In Anglo-Saxon countries it undoubtedly connoted "effective ownership," but in Italy it traditionally signified "vigilance" or "verification"! (Luigi Einaudi, p. 334.)

longer a question of "control" but of investigation to determine "whether the conditions of industry really required the reduction of wages that the industrialists declared to be necessary."[115]

The occupation of the factories ended in the defeat of labor because the goal of the movement remained unclear till the very end, and because the timing of the event, coming as it did on the eve of an economic crisis, could hardly have been better for the industrialists. According to Einaudi, many of them almost welcomed the movement as a means of liquidating their inventories and, at the same time, attributing the economic ills of the country to the irresponsible acts of labor.[116] For the Turin Socialists, who did not in fact originate the movement, the timing was especially bad, since their organization had not yet recovered from the strenuous events of April.

The "neutrality" of the government also contributed to the debacle, since it rendered the indecision of the Fiom and the PSI more damaging than ever. The Fiom leaders had staked their hopes of success on government intervention, without considering any other possible outcome. The Party directorate was unwilling to take either of the two paths that offered some hope of victory: join Giolitti's government or begin the Socialist revolution.

The result of the occupation of the factories was not just another defeat for labor. The Italian bourgeoisie came out of this conflict embittered, not merely because the workers had actually controlled their plants, but because they were convinced that the government could no longer protect their interests. The industrialists had lost their faith in the "liberal state," and had become receptive to political expedients of quite a different order.[117] The government, too, resolved to employ special, if only "temporary," measures to induce labor to return to more traditional forms of struggle. The hour of Fascism was at hand. Mussolini's movement, weak and negligible before September 1920, grew with extraordinary rapidity in the last three months of the year.[118]

Although Gramsci was pleased by the relative successes of the factory councils during the occupation, he had no illusions concerning the abysmal defeat of the occupation itself: "Our criticism of the Party and trade unions, both paralyzed by demagogic verbalism and bureaucratic arteriosclerosis, had unfortunately once again been confirmed by events."[119]

According to Gramsci, the Socialists did not attempt to seize power because the Party had no conception of the proper role of the revolutionary vanguard with respect to the masses. Their use of a referendum was a typical example of such ignorance; hence, Gramsci criticized this step in the most extreme Leninist terms:

The [present] leaders of the proletarian movement base themselves on the "masses"; that is, they ask the prior consent of the masses by proceeding to consult them in the forms and at the time that they [the leaders] have selected. But a revolutionary movement can only be founded on the proletarian vanguard and must be conducted without prior consultation, without the apparatus of representative assemblies. A revolution is like a war. It must be minutely prepared by a workers' general staff, just as a war is prepared by the general staff of the army. Assemblies can only ratify what has already happened, by either exalting successes or implacably punishing failures. The task of the proletarian vanguard is to keep the revolutionary spirit awake in the masses, to create the conditions in which the masses respond immediately to revolutionary slogans. In the same way, the nationalists and imperialists attempt . . . to create conditions in which the mob approves a war already decided upon by the general staff and by diplomacy. In the same way, no revolutionary movement will be decreed by a national workers' assembly; to convoke an assembly means to confess one's own lack of faith.[120]

In this statement lies the basic contrast between Gramsci and the Ordinovisti on the one hand, and traditional Italian Socialism on the other. The immediate task of the Party was not, said Gramsci, to establish another democracy upon existing models, but to create a revolutionary vanguard of high technical competence and great freedom of initiative. Otherwise, the progress of the revolution would be paralyzed by the inadequacies of the present.

6. Toward the Communist Party: Gramsci's Final Break with Maximalism

*La verità è che il Partito socialista
non era un' "urbe," era un' "orda": non
era un organismo, era un agglomerato
di individui.*

—*Gramsci, December 18, 1920*

Gramsci's conception of the role of the factory council and his Leninist view of the Party as the vanguard of the proletariat set him apart from traditional Italian Socialism. His experiences in Sardinia and Turin—especially his training in Crocean historiography—gave him a more sophisticated view of the role of such forces as anarchism, liberalism, Christian democracy, and the peasant movement than most of his fellow Socialists enjoyed. Many of his comrades were sincerely concerned about Gramsci's occasionally close relationships with these non-Socialist movements, although a closer examination would have demonstrated that such relationships did not lead Gramsci to any revision of his Marxist doctrine, but only to a greater understanding of these movements as historical forces.

Gramsci's views on these subjects did, however, play a part in his final break with Italian maximalism, in late 1920. These views, together with the defeats of the Turin labor movement in April and September and the results of the Second Congress of the Comintern in July–August, provide the background for understanding the long polemic between Gramsci and Serrati that destroyed the unity of the PSI and led to the foundation of the Italian Communist Party.

Gramsci and the Anarchists

The idea of the councils as forces for liberation of the working class attracted many anarchists to Gramsci's movement, to the great chagrin of some Socialist leaders. By midsummer of 1920, both of the Italian anarcho-syndicalist organizations had declared themselves in favor of collaboration with the Ordine Nuovo movement. Enea

Matta, an old militant, delivered a well-received speech on the councils at the Parma Congress of the Unione Sindacale Italiana.[1] In July the Bologna Congress of the Unione Anarchica adopted a manifesto supporting the councils as "the proper organizations for enrolling, in preparation for the Revolution, all manual or intellectual producers right on the job. [The councils] are, in accordance with the ends of anarchist Communist principles, absolutely anti-State organisms and possible nuclei for the future direction of industrial and agricultural production."[2]

A number of anarchists participated in the Turin council movement, above all Maurizio Garino and Pietro Ferrero, the director of the Fiom section in the city. Although the total number of anarchists in Turin was probably not great,[3] the contributions of men like Garino and Ferrero to the labor movement were considerable. For a time, even *Ordine nuovo* had an anarchist named Carlo Petri on its staff.[4]

Gramsci was particularly impressed with Garino, who, opposing Tasca, defended the Ordine Nuovo thesis that the principal function of the trade union was to advance the interests of the worker as a wage earner, not as a producer. For Gramsci, Garino's action was proof that "in the real revolutionary process, the whole working class spontaneously finds its practical and theoretical unity; that every worker, insofar as he is a sincere revolutionary, will ultimately collaborate with the whole class to carry out a task that is implicit in capitalistic society and not at all an end freely proposed by the conscience and the individual will."[5] Gramsci remarked that it mattered little to him if Garino and Ferrero were anarchists, so long as their activity remained "real and concrete."

By far the most significant support that Gramsci obtained from the anarcho-syndicalist camp came from Georges Sorel, the theoretician of revolutionary syndicalism. On October 5, 1919, in an interview with *Il Resto del Carlino,* Sorel exclaimed:

Rather than asking Kautsky and his emulators for the design of the city of the future, let [the workers] carry out their education by conquering more extensive powers in the factories. This should be the work of Communists! The experience they are undergoing in the Fiat plants is more important than all the writings published by *Neue Zeit.*[6]

Commenting on this judgment, Gramsci also stated his general evaluation of Sorel. This was surprisingly positive, although Gramsci made it clear that much of Sorel's doctrine was unacceptable to him. It was particularly necessary, moreover, to distinguish Sorel's work from that of his students and imitators in France and Italy, for whom Gramsci had only contempt. As for Sorel, "In his best qualities, he seems to recall in himself a little of the virtues of his two masters: the harsh logic of Marx and the restless, plebeian eloquence of Proudhon." Most important for Gramsci was Sorel's insistence that "the proletarian movement express itself in its own forms, give life to its own institutions." Such a belief made it possible for Sorel to appreciate the soviet movement in Russia and in Western Europe. For this reason, Gramsci felt that "Georges Sorel has truly remained what Proudhon made him, that is, a disinterested friend of the proletariat."[7]

Nonetheless, Gramsci's basic objections to anarchism were numerous, particularly since he feared that Socialist ineptitude was driving many workers into the libertarian camp.[8] True, since anarchism was a retrograde political movement whose strength varied in inverse proportion to the degree of industrialization in a given country, its appeal would gradually weaken.[9] In the meantime, however, Gramsci regarded certain anarchist doctrines as particularly pernicious, especially the anarchists' fear of the State as such.

Gramsci's position on the State is very simple: anyone who maintains under present conditions that a workers' State is not necessary to carry out the revolution corresponds, on the political level, "to the charlatan who offers a potion of barley water to a victim of typhus."[10] To demonstrate this, Gramsci uses two arguments, the first drawn from the Hegelian view of the State, the second from Lenin.

It is true, Gramsci observes, that communism is international, and hence anti-national economically and politically; however, if the national State is suppressed within the Communist International, the State as the concrete "form" of society or human collectivity is not. Society has always existed as a system and equilibrium of States, that is, of concrete institutions in which society acquires consciousness of its existence and development. "Each advance of civilization becomes permanent, is real history and not ephemeral and superficial episode, insofar as it is embodied in an institution and finds form in the State."[11]

Gramsci then applies this theory to the Socialist movement:

The Socialist idea remained a myth, an evanescent chimera, a merely arbitrary act of individual fantasy until it became incarnated in the Socialist and proletarian movements, in the institutions of organization and defense of the organized proletariat. In them and through them it took historical form and progressed. From them it generated the national Socialist State, disposed and organized to be capable of interlocking with other Socialist States, conditioned to be capable of living and developing only insofar as it adheres to other Socialist States for the realization of the Communist International, in which every State, every institution, every individual will find fullness of life and freedom.[12]

From the Marxist point of view, this argument at times seems close to being a positive defense of the State as an inevitable phenomenon; however, the real nature of Gramsci's disagreement with the anarchists becomes clear when he discusses the dictatorship of the proletariat. Although the limits of class competition and struggle have changed in a dictatorship of the proletariat, competition and classes remain. The workers' State must resolve the same problems as the bourgeois State, namely, internal and external defense. It would be disastrous for the working class to act as if these problems were already solved.

In fact, the rapid disintegration of the bourgeois State makes it essential to destroy certain prejudices "against all the forms of bourgeois domination," which both Socialists and anarchists have implanted. The defeat of capitalism will leave a residue of anti-State feeling: individuals and groups will want to be exempted from the service and discipline indispensable to the success of the revolution. But to suppress the State, a new State is needed; to suppress militarism, a new kind of militarism is needed. And unlike the bourgeois State, the Socialist State demands the active and permanent participation of its people in the life of its institutions.[13]

After defending the workers' State, Gramsci directly attacks anarchism. The anarchists are a "Masonic" or "religious" group who talk about "freedom" and "truth" as though they were absolutes, "revealed" rather than historically limited. Such notions have caused the anarchists to neglect the discipline proper to political parties, "a discipline born from the discussion of concrete political problems in relation to a fundamental political doctrine." Instead, they use irrelevant and misleading bonds to achieve political coherence: personal friendship or esteem, the prestige of a great name, the common fear of being called traitors.[14]

The anarchists' belief in absolute truth implies that such truth is "spontaneous" in the working class; hence, they are suspicious of attempts to govern and "direct" that class. To this, Gramsci answers:

Since we are more free spiritually [in the Marxist sense of understanding the limits of the historical situation] . . . than the libertarians, we perceive the facts themselves more clearly, and we do not judge as spontaneous (libertarian, voluntary, conscious) the action of a mob that has heard anarchist speeches, but we say: this mob is also governed. It too is under the influence of a power, and it is governed badly because the power is exercised chaotically.[15]

Gramsci also asked why, if the anarchists possess "revealed revolutionary truth," they have never succeeded in drawing the masses along with them. The anarchist movement has stagnated because it does not realize that a determined truth, not an absolute truth, is necessary to move the masses to action: "For the ends of human history, truth is only found in action . . . is only translated into deep movements and real conquests by the masses themselves." By realizing this, the Italian Socialist Party, as the party of the Italian working class, has grown and developed. Its very errors and shortcomings are those of the Italian working class itself.[16]

The anarchist doctrine—and its basis, the idea of freedom—is not specific enough. It cannot be reduced to a program; whereas the Marxists interpret freedom as the organization of the conditions in which freedom can be realized. At present, this means preventing the bourgeoisie from sabotaging the creative work of the proletariat and organizing all national and international production on the model of large industry. Only by making the proletarian way of life universal can relations between individuals be based on the industrial relations of production and not the political relations of class.[17]

Gramsci denied that anarchism was an ideology confined to the proletariat. In "The State and Socialism" (June 1919) he had only partly developed this idea. After declaring that anarchism as a political movement was doomed to extinction with the progress of industrialism, he nevertheless conceded that it would survive for some time as an "idealistic ferment." In fact, anarchism would "continue the liberal [anti-State] tradition insofar as this had imposed and realized human values that ought not to die with capitalism."[18] By the spring of 1920, however, Gramsci had gone much further in denying a positive role to anarchism in the future development of the working class:

Anarchism is not a conception proper to, and only to, the working class. . . . Anarchism is the elementary subversive feeling of every oppressed class and the diffused tendency of every dominant class. Because every class oppression took form in a State, anarchism is the elementary subversive conception that makes the State in and through itself the cause of all the miseries of the oppressed class. Every class, by becoming dominant, has realized its own anarchistic conception, because it has realized its own liberty.[19]

Thus the bourgeoisie, while opposing the control of the despotic
and aristocratic State, was anarchist. It remained anarchist, in a
sense, after its triumph because it had attained concrete liberty and
was living under its own laws. When the proletariat seizes power, the
bourgeoisie will again "be aware of a State" and return to their
former anarchism. Similarly, the proletariat is inclined to anarchism
because of its hatred of the bourgeoisie: anarchism has been the
"marginal" ideology of every oppressed class. But neither the proletariat nor the bourgeoisie is hostile to the "State" as a concept; they
oppose it in specific cases. The specific ideologies of the bourgeoisie
and proletariat have been, respectively, liberalism and Marxian Socialism. Unlike anarchism, Marxist doctrine is incomprehensible
when separated from the proletariat.[20]

Gramsci and Piero Gobetti

Gramsci had considerable influence on the younger and more militant liberals of Turin—like Piero Gobetti, with whom he had a remarkable relationship. In February 1918, while still a student at a
liceo, Gobetti had begun to publish a monthly review, *Energie nuove,*
to which Gramsci occasionally contributed. Later, in February 1922,
Gobetti directed and edited *La Rivoluzione liberale,* which became
the focal point of liberal resistance to Fascism.

In March 1924, Mussolini instructed the Prefect of Turin to "make
life difficult" for Gobetti.[21] As a consequence, Gobetti was twice
severely beaten by bands of Black Shirts. Finally, after the suppression
of *Rivoluzione liberale* in November 1925, he went to Paris to re-
cuperate from his wounds and to continue rallying anti-Fascist liberals around his publications. However, his physical constitution
had been entirely broken, and he died the following February at the
age of 26.

Gobetti's importance in the *primo dopoguerra* can hardly be exaggerated. As the formulator of a "revolutionary" liberalism, or "liberal revolution," he inspired many non-Marxists with a deep and
inflexible opposition to Fascism. Even today, his name is constantly
mentioned by those who wish to see a moral and political renewal of
Italy. The inspiration for Gobetti's highly original liberalism was provided by Benedetto Croce, by the "Southernist" movements of Gius-
tino Fortunato and Gaetano Salvemini, and by Gramsci.

From Croce, Gobetti learned that "liberalism as a doctrine explains
and justifies all parties dialectically, without coinciding with any of

them, not even the so-called Liberal Party."[22] Thus, liberalism is a form of historicism, which says that the mere existence of a political force proves that it has a real function—is meaningful. Yet, unlike many of the Croceians, Gobetti was not satisfied with knowing the historical function of a party, but also wished to lead it in a practical political struggle, which he called a "creative adhesion to history."[23]

From Fortunato, Salvemini, and other conservatives and liberals concerned with the failure of Italian democracy, Gobetti derived a negative view of the Italian ruling class and a deep belief that the Risorgimento, a "Risorgimento without heroes," would have to be completed in the present century if the nation were to survive.

It was Gramsci's influence, however, that pervaded all of Gobetti's thinking. Gobetti's close association with the Ordinovisti convinced him of the strength and vitality of this movement, and led him to write a long article called a "History of the Turinese Communists Written by a Liberal," one of the most important documents on the Gramsci of this period. Undoubtedly what attracted Gobetti to Ordine Nuovo was not its Socialism, but its creative originality. He thought of Ordine Nuovo as a movement capable of renewing Italian life through the agency of the working class. Gramsci's concern with the southern peasantry also attracted Gobetti, who knew that the rural masses were essential to the creation of a better Italy. Finally, Gramsci's absolute intransigence before Fascism provided a model, as it were, for Gobetti. Unlike many liberals, Gobetti never flagged in his opposition to Fascism, though this intransigence ultimately brought him death.[24]

Gramsci, for his part, had great respect for Gobetti's "intellectual loyalty and complete freedom from any vanity and meanness of a lower order."[25] Yet he recognized that Gobetti "was not a Communist and would probably never have become one."[26] Gramsci felt that Gobetti's direct experience with the working class, obtained through *Ordine nuovo*—in 1921 he became its regular drama critic—had enlarged his vision. Gobetti's real importance, to Gramsci, was as an "organizer of culture," as an intellectual who "established a line of no-retreat for those groups of honest and sincere intellectuals who in 1919–21 felt that the proletariat as a ruling class would have been superior to the bourgeoisie."[27] Gobetti represented a new stage in the development of Italian intellectuals: Gramsci later devoted much thought to this development, and derived a good part of his most important theoretical work from his reflections.

Gramsci and Christian Democracy

Gramsci's superior insight—and distinction from most other Italian Socialists of this period—is nowhere more evident than in his views on Catholic political action. This was a subject of great importance for Italian Socialism, since a Catholic party, the Italian Popular Party (PPI), had proved to be its only rival for mass support in the elections of 1919.

Gramsci had at first—with some truth, but rather flippantly—dismissed the formation of the PPI as motivated merely by the need for a "party of order," not too compromised by the war to mediate between the proletariat and the classes in power.[28] The decline of the liberal bourgeois parties had necessitated the rise of the PPI. By the fall of 1919, however, Gramsci realized that the new party would become an important political force. The result was an article entitled "I Popolari."[29]

The very foundation of the new party, says Gramsci, marks the "spiritual renewal of the Italian people," for it demonstrates that the Church hierarchy, and with it the peasant masses, are moving from the domain of religious myth to a world of historical action based on human motives.[30] Actually, the Popular Party was merely the culmination of a long-standing process. For several decades any number of Catholic institutions with an "earthly" character, proposing "earthly" ends, had arisen in Italy: mutual-aid societies, cooperatives, agrarian credit agencies, and trade guilds were only a few examples of this phenomenon. Expelled from "public things" by the new Italian liberal State, the Church took refuge in the countryside, in the daily social activities of the backward rural masses. Deprived of any direct influence in the management of the State, it now threatened that State by its control over the local economic and social interests of the peasantry—interests that the liberal State had largely ignored.

Thus Catholicism reappeared in the process of history—but in a modified form. "The spirit has become flesh—and corruptible flesh, like that of all human forms. It is dominated by the same historical laws of growth and decline that govern [all] human institutions." The Church has moved from a narrow, mystic hierarchy, the absolute ruler of the faithful masses, to a position identified with those masses and their material interests. Its fate now depends on "the good or bad results of the economic and political action of men who promise earthly goods, who offer terrestrial happiness, in addition to, or rather instead of, the city of God." Thus, the Church does not compete with liberalism and the secular State, but with Socialism, which promises the same ends. But this competition should not cause alarm. The Popular Party is a necessary phase in the development of the Italian proletariat toward Communism. It creates "associationism" and solidarity where Socialism could not, where the objective conditions of a capitalist economy do not exist. Although the postwar sense of bewilderment and disorientation also affects the countryside, the peasantry do not have the model of the great modern factory to guide them onto new paths.

Only "democratic Catholicism" could amalgamate this social group. But in so doing, the Church itself was committing sucide: once the peasant masses were organized, Socialism could influence them. When the peasantry became conscious of its real power, it would no longer want priests as spokesmen, but fellow peasants.

A few months after writing this article, Gramsci began debating the role of the Church in a Socialist State with a "Bolognese comrade." *Ordine nuovo* had stated that priests, monks, and nuns in a Socialist State should be treated as workers, insofar as they actually do work. The Bolognese was scandalized. He evidently feared that a new order of "Socialist" clerics would arise. Gramsci replied that some Socialists had similarly refused to support the establishment of soviets in Italy because they feared that a soviet at Bergamo (a stronghold of the PPI) would fall into the hands of priests. Gramsci asked the Bolognese what he would do in such an eventuality: "Should Bergamo be put to fire and sword? Should those workers and peasants who politically follow the left wing of the Popular Party be extirpated from Italian soil?" Gramsci asserted that Italian Socialism would have quite enough to do with its civil war against reaction without also beginning a religious war. Socialists must recognize that the Vatican did exist in Italy, that Catholicism was a real political force. The workers' State, like the liberal State, would be obliged to find a system of equilibrium with the spiritual force of the Church.[31]

Gramsci, the PSI, and the Peasant Question

The Socialist Party's greatest shortcoming, in Gramsci's opinion, was its weakness among the peasantry. In part, this was an organizational deficiency. The Party's only contact with the peasants came through the Federazione Italiana Lavoratori della Terra, a trade-union organization that included all agricultural workers, whether landholders or day-laborers. Because of the contrasting interests in this group, many of the small proprietors, tenants, and leaseholders preferred to join the Catholic agricultural organizations affiliated with the PPI.[32]

A more fundamental reason, however, for the impotence of Italian Socialism in the countryside was the ignorance of many Socialist directors concerning peasant problems. Moreover, a certain diffidence toward the peasantry prevented them from repairing their ignorance. This attitude is well illustrated in the official Socialist reaction to the forcible seizure of land by agricultural workers, a phenomenon that occurred frequently in the primo dopoguerra. In the words of Tasca, "the Socialist Party dealt with it [the occupation of land] very late and, in general, with suspicion and ill will."[33] Not a single Socialist deputy, for example, went to help the 150,000 peasants on strike in the province of Trapani, where such occupations were very frequent. The maximalist position on this question was clearly indicated by Serrati when he said, "Everyone knows that the movement for the occupation of lands—which was carried out, especially in Sicily, by veterans and Popolari—was a demagogic and petty-bourgeois movement aimed at entrancing the agricultural masses."[34]

This lack of understanding exasperated Gramsci, who thought such ignorance especially dangerous because of renewed attempts by the Giolittian liberals to encourage collaboration between northern capital and the working-class "aristocracies" of the industrial North, at the expense of the southern peasantry.[35] The Giolittians felt that the postwar alliance between workers and peasants, insofar as it existed at all, would eventually break down because of the peasants' fear that Socialism would reappropriate their recent gains in land, equipment, and livestock.[36]

Gramsci freely admitted that the Socialists did not regard the redivision of land as an adequate solution to the plight of the peasants. "Land to the peasants" must be interpreted as the control of agricultural establishments by the agricultural workers, organized in councils of poor peasants—who could never acquire capital sufficient to develop individual landholdings and raise the conditions and rewards of their agricultural production to the level of industrial production. Individualism was as inadequate on the land as in the factory. "The industrial proletariat, which is the basis of the workers' State, goes beyond plutocratic centralization, rather than destroying it."[37]

Gramsci believed that winning the peasants over to Socialism was absolutely essential, since they alone possessed the numerical strength to overthrow the bourgeois State. The rural masses would revolt only when the poor peasants and small landholders were "violently detached from the political parties of peasant coalitions" and, in particular, from the Italian Popular Party.[38] The peasants had to be shown that the industrial workers were the only class interested in increasing agricultural production, and ultimately in equalizing urban and rural levels of productivity. Once again, Gramsci pointed to the council as the instrument of education, and, indeed, asserted that an immediate task of the council movement should be spreading propaganda in the countryside.[39]

Gramsci's increasing bitterness against the directors of the PSI was partly founded in his conviction that they were doing nothing to further such a coalition of workers and peasants. After September 1920, with the rising counteroffensive of the industrialists and Fascists, it became apparent that the best chance for a worker-peasant alliance had passed.

The Disintegration of the PSI

The Turin general strike, the Second Congress of the Comintern, and the results of the occupation of the factories all divided the PSI into a number of factions so hostile that a schism became inevitable. This process of dissolution was completed from September to December 1920 by the argument over the adaptability of the "Twenty-one Points" to Italian conditions.

The Twenty-one Points, or conditions of affiliation to the Communist International, were promulgated at the Second Congress of the International, but they were not published in Italy until September 21.[40] On September 28 the Party directorate voted, seven to five, to accept these conditions without reservations.[41]

Serrati was unwilling to accept this decision: he was certain that it did not represent the majority opinion of the whole Party, and he was convinced that the very life of the Party depended upon its continued acceptance of the reformists. He was thus forced to oppose the Comintern openly and undertake a long and complicated polemic with Lenin and Gramsci. Serrati's stand split the maximalist group itself into two factions: the Left, led by Egidio Gennari and Nicola Bombacci, and the Right, led by Serrati and Adelchi Baratono. Thus Serrati's attempt to maintain Party unity merely resulted in further division. Certain features of this attempt are important in understanding the origins of the Italian Communist Party.[42]

In 1920 Lenin believed that the Socialist parties of Europe would succeed in their revolutionary tasks only if the reformists were purged from their ranks. In urging this step, he accused the reformists of treachery, although he did occasionally admit that they were traitors "without realizing it."[43] Serrati, however, vigorously defended the Italian reformists—men like Turati, Modigliani, and D'Aragona— against such charges. He correctly pointed out that they, unlike their counterparts in other lands, had definitely accepted uncompromising adherence to the class struggle, the historical necessity of the use of violence, the dictatorship of the proletariat, and a system of soviets to replace the Parliament.[44] Serrati justified the continued participation of the reformists in the Party on many grounds. He regarded their contributions as essential to the victory of the revolution in Italy: most of the directors of Socialist labor and of the communal governments held by the Party were reformists, as well as many of the deputies. He said the policy of the International was unfair, contradictory, and dangerous in demanding the expulsion of the reformists while permitting, and even encouraging, the adherence of those who, like Marcel Cachin in France, had taken a "social-patriotic" position during the World War. Finally, as representatives of the present position of many Italian workers, the reformists deserved a place in the Party of the working class.[45]

The reformists were not traitors: even Egidio Gennari felt compelled to defend them from Lenin's charge of treason, and preferred to term their behavior "an incomplete comprehension of the new functions" of the Party.[46] But Serrati was wrong in assuming that the Italian reformists were fundamentally different from their comrades in other countries. Although they had taken relatively left-wing positions on many issues, they were motivated more by force of circumstances than by principles. It was either "bourgeois illegality" or the "political immaturity" of their comrades, who comprised a majority, that impelled them to the Left. Fundamentally, they were social democrats, and hence regarded any but the strictly "democratic" method for coming to power as inadequate. For them, the only revolution that deserved to succeed was one that had already completely won over the masses and could be achieved with the technical capacity of the masses themselves. Serrati had to either accept the reformists while frankly recognizing this principle or admit that there was no room for reformism in the PSI; he was unwilling to do either.[47]

Ultimately, Serrati was driven to assert that the International, because it did not understand Italian conditions, was solely responsible for the demand to expel the reformists. According to him, not until the Second Congress of the Comintern did any member of the PSI seriously propose the expulsion.[48] In this, he was patently wrong, since Bordiga and his group had called for such a move as early as 1918.[49]

Long before the summer of 1920, Gramsci had also urged such a step. Bordiga, in fact, considered Gramsci overly cautious because he had accepted the unity of the Party until February 1920![50]

The principal weakness of Serrati's position was that he had no positive political line to oppose to Lenin's; in fact, he completely agreed with Lenin on most issues. Lenin argued that the chances for a successful proletarian revolution would be greatly increased if the PSI became highly disciplined and centralized in doctrine. Serrati's weak rejoinder was that the success of a revolution did not depend on whether a handful of reformists remained in the Party or were excluded:

The Revolution is not a magical act by this or that "leader," even if personal influences do have a value in themselves. The Revolution is the sum of varied and diverse circumstances, of multiplex elements that together add up and lead to the solution, in a given historical moment, of a crisis that has stubborn and deep economic causes. To believe that the "pure" Communists in Italy will produce the Revolution when they are free of Modigliani or Turati ... means to deny the importance and significance of the Revolution.[51]

This conception of revolution, whatever its other merits, meant that the Party could do little besides waiting for conditions to mature—this in a moment when reaction seemed the only force capable of "maturing."

Serrati's position was especially difficult because he was personally opposed to the politics of the reformists, was wholly loyal to the ideals of the Comintern, and, indeed, "looked to Moscow as to a beacon."[52] Yet he could not bring himself to disrupt the tradition of Italian Socialism, to reject the sacrifices and contributions to the Party made by leaders like Turati and Modigliani. Serrati was eventually successful in retaining the reformists in the Party—but this caused the defection of a much larger group of "pure" Communists. Hence, the PSI preserved a separate existence, still nominally a revolutionary party, though its total strength was much less.

This victory was a great tribute to Serrati's personal influence in the Party. In fact, the subsequent history of the Italian Socialist Party, the only large European Socialist Party that remained fundamentally Marxist despite the existence in the same country of a large and dynamic Communist Party, can be understood only in the light of Serrati's position in these months. Ironically enough, he admitted his earlier error in 1922, demanded the expulsion of the reformists, and, two years later, joined the Communist Party himself.

The reason for Gramsci's opposition to Serrati's political line ought to be clear from the article "Capacità politica" (see pp. 121–22), in which Gramsci called for the creation of a proletarian "general staff." Even more hostile toward the reformists than Lenin, he completely supported the Russian leader in this dispute. He especially insisted on greater discipline in the Party and the International, since he felt that the Italian revolution would need the support of the world proletariat: a revolution would certainly cause a blockade of Italy by the capitalists; moreover, the limited Italian economy had to be integrated with the economies of other Socialist countries.[53] Serrati's break with the International, therefore, particularly exasperated Gramsci. For him, expulsion of the reformists was warranted if it could be proved that they had not unconditionally accepted the Twenty-one Points, or had shown misgivings about Soviet Russia.[54] Since, at the beginning of October, the reformists had demanded "interpretative autonomy in the application of the Twenty-one Points according to the conditions of each country," Gramsci contended that they no longer belonged in the Party.[55]

At the end of October, representatives of all the "Communist" groups who agreed with Gramsci that the reformists should be expelled met at Milan to draft a program-manifesto for the coming Party Congress. This document bore the signatures of Gramsci, Terracini, Bombacci, Bordiga, Bruno Fortichiari, Francesco Misiano, Luigi Polano, and Luigi Repossi. It demanded a transformation of the PSI into a new and highly centralized Party, to be called "The Communist Party of Italy (Section of the Communist International)." The Party line was to be strictly in accordance with the directives of the Comintern. "Communist groups" were ordered to begin propaganda work in "all the trade unions, leagues, cooperatives, factories, farms, etc.," with the aim of winning majorities for the new party. This program, confirmed by a "Congress" at Imola on November 28, 1920, was the first document of Italian Communism. It was later accepted by many of the "Left" maximalists, including Egidio Gennari, Antonio Graziadei, and Anselmo Marabini.[56]

Despite these factional disturbances, the PSI was still supported by the majority of the working class and much of the northern peasantry in the municipal elections of October 5 and November 7, the first local elections since 1914. The Socialist Party duplicated its victory in the national elections of 1919, which meant a vastly increased role in the communal and provincial governments of Italy. From the 300 communes previously held, the PSI moved to the control of 2,162 (of a total 8,059) and obtained a majority on the councils of 25 out of 69 provinces. But the Socialists did suffer important defeats at Turin, Genoa, and Florence, caused partly by factional dissensions and partly because the opposition parties often combined against them.[57] At Turin, the Party section had declared that only "Communist" candidates would be presented. This decision automatically excluded Giulio Casalini, a reformist who in previous elections had always received many votes from the middle classes. The consequent bitterness, plus alleged fraud, and an alliance between the Giolittian group and the Catholics led to a Socialist defeat (though only by 300 votes out of a total of more than 100,000).[58]

This electoral campaign was the last political action undertaken by the Turin Socialists within the framework of the PSI. On October 17 the Piedmontese edition of *Avanti!* declared its complete independence from the Milan edition, and stated its intention to agitate on the national level as the organ of a "particularly advanced movement."[59] Shortly thereafter, the organization of the Communist faction at Imola, to which the Turin Socialists adhered *en bloc,* created the need for a newspaper expressing its point of view. Therefore, the executive committee of the Turin section voted unanimously (with one abstention) to merge *Avanti!* and *Ordine nuovo* into a new daily called *L'Ordine nuovo.* Its first number was to appear on January 1, 1921. Gramsci, who was appointed editor, described the position of the newspaper as "Communist according to the line laid down by the [2nd] Congress of the International and by the meeting [at Imola] of the Italian Communists, and according to the tradition of the Turinese working class and the majority of its Socialist section."[60]

Gramsci's Reputation at the End of 1920

Gramsci's development had been great indeed in the years since 1917. He had begun with a somewhat "idealistic" concern for the creation of an autonomous "Socialist" culture to replace the eclectic culture, of bourgeois origin, so often found among his comrades. Later, in the Ordine Nuovo period, he attempted to combine this need for cultural renewal with a real political movement. The result was the campaign to organize factory councils in Turin.

Outside of Turin the council movement had little success; however, it did focus the attention of the European Left on Gramsci, as the laudatory comments of Lenin and Sorel affirm. The Ordine Nuovo group was also praised by Henri Barbusse, who, by giving a benefit lecture, helped the newspaper to remain solvent.[61] *L'Humanité,* the organ of the French Socialist Party, complimented *Ordine nuovo* for its high intellectual level and its educational successes among the Turin workers.[62] Many non-Marxist Italian intellectuals were also impressed by the work of *Ordine nuovo*. Besides Gobetti, there were Benedetto Croce, who one day paid a visit to the newspaper, and Giuseppe Prezzolini, the editor of *La Voce,* who in November 1920 urged Gramsci to publish a collection of his lead articles from the Turin weekly.[63] More interesting—and ominous—is Mussolini's reference to Gramsci in a speech in December 1921. This "Sardinian hunchback and professor of economics and philosophy," said the future dictator, had "an unquestionably powerful brain."[64]

Of course, Gramsci had not yet attained the stature in the Italian Left of a Serrati, or even of a Bordiga. Outside Turin he was well known only to a small group of intellectuals and workers.[65] In 1921, however, with the founding of the Italian Communist Party, Gramsci was to receive his first opportunity to serve as a national leader of the Italian proletariat.

Part III

Gramsci and Italian Communism

7. Livorno, January 1921:
The Founding of the Italian Communist Party

*Il Partito comunista è lo strumento
della forma storica del processo di
intima liberazione per cui l'operaio
da esecutore diviene iniziatore, da
massa diviene capo e guida, da braccio
diviene cervello e volontà; nella
formazione del Partito comunista è
dato cogliere il germe di libertà che
avrà il suo sviluppo e la sua piena
espansione dopo che lo Stato operaio
avrà organizzato le condizioni materiali
necessarie.*
—Gramsci, September 4, 1920

The Congress of Livorno

The first issue of *Ordine nuovo*, the new "Communist" daily of the Turin labor movement, inaugurated the year 1921; however, its editors had no time for mutual congratulations, since preparations for the Party Congress had to begin immediately.[1] The Seventeenth Congress of the PSI had been planned for Florence in December, but the growing strength of Fascism in that city had forced the Party directorate to move the Congress to Livorno and postpone it to January 15, 1921. Strangely enough, this dislocation was scarcely referred to during the Congress; yet the menace of Fascism must be considered in any evaluation of the results of Livorno.

Before the Congress, five distinct factions in the PSI had been formally organized, each one intending to present its own motion on the political line of the Party.[2] The fundamental problem of each faction was defining its attitude toward the Comintern and the Twenty-one Points, which demanded the expulsion of the reformists. The reformists, led by Turati, Treves, Modigliani, D'Aragona, and many other parliamentary and trade-union leaders, organized as the Concentrazione Socialista. Their program was as ambiguous as their title. While insisting that the coexistence of different ideas in the Party was a source of strength, they denied that there were substantial differences between the factions "on fundamental principles of Socialism." They recognized that the dictatorship of the proletariat might be necessary under special conditions; yet it was not to be regarded as a "programmatic" obligation. Their motion added that more "demo-

cratically developed peoples" could not imitate the Russian example
of such a dictatorship. Finally, the Concentrazione, trying to satisfy
all the other groups, approved membership of the Party in the Third
International while reaffirming "interpretative unity [?] in the application of the Twenty-one Points according to the conditions of each
country." As previously stated, the reformists were basically social
democrats: the ambiguity of their program resulted from their refusal
to profess this unpopular position.

The "intransigent revolutionaries" were also closely tied to an
older tradition in Italian Socialism, although they, unlike the reformists, represented a leftist position. Traditionally, the intransigent
revolutionaries were opposed to reformism, but at Livorno they acted
as mediators between the Concentrazione and Serrati's "unitary Communists," not a very difficult job. Their principal leaders were Costantino Lazzari, Party secretary from 1912 to 1919; Angelo Filippetti,
the Mayor of Milan; and Vincenzo Vacirca. They were hostile to the
extreme Left, particularly the Ordine Nuovo group, and accused it
of not sufficiently appreciating the "glorious" history of the Party.
To the "voluntarism" and "opportunism" of the extreme Left—an
alleged tendency to reduce the problem of revolution to the purely
"political"—they opposed a rigid "economic determinism" and adherence to "inexorable economic laws."

The bulk of the Party supported the "unitary Communists," led by
Serrati and Adelchi Baratono. As previously explained, Serrati was
deeply attached to the Third International, but believed that the PSI
would suffer from the expulsion of the reformists. Both feelings were
undoubtedly sincere, but they were mutually contradictory; and the
more Serrati was identified with the retention of the reformists, the
more strained were his relations with the International. Serrati attempted to avoid the issue by calling the reformists "centrists," but
this was a purely verbal solution.[3]

The "Communist-unity" group, led by Antonio Graziadei and
Anselmo Marabini, tried to reconcile Serrati's group with the Communist faction. They pretended to no originality or leadership, but
wished to avoid the schism of basically Communist elements threatened by the controversy over the expulsion of the reformists. This
faction assumed that there was little fundamental difference between
Serrati's unitarians and the Communists, an assumption disproved
by the events of the Congress.

Finally, there was the "pure" Communist group, often so called to
distinguish it from Serrati's unitary Communists (hereafter referred

to as "unitarians"). The principal elements in this group were three: Bordiga's abstentionists, including Bruno Fortichiari, Luigi Repossi, and Luigi Polano; Gramsci's Ordine Nuovo group, including Terracini and Togliatti, who was left at Turin to direct the newspaper during the Congress; and a group of Left maximalists, including Nicola Bombacci and Francesco Misiano. In addition, the majority of the PSI directorate had decided to vote with the Communists, mostly out of loyalty to the Third International. They had no part in the formulation of the Communist program, and indeed could not wholly subscribe to it, since it contained many criticisms of the directorate; nevertheless, they felt that expulsion of the reformists was essential. The principal men in this group were Egidio Gennari, the Party secretary before Livorno; Ambrogio Belloni, a parliamentary deputy; and Giuseppe Tuntar, leader of the Left in Trieste.[4]

On the evening of January 4 the Turin Socialist section met to elect its delegates to the Congress.[5] After a row between the unitarians and the Communists, with the Communist-unity group attempting to mediate, the section decided to send three Communists and one unitarian, in proportion to the votes received in the section. Gramsci, Parodi, and G. Vota were the Communist delegates. The other factions did not have sufficient support to present motions, and hence were not represented.

About a week later, two days before the Congress, Gramsci's newspaper shocked Italian Socialists by publishing a telegram from the Executive Committee of the Comintern. Signed by Zinoviev and Bukharin, it declared that the reformists and centrists of Italy seemed "more to the Left than those of other countries" only because Italy was going through a revolutionary period. Yet it was increasingly obvious that Serrati's group was actually a "centrist faction." The telegram concluded with a warning that the decisions of the Second Comintern Congress required every Party to break with the reformists. "He who refuses to effect this schism violates an essential decree of the Communist International, and with this act alone puts himself outside the ranks of the International."[6] Henceforth, the unitarians would find it more and more difficult to insist on their loyalty to the Third International while also defending the reformists' right to a place in the PSI. Serrati took the only line still open, declaring that the International was misinformed: the Italian Right was not reformist but "centrist." Moreover, the telegram immediately pushed some of the Left unitarians closer to the Graziadei faction, and made a schism practically inevitable.[7]

Thus the Congress opened in an atmosphere of extreme political tension. There was also considerable confusion, because of the sudden move to Livorno. Although the Teatro Goldoni had been rearranged to accommodate the more than 2,000 delegates and guests, many were unable to find lodgings in the city and had to commute from Pisa every day. This problem and the late arrival of many delegates delayed the opening of the Congress until 3:00 P.M.

After the introductory speeches, Paul Levi, representing the Unified Communist Party of Germany, appeared on the platform to open the debate. Levi asserted that "in the history of the proletariat, the time arrives when we must recognize that yesterday's brother is not today's, nor will he be tomorrow's."[8] This comparatively mild request to expel the reformists was followed by the reading of the Comintern telegram and other statements of opinion from the various foreign Communist parties. All urged a break with the Right; the note from the Spanish Communists went so far as to call the Serratians "corrupters." Pandemonium broke out at this point, and order was rarely maintained during the following week.

After Secondino Tranquilli (better known as Ignazio Silone), the editor of *Avanguardia,* had announced that the Socialist Youth Federation would vote with the Communists, Misiano moved that the Party's political line be established before anything else was discussed. Only Lazzari protested, imagining with sentimental optimism that a prior discussion of the "real" problems of Socialism would reconcile doctrinal differences between the factions.

Graziadei was asked to deliver the first major speech, undoubtedly because the aristocratic Romagnole scholar regarded his task as strictly one of reconciliation—between the "Communist" groups. Still, his fluent speech only emphasized the inconsistencies in Serrati's position. He cogently pointed out that Article 16 of the Twenty-one Points (see pp. 105–6) was intended to allow autonomy in applying the Points, not to provide justification for evading them altogether. Graziadei admitted the importance of Party unity; but, for him, Communist unity was more important: if the unitarians believed they must choose between reformists and Communists, they had better choose the latter. Above all, international unity was preferable to national unity. To the argument that the Comintern was dominated by Russian influence, Graziadei replied that this domination was inevitable so long as Russia was the only Socialist country (Serrati himself shouted, "That is very true!"). But Graziadei differed from the Communist faction in refusing to automatically exclude all the reformists:

"All those who willingly accept the theses of the Third International and pledge to follow them immediately may remain in the Party."[9] The Communists felt that such a qualification would only allow a repetition of the events following the Congress of Bologna, where the reformists had joined the majority in formally accepting the Third International. Finally, Graziadei declared that, in case of a schism, his group would follow the Communists.

The second day of the Congress was almost entirely taken up by the speeches of Baratono and Khristo Kabakchiev.[10] Kabakchiev, a Bulgarian Communist, was an official representative of the Third International; hence, his speech was awaited with great interest.[11] Although Kabakchiev's position was well known, many were shocked by the violence of his attack on Serrati: "The truth, bluntly stated by Kabakchiev, offended too many persons, too many feelings, too many interests!"[12] For Kabakchiev, Serrati was fundamentally reformist in denying the revolutionary character of the occupation of the factories and the Italian situation in general, and in refusing to recognize the importance of the world colonial struggle. Each of the Bulgarian's charges was followed by shouts of "Non è vero!" from the unitarians and "Benissimo!" from the Communists, until the theater was sheer bedlam. At one point, Kabakchiev felt compelled to ask the Congress whether or not it even wanted to hear the statements of the Third International. He insisted on no interruptions from either side, a demand that Serrati hastened to second. Nevertheless, only the playing of the "Internationale" calmed the Assembly. Thereafter, this song proved remarkably successful in terminating controversy, for everyone was anxious to demonstrate his loyalty to the Comintern.

Adelchi Baratono, speaking for the unitarians, attempted to deny any serious differences between the factions, a task that involved the Florentine in a host of logical difficulties. Although presumably in the left wing of the unitarian group, Baratono had to defend the reformist leaders of the CGL against the Communist charge of treachery during the occupation of the factories. According to him, the plans of both the Party directorate and the CGL for solution of the occupation were "honest, but the one was revolutionary, the other syndical."[13] The Communists quickly pointed out that Baratono himself had just demonstrated the inability of the present Party to act as one in a specific situation. After vaguely hinting that the reformists might be expelled, Baratono advanced the familiar unitarian claims: the Italian Right was not really reformist, and it would have to sign an agreement accepting the Twenty-one Points; the unitarians and Communists were basically alike in their views, except for a few "extreme subjectivists" among the Communists. This speech did not begin to satisfy the Communist demand for expulsion of the reformists and greater Party discipline. In a meeting held after the session, the Communist faction almost decided to leave the Congress immediately; however, they finally agreed to wait for a vote on the various motions.[14]

By contrast with the preceding and following debates, the discussion of the third day, January 17, was relatively calm—mostly because Lazzari and Terracini were the principal speakers. Lazzari's forty years of service to Italian labor precluded violent objections to his ideas; Terracini carefully avoided demagoguery and irresponsible attacks, while pointing out to the unitarians the inevitable consequences of their ambiguous position.

Lazzari eloquently declared his opposition to any schism, to the "official" use of violence, and to changing the Party name.* He expressed a kind of implicit nationalism shared by many of these "Socialist" delegates by stating that the Comintern favored the French and English parties within it: this was so partly because the Russians were badly informed on things Italian. With this observation, he turned his fire on the Ordine Nuovo members, asserting that it was they who had misinformed the Russians. They were similar in their "voluntarism" to the anarcho-syndicalist conspiracies that he and other comrades had eliminated from the Party in 1892 and 1908. The young Turin intellectuals, said Lazzari, for all their wisdom, lacked feeling: "what we call fraternity and equality." They evidently did not understand the closing words of the Communist Manifesto, "Workers of the world, unite!" (Shouts from the floor: "Then why did you expel the anarchists?"[15]) After reproving Serrati for persuading the Bologna Congress to replace the "intransigent revolutionary" method with the cult of violence, Lazzari closed by warning the Ordine Nuovo group that the deficiencies of the Party would not be remedied by a schism. Lazzari's speech met with great applause, but it was certain that his group would be abandoned at the crucial moment, just as at Bologna.

Terracini opened his speech by declaring that the Communist faction intended to continue, not destroy, the past work of the PSI.[16]

---

* *Ordine nuovo* distastefully observed that Lazzari, with his "usual rancid sentimentality," often employed extra-logical modes of persuasion, such as suddenly displaying all his previous Party membership cards (about forty of them, including those of the Partito Operaio, the precursor of the PSI).

The majority of the Party directorate elected at the last Congress had, in fact, gone over to the Communists. Either the work of Bologna would be continued, or the results of the last Congress would be denied—in which case the Party would be expelled from the International. There was no way to avoid a schism. The Congress of Bologna and other recent events had shown that the reformists were unwilling to give up their ideas for the sake of discipline. Let them, then, seek support for their doctrines, but not in the Party, which could be disciplined only if it were homogeneous and cohesive. As for the use of violence, so repugnant to Lazzari and the reformists, the Party had to recognize that violence was sometimes unavoidable, and the only way to render it less brutal was to give it organization and discipline. Here, Terracini accused the trade-union leaders in the occupation of the factories of having thrown the working class into a terrible situation without providing them with arms.

Terracini then took up the question of agrarian policy. The reformists had charged that the Communist line in this area was the same as the Italian Popular Party's. Terracini did not entirely deny this allegation: the Popular Party was performing "a function for which the Communist Party ought to be grateful," since it had awakened masses that the Communists could not yet reach.[17] This idea, already familiar to those acquainted with Gramsci's views on the PPI, brought applause from the Communists but a storm of protest from the Right.

Terracini concluded his two-and-a-half-hour speech with the statement that the Third International had already decided the task of the Congress. The unitarians must make their decision: if they applied the Twenty-one Points without reservations, the Communists would be happy to stay in the Party. This conclusion was heard in absolute silence, broken dramatically by a great outburst of cheers from the Communists. Baratono, carried away by enthusiasm, rushed to the stand and declared that anyone rejecting the Twenty-one Points would be expelled; however, he was forced to eat his words later that evening, when he announced that his last remarks did not modify anything previously said by his faction.[18]

The proceedings of the fourth day exceeded all the others in violence. The speech of Gino Baldesi, an ultra-reformist trade-union leader, was perhaps on a higher level than the rest. He insisted—despite Baratono's declarations—that the unitarians and reformists were different! Baldesi exalted legislation as the only way to achieve control over production under capitalism. Political democracy would ensure the victory of Socialism when the South achieved the political consciousness of the North. Voices from the floor shouted that then the bourgeoisie would stop Socialism by force; Baldesi replied that in such a case a dictatorship would be morally justified, because it would be of the majority. The Communists demanded that he explain how the reformists would prepare the workers to exercise this dictatorship: he retorted that a dictatorship of the Party over the proletariat, which the Communists presumably advocated, would be suited only to backward countries, not to those having a long democratic tradition. The reformists would renounce some of their points for the sake of Party unity, but insisted that the Twenty-one Points be revised to "adapt them to the conditions of Italy."

Vincenzo Vacirca, who then spoke for the intransigent revolutionaries, had just published a letter in *Avanti!* that accused Bombacci of abandoning Bologna while the Fascists were running amok there. Vacirca's speech strongly implied that the PSI "cult of violence," adopted at the Congress of Bologna, had touched off the present violence of the Fascists. The Congress broke into an uproar. Ennio Gnudi, the newly elected mayor of Bologna, rushed to the stage and attempted to answer Vacirca—who turned to Bombacci, shouted "Rivoluzionario del temperino!," and displayed a "pocketknife" to emphasize his point. Vacirca really meant to say that Bombacci, with his cult of violence, was encouraging bloody revolution instead of a real political movement. Bombacci replied by drawing a pistol. Although it seems that he did not actually point it at Vacirca, Bombacci was nearly thrown out of the session.[19]

After a few remarks by Ernesto Schiavello (Communist-unity) and Pietro Abbo, a "peasant deputy" who made a pathetic and sentimental appeal for unity, this stormy session came to a close.

By now the principal arguments had already been stated, a schism in the Party was inevitable, and nothing remained but the vote. Still, it was decided to permit another round of speakers—perhaps in a desperate hope that the atmosphere of the Congress might change, perhaps in order to give the floor to more of the leading Party members, perhaps because "God gave Italy the gift of gab," as Silone has put it. In any event, three reformists, one unitarian, two members of the Communist-unity group, and three Communists spoke on the fifth day of the Congress.[20]

Bordiga, the first speaker, emphasized the social-democratic character of Italian reformism. For the reformists, the revolution was not really inevitable; in fact, the only realities were the day-to-day problems of Socialism. The movement was everything; the end, nothing. The reformists were always able to show that the time for revolution had not arrived: before the war they had said the bourgeoisie was too strong; now they said that its weakness had created a mess for which the Party should not take responsibility. The refusal of the Italian reformists to collaborate with the bourgeoisie should not be used to demonstrate their intransigence. "Intransigence" might have meant that before the war; it now meant no less than the total conquest of power by the proletariat.[21] The unitarians admitted that the revolution was impossible because the proletariat was not prepared. But the whole purpose of the Communist program was to achieve such preparation. The cooperatives, trade unions, Socialist municipalities, etc., were not organs of preparation, as Serrati seemed to think. They had no meaning unless a Party determined to destroy the power of the bourgeoisie existed. The PSI was not such a party. To Baratono's question "What are you going to do?," Bordiga eloquently replied:

It is quickly said. The Third International has obliged us to separate from the reformists. The Unitarians offer them a way of remaining. . . . We cannot follow the Unitarians in that. For this reason, we shall leave.

But you tell us that we shall end up like all the others who left the Party [the anarchists in 1892, the syndicalists in 1908, etc.]. That shall not be, since two qualities distinguish us from those who left earlier. We are, and we feel we are, the true heirs of the Italian Marxist Left. If we must go, we shall take with us the honor of your past. Then, there is another reason: we are sincerely following the Communist Third International.[22]

The Congress was strangely silent after Bordiga's address; but Serrati's speech, which followed, brought chaos. Because of the contradictions in his position, Serrati was reduced to two arguments: the Comintern was discriminating against the PSI in favor of other Socialist and Communist parties, and the Communist faction was already riddled with internal differences, despite its declared intention of creating a party of discipline.[23] Serrati's statement that "There is a profound difference between Gramsci and Gennari, between Gramsci and Bordiga" was basically true, and strikingly predicted the future development of Italian Communism; however, at Livorno, Serrati used the argument solely to avoid expulsion of the reformists.[24]

Filippo Turati, the leader of Italian reformism, was the next speaker. Because Turati made no attempt to hide his honest differences with the extreme Left, the whole assembly felt his sincerity; and he was sometimes applauded by even the Communist faction. "When the Russian myth has passed," said Turati, "our classical conception

of Socialism will again come to the fore. The soviet will never replace
a proletarian parliament of technicians." Turati acknowledged the
fitness of the Russian Revolution for more backward peoples, but
denied its usefulness as a model for the West: "The Russian Revolution will bring all the new peoples of the Orient to the stage of history, but it must not hinder proletarian unification in more developed
countries." Nevertheless, Turati, for the sake of national and international unity, was also anxious to continue membership in the Third
International.[25]

Three short speeches followed. Nino Mazzoni declared that the
Moscow decisions on the agrarian question were "excessively reformist" ("Neither God nor Lenin will tear us from Socialism!").[26] Bombacci asserted that the alleged presence of opportunists in the French
party provided no justification for opportunists in the PSI. Anselmo
Marabini declared that the Communist-unity group would vote with
the Communists, since it was evident that the unitarians would persist in their own program, essentially hostile to the Comintern. However, a minority of the Graziadei-Marabini group, led by Giulio
Cavina, a Tuscan trade-union organizer, declared for the unitarians.

Finally, Egidio Gennari explained why the majority of the Party
directorate was supporting the Communists. Ciccotti's articles openly
urging collaboration with the bourgeoisie; Nofri's slanderous book
on Russia; Turati's attacks on the soviet; Modigliani's project for a
social-democratic republic—all showed that the PSI was continually
in danger of corruption by social democracy so long as the reformists
remained in the Party. The reformists wished to stay in the Party only
to maintain contact with the masses, as Turati himself had stated.
Outside the Party they would lose all influence. The occupation of
the factories was a good example of the Party's inability to act so long
as it was fundamentally divided in doctrine.[27] After Modigliani was
given an opportunity to defend himself against Gennari's accusation,
the fifth and last day of debate ended at 10:00 P.M.

The following morning, after Lazzari announced that his faction
would withdraw its motion[28] and vote with the unitarians, there remained only the final address by Kabakchiev and the vote itself.
Kabakchiev first defended the Comintern against Serrati's charges,
and then went on to expel both unitarians and reformists from the
International:

After extending a fraternal hand to Comrade Serrati and seeking to detach
him from reformism—since he persists in rejecting the International and
retaining the reformists in the name of Party unity—I declare, in the name

of the International, that we must remain firmly intransigent; and therefore, all the factions that do not completely accept the theses of the Communist International will be excluded from it.[29]

The PSI would be expelled if the reformists remained. Kabakchiev followed this statement with a long declaration of principles, which drew violent objections from the unitarians and fervent applause from the Communists.

Although the voting took place on Tuesday afternoon, final results were not determined until midnight. The outcome was much as expected: of a total of 172,487 votes, the unitarians received 98,028, the Communists 58,783, and the reformists 14,695.[30] The Communists had majorities in only fifteen provinces: Turin (the strongest Communist province of all) and Cuneo in Piedmont; Mantua and Sondrio in Lombardy; Forlì in Emilia-Romagna; Arezzo, Florence, and Massa in Tuscany; Macerata, Ancona, and Pesaro in the Marches; Trieste in Venezia Giulia; Campobasso in the Molise; Lecce in Apulia; and Sassari in Sardinia. The Communists also received a majority among the Italian Socialists living abroad, and came very close to the unitarians in the following provinces: Alessandria (Piedmont), Bologna (Emilia-Romagna), Treviso (Venezia Euganea), Naples (Campania), and Girgenti and Catania (both in Sicily). The unitarians achieved solid victories in the remaining 48 provinces.[31]

The next morning, January 21, 1921, the last meeting of the unified Italian Socialist Party took place.[32] It was quickly terminated. Bordiga declared that "the majority of the Congress, with its vote, has placed itself outside the Third International. The delegates who voted for the Communist motion are to leave the hall. They will meet at eleven o'clock at the Teatro San Marco to write the constitution of the Communist Party, Italian Section of the Third International."[33] To the cry of "Viva l'Internazionale!" the Communist delegates left the Teatro Goldoni. Even though all the representatives of the International and the foreign Communist parties left with the secessionists, many of the remaining delegates could not believe that the rupture with the International had actually occurred. Modigliani suggested that Kabakchiev's remarks had merely "been written at Livorno." This was of course true; but Serrati, who had been a member of the International's Executive Committee, pointed out that the Comintern would never repudiate its own representative. Baratono, in a last effort to push the reformists to the left, delivered a little sermon to Turati, who obliquely but firmly rejected it. A new central committee was elected, and the Congress was dissolved.

Meanwhile, at the Teatro San Marco, the Communist Party of Italy was organized.[34] After complimentary speeches by Kabakchiev and other foreign Communists, and the reading of several congratulatory telegrams—the Turin Chamber of Labor announced its adherence to the PCI—the Communists discussed their program. The line of the Communist deputies and members of local government was decided, as well as procedures for the formation of Party sections. The Party headquarters would be at Milan, perhaps with the aim of winning over part of the large unitarian majority there. Because it was published at Turin, *Ordine nuovo* could not, therefore, be recognized as the official Party organ; the Party, however, would "distribute and protect" it. In addition, an official biweekly, *Il Comunista*, would be published at Milan. Lastly, the Party selected its central committee. It consisted of those who had signed the Imola Manifesto, plus a few leaders won to the Party during the Congress: Gramsci, Fortichiari, Bordiga, Repossi, Misiano, Bombacci, Polano, Terracini, Gennari, Marabini, Parodi, Ludovico Tarsia, Ambrogio Belloni, Ruggiero Grieco, and Cesare Sessa.[35]

The Congress ended at 6:00 P.M. The central committee met in the evening and chose the executive committee (Bordiga, Fortichiari, Terracini, Grieco, and Repossi) that would operate at Milan.[36] Gennari was selected as the Party's representative to the Third International, and Bordiga announced the dissolution of the abstentionist faction, now that its principal task, the founding of a new Party, had been achieved by the Congress.[37] The schism had been effected, and the PCI was a reality.

The Meaning of the Congress

The Congress of Livorno and the bifurcation of Italian Socialism are synonymous; hence, an evaluation of the Congress depends on one's judgment of the schism. Most books on the Italy of this period insist that the breaking of Socialist unity at that time was a mistake. They portray an academic, though unruly, debate over obscure and irrelevant matters of doctrine, while the real problem of the moment —the rise of Fascism, which threatened the very existence of the Italian labor movement—was ignored. A Socialist "Congress" might reasonably be expected to spend much time discussing the specific political conditions in its own country. Livorno, however, was not really a "Congress." Its sole purpose was to determine how far and in what ways the Italian Socialist Party would split, and current political conditions were only one of the factors to be considered. Many of the delegates had already suffered personally from Fascist violence, and were therefore aware of its danger; however, they were convinced that the Socialists could not properly combat this new menace until the general political line of the Party (or Parties) was established.

Nonetheless, the customary historical judgment insists that any schism at that time was a mistake, that the PSI should have remained united in order to fight Fascism more effectively. But one of the facts most clearly demonstrated at Livorno—not only by the Communists, but also, if grudgingly, by Baratono and the unitarians—was that the PSI had not obtained unity of action in any area but electioneering in the fifteen months since Bologna. The next five years would show that there were just as many ways for Socialists to deal with Fascism as there had been for them to deal with the Turin general strike and the occupation of the factories. Hence, discipline and truly unified action, albeit on a more restricted scale, could only have been achieved by a schism. The Communists were certainly wrong, and perhaps irresponsible, in calling men like Turati traitors, even though Communists and reformists were profoundly different. They were probably wrong in assuming that the Italian situation in January 1921 was still "revolutionary"; historians, with the advantage of hindsight, have easily proved them incorrect on this point. Yet, even at Livorno, many Communists insisted that a homogeneous and disciplined Party was essential, regardless of present conditions. This basic principle of Leninism was clearly not understood by the majority of the delegates, however enthusiastically they applauded the Russian leader.[38]

Although a schism of the Party seemed warranted by the facts, the particular schism that occurred at Livorno was disastrous. Thanks to that Congress—and to Mussolini—the Italian Left was eliminated from political life for the next twenty-two years. The PSI had 216,000 members in 1920. Scarcely 100,000 of these extended their membership—in either the PSI or the PCI—into 1921, and the PSI experienced other schisms in 1922 and 1924.[39] The results of Livorno were in no small measure responsible for this chaos.

Pietro Nenni's statement that Livorno caused a "schism of those in agreement and an agreement of those in disagreement" assumes too much; however, it does point directly to certain tragic weaknesses in the Italian Left, which Livorno had made unavoidable. The unitarians left the Congress without a clear idea of where they were leading the PSI. They insisted that there were no fundamental differences between themselves and the Communists, and, in fact, devoted most of their energies for some time to regaining a place in the International. The reformists were even more hamstrung, since the unitarians had bound them to a political position that was utterly opposed to the principles of reformism. In 1921 Serrati was viciously attacked by the Communists, but he absolutely refused to take up the struggle against them. The few differences between the PSI and the PCI that Serrati admitted were envisioned in purely sentimental terms. The result was a total cessation of political action by the Italian Socialists.

The inescapable conclusion is that many, if not all, of the unitarians should have gone over to the Communists at Livorno—especially since Serrati and his group finally did expel the reformists in 1922! Kabakchiev was perfectly correct in pointing out that there were "two fundamental schools of Socialism" conflicting at Livorno. These were reformism and Communism: every point of practical or doctrinal significance at the Congress was made by spokesmen of these two positions. The unitarians who really were "Communists"—and certainly many like Serrati were—should have accepted the discipline of the International and joined the PCI; those who were essentially reformists should have been permitted to take the PSI in hand and give it a political direction that provided a significant alternative for those on the Left who were not Communists.

The tragedy of the schism at Livorno had a deep effect on the Communist Party. The Ordine Nuovo group, the only one in the Party capable of making original contributions to Communist theory and practice, was isolated between the demagoguery of Bombacci and the ultimately sterile sectarianism of Bordiga. The relatively small PCI was dominated for some time by former abstentionists, who were the most numerous and best organized faction in the new Party. True, Gramsci's point of view eventually won over most of the PCI. But meanwhile, precious time was lost, and it is impossible to know how much Gramsci's own flexibility and richness of thought suffered in this process.

Gramsci himself played a very small role at the Congress of Livorno. He delivered no speeches, and he rarely participated in the discussions.[40] This passivity can be explained by Gramsci's excessive personal modesty, by his physical condition, which was worse than ever, and by the constant attacks of his opponents in the PSI on his alleged "interventionism" and "voluntarism."

Another year passed before Gramsci overcame his reluctance for public speaking. In the meantime, Umberto Terracini usually expressed Gramsci's ideas in public, as at Livorno, since the young Genoese was an accomplished speaker. Certainly, the Ordine Nuovo group, of which Gramsci was the undisputed founder and leader, was recognized at Livorno as the intellectual center of Italian Communism. In this sense, the frequent attacks made there by Turati, Lazzari, and Serrati were a tribute to the Ordinovisti.

Terracini, rather than Gramsci, was elected to the executive committee of the new Party, partly because Gramsci, as director of the newspaper in Turin, was unable to live near PCI headquarters at Milan. But the Party press was firmly controlled by Gramsci and his Turinese supporters. A few months after Livorno, there were three Communist daily newspapers: *Ordine nuovo* in Turin, edited by Gramsci; *Il Comunista* in Rome, edited by Togliatti; and *Il Lavoratore* in Trieste, edited by Ottavio Pastore.[41] Eventually, this control of the press, in addition to the support of the International, helped the former members of Ordine Nuovo dominate the Italian Communist Party.

After January 1921 the Ordine Nuovo movement, as a separate faction, ceased to exist and was absorbed by Italian Communism. In the same way, the previously unruly Turin labor movement thereafter accepted the discipline of the PCI. One historical period had ended; in the next period, Gramsci and his supporters gradually rose to uncontested leadership in the PCI. The Ordinovisti necessarily lost much of their youthful idealistic fervor in achieving this victory; there is, however, a direct line of descent from the earlier Turin movement to Gramsci's "Quaderni del Carcere" and Togliatti's editorials in *Rinascita* from 1945 to 1964. The movements to organize the peasant masses of the Mezzogiorno, to create a specifically Socialist culture based on the dignity of the worker as producer, to establish a discipline patterned after that of the Turin working class—all entered the permanent legacy of the Italian Communist Party.

8. Gramsci, the PCI, and the Third International

Ricevo ora molte lettere dai compagni itali-
ani. Vogliono da me la fede, l'entusiasmo,
la volontà, la forza. Credono che io sia
una sorgente inesauribile. . . . Domandano troppo
da me, si aspettano troppo e ciò mi impres-
siona sinistramente.

—*Gramsci, March 6, 1924*

A definitive account of Gramsci's role as a leader of Italian Communism would require a satisfactory history of the PCI's early years. No such history exists; and it was not possible to produce one until quite recently. Previously, many essential documents were unavailable, and the immediate political interests of Communist, non-Communist, and anti-Communist scholars precluded the minimum of detachment necessary for good historical writing.

At last the documents are beginning to appear. Most important is Palmiro Togliatti's *La Formazione,* a collection of personal and supposedly confidential letters exchanged by Gramsci and his friends—especially Togliatti, Terracini, and Mauro Scoccimarro—that reveal the inner life of the PCI and the process whereby Gramsci became its leader.[1]

Another new source for Party history in these early years is Gramsci's correspondence of 1922–26 with Giulia Schucht, his Russian wife. In 1962 *Rinascita,* the official weekly of the PCI, published some 55 of these letters. Highly personal, they document Gramsci's thoughts and feelings in the frankest possible way, often providing material of general historical value. We observe, for example, Gramsci's consternation when he discovered that his Italian comrades expected *him* to save the Party and themselves: "I have received many letters from my Italian comrades. From me, they expect faith, enthusiasm, will, and force. They think that I am an inexhaustible source, that I have all these qualities in sufficient measure for ample distribution.

... They are asking too much from me, they expect too much, and this disturbs me."[2]

Gramsci's articles of 1921–26 are, in a way, also a new discovery. Modest and self-effacing, he rarely signed these articles. Historians had to tentatively separate Gramsci's work from that of his comrades on the basis of stylistic or topical evidence. Now an annotated collection of Gramsci's more important articles from those years is available.[3] Two journals—*Rinascita*, edited by Togliatti until his death in August 1964, and *Rivista storica del socialismo*,[4] whose content reflects a variety of political positions—have also published many documents on the PCI's early history.*

Gramsci, Bordiga, and the Comintern, 1921–26

In many ways, the years 1921–22 were among the most difficult of Gramsci's life; indeed, they recall his youthful periods of bleakness and uncertainty at Cagliari and at the University of Turin. His intense efforts during the great Turin labor struggle of 1920 had pushed Gramsci to the verge of a nervous breakdown, which actually occurred in 1922. There were also political reasons for his depression. The PCI had been founded at an unfortunate time. Fascist violence and aggression against working-class institutions was about to reach its peak. Then, too, Livorno had shown that the Communists were definitely a minority compared with the Italian Socialists.† The Ordine Nuovo group had been reduced to a minority in the PCI; Gramsci himself was not even on the executive committee. Also, Bordiga's hostility had forced Gramsci to suspend work on the factory councils. But Gramsci was not completely inactive. As editor of the daily *Ordine nuovo* he had great responsibilities, and he wrote many articles in this period.

April and May of 1921 were particularly unpleasant months for Gramsci. On April 25 the Fascists burned the Casa del Popolo in Turin. In the May elections Gramsci, as a candidate for the Cham-

---

* While no satisfactory history of the PCI has yet been produced, Italian scholars are evidently not alone in their failure. As E. H. Carr remarked recently, "The only two reasonably adequate histories of Communist Parties hitherto published have been Mr. J. Rothschild's history of the Bulgarian Party and Mr. Theodore Draper's of the American Party; and these were not very important Parties" (Carr, pp. v–vi). The few histories of the PCI that have been published are indeed excessively tendentious. See my annotated bibliography of the PCI in *Soviet Foreign Relations*, pp. 520–39.

† In the elections of May 1921 the PSI won 1,600,000 votes, and the PCI only 300,000 (the PSI elected 123 deputies, the PCI only 15).

ber of Deputies, was defeated, though other Communists, Misiano and Rabezzana, were elected in Piedmont. Once again the issue of Gramsci's "interventionism" was raised, this time by some ex-abstentionists in the Turin section.[5] Earlier in the month, the Fiat workers suffered another defeat, after management responded with a lockout to protests against layoffs of 10 per cent of the labor force. Gramsci's article on this event showed deep compassion for the plight of the workers.[6]

About the same time, Gramsci attempted, for some reason, to establish contact with Gabriele D'Annunzio. The former Comandante of Fiume had previously had vague ties with other European radicals, and in 1921 even Lenin thought he might be a "revolutionary." In an article of January 11, Gramsci had already implied a desire that the Party examine the politics of the Fiumean "Legionnaires" more closely.[7] In April 1921, accompanied by a Legionnaire from Turin, Gramsci went to Gardone, where he hoped to see D'Annunzio. For various reasons, the plan fell through. Perhaps the most lasting result of the episode was a portrait of Gramsci at that time:

Good, almost sweet, with that large intelligent face on that greatly deformed body, quick to smile and every word full of thought, born for conversation though speaking at length tired him . . . , Gramsci was charming from the beginning, for all his monstrous appearance. He dressed very badly, and demonstrated that he gave little importance to personal cleanliness.[8]

During 1921–22, Gramsci was chiefly concerned with the relationship of the Socialists and Fascists to the old ruling parties. He was as harsh as other Communists in the constant disputes with the PSI on this question. Often, however, he suggested that the PSI would soon enter the government, "because today this is their single will"; that is, the PSI was no longer a revolutionary party and could only turn "reformist." Gramsci's statement was intended partly as an "exposé" and partly as a proposed method for isolating the Fascists. Perhaps this was the meaning of G. M. Modigliani's remark of February 1922: "The Communists, outside of [the Chamber of Deputies], are most insistent that the Socialist Party assume its responsibilities."[9] In 1922, however, neither the Socialists nor the "democratic" parties were prepared for an "opening to the Left" like that in the 1960's.

Neither Gramsci nor any other Communist of the time thought that Fascism would seize power on its own—for that matter, neither did Giolitti, who continued to use Fascism as an annoying but convenient instrument for controlling the labor movement and its parties.[10] But Gramsci by no means overlooked the possibility of a Fascist alliance with other groups in a reactionary coup d'etat. He had predicted a turn to reaction as early as the summer of 1920, and Leon Trotsky wrote in 1932 that none of the Italian Communists "except Gramsci" had seen the possibility of a Fascist dictatorship."[11]

On this point, as on many other political questions, Bordiga's views differed from Gramsci's. For many years (*ca.* 1930 to 1960), the Bordiga case was the outstanding Italian example of the Stalinist reduction of disaffected leaders to "un-persons." The later editions of Giovanni Germanetto's famous *Memoirs of a Barber* systematically eliminated Bordiga's name. When Bordiga was mentioned in official literature, he rarely appeared as other than a "fanatic," or at best a "mediocrity." In more recent documentation, especially the letters published by Togliatti, Bordiga as a personality appears very differently. Togliatti wrote to Gramsci on May 1, 1923, that "Amadeo's personal will and strength of character are an asset to the Party, and should not be lost."[12] Gramsci asserted a year later that replacing Bordiga with any single person would not be easy, since "for general capability, and for work, he is worth at least three."[13] Karl Radek called Bordiga "one of the few capable of taking the leadership of the International."[14] Bordiga was still respected in February 1926, at the Sixth Plenum of the ECCI, even after Gramsci had completely destroyed his political position. Besso Lominadze, who scorned "left-wing" Communism, described him as "a sincere, straightforward, convinced, honorable, leftist oppositionist."[15] The rarest compliment of all was Stalin's, since Bordiga at this time, like the Pope in World War II, had "no divisions behind him": the Bolshevik leader said he could "respect and believe Bordiga ... because he says what he thinks."[16]

Bordiga's straightforward character, however, led him to refuse any reconsideration of his fundamental views. Gramsci was "convinced that he is unmovable. . . . His very character, inflexible and tenacious to an absurd degree, obliges us to consider building the Party and its center without him."[17] Bordiga's greatest fear was that the Communist movement would be "contaminated" by the values of "bourgeois liberalism" and democracy, whether these values were expressed by traditional "democrats" or Italian Socialists.[18] There could be no collaboration of any sort with these ideas: indeed, winning a majority of the working class was for him less important than preserving the "purity" of the new Party. The only essential prerequisite for a successful revolution was a truly revolutionary elite ("pochi ma buoni"), which would apply the intransigent tactical system that Bordiga had worked out from Marxist texts. Here there was no room for internal discussion or Party schools. Orders came down from the executive committee in the manner of a "barracks party."[19]

Gramsci had opposed Bordiga's views for some time, and their relations had been strained. But when the Comintern formulated its "united front" policy (at the Third Congress of the International, June–July 1921), it threw open the whole question of the PCI's future development and leadership. The policy, rather vague at first, was spelled out in greater detail in the ECCI's circular of December 15, 1921.[20]

The united front policy called for collaboration on specific issues with the other parties of the proletariat. Radek, Zinoviev, and others went to great pains to show that the new program did not contradict the policy of schism advocated by the Second Congress. Logically, they were correct: the various Communist parties could now make "concrete" agreements with other parties from an independent base. Practically, the difficulties were enormous, especially in Italy, where the PCI and the PSI were in close competition, where the split had been so recent, and where so much rancor existed between the respective leaders.[21] But the Comintern leaders insisted that there was no choice:

Had the Red Army in 1920 taken Warsaw, the tactics of the C.I. today would be other than they are.... The strategic setback was followed by a political setback for the whole workers' movement. The Russian proletarian party was compelled to make extensive concessions. That slowed down the tempo of the proletarian revolution, but the reverse is also true; the setback which the proletariat of the western European countries suffered from 1919 to 1921 influenced the policy of the first proletarian state and slowed down the tempo in Russia.[22]

At the Third Congress, the Italian, German, and Austrian parties had refused to vote for the united front proposals of the Russian delegation unless various amendments were added to them. Terracini, following Bordiga's lead, had asserted the virtues of the small Party and decried the Russian emphasis on gaining majorities. Lenin's reply to Terracini's speech was perhaps one of the best defenses of united front tactics: "To win the sympathy of the masses is necessary. An absolute majority is not always necessary; but to win, to stay in power, we must win over not only the majority of the working class [industrial proletariat] ... but also the majority of the exploited and of the agricultural workers."[23] At the first enlarged plenary session of the ECCI (February 21–March 4, 1922), involving 105 delegates from

36 parties, the Italian, French, and Spanish delegates opposed the united front theses, which were nevertheless adopted, 46 votes to 10.[24]

Immediately after the First Plenum of the ECCI, the PCI held its Second Congress (Rome, March 20–24, 1922). The main task of the Congress was defining the Party's position on the united front tactic. To this end, Bordiga drew up a series of resolutions, known in Party history as the "Rome Theses," that are outright attacks on the united front tactic:

It is an error to suppose that one can, by expedients and maneuvers, expand the Party base among the masses at any time, since relations between the Party and the masses depend in great part on the objective conditions of the situation. The controversy between us leftists and other factions lies in our belief that variations in the situation should not change the fundamental program, organization, and tactics of the Party. As we see it, Party influence among the masses will grow when the situation becomes more revolutionary, provided that the Party holds firmly to its preconceived organization and tactics. The other factions apparently see the problem of "conquering" the masses as a problem of will; but actually, they fall into opportunism by continually adapting themselves to specific situations. Thus they so deform the nature and functions of the Party that it is incapable of conquering the masses, or of performing its supreme tasks when the right situation does occur.[25]

Bordiga declared his opposition to any direct dealings with the PSI and to any political agreement with its leaders. The united front should be confined to the trade-union level. Thus the Rome Theses directly challenged the Comintern's conception of the united front. Although Gramsci succeeded in having them presented to the Congress only as a "basis for future discussion" at the next Congress of the International, and managed to modify two articles, they were accepted at Rome by a vote of 31,089 to 4,151.[26]

Bordiga claimed that Gramsci originally accepted the basic ideas of the Rome Theses wholeheartedly, but later rejected them for opportunistic reasons. Bellini and Galli, in their Trotskyist-oriented work, support this view. But Togliatti and Tasca (though Tasca had some reservations) have held that he accepted the Theses for contingent reasons—the weakness of his own group compared to Bordiga's and the danger of giving the right-wing "minority" an opportunity to split the Party. Gramsci's recently published correspondence does support the second view, but it also shows that Gramsci did substantially nothing to combat the Theses until late in 1923. A letter of February 9, 1924, to Togliatti and Terracini, shows that Gramsci opposed the Theses from the beginning; however, we are forced to trust Gramsci's memory, since corroborating evidence is apparently not available:

Sometime before the Rome Congress, in my speech to the Turin section, I said rather clearly that I accepted the [Rome] Theses on tactics only for the contingent reason of Party organization; but I also said I was in favor of the united front right up to its culmination in a workers' government. Moreover, the Theses as a whole had never been thoroughly discussed by the Party. And, at the Congress of Rome, the question was quite clear: if the EC [of the PCI] had not agreed with the delegates of the Comintern to present the Theses only as a basis for discussion and to change them after the Fourth Congress [of the International], it is not very probable that the majority of delegates would have stood with the leadership. Certainly, I would [not] have done so, and neither would the Piedmontese delegation, with whom I met after Kolarov's [the representative of the International] speech and with whom I established an agreement: prevent the minority from suddenly conquering the Party, but do not attribute any meaning but an organizational one to the vote.[27]

The second Rome Thesis declared that individuals could not exhibit "consciousness and will," since these faculties were realized only by the integration of many individuals in one collective organism. In the same letter, Gramsci attacked this view:

This concept, correct in reference to the working class, is mistaken and extremely dangerous when applied to the Party. Before Livorno, Serrati contended that the Party as a whole was revolutionary, even if Socialists of many different stripes coexisted within it. And at the Congress that split Russian social-democracy, the Mensheviks upheld this concept, saying that the Party itself was important, but not its individual members.

This attitude had stultified all action by individuals: the mass of the Party was passive. The rank and file continued to believe that revolution depended solely on an apparatus like the Party, and even thought that the Party's mere existence guaranteed the eventual outbreak of revolution.[28]

Gramsci was chosen as the PCI delegate to the ECCI in Moscow, probably because of his ability to work with Vasilii Kolarov, the representative of the International at the Rome Congress. In the jargon of the PCI's private communications the Comintern representatives in Italy were usually referred to as "flamingos" (*fenicotteri*). Of the many "flamingos" in the early 1920's, three stand out: Dmitrii Manuilsky, Matyas Rakosi, and Jules Humbert-Droz. The Italians assigned each of them an ornithological label. Manuilsky became *il Pellicano,* for according to legend the pelican will wound itself to feed its children. Manuilsky had brought difficulties on himself in Moscow by defending the allegedly sectarian views of the Italian Party. Rakosi was called *il Pinguino*, probably because his behavior seemed about as intelligent and graceful as a penguin's. Humbert-Droz became the *Colibrì* or *Uccello Mosca*: both words mean hummingbird, but the latter also means "Moscow Bird"! Togliatti suggests that perhaps he was given that name "in consideration of his more refined political activity."[29]

Gramsci's first important contact with a representative of the International was not with one of these, but with a certain Chiarini—who, despite his Italian name, was a Russian national. In the fall of 1921, he advised Gramsci to enter the ECCI with the aim of replacing Bordiga. Chiarini said that Terracini's weakness and the incapacities of Repossi and Fortichiari had made Bordiga's views predominant: the Comintern had wished to give the Turin group leadership of the PCI.[30] Gramsci warmly replied that he "did not want to lend myself to intrigues of that kind, that if they wanted another leadership, they should make it a political question."[31]

Gramsci left for Moscow in May 1922. Although very ill, he did take part in the Second Plenum of the ECCI (June 7–11). Afterward he retired to a rest home at Serebranyi Bor on the outskirts of Moscow, where he remained for about six months. He had evidently suffered a complete breakdown—constantly high fever, tremors in the arms and legs. Even after his recuperation, "the exhaustion persisted" for some time, and he could not work "because of amnesia and insomnia."[32] Yet these months, and those immediately following, were perhaps the only really joyful period in Gramsci's life. In Serebranyi Bor he met Giulia Schucht, who was later to bear him two sons, Delio and Giuliano.[33] Gramsci was deeply affected by his attachment to Giulia, as we have learned from his recently published letters to her.[34]

By November of 1922, Gramsci was well enough to attend the Fourth Congress of the Comintern. Moscow had just learned of the March on Rome and of the Rome Congress of the PSI (October 1922), where the reformists were finally expelled. The Fourth Congress went beyond the united front theses of December 1921, and proclaimed the slogan of a "workers' government" (or a "workers' and peasants' government") as the new tactic of the International. In countries where the new slogan could be applied—that is, where popular forces had a chance of assuming state power—"Communists must declare themselves ready to form a workers' government with non-Communist workers' parties and workers' organizations."[35] Presumably Italy was regarded as one of those countries. Bordiga was, of course, even more opposed to this slogan than he had been to the united front. His unequivocal opposition at the Congress was the real beginning of his break with the Comintern.

The Comintern leaders had decided that the PSI's belated acceptance of the 21 Points called for a "fusion" of Italian Socialists and Communists. Bordiga was solidly opposed to fusion of any sort—for him the issue was bound up with what he called "Communist revisionism" in the International. Tasca and the right-wing minority accepted the plan. Gramsci himself compromised. At first he argued that only the "Third-Internationalist" faction ("Terzini") of the PSI should be merged with the Communist Party. Afterward, however, he also accepted the Comintern plan, and was appointed to the joint committee for arranging the merger.[36] Gramsci later insisted that the bleak outlook for the PCI at the beginning of 1923 left him no choice but vacillation and compromise: the complete support of the International was essential. An open break with Bordiga was not feasible, since Gramsci then believed that only the Neapolitan leader could hold the Party together.[37] Gramsci's "wriggling," as he called it, evidently satisfied no one. Zinoviev complained that Gramsci "makes vague promises; and when he fulfills them, they have an effect contrary to what was expected."[38]

Gramsci may have been ineffective in his efforts, but he was probably sincere. During the Congress, he was approached by Matyas Rakosi. The Penguin, "with the diplomatic delicacy that distinguishes him, assaulted me, once again offering me the leadership of the Party at Amadeo's expense."[39] Gramsci replied that in view of Bordiga's prestige and position, he could not be replaced without a great deal of preliminary work. He was appalled by the political confusion of the Italian delegation—he himself had not been in Italy since May—and also by the strength of Tasca's minority. "If the Penguin, instead of being a fool, had an ounce of political intelligence, the Party would have cut a miserable figure."[40] That is, if Rakosi had been adept enough to convince Gramsci, then Gramsci could easily have won over most of the Italian delegation; but this method would have ruined the Party.

In any case, nothing came of the proposal for fusion. Pietro Nenni had formed a "Committee for the Defense of the Party," taken over *Avanti!*, and won over a majority of the PSI leadership with a program opposed to fusion. Serrati was arrested immediately after his return from Moscow, and could do little to counter Nenni's action. Zinoviev, on hearing of these events, called for a "bloc" of the two parties in place of a fusion, but this proposal proved even more distasteful to most of the PCI.[41]

On February 3, 1923, Bordiga and Grieco, the main PCI opposition to the line of the Third International, were arrested. Terracini, as a member of the executive committee, immediately appointed Scoccimarro, Camilla Ravera, Tasca, and Graziadei to the central committee, and brought Togliatti and Scoccimarro into the executive committee itself. As Togliatti has said, this move was not a deliberate attempt to change the Party line, but it did "create some of the conditions that later made the beginning of the renewal necessary and possible."[42]

In April 1923, Bordiga decided to take the offensive against the International's program for the PCI. Though still in prison, he wrote an "appeal to the comrades of the PCI," which openly attacked the views of the Fourth Congress on the united front, "workers' government," and fusion. His concluding points were an out-and-out challenge to the International: he called for a discussion by the Party leaders of the whole "programmatic and tactical direction" of the Party and a discussion by the "competent organs of the International on the conditions of the proletarian struggle in Italy"; if the PCI debate did not produce a "substantial consensus," the present leadership, though remaining in the Party, should "not take part in the leading organs of Party direction." Bordiga added that he was very interested in a distribution of the manifesto in other countries: "We would be very grateful to whoever does this in the form of a translation."[43]

On May 1 Togliatti, who had previously opposed Bordiga's views on fusion, wrote Gramsci and urged him to sign the manifesto; Gramsci refused to accept the document.[44] This refusal opened a debate between the former members of the Ordine Nuovo movement, which continued till February and March of 1924, when Togliatti, Scoccimarro, and Terracini all accepted Gramsci's views.

The Third Plenum of the ECCI (June 12–23, 1923) selected an entirely new executive committee for the PCI including Togliatti, Scoccimarro, Tasca, Vota, and Fortichiari, who resigned and was replaced by Gennari. The Plenum also decided to make Terracini the PCI representative to the Comintern. Gramsci would move to Vienna, partly to head the new office of the Comintern in that city and partly to facilitate his assumption of active leadership in the Italian Party by getting closer to the scene of action.

Shortly before leaving Moscow, Gramsci communicated with the executive committee of the PCI, outlining his plans for a new daily newspaper, to be published jointly by the Party and the "Terzini" group that had been expelled from the PSI. This letter was Gramsci's first practical move toward the implementation of those broad and flexible tactics that later became identified with his political approach and, in fact, with that of the whole Italian Communist Party. The newspaper, said Gramsci, "ought to be published so as to ensure its legal existence for the longest possible time," which really meant that it should not appear as an organ of the Party. Gramsci proposed as a title *L'Unità*, "which will have meaning for the workers, and even a more general meaning." At this point, for the first time, Gramsci suggested that the PCI give a special importance to the "Southern Question." That was not simply a matter of allying workers and peasants, which was central to the program of the International; it was "also and especially a territorial problem, that is, one of the aspects of the national question."[45] The first issue of *L'Unità* appeared on February 12, 1924. Its regular publication ended in November 1926, when all the anti-Fascist parties were outlawed; but it was occasionally published clandestinely during the years of the Fascist dictatorship. Since the end of World War II it has been the official newspaper of the PCI.

In November 1923 Gramsci left for Vienna.[46] Once there, he began a period of very intensive work. He planned to publish a new theoretical Party journal, *Critica proletaria,* which would provide a forum for all elements in the Party—even Bordiga, who had recently been released from prison. This journal never materialized, but Gramsci did succeed in establishing a new series of *Ordine nuovo,* this time as a biweekly published at Rome. The first issue appeared on March 1, 1924, and sold 6,500 copies on the day of publication. According to Gramsci, this was 1,500 more than an *Ordine nuovo* issue of 1920 usually sold.[47]

Above all, he increased his correspondence with Togliatti, Terracini, Scoccimarro, and Leonetti in an effort to imbue them with a new and more flexible conception of the Party. Gramsci began this task with the advantage of great prestige among these men. Leonetti confided to Gramsci on January 20, 1924, that "you alone are the person who can and must assume the initiative to save the Party from a schism with the International on the one hand, and from falling into chaos and the most degrading inertia on the other hand."[48] Terracini, for his part, confessed that he, Scoccimarro, and Togliatti during "the whole past life of the party" merely "constituted the bridge between

Amadeo and Masci [Gramsci]."[49] Gramsci was not overly pleased with this image: "You, Negri [Scoccimarro] and Palmi [Togliatti], must also decide for clarity, for a position closest to your intimate convictions, and not for your function as 'bridges.' "[50]

Gramsci's other advantage in this debate was that he really believed in the program of the International, although he did have his own interpretation of that program. The whole policy of the Third International from 1921 to 1924—and in some respects until 1928—assumed that the revolutionary wave had receded and the working class was once again on the defensive. True, this simple principle was often hedged, and even contradicted, by many Comintern leaders, but it was still the basis for policy in those years. In October 1922 Trotsky therefore advised a policy of maneuver and consolidation for the non-Russian parties of the International. Gramsci went much further than the Comintern in his evaluation of the situation. On May 18, 1923, he wrote:

Three years of experience have taught us, not only in Italy, how deeply rooted are social-democratic traditions, and how difficult it is to destroy the residue of the past with simple ideological polemics. A vast and detailed political action is necessary to disintegrate this tradition by disintegrating the organism that personifies it. The policy of the International is adequate for that.[51]

The next year, Gramsci advanced his theories to an entirely different (and prophetic) level. Bordiga, he said on February 9, 1924,

thinks that the tactics of the International reflect the Russian situation, produced by a backward and primitive capitalist civilization. For him the tactics are excessively voluntaristic and theatrical, because only by a supreme effort of will can the Russian masses be moved to revolutionary action when this action is not determined by the historical situation. He thinks that, for the more advanced countries of Central and Western Europe, this program [united front, workers' government] is inadequate or simply useless. In these countries the historical mechanism functions according to all the Marxist sacraments; there is a determinism that was lacking in Russia: and therefore the dominant task must be the organization of the Party in itself and for itself.

I believe that the situation is very different. First, the political conceptions of the Russian Communists were formed in an international context, not a national one; secondly, the development of capitalism in Central and Western Europe not only determined the formation of broad proletarian strata, but also created an upper stratum, the working-class aristocracy with its annexes of trade-union bureaucracy and social-democratic groups. The direct determinism that moved the Russian masses in the streets to revolutionary assaults was complicated in Central and Western Europe by all the political superstructures created by the greater development of capitalism; it rendered mass action slower and more cautious, and therefore demands from the revolutionary Party a system of strategy and tactics much more complex and long-range than those used by the Bolsheviks between March and November 1917.[52]

Gramsci's analysis of the world situation could only lead to a Party line of maneuver toward class alliances. In the process, Party ideology would certainly run many risks of "contamination"; but social democracy was a reality in Western Europe, and mere intransigence could not defeat it. Thus Gramsci was firmly convinced that the International's tactics were generally correct. Like all Communists of the 1920's—Bordiga included—Gramsci wholeheartedly believed in the international character of the movement.[53] But he also believed that the individual parties could only be effective through their own autonomy and strength. The problem was one of reconciling national traditions with an international framework. One reason for the meager results of the united front and workers' government campaigns was "the way in which the so-called centralism of the Comintern has been understood: up to now no one has succeeded in developing autonomous, creative parties that are automatically centralized by means of their response to the general plans of action arrived at in the [Comintern] Congresses."[54]

Gramsci wanted the PCI to regain the faith of the masses before the Fifth Comintern Congress (June–July 1924) so that "we can assume an independent position, and also permit ourselves the luxury of criticism. Presently it seems to me that we must still tack [*louvoyer*] for some time, to avoid increasing the confusion and crisis in faith and prestige that is already widespread." The ominous break between Trotsky and Zinoviev–Stalin led to a particularly significant reflection: "We must work to build a strong Italian Party, tightly organized politically, with its guiding principles firmly impressed on the mind of each individual member, so that matters like this will not cause its disintegration."[55]

In a letter of February 9, 1924, Gramsci explained his past views and his plans for the Party's future. His fundamental assumption was that the PCI had to become a mass Party, but that this was not likely in the immediate future. Even with a political revival in Italy, "Our party will still be a minority..., the majority of the working class will go to the reformists and ... the bourgeois democrats will still have much to say."[56] This situation called for tactics like those proposed by the International, and for a policy making the Southern

Question central in Party activities. On February 23, 1924, Togliatti abandoned his reservations and joined Gramsci; Terracini followed suit on March 26. The old Ordine Nuovo group was again united.

On May 12, 1924, after having been elected to the Italian Parliament, Gramsci returned to Italy and took up his duties as leader of the PCI.[57] A few days later, the first National Conference of the Party met secretly in the vicinity of Como. There Gramsci learned that most of the Party cadres were still solidly Bordigan, though his own position as Party leader was not challenged. The Bordigan view was not reduced to a marginal position until the latter part of 1925. At the Fifth Congress of the International (June 17–July 8, 1924), Bordiga was even elected to the ECCI, though he refused this office just as he had refused all others since 1923.

After Como Gramsci moved to Rome, where he led the Communist parliamentary group. He began transforming the Party into a semi-clandestine organization, so that it could continue in case of complete suppression.* He also tried to organize a democratic united front against the Fascist dictatorship: in spite of Bordiga's objections, he even participated in the Aventine opposition that followed the assassination of Matteotti in June 1924, until it was clear to him that the liberal and Socialist parties intended to limit their opposition to a "moral protest." Gramsci then returned the Party to the regular Parliament, where, directly confronting the Fascists, he hoped to win the national audience that only a national legislative body could provide.

Gramsci's united front policy was far from completely successful. He did succeed in merging Serrati's "Third International" faction of the PSI with the PCI in 1924, but was generally unable to overcome the diffidence of other leftist groups toward the Communists. The extremism of the PCI under Bordiga's leadership had made a rapprochement with other parties extremely difficult; moreover, the other parties were unwilling to employ general strikes and armed

---

* Renzo De Felice has recently published a report compiled in the fall of 1926 by the Fascist state police; it concerns "the situation of the anti-Fascist parties on the eve of their suppression." According to De Felice, who is certainly not a Communist, the report describes crises in all the parties except the PCI. "In general, it had not only succeeded better than the others in maintaining ties with the masses but, having become semi-clandestine, it had also partly salvaged the essential structure of its organization." Gramsci's leadership was responsible for this successful transition to a clandestine organization. See De Felice, ed., "La Situazione dei partiti antifascisti alla vigilia della loro soppressione secondo la polizia fascista," *Rivista storica del socialismo*, VIII, 25–26 (May–Dec. 1965), 79–80.

resistance, which the PCI insisted were necessary to overthrow the Fascist dictatorship.

Still, if Gramsci's policies had little effect during his active leadership, in the long run they transformed the PCI from a "sect" into a "mass" Party. His contributions were theoretical, and often looked beyond the immediate problems of the Party. For example, his essay "Alcuni Temi" (1926) was the first detailed examination of the Southern Question and expressed many of the themes that occupied Gramsci in his later Prison Notebooks: the problem of the South as the key problem of the Italian revolution; the importance of the intellectuals, especially Croce, in maintaining the Southern status quo; the consequent need to swing the intellectuals to the Left. Yet this important work was not published until 1930, long after Gramsci had gone to a Fascist prison.[58]

"Alcuni Temi," however, was a far less important contribution to Italian Communism than the Lyons Theses, which Gramsci delivered at the Third Congress of the PCI (January 1926). With the Theses, he gave the Communists a "national" as well as a class attitude. Thereafter the PCI imagined itself the only force capable of completing the work of the Risorgimento, of creating a vigorous, democratic Italy.

The Lyons Theses

The exact authorship of the Lyons Theses is uncertain. In a more or less "official" work, Ferrara and Ferrara say: "Gramsci came secretly at night to Togliatti's house, and stayed there for two days. They talked, decided on the main points, and prepared an outline. Then the Theses were written out by Togliatti."[59] It has been implied that Togliatti gave himself too much credit;[60] but in a work of 1958, he stated directly that the document was written "under Gramsci's direction."[61] In any case, the final product, as S. F. Romano says, "bears the clear imprint of Gramsci's personality."[62]

Italian Communists have always regarded the Theses as an important milestone in their Party history. For Velio Spano, Lyons was a "rebirth of our Party." In 1956, he argued that "all our cadres, especially today, after the Twentieth Congress of the CPSU," should devote "serious study" to the Theses.[63] Togliatti later emphasized that the importance and the novelty of the Theses lay in their "rigorous scientific and historical analysis" of the Italian social structure, the development of the labor movement, and the nature of Italian capitalism.[64] Non-Communists have also admired some aspects of the document. Garosci wrote that it contained "particularly interesting views on Italian history, closely tied together."[65] And S. F. Romano asserted that the Theses, as well as "Alcuni Temi," were more effective than the clandestine organization of the Party in attracting young intellectuals during the years of Fascism.[66]

The Theses completely changed the intellectual outlook of the Party. Before Lyons, the Party's extremism had infected it with a fatalistic acceptance of historical determinism: the Party members had assumed that "history would prove us right." Gramsci's repeated assertions (Thesis 14) that the Left had been defeated in 1922 because of its own political deficiencies made the rank and file realize that "history would prove us right in the measure we deserved!"[67] He managed to give the Party an active historical view. Those sections of the Theses devoted to an analysis of recent Italian history and society are still impressive in their insights and breadth of understanding.

The opening paragraphs of the Theses, however, as well as Thesis 19 and all those following it, are very far from these broad considerations. The Third, or Lyons, Congress of the PCI had the specific task of defeating and isolating the Bordigan group, but also the more general task of "bolshevizing" the Party, in accordance with the prior decisions of the ECCI's Fifth Plenum (March-April 1925).[68] In analyzing the Theses, it is important to separate the more specifically Gramscian ideas (Theses 3–18) from those we shall consider first, which are no more than a "translation" into Italian terms of the Fifth Plenum's work.

The Theses begin by declaring that "transformation of the Communist Parties . . . into Bolshevik Parties" is "the fundamental task of the Communist International."[69] Attacks by the extreme Left against the Comintern "as an organ of the Russian state" must be fought by demonstrating how the Russian party is historically justified in playing the "leading role in building the Communist International."[70] Bolshevization meant unifying and centralizing the Party, on both ideological and organizational levels. Ideologically, a complete acceptance of Lenin's form of Marxism was necessary; Gramsci justified this dependence by noting that the PCI "did not find in the history of the Italian labor movement a vigorous and continuous current of Marxist thought to which it could appeal."[71] Organizationally, bolshevization required a Party "led by the central committee, not only in words but in deeds."[72] Internal democracy in the Party was still limited by the repressive acts of Fascism, and by the "political capacity of the peripheral organs and single comrades working on the periphery"; that is, by the degree of *bordighismo* inherent in the Party cadres. The work of the Party leadership to increase this political capacity would "make possible an extension of democratic 'systems,' and steadily reduce the system of appointment and intervention from above in regulating local organizational questions."* The process of centralization would not rule out "contrasts of tendencies" that contributed to the dialectical development of the Party; but "organized groups that assume the character of factions" should henceforth be forbidden.

Gramsci's views on the social composition of the Party were closer to his characteristic thoughts and style of expression. The Bordigans maintained that the Party was an "organ" of the working class, implying that it was an institution representative of the workers because it knew and stood up for their interests. Yet the Party was not in the class. This was a natural development of the Bordigan view: the Party had to establish principles of strategy and tactics and remain faithful to them; they must not "contaminate" them by adjusting them to momentary situations. A Party like this was created by unifying individuals who had learned and accepted these principles. There was an indirect link between the Party and the working class, since Party principles would presumably reflect the workers' real and permanent interests; but the Party itself could be made up of "heterogenous" individuals. For Gramsci, this was a thoroughly ahistorical view of the political party's role—or of any human institution's, for that matter. As he later said in the "Quaderni del Carcere," political parties are the "nomenclature" of social classes.[73] In Theses 27 and 29, he asserted that the Party must be a "part" of the working class. This meant, as he said a few weeks later in his report on the Lyons Congress, that the PCI was a class Party "not only abstractly" but "physiologically"—the great majority of its members should be proletarians.[74] The Italian social structure had many economically destitute and anti-capitalist elements that were non-proletarian. These might flood the Party, diluting its program with non-Marxist ideologies and preventing the Party-class dialogue needed to make the working class an effective ruling class. But "the Communist Party

---

* From any really "democratic" standpoint, Gramsci was on dangerous ground here. He ultimately justified the need for centralization by pointing to the abnormal conditions created by Fascism and stating that the PCI "is not a democratic Party, at least in the common sense of this word. It is a centralized Party, nationally and internationally. In the international field our Party is simply a section of a larger Party, a world Party." (Ferrata and Gallo [12], I, 747.) Gramsci himself believed this, though sometimes "with a grain of salt" (see Note 55). The question was whether the rank and file of the PCI, or the Italian people, also believed it.

cannot be just a workers' Party. The working class cannot do without the intellectuals, nor can it ignore the problem of gathering around itself all those elements driven in one way or another to revolt against capitalism."[75] The "nature" of the Party was clearly a difficult theoretical and practical problem, but Gramsci thought it could be solved, if only the "proletariat is guaranteed a ruling *function* in the Party."

Gramsci had lost none of his *Ordine nuovo* spirit regarding relations between the Party and the working class. The Party had to lead the workers, but not by an "external authoritarian imposition," either before or after the conquest of power.[76] The Party could not lead the working class by "proclaiming" itself as a revolutionary organ; it had to make itself part of the working class, unite itself with all the sections of the class: "Only as a consequence of its action among the masses can the Party obtain recognition as 'their' Party."[77]

Party work in the labor movement, an obviously essential part of this "action among the masses," was difficult to carry on in 1926. The General Confederation of Labor was almost dead;[78] and, although the Communists still insisted that the CGL "historically expressed" the traditions of the Italian labor movement more effectively than other organizations, working in it was hardly "action among the masses."[79] Thesis 37 proclaimed that no organizations through which the Party could contact the workers should be abandoned.[80] Yet neither the Theses nor Gramsci's report on the Congress advised the PCI to penetrate the Fascist trade unions, where the "organized masses" were at this time—even though the Fifth Plenum of the ECCI specifically called for work in those unions.[81] At the Lyons Congress, the Left opposed concern with any of the existing trade unions. Gramsci evidently did not care to risk a fight with the Bordigans on the issue of "working with Fascists." As it was, the Left attacked him at Lyons as a "Proudhonian" and a "Crocean."[82]

If effective trade union work was problematical in 1926, there was another way to reach the working masses: create representative bodies "that adhere to the system of production."[83] This meant reviving the internal committees of the first years after World War I. In Thesis 30, which dealt with Party reorganization based on centers of production ("cells") rather than geographical areas ("sections"), Gramsci recalled his earlier experiences in Turin:

The factory movement in 1919–20 demonstrated that only an organization tied to the place and system of production allows contact between the upper and lower strata of workers [skilled, unskilled, and laborers] and prevents the establishment of any "labor aristocracy." Organization by cells provides the Party with many elements [cell secretaries, members of cell committees, etc.] that are part of the masses; and even though they exercise ruling functions they remain part of the masses, unlike the secretaries of territorial sections, who were necessarily detached from the workers. The Party must give special attention to educating these comrades, who form the connective tissue of the Party and unite it with the masses.[84]

This Thesis recalls the content and spirit of the old *Ordine nuovo*, especially Gramsci's plan in the summer of 1920 to organize "Communist groups" for educational work in the factories.* The connecting idea, present in every stage of Gramsci's thought, is the supreme importance of constant contact between the base and the ruling elements, the masses and the intellectuals.

For the Communist movement in 1926, work among the masses had only one justification: awakening the "motive forces of the Italian revolution."[85] Those forces were the working class, the "agricultural proletariat" (the rural day-laborers of the Po Valley, who had always been numerically important in the Italian Left), and "the peasants of the South, the islands, and the other parts of Italy." The industrial and agricultural proletariats had to achieve a "high degree of organization and combativeness." The peasantry would be essential to the revolution in a country like Italy, but only after an alliance with the proletariat; for a number of reasons, Gramsci regarded the peasants of the South and the islands as particularly important.[86]

But at the moment, these revolutionary forces were only potential. The Party had to mobilize them, and therefore had to take part in every struggle for immediate, non-revolutionary, or "partial" demands.[87] Gramsci wrestles with this problem time and again in the Theses, most unequivocally, perhaps, in Theses 39 and 40:

[The Party] leads and unifies the working class by participating in all struggles of a limited character, and by formulating and promoting a program of immediate interest for the working class. Partial, limited demands are considered a necessary opportunity for achieving the progressive mobilization and unification of all the forces of the laboring class.[88]

Gramsci then moved considerably beyond the framework of the Fifth Plenum: "All the legislation with which the Fascists in Italy suppress even the most elementary freedom of the working class ought to

---

* Interestingly, the word "council" never appears in the Theses—or in Gramsci's report, where he made a special effort to historically justify labor organizations within the factory. When such groups are discussed (e.g., in "La Relazione" [32], p. 522), he refers to them as "internal committees." Perhaps the earlier attacks of Bordiga and others had taught Gramsci and Togliatti that the past could be an "insidious companion" (See Ferrata and Gallo [12], I, 703).

furnish the Communist Party with material for stirring up and mobilizing the masses." Gramsci's exposition is much more positive toward limited struggles than Bordiga's chary attitude. As Spano has said, the Lyons Theses struck a powerful blow against the determinism inherent in the early PCI, and made the Party a permanent fixture in Italian politics.

Gramsci calls mobilization of the masses and unification of the working class the "positive" aspects of the united front tactic.[89] The struggle for partial demands was the implied "negative" aspect, designed to demonstrate to the masses that no important changes were possible, short of revolution. It must be said that Gramsci had little room for maneuver on this question because the International had imposed very narrow limits on the ultimate possibilities of limited struggles:

... Bolsheviks make use of every partial demand to explain to the masses the necessity of revolution, to show the masses, by the concrete facts of the case, the impossibility of even a moderately serious and lasting, let alone fundamental, improvement in their position so long as the power of capital is maintained.

At the same time the communists demonstrate to the masses in the light of experience that it is precisely the reformists who sabotage every serious struggle for partial demands, while it is the communist party which is alone able to lead a consistent struggle for the day-to-day interests of the working masses and ward off attacks on their standard of living.

Bolsheviks place every concrete demand to which the workers rally in the perspective of the fight for the revolution.[90]

Gramsci filled the Lyons Theses with safeguards against the perfidy of any potential political allies in the struggle against Fascism. He posited a "chain of reactionary forces" extending from the Fascists to the maximalist Socialists:

Beginning with Fascism it includes the anti-Fascist groups that do not have large mass bases (liberals), those that have a base in the peasants and petty bourgeoisie (democrats, veterans, Catholics, Republicans) and in part also in the workers (reformist party), and those that have a proletarian base but tend to keep the masses in a state of passivity and lead them to follow the politics of other classes (maximalist party).[91]

Of course, Gramsci and his party were attacked just as violently by the other groups of the Left. Moreover, considering Gramsci's whole way of thinking, it is probable that here he meant only that the maximalists were "reactionary" because their inability to develop an "autonomous" class line in effect placed the masses of that Party under the "hegemony" of the ruling classes.

In Thesis 20, however, Gramsci called the whole "democratic" opposition to Mussolini a sham. His experience with the Aventine groups had convinced him that the function of the "bourgeois democratic opposition" was "to collaborate with Fascism in preventing the reorganization of the working class."[92] This democratic opposition would return to power only when the methods of Fascism no longer prevented "the unleashing of class conflicts." Fascism and bourgeois democracy were merely two responses of the same ruling class to the same proletarian threat. Gramsci's view in this Thesis—unlike some of his earlier ideas—leaves little room for the political impact of the organized proletariat. It may be true that the "ruling class" in question held this position, but the mass forces behind the two responses would necessarily be very different.

Thus the "negative" aspect of the united front tactic was simply an exposure of all non-Communist elements as reactionary forces. The PCI should engage in partial struggles to demonstrate the "impossibility that the workers' conditions can improve in the period of imperialism," and to demonstrate that the nature of the Fascist regime would not undergo radical changes until a massive anti-Fascist struggle was begun, "which will inexorably develop into a civil war."[93]

Velio Spano reflected in 1956 that in the Lyons Theses, "we offered to the others, as the program of united action, not a platform that was truly common, but a program and an objective that were really our own."[94] But Spano does not indicate that the program and its boundaries had been previously established by the Comintern. Gramsci's own original contributions came in Theses 3–18, and these Theses contain material of greater importance and far more general value. Gramsci intended them as an introduction to the Comintern-inspired Theses dealing with the nature and role of the PCI: actually, the "introduction" presented a broad history, or "sociological" analysis, of Italian social structure, labor movements, bourgeois politics, and Fascism.

In his discussion of Italian class structure Gramsci intended to emphasize certain unusual characteristics of Italian society—Italian "exceptionalism," as it were—that might have spurred the PCI to action. Three of these presumed characteristics are still of interest as historical problems: the relative weakness of Italian capitalism, and the political and economic consequences of this weakness; the regional aspects of relations between industry and agriculture in Italy;

and the greater revolutionary importance of the Italian proletariat compared with the same class in other European countries.

Although capitalism had become the dominant element in Italian society, the industrial base of the country was still very weak. Agriculture still employed many more hands than industry. To control the State and the economy, the industrialists had to make economic compromises with the great landowners; hence, the "traditional economic struggle between industrialist and agrarian interests" did not occur in Italy, nor did the usual "rotation of ruling groups." These compromises had adverse effects on the entire economy: a slower rate of economic development, a chronic budgetary deficit, and endemic unemployment that caused extensive emigration. The State itself was also a compromise. To strengthen and defend it, the industrialists were forced to grant important posts and influence to those groups over which they held a "limited hegemony," especially the agrarian interests and the petty bourgeoisie.[95]

Industrial-agricultural relations had a "territorial base" in Italy. Industry was almost exclusively concentrated in the North, and the agricultural workers there were highly proletarianized; to strengthen its position, the bourgeoisie had to ally itself with ruling elements in the South. As a result, the Southern laborers became a "colonial" population. Northern industry assumed the role of a "capitalistic metropolis"; the great landowners and middle bourgeoisie of the South had the same function as those colonial groups (feudal elements and "compradors") that "ally themselves with the metropolis to hold the mass of the working people in subjection."[96] Gramsci also likened the relative functions of the South and North to an immense countryside linked with an immense city.[97] For him, one of the main effects of this relationship was to make the Southern peasantry the chief potential ally of the proletariat. It also imparted a "national" character to the Socialist revolution in Italy, since only such a revolution could complete the unification of the country by ending the "colonial" subjection of the South.

The Gramscian image of the "colonial" South as one immense countryside and the North as one great capitalist city has interesting similarities to recent ideas expressed by the Chinese Communist Party.* In an article of September 3, 1965, Lin Piao, Vice Premier

---

* In fact, the working theories of Chinese Communism, as developed by Mao Tse-tung, are sometimes quite Gramscian in character. In the late 1920's and the 1930's Gramsci and Mao were outstanding figures in the Communist movement— Gramsci was marginal because of imprisonment, Mao because of geography and

and Minister of Defense of the Chinese People's Republic, applied
the idea of rural and urban areas to the whole world:

Taking the entire globe, if North America and Western Europe can be called
"the cities of the world," then Asia, Africa, and Latin America constitute
"the rural areas of the world." Since World War II the proletarian revolutionary movement has for various reasons been temporarily held back in the
North American and West European capitalist countries, while the people's
revolutionary movement in Asia, Africa, and Latin America has been growing vigorously. In a sense, the contemporary world revolution also presents
a picture of the encirclement of cities by the rural areas.[98]

In this theory the whole underdeveloped world becomes a vast Mezzogiorno. The principal difference is that for the Italian theorist of
1926, the revolutionary impulse originated in the cities, though its
success depended on support from the rural areas. For the Chinese
theorist of 1965, the revolution has its primary center in the countryside, and support from the cities may even be unnecessary.

The "heterogeneity" and contradictory interests of the Italian ruling classes gave the proletariat "a greater importance than it has in
other European countries, even those of a more advanced capitalism."[99] Only the proletariat could unify and coordinate the whole
society; and its program alone would "not deepen the contrasts between various elements of the economy and society." Italy confirmed
the thesis that the most favorable conditions for proletarian revolution were not always in countries where capitalism and industrialism
had developed furthest; instead, the revolution could occur where
the capitalist system offered less resistance to revolution because of
its structural weaknesses.[100]

In Theses 10 to 14, Gramsci expounded his views on the politics of
the Italian bourgeoisie, from 1870 to the *primo dopoguerra*. Again
remarking on the varying compromises that the bourgeoisie undertook to maintain control of the State, he analyzed the methods used
by the ruling class to control the masses: either direct repression
(Crispi), or the "exterior methods" of "democracy" and "political cor-

---

the place assigned to him by Soviet foreign policy. Key problems in comparing the
thought of the two men are their views of the revolutionary process and the place
of the peasantry, intellectuals, and "national" bourgeoisie in that process. Some
basic materials for the study of these points are Stuart Schram's remarkable edition
of the *Political Thought of Mao Tse-tung* (New York: Praeger, 1963) and two
contributions by the Italian Marxist scholar Enrica Collotti Pischel: *La Cina rivoluzionaria: Esperienze e sviluppi della "rivoluzione ininterrotta"* (Turin: Einaudi,
1965), and "Su alcune interpretazioni della figura di Mao Tse-tung," *Studi storici*,
VI, 4 (Oct.–Dec. 1965), 749–84.

ruption" to secure the cooperation of a "labor aristocracy." Especially important for Gramsci was the role of the Church at each stage of development.[101]

Finally, Gramsci tried to analyze the nature of Italian Fascism. As a movement of "armed reaction," it was at first favored by all the old ruling groups, especially the agrarian interests. The social base of Fascism was, however, in the urban petty bourgeoisie, and in a "new agrarian bourgeoisie" created by changing relationships in rural land ownership during the war. This new social base and the "ideological unity" provided by the militaristic legacy of the Great War enabled Fascism to conquer the State in opposition to the old ruling classes. Although Fascist "revolutionary" pretensions were absurd, the groups gathered around Fascism did have a "homogeneity" and a psychological outlook characteristic of "nascent capitalism" that distinguished the movement from anything in earlier Italian history. Thus Gramsci, unlike many other Communists of the time, did understand the novel aspects of Fascism. Its social composition allowed the Fascist movement to oppose the political leaders of the past and develop an ideology contrary to traditional bourgeois theories of the State; at the same time it could devote its main energies to fighting the same common foe, the organized proletariat.[102]

Gramsci asserted that the Fascists had developed a new program for maintaining the supremacy of the bourgeoisie: Fascism replaced the old agreements and compromises between elements of the ruling classes with the proposal to unify the bourgeoisie in one "political organism, under the control of one central authority that would at the same time lead the Party, the government, and the State." As a program for all-out resistance to revolution, this would attract to Fascism "the most reactionary part of the industrial bourgeoisie and agrarian interests."[103]

The new Fascist methods would eventually put even more strain on the social structure. To promote this bourgeois "organic unity," the Fascists had already made many concessions to the industrialists and landowners, thus provoking "discontent in the petty bourgeoisie, who thought the era of their dominion had come with the arrival of Fascism." Meanwhile, in 1926, Fascism had not yet created the "organic unity": two bourgeois groups still remained outside the system. Giovanni Giolitti's group—including *La Stampa* and part of the industrial bourgeoisie—remained true to a program of reformism based on the support of the upper strata of the working class and sections of the petty bourgeoisie. F. S. Nitti's group—including the

Milanese newspaper *La Corriere della sera* and another part of the industrialists—argued that the State should be based on "a rural democracy in the South and the 'healthy' part of northern industry."

In commenting on this struggle between bourgeois factions, Gramsci made a point rarely presented by other Communists of this period; possibly here we can see the hesitant origins of the later popular front policy. "This struggle—which, willingly or not, indicates a fracture in the bloc of conservative and anti-proletarian forces—can under certain circumstances favor the development and the affirmation of the *proletariat as a third and decisive factor* in a political situation."[104]

Gramsci singled out the "crowning glory" of Fascism as its tendency toward imperialism. Fascism would attempt to resolve "the crisis of Italian society outside the national field." Gramsci ominously concluded: "In this are the germs of a war, which will ostensibly be fought for Italian expansion but in which Fascist Italy will actually be an instrument in the hands of one of the imperialist groups struggling for domination of the world."[105]

Gramsci and the Comintern, 1925–26

In some ways the Lyons Theses, dependent on the decisions of the Fifth Plenum for much of their content, may be regarded as one aspect of Gramsci's relationship to the Communist International. Although he had attended the Fifth Plenum, his relations with the International were not always smooth during the last period of his active political life. He did believe that the PCI had its responsibilities toward the Comintern, but the reverse was just as true. Therefore, he did not hesitate to speak out whenever he was convinced that Moscow was betraying those responsibilities.

In early 1925 Dmitrii Manuilsky, the "Pelican," wrote a pamphlet ("Bolshevization of the Communist Parties") containing a criticism of the PCI for its alleged tendency to rely on illegal methods rather than open political activity. The Pelican, in the true spirit of "bolshevization," urged that the Italians take a lesson from the Russian Bolshevik Party, which, "on the eve of October 17, 1905, succeeded in breaking out of the police barriers that were suffocating it."[106] Gramsci replied with a sharp and uncompromising letter to the ECCI. He pointed out that the PCI had tripled its membership from April 1924 to April 1925, and, alone among the proletarian parties, maintained its vote in the elections of 1924 at nearly the levels of 1921. He also dared to suggest that the PCI, confronted with a reactionary outburst, faced problems that the Russian Bolshevik Party had never needed to resolve.

Let us therefore ask Comrade Manuilsky for a bit more caution and precision in formulating judgments on our Party like those published by him. It is absurd for responsible comrades like Manuilsky to make assertions so devoid of foundation in an essay that should help form the opinion of delegates to an international conference [probably the Fifth Plenum of the ECCI, March–April 1925].[107]

On October 14, 1926—when Stalin and his new allies faced the combined opposition of Trotsky, Zinoviev, and Kamenev—Gramsci, in the name of the "political office" of the PCI, sent a long letter to the leaders of the Communist Party of the Soviet Union.[108] It is a rich letter, containing a capsule theory of relations between the CPSU and the "brother" parties. The tone was both deferential and anguished, for Gramsci feared that the International and the Italian Party would be torn apart by the great struggle between the Russian leaders:

Comrades, in these nine years of world history, you have been the organizing and motivating element for the revolutionary forces in all countries. In the whole history of mankind, there has been no precedent for the scope and complexity of your work. But today you are destroying your work. You are degrading, and running the risk of nullifying, the ruling function that the Communist Party of the USSR conquered through Lenin's work. To us, it seems that the violent passion of Russian questions is making you lose sight of the international aspects of the Russian questions themselves, making you forget that your duties as Russian militants can and must be fulfilled only within the framework of the interests of the proletarian International.[109]

Gramsci did not defend Trotsky and his comrades; rather he called their opposition an attack on the "hegemony of the proletariat" in Russia. Yet, in his own way, he had to defend them:

Comrades Zinoviev, Trotsky, and Kamenev have made powerful contributions toward educating us for the Revolution. At times they have corrected us energetically and severely; they have been our teachers. To them especially we turn, as those most responsible for causing the present situation, because we want to be certain that the majority of the Central Committee of the USSR does not intend to overly exploit its victory in the struggle and is disposed to avoid excessive measures.[110]

Togliatti tells us that he immediately consigned the letter to Nikolai Bukharin, then on the Secretariat of the International, who in turn called it to the attention of the Political Office. Humbert-Droz, the Hummingbird, was sent to Italy to explain the situation to the PCI's executive committee.

This letter to the CPSU was Gramsci's last important political act as a free man. Following the attempted assassination of Mussolini on October 31, 1926, the Fascists passed the Exceptional Laws, which ordered the immediate dissolution of all opposition parties. They established a "Special Tribunal" for the "defense of the State" and carried out mass arrests. Gramsci, though a deputy in the Italian Parliament, was among the first to face the Tribunal. On the advice of the prosecutor, who urged that "We must stop this brain from functioning for twenty years," Gramsci was sentenced to twenty years, four months, and five days of imprisonment, on six different charges of treason. He was actually confined for more than ten years, most of it at the Penal House of Turi, near Bari.

Turi di Bari, 1930

At the end of 1964, *Rinascita* published a remarkable document that for the first time gives us some direct knowledge of Gramsci's views on current politics during his imprisonment: a report originally sent by Athos Lisa to PCI headquarters in March 1933. It summarizes a number of political discussions held by Gramsci with his fellow prisoners at Turi in late 1930. Lisa, a Tuscan Communist of some importance, was among those present, and wrote this report shortly after his release from prison. Other former political prisoners, Giovanni Lay and Gustavo Trombetti, have since added their memoirs to Lisa's.[111] According to Franco Ferri, who has written an important introduction to Lisa's report, others who participated in the discussions were Enrico Tulli, formerly a reporter for *L'Unità*; Giovanni Lay, a Sardinian Communist; Francesco Lo Sardo, previously the PCI representative from Messina in the Chamber of Deputies; two other Communists, Bruno Spadoni and Angelo Scucchia; and two anarchists, Piacentini and Ceresia, who were "particularly close to Gramsci."[112]

The discussions took place over a period of several weeks. Lay recollects that all seemed to go well until Gramsci suddenly decided to suspend them for six months. He was convinced, by "false information" says Lisa, that the work was only causing factionalism among the political prisoners.[113] Lay, however, insists that Gramsci's information was not false: "Often, too often in my opinion, [the cellmates] descended to gossip, and even calumny, with personal opinions of Gramsci that sometimes went as far as denigration."[114] Angelo Scucchia—in Lay's judgment, the most reprehensible in this respect—claimed that Gramsci's views had become "social-democratic, that Gramsci was no longer a Communist, that he had become a Crocean by opportunism, that his sabotage should be denounced to the Party, and that meanwhile he ought to be thrown out of the exercise-yard."[115] When Gramsci learned of these denunciations, he immediately suspended the talks.

In part, the origin of these violent disagreements was in Gramsci's own personality, or rather his projection of it at this time. His total dedication to his work, his hopes of accomplishing something of lasting importance, his desperate attempts to avoid the moral degeneration that usually accompanies long imprisonment—all prompted him to resume the behavior that he often likened to the actions of a "bear in a cave." Before coming to Turi, Lay had learned that "Gramsci did not have an easy temperament; that he was irritable, would not admit weaknesses, conceded nothing to feelings; that he was a great political brain and a great revolutionary leader, with whom it was difficult to maintain relations that were not political."[116]

No doubt there was also jealousy because Gramsci, after persistent demands going all the way to the "head of the government" (Mussolini), finally received official permission to obtain certain books and to have pen, ink, and paper in his cell. Gramsci had constant trouble maintaining these privileges; indeed, in 1933, his permitted writing periods were reduced to two hours a day.[117] Nonetheless, some of Gramsci's comrades who were unwilling or unable to make use of the laborious and almost interminable legal procedures for obtaining such rights were resentful. Indeed, they found his whole "legalitarian" approach extremely irritating. Many of them were ready to challenge prison regulations on any occasion, and commit impulsive acts that naturally led to isolation, bread-and-water diets, and deprivation of "privileges" like the daily period of fresh air. Such *beaux gestes* were always distasteful to Gramsci, but under prison circumstances he considered them actually harmful. Many of the prisoners with shorter terms than his would be released in a few years; their lives and health would still be important to the Party.[118]

But there were more important reasons for dissension among the Communists at Turi than personal feelings. Gramsci's ideas as presented in Lisa's statement were objectively out of tune with the Party line in those years, and consciously criticized many ideas that characterized the program emerging from the Ninth Plenum of the ECCI (February 1928), the Sixth Comintern Congress (July–September 1928), and the Tenth Plenum (July 1929). The policies of the PCI had conformed with this program.[119] This was the "Third Period" of the Comintern, during which it held that the predicted economic crisis of capitalism would bring a rapid leftward movement of the masses. In such a situation, social democracy, or "social Fascism," became the vanguard of reaction, and all "democratic illusions" or "intermediate stages" between bourgeois rule and the dictatorship of the proletariat must be rejected out of hand.

Gramsci, in his prison talks of 1930, repeatedly attacked certain "maximalist" attitudes allegedly still prevalent in the Party:

Too often we are afraid of all those designations that are not part of the old maximalist vocabulary. We think of the proletarian revolution as a wholly completed thing that happens at a certain time. Any tactical action not in tune with the subjectivism of the dreamers is held to be a general deformation of the tactics and strategy of the revolution.[120]

Gramsci then had the temerity to suggest an Italian Constituent Assembly as the immediate political goal, or at least slogan, of the PCI (to the typical "maximalist," said Gramsci, the idea of a *Costituente* was like a "punch in the eye"). This goal was examined first and above all as a tactic for winning "allies of the proletariat." In 1930 the Party itself had almost been obliterated in Italy, although the resolute (at the time, some said reckless) action of Togliatti, Longo, Camilla Ravera, and Pietro Secchia soon reconstructed its organizational framework and reestablished its presence there. But in the meantime, Gramsci argued that since the Party had been deprived of its organization and could not engage in legal activities, the "relatively rapid" achievement of working-class predominance was no longer possible. Thus class alliances became extremely important; yet certain Italian conditions made it "extremely delicate and difficult" for the proletariat to construct these alliances. Italy was a predominantly agricultural country, but it had an industrialized nucleus in the Turin-Milan-Genoa triangle. In addition, great regional differences, especially the North-South problem, had created unusual differentiation "even among the social strata of the working class." Thus class allies were difficult to find in Italy, but absolutely necessary. Without them, "any serious revolutionary movement is impossible for the proletariat."

Under the prevailing circumstances, the peasantry and the rural petty bourgeoisie were not prepared to accept the Communist Party, with its *full* program, as their party. They could be won to this program only "by stages." By raising the "constitutional and institutional problem" as a first step, the PCI could make common cause with all Italian anti-Fascist parties. The Party must take this step immediately if it wished to lead such a coalition.[121]

Gramsci, like any Communist of this period, wholly accepted the dictatorship of the proletariat, but its ultimate achievement depended upon the proper use of intermediate tactics: "On the Party's ability to maneuver in these phases of the struggle, on the level of its political capacity, will depend the possibilities of going beyond the intermediate slogans that mark the stages of thawing in the social strata to be won over." Even if current conditions did weaken the strength of Fascism in Italy—a view then advanced by the PCI and the Comintern—the Party would still be faced with great difficulties. At most, it could rely on about 6,000 organizational leaders on a provincial level.[122] Under these circumstances, the most favorable outcome that the Party could expect would be a "period of transition" rather than a direct conquest of State power. Therefore, the PCI should adopt the slogan of a "constitutional assembly" and use it as "the basis for an agreement with the anti-Fascist parties." Future political developments would give the Party ample time and opportunity to demonstrate the inability of reformist programs to meet the fundamental needs of the working class and its allies.

Gramsci especially emphasized that the world economic crisis, or rather the form it took in Italy, was not a sufficient stimulus for the onset of a revolutionary period like that of 1917–21: the Party was in no condition to force the situation, although the crisis would provide ideal circumstances for launching the campaign for a constituent assembly. Characteristically, he placed little importance on the "objective conditions" for revolution, such as the existence of a great economic depression. In any case, "objective conditions for the proletarian revolution have existed in Europe for more than fifty years."[123] The principal requisite was to "be more political, to know how to use the political element, to be less afraid of making politics."

Gramsci was thus asserting the importance of "immediate democratic objectives" even more forthrightly than at the Congress of Lyons. As Ferri puts it, Gramsci believed such a program was needed to establish "new political relations, within which the Communist Party could extend its influence, affirm its own program of struggle, confront the programs of other parties, acquire a mass influence, and exercise its national ruling function."[124] He evidently believed also that this program was essential to the Italian revolution, whatever the prevailing views of the Comintern might be. In 1930, the Communist movement was not ready for a change like that. But a few years later, the entire leadership of the PCI accepted this line, which culminated in August 1934 in the pact of united action between the PCI and the PSI; a year later the program of the Popular Front was established at the Seventh Congress of the Comintern.[125]

Luigi Cortesi has recently observed that Lisa's report provides a missing link in the history of the PCI.[126] There is indeed a continuity from the Ordine Nuovo period to the political letters of 1923-24, from the Lyons Theses to the Popular Front. Opponents of this kind of Communism have denounced it as "opportunism" and "reformism," but others have interpreted it as a "realistic" response of the Communist movement to the economic, political, and cultural conditions existing in modern capitalist states.

Part IV

The Quaderni del Carcere

9. The Nature and Tasks of the Political Party

Non credere che io non continui a studiare,
o che mi avvilisca perchè a un certo punto
non posso condurre più avanti le mie ricerche.
Non ho perduto ancora una certa capa-
cità inventiva nel senso che ogni cosa im-
portante che leggo mi eccita a pensare:
come potrei costruire un articolo su questo
argomento?

—*Gramsci, September 7, 1931*

"Prison," observed Gramsci, "is a poor place to study." Yet almost from the beginning of his confinement he attempted to organize his life so that he could study and write. By March 1927 he had already selected several topics for development, chief among them "a study of the Italian intellectuals, their groupings according to cultural currents, etc." Gramsci wrote his sister-in-law that this interest had developed from his "hasty and very superficial essay on Southern Italy and the importance of B. Croce." Now Gramsci wished to fully explore this theme, but "from a 'disinterested' point of view, *für ewig.*"[1]

Conditions for serious study in prison were almost insurmountably difficult, with censorship the worst problem. Twenty-one of Gramsci's notebooks bear the stamp of prison authorities; to continue writing, he had to almost completely abandon traditional Marxist terminology and alter the names of most world Communist leaders: Marxism itself became "the philosophy of praxis"; the dictatorship of the proletariat, "State-force"; Lenin, "the greatest modern theoretician of the philosophy of praxis," or simply "Ilici"; and Stalin, "Giuseppe Bessarione." The consequent scarcity of references to specific events and persons sometimes gives the Notebooks an abstract air that was completely foreign to Gramsci's nature. Moreover, bibliographic materials, even the books and periodicals Gramsci was authorized to receive, were sometimes arbitrarily withheld from him. These conditions inevitably produced a set of "prison notebooks," not exhaustive treatises. Still, Eugenio Garin has asserted that even the more fragmentary writings of the Quaderni have a "consistency of themes" stemming from the "profound unitary context" of Gramsci's work.[2]

The Quaderni del Carcere were published between 1948 and 1951; by 1957 nearly 400,000 copies had been sold, an astronomical figure by Italian standards.[3] The Quaderni are almost certainly responsible for much of Italian Communism's postwar success, notably among intellectuals; commentaries on them are already numerous, and it seems certain that Gramsci's work, over the decades to come, will develop a whole literature as footnotes to the original text.* Though still available for the most part only in Italian, these prison notebooks may eventually be recognized as one of the masterpieces of twentieth-century political thought. The size of the work—2,848 manuscript pages—is monumental, its insight is impressive, and its major themes are of special interest to intellectuals of the present day. Luigi Russo, the late Croceian literary critic, said:

[Gramsci] must now be considered among the most notable thinkers of contemporary Europe. . . . He belongs not only to the Communist Party, but also to European thought. . . . Gramsci's thought, notwithstanding its contact with the Eastern world, is completely infused with the Western spirit. We might also say, making a concession to the *idola tribus* and the *idola fori,* that it is a thought essentially rooted in the Italian tradition.[4]

Russo clearly indicates why Gramsci's work has strongly affected Italian intellectuals. Marx, and most leaders of the world Marxist movement, had drawn primarily on experience in England, France, Germany, and Russia. Gramsci was the first Italian to seriously apply the Marxist interpretation to all aspects of Italian history and culture. Both the form and content of his thought are much more familiar to "Western" intellectuals than the work of other Marxists. In great part, this is because Gramsci dealt primarily with the "superstructure"—the whole complex of political, social, and cultural institutions and ideas—rather than its "economic foundation." This choice was deliberate; Gramsci believed that "cultural" problems were especially important in periods following revolutionary activity, as in Europe after 1815 and again after 1921. At such times, he said, there are no pitched battles between classes: the class struggle becomes a "war of position," and the "cultural front" the principal area of conflict.

But a "cultural" battle was not easy: Marxism had retained too many elements of materialism, determinism, and economism. "In its

---

* A few years ago a British writer, Gwynn Williams, asserted that the Quaderni established Gramsci as "the most significant thinker in the enigmatic tradition of 'liberal Communism,' and have created what is virtually a Gramsci cult in his homeland" (Williams, p. 586). For a good example of the kind of reaction produced by the Quaderni in Italy today, see the Appendix.

most common form of economistic superstition, the philosophy of praxis loses its cultural expansiveness in the upper sphere of the intellectual group, however much it acquires among the masses and among mediocre intellectuals who do not want to tire their brains but wish to appear very shrewd."[5]

Gramsci's Marxism was a radical historicism, differing greatly from "orthodox" schools. Bukharin's work, he thought, especially suffered from determinism, mechanicalism, and "vulgar" materialism.[6] Marxism could become a self-sufficient philosophy only by emphasizing its dialectical and historical aspects, by "undertaking the same reduction of Croce's philosophy as the first theoretician of the philosophy of praxis did of Hegel's."[7] Only through serious work of this kind would Marxists learn to avoid simplistic attempts at solving complex problems. An all too frequent example of current Marxist thought was its blanket statement that the "anatomy of society is determined by its economy."[8]

Although he declared that Karl Marx, "the writer of *concrete* historical works," was not guilty of such naïveté, Gramsci carried disagreement with economic determinism much further than Marx. Material forces as "content" and ideologies as "form" are a "historical bloc"; material forces are inconceivable without form, and ideologies merely individual dabbling without material forces.[9] An ideology like Marxism, aware of the organic relationship between "structure" and "superstructure," can achieve a reciprocity between the two. The Marxist intellectual develops the principles and the problems created by the masses' practical activity, and the conclusions of this theoretical activity are then used to change the practical realm. The change produces a new and higher praxis, which in turn brings up new problems for theoretical consideration.[10]

Gramsci's "voluntaristic" approach to fundamental Marxist problems—perfectly consonant with his thought in the Ordine Nuovo period and in 1923–26—makes his work especially appealing to intellectuals, many of whom had thought Marxism wholly deterministic. Moreover, he is able to express his Marxist thought in the language of other philosophies, often exposing the weak points of those systems by comparing them, in their own language, with corresponding Marxist concepts.[11]

There is a tendency to place Gramsci's work, described as "left-wing idealism," midway between Croce and Marx or between totalitarianism and historicism.[12] Undoubtedly, Gramsci's extreme historicism sometimes led him away from the opinions generally accepted by Marxists. Thus he implied that economic laws are not really laws in the "naturalistic sense," but "laws of tendency" in the historicistic sense, recognized because the bourgeoisie had formed a world market "dense" enough for economic tendencies to be isolated and studied.[13] Gramsci also doubted the wisdom of "mechanically" asserting the objective reality of the external world—as though the world could be understood apart from human history.[14]

Nevertheless, Gramsci had no intention of revising Marx, and his final conclusions are rarely very different from those of other Marxist thinkers. He had been accused of "voluntarism" and "idealism" since the days of La Città futura; however, such accusations did not prevent him from rising to leadership in the PCI—with the explicit approval of Lenin and the Comintern. He thought of himself as carrying on Lenin's work by continuing to purify the philosophy of deterministic elements, and Marx's by relating himself to Croce in the way Marx was related to Hegel.

Gramsci wrote the Quaderni within the broad outlines indicated above. Because he emphasized the importance of the "cultural front," he devoted many of his notes to sweeping analyses of problems in philosophy and literature; and even a brief summary of the entire Quaderni would require a book to itself. Since our chief concern is with Gramsci's political and intellectual life, we shall examine only two major concepts from his notebooks, concepts that Gramsci himself considered closely related to his actual political activity. The remainder of this chapter will deal with his views on the political party, and Chapter Ten will outline his conception of the historical role of Italian intellectuals.

The Nature and Tasks of the Political Party

Some years ago Palmiro Togliatti observed that "Gramsci was a political theorist, but he was above all a practical politician."[15] This remark might surprise the reader, considering the intense intellectuality of Gramsci's writing. Yet none of his more important work— even work that seems abstract and objective—can be understood outside the context of the political struggle in Italy during the first quarter of this century. This is especially true of his analysis of political parties, for him the principal and indispensable agents for social change.*

* Much of Gramsci's commentary on the nature of political parties is collected in the fifth volume of his works, Note sul Machiavelli, sulla politica, e sullo stato moderno. For Gramsci, the political party was the "Modern Prince," and he regarded Machiavelli as the chief figure in the rich tradition of Italian political thought. See pp. 209–12 of this work.

Gramsci began his analysis of political parties in a fairly orthodox Marxist manner: "The first principle is that there do exist governors and governed, rulers and ruled."[16] This simple point was not always accepted, even in Gramsci's generation. Some critics insisted that in modern democratic states quantitative majorities controlled the direction of politics. The effect of a ballot on the actual conduct of the State apparatus, especially in Europe, is no simple matter, given the detachment of bureaucracy and administration from the legislature. And, as Gramsci noted, "Counting 'votes' is the terminal manifestation of a long process, in which the greatest influence belongs to those who 'dedicate to the State and to the nation their best forces' "; in other words, those in power.[17] Under normal conditions it would indeed be surprising "if this presumed group of *optimati,* possessing unlimited material force, did not win the support of the majority." If it does not, it is either inept or totally unrepresentative of the "national" interests.[18]

Classes are historical realities, and the various political parties are their "nomenclature."[19] Still, political parties rarely, if ever, represent one class totally and exclusively; a party stands for its class under "certain given conditions." Thus the progress of its group will normally come about with the "consensus and aid of allied groups, if not even of decisively opposed groups."[20] Therefore, a party must involve itself actively in the "public arena," manipulating the real world to reach an "ideal" world.

Sometimes, though, what seems a political party is often much less. In many countries the basic parties, from struggle or other causes, break into factions, each assuming the name of "party" and often becoming an independent party.[21] Here Gramsci clearly recalls the fragmentation of the left-wing Italian parties following World War I; nonetheless, the same processes occur in other parties. Often the "intellectual general staff" of a movement does not belong to any faction, "but operates as though it were a ruling force in itself, superior to the parties; and sometimes it is even believed to be such by the public."[22] A great newspaper frequently plays such a role: Gramsci mentions the *Times* of London and the *Corriere della sera* of Milan as examples.[23]

In a totalitarian regime the role of opposition parties is eliminated by definition. Nevertheless, political activity is not absent under such circumstances; it is merely "indirect": "If legal opposition parties do not exist, de facto parties and legally irrepressible tendencies always exist." In "parties" of this kind, however, "cultural functions predominate, and political questions are disguised as cultural questions," a poor way to deal with politics, but inevitable under the circumstances. For that matter, the totalitarian party itself is not really political. It may have technical, propagandistic, police, or cultural functions, but it does not openly represent the values of its social group or groups in political struggle.

Thus two kinds of parties avoid immediate political action: the elite type, composed of intellectuals who, from an "independent" position, formulate the general ideology of related parties that are often fractions of the same basic party; and the more recent mass totalitarian party, whose members display only generic loyalty of a military type to their political center. The "mass" is simply for backing, and is placated by moral sermons and messianic myths pointing to a golden age.[24]

Gramsci placed a high value on the political party in the life of modern states. There is nothing conspiratorial or sectarian in his view; the party is above all an instrument of education and civilization:

If the State represents the coercive and punitive arm of the country's juridical rule, then the parties, which represent the spontaneous adherence of an elite to that rule (considered as a collective organization to which the whole mass must be educated), must show in their internal life that they have assimilated as principles of moral conduct the rules that in the State are legal obligations. In the parties, necessity has already become freedom, and from that derives the great political value ... of internal party discipline.... From this point of view, the parties may be considered as schools of the life of the State.[25]

Political parties are an integral part of the legal, political, and social structure of a country at a given time: thus they must, among other things, accept the "rules of the game." Even if a party is—like the Communists—working toward a "higher end," the task begins within the State's "present juridical rule." This rule, like any human institution, is not "permanent," but meanwhile the party's rank and file must be educated in the rule. By the phrase "In the parties, necessity has already become freedom," Gramsci means that only through the organization and discipline of a party can a "subaltern" class achieve its goals.

Party discipline is important to Gramsci, but discipline is

certainly not a passive and supine acceptance of orders, a mechanical execution of assignments (though even that would sometimes be necessary: during an already decided and initiated action, for example), but a conscious and clear understanding of the aims to be realized. Discipline in this sense does not annul individual personality . . . , but merely limits the will and irresponsible impulsiveness.[26]

In evaluating the role of party discipline, everything depends on the "origin of the power that enforces the discipline":

If the authority is a specialized technical function, and not an "arbitrary" force or an external imposition, discipline is a necessary element of democratic order and freedom. A specialized technical function exists when the authority is exercised within one socially (or nationally) homogeneous group; when it is exercised by one group over another group, discipline will be autonomous and free for the first, but not for the second.[27]

In a way, Gramsci's view of discipline (or democratic centralism) is not very different from the Church's view of salvation. He himself (though perhaps with tongue in cheek) quotes from the Catholic Alessandro Manzoni's *Pentecoste*: "The individual 'willingly' accepts the divine will."[28]

One other aspect of the political party was of extreme interest to Gramsci, given the conditions under which he wrote the *Quaderni*: the assurance of his Party's survival. More generally, the question might be: "What are the conditions that historically justify the existence of any political party?" First, the party must have a solid base in a particular social group (parties as the "nomenclature" of classes). In addition, the organization must have a political tradition, a sense of historical continuity similar to the kind of permanence normally identified with the State itself (*spirito statale*). Each member must be aware of intangible forces, "which are nevertheless felt to be operating and active, accounted for as if they were 'materially' and bodily present." The solidarity of a movement depends upon consciousness of its historical continuity: "We must feel solidarity with the old men of today, who represent the past still living among us, with which we must come to terms, and also with the children and growing generations, for whom we feel responsible."[29]

A party justifies its historical existence when it develops three basic elements: (1) the rank and file, "a diffuse element of ordinary men whose participation is characterized by discipline and faith, not by a creative or organizational spirit"; (2) leadership, "the principal cohesive element, centralized in the national field and developing efficiency and power in an ensemble of forces that are worthless individually"; (3) party cadres, "a middle element that articulates the first with the second element by putting them in contact 'physically,' morally, and intellectually."[30]

Gramsci emphasizes that a party cannot exist with the rank and file and the cadres alone; leadership is of primary importance: "We speak of captains without an army, but in reality it is easier to form an army than to find captains. It is surely true that an already existing army will be destroyed if it lacks captains; whereas a group of captains, cooperative and in agreement on common ends, will not be slow in forming an army, even where none exists."[31] Thus the presence of leadership will ensure the existence of a whole party structure. Competent leaders must be able to demonstrate "that necessary and sufficient conditions already exist so that certain tasks can, and therefore should, be resolved historically (*should*, because any failure in one's historical duty increases disorder and prepares graver catastrophes)."[32] Gramsci denies that immediate economic crises produce revolutions directly. They can only create a more favorable environment "for the diffusion of certain ways of thinking."[33] Competent leadership is responsible for exploiting this more favorable environment.

Here we have characteristic examples of the dialectical unity of objective and subjective factors in Gramsci's historical analysis. Many of Gramsci's contemporaries regarded him as a champion of idealism or "voluntarism," in opposition to an older Marxist tradition that was supposedly a form of "historical determinism." Gramsci himself merely thought he was further developing the "anti-economistic" ideas of Lenin.[34] Gramsci was definitely a Leninist, but he emphasized "voluntarism" in his analysis of the political party more consistently than Lenin. Moreover, Gramsci's style and approach to this question were naturally more attuned to Western intellectual traditions:

If it is true that man can be conceived only as historically determined man— that is, that he has developed and lives in certain conditions, in a specific social complex or ensemble of social relations—can one conceive of sociology as only the study of those conditions and the laws that regulate their development? Since one cannot exclude the will and the initiative of men themselves, this concept can only be false. Consider the problem of "science." Is not science itself "political activity," and political thought, insofar as it transforms men, makes them different from what they were before?[35]

Gramsci insisted on a thoroughly non-mechanical interpretation of Party doctrine: "Ideology" or doctrine should be considered not something artificially superimposed ("like a suit, and not like the skin, which is organically produced"), but something historical, developing through incessant struggle. A party must integrate three elements: its doctrine, the specific historical nature of its personnel, and the "real historical movement," the dynamics of the particular culture in which the party operates. "The first and second elements can be controlled by the associated and deliberating will [the Party]. The third element constantly reacts with the other two and causes an incessant struggle, theoretical and practical, to raise the organism [the Party] to ever more elevated and refined collective consciousness."[36]

But if doctrine must be continually developed in ever-changing circumstances, then we cannot expect any "specific conception of life and the world" to have an *intrinsically* superior capacity for foresight.[37] This statement seems a striking admission of futility, coming from a Marxist theoretician and Communist political leader—a negation of Gramsci's own views on the importance of the creative will in history. However, Gramsci's interpretation of foresight is far from either futility or determinism:

Foresight means nothing but clearly seeing the present and past as movement: that is, precisely identifying the fundamental and permanent aspects of the process. But it is absurd to imagine a purely "objective" foresight. The man with foresight has, in reality, a definite program in mind; and foresight is an aid to reaching that goal. This does not mean that foresight must always be arbitrary and gratuitous, or always tendentious. Indeed, one may say that the objective aspects of foresight are really objective only insofar as they are connected with a goal: (1) because only passion sharpens the intellect and cooperates to render intuition clearer; (2) because reality comes from applying human will to the society of things (like a machinist and his machine); ignoring any voluntary element, or calculating only *another*'s will as an objective element in the process, mutilates reality itself. Only he who strongly wills identifies the elements necessary to realize his will.[38]

This judgment led Gramsci to condemn the popular idea of the "realistic" politician as one who deals only with "effectual reality," and not reality as it "ought to be." A true statesman has a program; he wishes to create new relations of forces, and therefore must consider what "ought to be." He bases himself on effectual reality—but what is effectual reality? It is not something static or immobile, but a pattern of forces continually moving and changing equilibrium. A man must apply his will to create a new equilibrium of concrete forces, selecting the force he sees as progressive and working to strengthen it; then he is working with effectual reality, but is able to dominate it.[39]

Gramsci's political ideas were not abstract reflections, but derived from his own political experience before his imprisonment; and opposition to the reformist point of view was a constant stand in his political and intellectual life. The reformist, asserts Gramsci, does not conceive of the Socialist movement as independent and autonomous, but as part of a larger movement, bourgeois democracy, in which its task is reforming "certain presumed or real evils."[40] He assumes, in effect, that a "natural" political order exists, which needs no more than adjustment or retouching. In a crisis, as in 1921–22 in Italy, the reformist leaders return to their "real" party (the party representing the "natural" order) and leave the masses, who have very different political interests, disoriented and ineffective. Therefore Gramsci insists—in the light of his "theoretical truth" that every class has one unique party—that a party should be founded on a "monolithic" basis, and not on secondary questions, "on the basis of an autonomous conception of the world and the role of the represented class in history." Elsewhere, Gramsci analyzes the "marginality" of reformism more brutally. He tells the fable of a beaver pursued by hunters who wished to cut off its testicles to extract certain medications. What does the beaver do to solve this predicament? He himself cuts off his testicles to save his life![41]

Here Gramsci suggests why there was no adequate defense against Fascism. The reformist leaders were paralyzed by their "fatalistic and mechanical conception of history," and did not recognize the *autonomous* interests of the class they presumably represented. In reality, they had "no comprehension of its fundamental needs, its aspirations, its latent energies."[42] As far back as 1917 (the Florence Conference), reformist leaders had accused Gramsci of voluntarism, in opposition to their own declared determinism. However, Gramsci noted that if reformism were opposed to voluntarism, it ought to appreciate "spontaneity," that is, the unpremeditated political action of the masses. Instead, the reformist leaders regarded the " 'spontaneous' as an inferior thing, not worthy of consideration, not even worthy of being analyzed." For Gramsci, "spontaneous" events, especially those in 1919–20, clearly proved the ineptness of the PSI in those years. The very spontaneity of these events, and their repudiation by the Party leadership, induced the climate of "panic" that enabled the ruling classes to unite in a more effective repression of these and other events.[43]

Gramsci asserted that "pure" spontaneity did not really exist. In the "most spontaneous" movements, "the elements of 'conscious leadership' are merely invisible. They have not left any ascertainable traces."[44] It follows that the most "peripheral" of the "subaltern" classes will characteristically express themselves "spontaneously," since they have no effective leadership or class consciousness.[45] Here Gramsci seems to employ the term "spontaneity" in a negative sense. But elsewhere he uses it in referring to the actual ideas and values held by a working class that has not yet been educated and disciplined. However crude and contradictory these notions may be, they cannot be neglected by a responsible leadership. For this reason, the Turin factory-council movement in 1919–20 completely opposed the scornful rejection of spontaneity by the reformist leaders. The Turin movement "applied itself to real men":

"Spontaneity" was not neglected, much less scorned: it was *educated*, directed, purified of everything that hindered its fusion—in a living, historically efficient way—with modern theory [i.e., Marxism]. The leaders themselves sometimes spoke of the "spontaneity" of the movement; it was right that they spoke of it: ... it gave the mass a "theoretical" consciousness of creating historical and institutional values and being a founder of States. The union of "spontaneity" and "conscious leadership," or "discipline," is the real political action of subaltern classes, since it is mass politics and not simply an adventure of groups who address themselves to the mass.[46]

Gramsci's long struggle with Bordiga also led him to consider the effects of "extremism" (or "sectarianism") on political parties. Many of his remarks on reformism are also applicable to extremism. Extremism, however, is rigidly averse to compromise because of its "iron conviction that there are objective historical laws, similar to natural laws"; this combines with an almost religious fatalism.[47] If one believes that favorable conditions must inevitably develop, then of course "any voluntary initiative aimed at arranging these situations according to a plan" is useless, perhaps harmful. This view is a form of "economism," the belief that economic conditions irrevocably determine the human situation. Yet this thinking was fallacious precisely because it did not take account of the "real economy," the mass ideological facts that always lie behind mass economic facts. Political initiative is always needed to "free the economic thrust from the shackles of traditional politics," to change the political direction of certain forces that must be absorbed in order to form a new "economic-political, historical bloc, without internal contradictions."[48] Gramsci condemns "economism," a form of sectarianism, in "economic" language: if consciousness follows economic realities, then the politician must repair the gap by raising the level of consciousness!

The sectarian confuses the Party's "technical organization" with the needs of the real historical movement of which the party is merely an instrument.[49] Thus "the sectarian will extol the petty internal events [of party life]," whereas the historian or politician will "emphasize the real efficiency of the Party ... in contributing to events, or even in preventing other events from occurring."[50] The irresponsible sectarian neglect of the represented class's actual condition causes a wholly unwarranted optimism: "One looks on the 'will to believe' as a condition of victory, which would not be mistaken if it were not conceived mechanically and did not become a self-deception" (that is, confuse mass and leaders and lower the leader to the level of the most backward follower).[51] Characteristic of this self-deception is a tendency to "belittle the adversary." But, asks Gramsci, if this adversary presently dominates you—although you are "superior" to him—"then how did he succeed in dominating you?"[52]

Finally, the sectarian politician is all too ready to resort to arms, although this tendency would seem contradictory to the deterministic sectarian view. The answer is that the extremist believes that the "intervention of the will is useful for destruction, but not for reconstruction." A little push, as it were, will facilitate the final victory of history's underlying currents. While coercion is certainly unavoidable in some cases, Gramsci did not view it as even theoretically desirable in creating a fusion of related forces: "The only real possibility is compromise; force may be employed against enemies, but not against a part of oneself that one wants to assimilate rapidly and from whom 'good will' and enthusiasm are required."[53]

10. The Historical Role of Italian Intellectuals

*Autocoscienza critica significa storicamente
e politicamente creazione di una elite di intellettuali:
una massa umana non si "distingue" e non diventa
indipendente "per se," senza organizzarsi (in senso lato)
e non c'e organizzazione senza intellettuali.*

—Gramsci, *"Il Materialismo storico"*

Types of Intellectuals

Gramsci's analysis of parties may serve as an introduction to his abiding interest in the role of intellectuals, for him (as for others in our own time) a key cultural and political question. He was dissatisfied with previous criteria for classifying groups as "intellectual" or "non-intellectual" because he believed these criteria were based almost exclusively on comparative evaluations of the cerebral activity involved in any act. On this basis, everyone would be an "intellectual" to some extent: every man, apart from his profession, "exhibits some intellectual activity, . . . shares a world-view, has a conscious line of moral conduct, and therefore contributes to sustaining or modifying a conception of the world."[1] A more precise and perhaps more fruitful method for classifying intellectuals would describe their "social function."

From this "functional" point of view, Gramsci considers as intellectuals all those who exercise "technical" or "directive" capacities in society—e.g., industrial managers, administrators and bureaucrats, politicians, and "organizers of culture" like artists and scholars.[2] Some of these categories are only adapted to the basic activities of certain social groups. Thus industrial managers and foremen are "specialists" in organizing industry for the capitalists. But society also needs men of a larger, broader, or more "political" vision—in short "directors," who will organize society in general to "create the most favorable conditions for the expansion of the class" whose interests they serve.[3]

Besides this "vertical" distinction of intellectual types (the special-

ists and the directors), Gramsci also makes a "horizontal" distinction
between "traditional" and "organic" intellectuals.[4] The "traditional" group is the totality of creative artists and learned men in society,
those who are usually thought of as "intellectuals." Their outstanding characteristic is a feeling that they represent a "historical continuity uninterrupted by even the most radical and complicated
changes of social and political systems."[5] This attachment to past
intellectuals has important political consequences: for example, traditional intellectuals feel that they are "autonomous, independent
of the dominant social group."[6]

Gramsci does not attempt to establish the actual degree of coordination between "traditional" intellectuals and the social group that
dominates economic production; indeed, he would have rejected any
such effort as the purest abstraction. But he does assert that, generally
speaking, this relationship is not "immediate," but "mediated" by
many elements in society's superstructure.[7] For example, the "traditional" intellectuals of the ecclesiastical hierarchy, as conscious
heirs of the apostolic tradition, have never completely shared the
world-view of the socially and economically dominant classes. Even
so, they achieved—or were granted—a near monopoly of important
social activities, such as education, philosophy, and science.

The "organic" intellectual is more directly related to the economic
structure of his particular society: new categories of them are, in fact,
created by "every social group that originates in the fulfillment of an
essential task of economic production."[8] The "organic intellectual"
gives his class homogeneity and awareness of its own function, in the
economic field and on the social and political levels. The capitalist
entrepreneur brings forth the industrial manager, the political scien-
tist, the cultural innovator, a new law, and so on.[9]

Obviously, the two types of intellectuals are not rigidly separated.
Every intellectual has some connection with a basic social group,
although his interests may not be identical with that group's. For
example, the Church, at any given point in its history, has had to
come to terms with the dominant socio-economic group; nonetheless,
its interests are not *identical* with that group's. The interests of the
organic intellectual are, however, more nearly identical with those of
the dominant class of the time than the traditional intellectual's.
Moreover, when there are many traditional intellectuals hostile to
the interests of the dominant class, the dominant class must campaign
for their "assimilation and 'ideological' conquest."[10]

Under normal conditions, the organic intellectuals of the "historically (and realistically) progressive class" will be able to dominate the intellectuals of subordinate classes. The result is solidarity among all intellectuals, who are held together by "bonds of a psychological order (vanity, etc.) and often of caste (technico-juridical, corporative, etc.)." As long as a dominant class remains progressive and truly advances the interests of most of the society, this "system of solidarity" is likely to continue.[11]

Geography and class origin provide a third basis, especially in Italy, for classifying intellectuals: differing types derive from urban and rural bourgeoisie. The provincial middle classes "specialize" in producing state functionaries and members of the liberal professions, while the metropolitan bourgeoisie produce technicians for industry.[12] Hence, intellectuals of provincial origin are usually traditional, whereas urban intellectuals are mostly organic. Still, traditional southern Italian society also has some organic intellectuals in the so-called *pagliette* (literally, "straw hats"),[13] who act as middlemen between the peasants on the one hand and the landowners and government on the other.[14]

Although every social group develops its own organic intellectuals, the industrial proletariat has relied mostly on "assimilated" traditional intellectuals for leadership. Gramsci always regarded this as one of the chief problems of the working class; a principal aim of Ordine Nuovo was the development of leaders originating in the proletariat, and in the Quaderni he returned to this theme. The initial stage in forming the new organic intellectual would be a technical and industrial education obtained directly in the shops. At the same time the select worker would strive to rise above this level: "From technical work he arrives at technical science and historical humanistic views, without which he would remain a 'specialist' and would not become a 'director' (that is, specialist plus politician)."[15]

In classifying intellectuals, Gramsci distinguished two different areas in the superstructure of society, partly following a distinction already made by Hegel, Giannone, and Vico: "political society" is made up of public institutions and organs of coercion (the army, the courts, the State bureaucracy); "civil society" is the totality of private institutions (Church, schools, political parties).[16] While analyzing political parties, Gramsci had pointed out that they were elements of civil society; unlike "political" elements, they tried to obtain free consent to a given economic situation. Organic intellectuals, part of the dominant class, provide personnel for the coercive organs of political society. Traditional intellectuals, important in civil society, are more likely to reason with the masses and try to obtain "spontaneous" consent to a social order.[17]

The Concept of Hegemony

Gramsci's thoughts on intellectuals led him to consider the Marxist view of the State. As he wrote Tatiana Schucht in 1931, Marxists usually think of the State as "political" society, not as an equilibrium of political society with civil society—the hegemony of one social group over the whole society, "exercised through so-called private organizations, such as the Church, trade unions, schools, etc."[18] A British student of this phase of Gramsci's thought has provided us with a useful introductory definition of the problem: hegemony is "an order in which a certain way of life and thought is dominant, in which one concept of reality is diffused throughout society in all its institutional and private manifestations, informing with its spirit all taste, morality, customs, religious and political principles, and all social relations, particularly in their intellectual and moral connotations."[19] It follows that a hegemony is the predominance, obtained by consent rather than force, of one class or group over other classes. Hegemony is therefore achieved by institutions of civil society.

In its general sense, hegemony refers to the "spontaneous" loyalty that any dominant social group obtains from the masses by virtue of its social and intellectual prestige and its supposedly superior function in the world of production. Thus the Italian bourgeoisie exercised an almost unchallenged hegemony over the workers and peasants from 1870 to 1890, following its successful conclusion of Italian unification and before the birth of the Italian Socialist Party, with a competing and "autonomous" ideology.[20] In a more restricted sense, Gramsci uses the term "hegemony" to refer to projected alliances of a predominant working class with other "subaltern" but "progressive" social elements, especially the peasantry, parts of the petty bourgeoisie, and the intelligentsia. Even in a Socialist state, the term "hegemony" would still be useful to indicate the social (or civil) form of the workers' State based on consent—in contrast to the "dictatorship of the proletariat," based on force, which would be the state's political form.[21]

The development of hegemony depends on the "level of homogeneity, self-consciousness, and organization" reached by a given social class. Mere awareness of economic interests is not sufficient: the class must be convinced that its "own economic interests, in their present and future development, go beyond the corporative circle of a merely economic group, and can and must become the interests of other repressed groups. This is the most purely political phase, which marks the passage from structure to the sphere of complex superstructures." At this point, the class has truly become a party, and it must now fight for its intellectual and moral values, as well as its economic and political ends. The leading class must also coordinate its interests with those of "allied" classes. In this new equilibrium the "interests of the dominant group will prevail," but not to the point of fully achieving only its own "crude" economic interests.[22]

The fundamental assumption behind Gramsci's view of hegemony is that the working class, before it seizes State power, must establish its claim to be a ruling class in the political, cultural, and "ethical" fields.[23] "The founding of a ruling class is equivalent to the creation of a *Weltanschauung*."[24] This idea, of great theoretical importance for the development of Socialism, was basic to Gramsci's work at least as far back as the days of *Ordine nuovo* and the factory-council movement. For Gramsci, a social class scarcely deserves the name until it becomes *conscious* of its existence as a class; it cannot play a role in history until it develops a comprehensive world-view and a political program.[25]

The "orthodox" school of Marxism, in the late nineteenth and early twentieth centuries, was riddled with "economism" and materialism, a climate that left no room for problems of hegemony. For Gramsci, it was Lenin who revived Marxism as a creative philosophy: Lenin, "in opposition to various 'economistic' tendencies" reaffirmed the importance of hegemony in his conception of the State and gave the cultural "front" as much emphasis as the economic and political fronts.[26] Lenin's struggle against "economism" and "tail-ism" (or "spontaneity") led him to stress the necessity of educating the masses in a revolutionary sense. Moreover, his theory of the political party was founded on the conviction that conscious organization was essential for victory. Perhaps most important of all, he insisted on establishing a "hegemonic" relationship between working class and peasantry as a prerequisite for the revolution.

Still, Gramsci seems to have doubts about Lenin's thoroughness in examining the hegemony of the working class and the "cultural front." In reality, Gramsci went far beyond Lenin in seeing hegemony as a political and cultural predominance of the working class and its party aimed at securing the "spontaneous" adherence of other groups.[27] Hegemony—rule by consent, the legitimatization of revolution by a higher and more comprehensive culture—is the unifying

idea of Gramsci's life from the days of *La Città futura* to those of the
Quaderni del Carcere.

In his later work Gramsci stressed the problem of "civil society,"
hegemony, over the problem of "political society," which is—for
Marxists—the dictatorship of the proletariat. The shift in emphasis
was caused by Gramsci's increasing awareness of differences between
the Russia of 1917 and Western Europe after 1923. Problems of hegemony, said Gramsci, become particularly important in periods that
follow a phase of revolutionary activity. Gramsci believed that the
class struggle then changes from a "war of maneuver" to a "war of
position" fought mainly on the cultural front.[28] The Quaderni were
written during such a period, and this partly accounts for their emphasis on hegemony.

In the united front policy Lenin himself, said Gramsci, indicated
the need to shift from a war of maneuver, which had succeeded in
Russia in 1917, to a war of position, "the only possible one in the
West."[29] But the shift was the responsibility of Western Communist
leaders because of certain fundamental differences between Russia
and Western Europe. "In the East the State was everything, and civil
society was primordial and gelatinous; in the West there was a correct relationship between the State and civil society." However unstable the State might have appeared to be, behind it stood "a robust
structure of civil society."[30] Under these conditions, the seizure of
power by a new class is unlikely to succeed without a prior victory in
the area of civil society; hence, the struggle for hegemony, for cultural
and moral predominance, is the main task of Marxists in the advanced
countries of the West.

Notes on the Development of Italian Intellectuals

Gramsci had a thesis concerning Italian intellectuals: they were in
the main "cosmopolitan," "supra-national," and "non-popular" (*non-
nazionale-popolare*).[31] These were negative qualities, all the more so
considering the great importance that Gramsci assigned to intellectuals in the revolutionary process. It was therefore important to establish in what historical periods and under what conditions the Italian
intelligentsia had become detached from the "nation" and the
masses.

Gramsci dismissed Mussolini's "Roman tradition" as pure rhetoric.
But, although national virtues were totally unrelated to those of
ancient Italy, the detachment of Italian intellectuals might have begun in antiquity. Roman intellectuals were originally composed of

two main elements: Greek and oriental freedmen who served in the imperial bureaucracy, and a large number of gifted men, deliberately enticed by offers of citizenship to establish their residence in the capital.[32] Italy thus became the center for the cultivated classes of the whole Empire; the intellectuals there were consequently more cosmopolitan than national. Even before the collapse of the Empire, the Church had assured the continuation of this cosmopolitan detachment by taking many intellectuals into its hierarchy—of necessity trained for service to the whole Catholic world. Moreover, Catholicism's dual role as a sacred institution and a secular power determined its opposition to the Italian national spirit.

The history of the Italian written language was a significant reflection of detachment.[33] Latin, as both an ecclesiastic and a learned language, was common to all Europe, but the language gap between the intellectuals and the masses was much greater in Italy than elsewhere. The French clergy, for example, was required to preach in the vulgate as early as the ninth century, but this practice did not become general in Italy until the thirteenth century. The written Italian language had little connection with the masses, owing to its Latin syntax and specifically Florentine vocabulary and phonetics. Italian scholars, with the partial exception of the poets, wrote for Christian Europe, not for Italy. Hence Gramsci concluded that even the tools of the intellectuals—Latin and Italian—were learned languages, and the final supremacy of Italian had little popular importance.[34]

Gramsci asserted that the bourgeoisie of medieval city-states did develop its own category of organic intellectuals—popular poets like Cavalcanti and humanist administrators like Salutati. These men, in many ways, expressed the concrete aspirations of their class. The burghers did not, however, "assimilate" the traditional intellectuals, especially the clergy, or establish a hegemony over other social groups.[35] By their particularism, they attempted to destroy what unity was still to be found in the universal institutions of Church and Empire, and yet were unable to establish a new kind of unity.

Gramsci found a reason for this failure of the early bourgeoisie in its primitive conception of the State—a view limited solely to the economic organization of society which he calls "economic-corporativism." All the institutions and policies of the city-state were accepted or rejected on a purely economic basis. Obviously enough, the classes whose interests countered the policies of the ruling class needed some ideological or political persuasion. Instead of developing ideological tools for obtaining the "consent of the governed," however, the city-state rulers turned to the ready-made formulas of the Church and Empire, despite the basic hostility of these two institutions to the interests of the city-state. This ideological poverty explains why every city in medieval Italy called itself either Guelph or Ghibelline, Papal or Imperial. It was not that the early Italian bourgeoisie and its intellectuals were less capable politically than the same class in France or England; but in countries less burdened with cosmopolitan universalism a national monarchy could be developed as a "superstructure" that adequately met the needs of this early bourgeoisie.

The outstanding political fact of the Italian Renaissance was the final destruction of the particularistic city-states by forces that claimed to represent medieval universalism, the Church and the Empire. From the "national-popular" point of view, the whole movement was regressive: first, because the Italian bourgeoisie, by exhausting itself in impossible attempts to found autonomous states, also lost its economic initiative; second, because even the rudimentary popularism of the city-state intellectuals was then destroyed. From then on, the political capacities of the intellectuals were directed toward personal affairs, toward the maintenance of the family and other concerns of civil society.[36] Intellectual activity was unrelated to Italian political problems, and was commonly regarded as its own justification: it was of no concern to Cellini and Leonardo whether they were employed by an Italian prince or the King of France.

In his discussion of humanism, the major intellectual movement of the Renaissance, Gramsci followed Giuseppe Toffanin's thesis that humanism was an entirely orthodox Catholic development.[37] Through its belief in the universality of culture as embodied in classical antiquity and the Church, humanism only intensified the cosmopolitanism of Italian intellectuals and increased their detachment from the masses. By this interpretation, humanism and the Reformation would be antithetical rather than complementary. Gramsci called humanism "a Counter-Reformation in advance ... a barrier against a rupture in medieval universalism that was implicit in the city-state."[38]

The Counter-Reformation itself confirmed the aloofness of Italian intellectuals, which the Church increased in two ways: by forcing the emigration of intellectuals who did not wish to submit to her discipline, and by selecting more and more Italian intellectuals for positions in the Church hierarchy, leading these intellectuals to identify themselves even more with the supra-nationality of the Church.[39] The Papacy was forced to begin this transformation to protect itself from domination by the "national" monarchies of Spain and France.

But this ostensible "nationalization" of the Church was really very different from a movement like Gallicanism, precisely because its aim was to preserve the universality of the Church. The existing "supranationalism" of Italian intellectuals furthered this aim.

For Gramsci, the tradition of "non-popular" cosmopolitanism was a major barrier to the unification of Italy, and seriously hindered twentieth-century Italian intellectuals in performing their proper "hegemonic" role. Niccolò Machiavelli was, however, one earlier Italian intellectual who epitomized qualities that Gramsci thought necessary for establishing a more complete and harmonious state.

Niccolò Machiavelli, "The First Italian Jacobin"

Liberation of Italy from the "barbarians" was the goal that led Machiavelli to create an entirely new conception of the State. In the course of his reflections, he developed a specific program for establishing a "modern" Italian State capable of defending its autonomy. Gramsci refers to Machiavelli's theory and his specific political program as a "precocious Jacobinism."[40] Jacobinism as theory is a purely "political" approach to the problems of society, with the aim of radically changing that society. The Jacobin establishes a pattern for society, and then employs all his force to create it; he knows what he wants and how to get it. As a specific political program, Jacobinism would aim at founding a coordinated national state by allying major urban classes, such as the proletariat and the petty bourgeoisie, with the peasants. This alliance can be initiated by establishing a national militia, drawing members from all these classes; it is strengthened by a series of myths (based on reality) that the populace will enthusiastically accept.

This is the abstract program of "Jacobinism." But it is also important to examine the real historical role of the French Jacobins, those "energetic and resolute men," those "creators of irreparable *faits accomplis*" who impelled the bourgeoisie forward with "kicks in the behind."[41] Important in the ultimate success of the Jacobins, said Gramsci, was the heterogeneity of the Third Estate. Its principal elements were an economically advanced but politically moderate group and a "disparate" intellectual elite; thus the class expressed a variety of political positions, depending upon general circumstances. At the beginning of the Revolution, the Third Estate had, in fact, demanded only reforms that interested the "actual physical components" of its social group—that is, reforms that satisfied its immediate "corporative" interests. But this stage was ended by the resistance of the old

social forces and by foreign threats to even these limited revolutionary gains.

At this point the Jacobins, "a new elite," stepped forward. They
thought of the bourgeoisie as "the hegemonic leadership of all the
popular forces." The Jacobins consequently opposed any compromises
that might isolate the bourgeoisie from its popular base, and this intransigence gave them a special role in the Revolution. They stood
for the present and future needs "of all the national groups that were
to be assimilated by the fundamental existing group." Particularly
important for Gramsci, because of the class structure in Italy, was the
acceptance of Jacobin rule by the peasantry, which eventually understood that the Old Regime could be defeated only by a peasant alliance with the "most advanced forces of the Third Estate, not with the
moderate Girondins." True, the Jacobins "forced the hand" of the
revolutionary movement; but they did this on a solid historical basis
by making the bourgeoisie both the dominant class (the class hold-
ing State power) and the "hegemonic" class.

Gramsci concluded that "Jacobinism was a categorical incarnation
of the Prince,"[42] or conversely, that Machiavelli was the first Italian
Jacobin. All of Machiavelli's political and historical work should be
interpreted in this light; the *Prince* and the *Art of War* are especially
relevant.[43] Much misunderstanding and dislike of Machiavelli was
occasioned by failure to see him as a man of his age.[44] Machiavelli is
often accused of fostering despotism, but considering the political
immaturity of the early bourgeoisie and the inherent limitations of
the economic-corporative city-states, absolute monarchy was really an
instrument of revolutionary progress, an essential element in forming
a superstructure organically related to the State's economic life. In
reality, the *Prince* was primarily not a systematic treatise on political
science, but an appeal for the organization of an Italian State, formulated in a truly Jacobin manner.[45] In the main body of the text, Machiavelli outlined, with scientific detachment, exactly what was necessary to achieve this goal; in the epilogue, he appealed with great
eloquence and passion for popular support in fulfilling his plan.

Gramsci also rejects the common notion that Machiavelli was a
"visionary" and not a "realist."[46] He was not a realist in the sense
that he limited his attentions to the sphere of political actuality. Instead, he was concerned with "what ought to be"—realistically—and
therefore applied his intellect and will to projecting a new relationship of classes and institutions in Italy. But these classes and institutions were "real" entities, and Machiavelli analyzed them in a thor-

oughly "Jacobin" manner: beginning with the actual social structure, he established a goal that was attainable through resolute political direction of forces in the structure. Gramsci, in fact, concluded that only this Jacobin attitude is realistic, because it alone can deal with historical reality.

If the *Prince* indicated Machiavelli's Jacobin attitude, then the *Art of War* was proof of his Jacobin program.[47] In it Machiavelli outlined plans for creating a national militia, a citizen army composed of both urban and rural classes. Gramsci emphasized the Florentine statesman's awareness that neither an effective militia nor a powerful state could be created without bringing the peasants into political life. The similarity of this program with that of the later Jacobins was important evidence that Machiavelli was a sixteenth-century "Jacobin."*

It was certainly not Machiavelli's cultural "nationalism" that appealed to Gramsci. This was an old motif in Italian culture, and in any case Gramsci was not a "nationalist." There are, however, three ideas in the *Prince* that are remarkably close to the spirit of Jacobinism. First, the last chapter of the *Prince* was an "Exhortation to Liberate Italy from the Barbarians"; Machiavelli appealed directly to the masses, over the heads of various Italian State governments. This was unique for an Italian intellectual of that time.[48] Second, Machiavelli knew that force alone would not guarantee the success of his political program. Ultimately, the "best fortress [of the Prince] is the love of the people; for although you may have fortresses, they will not save you if you are hated by the people."[49] This was an early statement of the crucial importance of "spiritual" leadership—hegemony—in the political struggle, not unlike that practiced by the Jacobins. Finally, it would be hard to find a better example of the Jacobin propensity to deal with problems in a "purely political" spirit—and with "energy and resolution"—than Machiavelli's introduction to the 17th Chapter of the *Prince*:

I say that every prince must desire to be considered merciful and not cruel. He must, however, take care not to misuse this mercifulness. Cesare Borgia was considered cruel, but his cruelty brought order to the Romagna, united it, and reduced it to peace and fealty. If this is considered well, it will be seen

---

* Whether or not Gramsci's picture of Machiavelli corresponds to historical reality may be unimportant. Certainly, it is not within the scope of this work to examine the vast literature on the meaning of Machiavelli. But cf. the remarks on Gramsci's interpretation of Machiavelli in the following works: Chabod, "L'Età," I, 155; Matteucci, p. 63; Garin, pp. 414–16.

that he was really much more merciful than the Florentine people, who, to avoid the name of cruelty, allowed Pistoia to be destroyed.[50]

There is a whole new world of politics in this statement. It may not yet be "Jacobinism," but it is even further from the cosmopolitan detachment of intellectuals contemporary with Machiavelli.

We have concerned ourselves with only a few aspects of the Quaderni, those that are most closely connected with Gramsci's active political life. He covered many other fields of political, artistic, and philosophical thought in his Notebooks; and, although his themes are broad, his treatment does them full justice.

Gramsci was released from confinement in 1937. But the strain of prison deprivations had been too much for his delicate constitution. He died on April 27, 1937, at the age of 46—only a few days after he was formally freed, and as a direct result of his confinement.

Antonio Gramsci was a man of extraordinarily varied interests and capabilities. Still, his best and most serious efforts, from the liceo at Cagliari to the prison at Turi, were always devoted to understanding a person, an idea, an institution, or a people—not as abstractions, but as living realities in the process of history. Gramsci's epitaph might well be a remark from his last letter to his son Delio:

I think you will like history, as I liked it when I was your age, because it deals with living men and all human problems. Contemplating all the men of the world, who come together in society to work, struggle, and better themselves, cannot but please you more than any other thing.[51]

Appendix: Gramsci and the Risorgimento

Gramsci's thought on the political party and the historical role of intellectuals profoundly influenced his interpretation of the Risorgimento. This interpretation has occasioned an interesting controversy between liberal and Marxist historians. Rosario Romeo, author of an important book on the Risorgimento in Sicily, began the polemic by publishing two articles in *Nord e Sud* in 1956 and 1958.[1] Although the first article was supposedly a general survey of Italian Marxist historiography, its main purpose—and the sole purpose of the second article—was to refute Gramsci's interpretation of the Risorgimento. Romeo justifies this emphasis by asserting that Italian Marxists almost "universally accept Gramsci's theses on the Risorgimento."[2] An examination of these theses and the opinions of Romeo and others regarding them will provide an excellent example of Gramsci's impact on present-day Italian culture.

Considering Gramsci's views on political parties and intellectuals, it is not surprising that his interpretation of the Risorgimento centered on the political leadership of its "revolutionary" social classes and groups.[3] This leadership was supplied by only two parties: the "moderates," led by men like Cavour, D'Azeglio, and Balbo, were a relatively homogeneous group made up of the bourgeoisie, those members of the nobility whose economic activities were capitalistic, and most of the "upper" intelligentsia; the "Party of Action," led by men like Mazzini, Garibaldi, and Pisacane, was a more diverse group supported by the radical petty bourgeoisie (artisans, small entrepreneurs, and many professional intellectuals) and the exiguous urban proletariat.

The moderates managed to establish a hegemony over the Party of Action by a "gradual but continual absorption" of actionist elements. This process made the Risorgimento a movement "without 'terror,' a 'revolution' without a 'revolution.' " While the moderates were "organically" related to the bourgeois-aristocratic forces—indeed, they were the "organic intellectuals" of this group—the actionist leaders had no close connection with the heterogeneous classes they supposedly represented. Consequently, the actionists never established a "concrete program of government." To effectively counter the moderate program, they had to create an alternative program that would attract the rural masses, almost four-fifths of the people. Only an economic and social program of the "Jacobin" type would have offered a viable alternative to moderate politics. Gramsci's analysis of the Risorgimento aimed at showing why the Party of Action did not develop a "Jacobin" program—that is, why the Italian Revolution of 1859 was not the French Revolution of 1789.

To begin with, the petty-bourgeois social base of the actionists retained a semi-agrarian character that limited its autonomy vis-à-vis the older landowning class and also made it fear the possible economic demands of the peasantry. The political interests of the European and Italian bourgeoisie in 1859 were very different from those of 1789. The "specter of Communism" had made them cautious: it seemed that a "proletarian" alternative to bourgeois rule was at least possible. In addition, the political weakness of Italy, its lack of national "autonomy," limited effective action by the Italian bourgeoisie. The audacity of the Jacobin spirit was "certainly related to the hegemony so long exercised by France in Europe." Finally, the "national" character of the Risorgimento—its goal of expelling the Austrians and forming an Italian State—made it easy for the moderates, and even some actionists, to neglect the social character of the revolution in the interests of achieving the largest possible unity of action. Gramsci did not believe that these conditions necessarily and absolutely paralyzed the actionists. He insisted that in spite of these difficulties "an alliance with the peasants was certainly always possible." Still, historical complications are a major reason for the limited, moderate character of the Risorgimento and the inherent weaknesses of the more democratic groups participating in the movement.

According to Romeo, the core of Gramsci's thought on the Risorgimento is a criticism of its leaders, both moderate and democratic, for failing to promote agrarian revolution (pp. 19–21).* Working on this assumption, Romeo then attempts to demonstrate: (1) that Gramsci's conclusions resulted from his political position, and not from "serene" historical examination; (2) that his work was vitiated by using the French Revolution as a model to demonstrate the inadequacy of the Italian Revolution; (3) that his belief in the possibility of an agrarian revolution in the nineteenth century was mistaken; (4) that in any case a revolution would have seriously delayed the development of capitalism in Italy, a situation that Gramsci, as a Marxist, should have deplored.

Romeo believes that almost all Italian Marxist historical writing—not just Gramsci's—exhibits unhistorical political attitudes. "Quite a few Italian historians," he writes, came to Marxism from complex motives, "among which politically contingent passion and attitudes played a predominant role" (p. 94). Italian Marxist historiography shows political bias with its lack of interest in periods preceding the French Revolution and the Risorgimento. Gramsci's work is merely part of a "revisionist" tendency in Italian historiography, stressing what the Risorgimento did *not* do rather than what it did. Romeo follows Benedetto Croce, Carlo Antoni, and Federico Chabod (pp. 20, 46) in charging that Gramsci "anachronistically" reflected the twentieth-century interests of the PCI in stressing the importance of the peasant movement and the Southern Question during the Risorgimento, in underestimating the influence of the European powers on the Risorgimento, and even in using terms like "national-popular," supposedly derived from the Russian term *narodnost* (p. 25, n. 12).

Romeo has a special dislike for Gramsci's alleged tendency to use the French Revolution as a "model" for analyzing Italian history; the much greater industrial development of France invalidates the comparison (p. 26). Romeo does not object to the comparative method for studying revolutionary processes, though he tends to regard it as "arbitrary and incomplete"; he does object strongly to the "assumption that French historical development is an 'exemplary' model for a modern bourgeois and capitalist country" (p. 44): from the economic and social points of view, the "Prussian way" is "far more energetic and expansive." Romeo follows Lenin in defining the

* Page numbers in parentheses refer to Romeo's book *Risorgimento e capitalismo.*

"Prussian way" as a "compromise of the capitalistic bourgeoisie with feudal elements" (p. 39), and recognizes that it is undoubtedly less "democratic" (p. 40) than the French way. Romeo attributes the tendency of Italian Marxists to exalt French history to a "certain Francophilia of our democratic thought" (p. 44). He even asserts that Italy was fortunate in not following the pattern of the French Revolution, especially among the peasants, since French industrial and agricultural development had been hindered by the Revolution's changes in the relations of production in the countryside.

Romeo flatly denies the possibility of an Italian agrarian revolution in the nineteenth century (or indeed of any "alternative to the Risorgimento as it was concretely realized"). Despite innumerable peasant insurrections and the admitted existence of grinding rural poverty, an agrarian revolution would not have been tolerated by the great powers (p. 22). Although Romeo admits that Gramsci recognized this problem, he finds it contradictory that Gramsci could still assert the possibility of "alliance with the peasants."[4]

Finally, Romeo thinks it fortunate that an "agrarian revolution" did not occur in Italy. Employing the Marxist concept of "primitive capital accumulation" and modern theories of economic development, he attempts to show that an agrarian revolution would have increased the consumption of the peasants, then more than eighty per cent of Italy's population, and therefore would have severely retarded capital accumulation. Italian agricultural production increased greatly in the period 1861–80, but the surplus was not absorbed by the rural masses; instead, it took the form of rents and profits, providing capital for investment, especially in the "infrastructure" of society (public utilities, transportation, communication). True, high taxes and foreign investment also built up Italian capital, but the bulk of it came from low rural consumption accompanied by higher production. If agrarian reforms had been carried out, the peasants would themselves have consumed any meager surplus they might have gained from the inherently inefficient small holdings that a revolution would have created.

The agricultural crisis of the 1880's ended the flow of capital from country to city. By then, however, investments were derived mainly from the profits of commerce and industry (p. 174). Romeo optimistically concludes that Italian industrial development in the 1880's was "probably the most rapid in the history of the Italian industrial economy" before the twentieth century (p. 188). "Because of the sacrifice imposed for so many decades on the countryside and the

South, Italy, poor in territory and natural resources, was the only country in the Mediterranean area to create a great industrial complex and a highly developed urban civilization" (p. 197).

The tone of Romeo's work is often harsh and condescending, which explains the none-too-gentle response of Italian Marxists. Although the dispute is not yet over, it is now possible to summarize the principal Marxist criticisms of Romeo's theses, as well as some observations made by other scholars.

Gramsci himself was strongly opposed to "immediate and ideological, non-historical" interpretations of the Risorgimento.[5] It is nonetheless true that any history of the Risorgimento immediately excites political interests. Giorgio Candeloro, writing of the conflict between tendencies to exalt and to denigrate the Risorgimento, urges the avoidance of either extreme, but further explains that these positions

have an ideological foundation that goes back to the Risorgimento itself, and to the politico-social situation deriving from the events of a hundred years ago. Those events have preserved an immediacy that continues to stimulate discussion of them in substantially political terms ... chiefly because they gave birth to new problems (or a new face to old problems) central to the later history of Italy—problems that still exist today, albeit partly changed in some respects.[6]

Candeloro concludes that any discussion of the Risorgimento must keep in mind the fundamental characteristics of both the Risorgimento and "united Italy and its social and economic development."

Romeo's case for the "non-historical" character of Gramsci's work on the Risorgimento rests on the assertion that Gramsci's concern with the "agrarian question" reflects a political problem of twentieth-century Communism, and is an "anachronism" when applied to the "concrete reality" (p. 20) of the Risorgimento. Was agrarian revolution only Gramsci's problem or also a problem in 1848 and 1860?[7]

Awareness of the need for agrarian reform, however vaguely expressed, was certainly widespread among radicals before the Risorgimento. For example, the left wing of the Carbonari (c. 1820) required its more advanced members to swear to "favor with all my forces and at the cost of my life the promulgation and execution of the agrarian law—without which there is no liberty, since private property is an offense against the rights of humanity."[8] There was also the social program of Carlo Bianco di St. Jorioz, who urged that at the successful conclusion of the "national war of insurrection" the combatants receive "the lands and private possessions of the princes and the enemies of liberty."[9]

Although these statements may be dismissed as the expression of an insignificant lunatic fringe, two recent works by Italian Marxists have shown how important the question of agrarian revolution was by 1860.[10] Indeed, a principal reason for the support given Garibaldi by the Sicilian peasantry was his promise to "divide up the large estates and distribute the land."[11] Very little came of this promise, it is true; the point is merely that the question of "agrarian revolution" originated in the Risorgimento, and not in the twentieth century. Almost immediately after the completion of national unity, the agricultural question became a major issue for both democrats and moderates—as the famous parliamentary inquiry into agriculture demonstrated.* Gramsci's concern with the agrarian question (which is inseparable from the question of the South) is the culmination of a specifically Italian tradition going back through Gaetano Salvemini and Antonio Labriola to Carlo Cattaneo. Even the idea of allying southern peasantry and northern workers is not "Bolshevik" in origin: this very alliance had been demanded by Salvemini in 1900.[12] The tradition culminates in Gramsci because only after World War I did it seem "concretely possible to overcome the social contradictions inherited from the Risorgimento."[13]

According to Romeo, the French Revolution unduly influenced Gramsci's view of the Risorgimento; but since social and economic conditions were entirely different in the two countries, any comparison of their respective historical developments would have been gratuitous. Indeed, Gramsci did emphasize the failure of Italian revolutionists to develop a Jacobin-like program during the Risorgimento, involving an alliance of urban bourgeoisie and peasantry.† He believed that the absence of Jacobinism greatly influenced the outcome of the Risorgimento, and he gave many reasons for the underdevelopment of Italian Jacobinism. The success of the moderates and the failure of the actionists to develop a Jacobin program established the fundamental character of the united Italian State: a compromise of the old (the landed aristocracy) with the new (the commercial and industrial bourgeoisie). Gramsci wished to prove that under the limi-

---

* Ironically, Romeo himself, in another work, makes a judgment on the importance of the agrarian question that is almost identical with Gramsci's. Discussing why the thirteenth-century Della Torre lords of Milan did not attack feudalism in the rural areas, Romeo concludes that the "lack of concrete support in the countryside, which they were unable or unwilling to find in the peasants, made effective control of the realm much more difficult for the powerful city." As quoted in *Studi Gramsciani*, p. 383, n. 1.
† See pp. 209–10.

tations imposed on the Italian bourgeoisie, where essentially *political* problems like national independence and unity prevail, a limited bourgeois revolution is possible without an alliance with the peasants and masses but through an alliance with the previous ruling class.[14]

Is Gramsci's use of the Jacobin idea as a tool for analysis valid? Certainly not, if he meant to establish the French Revolution as an abstract model for all other bourgeois revolutions. That Gramsci never intended this is shown by his disapproval of Giuseppe Ferrari (1811–76), a federalist republican who tried to apply "French schemes" to Italian questions.[15] But Gramsci reasoned that to know what the Risorgimento was, it was also necessary to know what it was *not*. The "comparative method" could show why Italian developments were different from French. As a matter of fact, the comparison itself was an old tradition in Europe. In 1801 Vincenzo Cuoco had developed the idea of "passive revolution"—i.e., revolution from above, or because of external pressures—as contrasted with the "active revolution" that occurred in France. In the 1860's Alessandro Manzoni wrote *La Rivoluzione francese del 1789 e la rivoluzione italiana del 1859,* defending the Risorgimento as "legal" and attacking the French Revolution for its violence. The comparison is even more valid today, as is shown by Albert Soboul's recent essay on "Risorgimento et révolution bourgeoise."[16] Giuseppe Talamo seems equally unable to avoid a Gramscian interpretation in discussing the Risorgimento. With regard to the first constitutional ministry in Naples during the revolution of 1848, he says:

In the rural areas, and in all the provinces in general, the position of the constitutional ministry was very weak. The age-old question of assigning the common domains, arbitrarily occupied by the landowners, was not even discussed. This was undeniably to the advantage of the king, who (as Spellanzon has written) would later be able to take advantage of widespread discontent among the agricultural masses in his opposition to the political aspirations of the bourgeoisie.[17]

Thus Italian political leaders of every camp, from the Risorgimento to the present, have deplored the lack of change in the agrarian economy. But Romeo charges that Gramsci asserts the *possibility* of an agrarian revolution and makes it central to his "indictment" of the Risorgimento. Actually, the main point of Gramsci's work is to show why such a revolution *did not* occur in Italy: he outlines the reasons for the failure of the Party of Action and the success of the moderates.[18] Perhaps Gramsci's only concrete reference to a real possibility of enrolling peasants in the national movement comes when he accuses the actionists of not effecting an "alliance with the peasants, [which] was certainly always possible."[19] But this vague charge follows a discussion of that very party's weakness. Elsewhere Gramsci explains very clearly why such a movement was not historically possible: "Did any of the conditions exist in Italy for a movement like that of the French Jacobins? For many centuries France was a hegemonic nation: its international autonomy was extensive. Italy had nothing of the kind: it had no international autonomy."[20] Agrarian revolution was impossible because of the strength of the moderates: Cavour and his party "represented the only correct politics of the era, since they had no strong, politically intelligent competitors."[21] An undistorted view of Gramsci's historiography forbids the arbitrary removal of any one idea from its context, be it the absence of Jacobinism or of agrarian revolution. In his own words,

The Risorgimento is a complex and contradictory historical movement, which achieves wholeness from all its antithetical elements: its protagonists and antagonists, its struggles and the reciprocal modifications those struggles brought about, the action of latent and passive forces like the great agricultural masses, and the preeminent consideration of international relations.[22]

His historical justification of the moderates does not prevent Gramsci from pointing out the unfortunate results of their victory in the long run. The moderates

said they proposed to build a modern State in Italy, and they produced a kind of bastard; they proposed to develop a numerous and energetic ruling class, and they did not succeed; [they proposed] to include the people in the life of the State, and they did not succeed. The consequences of this deficiency were the poverty-stricken political life of 1870–1900, the basic and endemic unrest of the lower classes, and the crude, petty existence of a cynical and idle ruling class. Another consequence was the international position of the new State, deprived of effective autonomy because it was undermined by the Papacy and the stubborn passivity of the great masses. Hence, the right-wingers of the Risorgimento were really great demagogues. They made an instrument and an object of the democratic nation by degrading it, and therein lies the greatest and most contemptible demagoguery.[23]

Aldo Berselli, a liberal, recognized that Gramsci's views cannot be included in the "general category of 'Risorgimental revisionism.' "[24] Similarly, A. W. Salomone recently attacked revisionist tendencies in the historiography of the Risorgimento, but treated Gramsci's work with considerable respect.[25] Romeo's charge of "present-mindedness" in Gramsci might better be applied to himself. He attempts to "idealize" the past, to demonstrate that what "really" happened was for the best and, indeed, could only have happened as it did. This is a far from disinterested examination of the past. As Aurelio Macchioro has said, it may be dangerous to hypothesize alternative possibilities in history, but it is more dangerous "to make what happened in the past not only the real history—which it is—but also the ideal history."[26]

Gaetano Salvemini's discussion of his own apparently contradictory evaluation of Cavour expresses the Gramscian view:

We must distinguish "historical" judgment from "political" judgment. One can recognize "historically" that the Italian democratic parties produced an excessive number of inconclusive windbags; and that, granted their incapacity and the objective conditions under which they worked, their defeats were not only inevitable, but deserved—however, one is not therefore obliged to condemn their ideals for all times and all places. One can recognize the superior political capacities of the conservatives compared with the democrats, and still not pass over bag and baggage to the official historians of the conservative parties. . . . As a "historian," I must see men as they were; as a "man of politics"—which is not the same thing as a "politician"—or as a "moralist" (to add a note of Crocean contempt), I do not remove my hat before accomplished facts, and, if necessary, shall even take a stand for the defeated.[27]

But for Romeo the actual course of Italian history was "the quickest and shortest historic road for Italy to the structure and characteristics of a modern country."[28] True, he cannot ignore the continued ailments of the South, but these he regards as an aspect of "potentializing the city at the expense of the country."[29] And southern backwardness is a "temporary condition (even if protracted for many decades), destined to be corrected by the internal development of northern industrialism."[30] Capitalism must continue because it will eventually provide for all, and any violence committed along the way is justified once the pieces have been picked up.[31] But recent statistics show that the regional contrast in Italy is increasing rather than decreasing. Romeo seems to be the one imposing "abstract schemes" on historical development. Gramsci's approach is much more sensible—and ultimately more "historical":

The hegemony of the North would have been "normal" and historically beneficial if industrialization had been able to widen its confines rapidly to incorporate new economic zones. Then this hegemony would have been the expression of a struggle between the old and the new, between the more productive and the less productive. . . . [However,] it was not so. The hegemony was presented as permanent: the contrast was presented as a historical condition necessary for an indeterminate time—and therefore apparently "perpetual"—to the existence of northern industry.[32]

Romeo's last point, that development of a modern capitalistic Italy came about chiefly because there was no agrarian revolution, has received as much attention from scholars as his critique of other aspects of Gramscian historiography. In sum, criticism of the thesis has been on four grounds: (1) Romeo's version of "primitive accumulation" of capital is mistaken; (2) his assumption of a direct relationship between the growth of small peasant property and increased consumption is unwarranted; (3) his belief that large landholdings are necessarily more progressive than small peasant holdings is, for the nineteenth century, often untrue; and (4) his data on the reasons for and extent of economic growth in Italy compared with other countries are often misleading and exaggerated.[33]

The whole controversy has generally demonstrated the inadequacy of Romeo's critique of Gramscian historiography and his view of capital formation in Italy. Nevertheless, he has unintentionally rendered great service to Italian Marxist scholars by forcing them to avoid unhistorical condemnations of the past and apply Gramsci's method to a more concrete and creative study of Italian history.

Notes

Complete authors' names, titles, and publication
data will be found in the Bibliography, pp. 274–97.
Numbers in brackets refer to the numbered list of
Gramsci's writings at the beginning of the Bibliography.

Chapter One

1. *Passato e presente* [8], p. 174.
2. S. F. Romano, p. 8.
3. There is a village in southeastern Albania named Gramshi. See *Lettere* [2], p. 508, n. 4.
4. For details of Gramsci's family background, see Lombardo Radice and Carbone, p. 9; S. F. Romano, pp. 9–10; and the "Cronologia della vita di Antonio Gramsci," in *Lettere* [2], p. xxi. See also G to Tatiana, 12.x.31, *Lettere* [1], p. 150. The most important book on Gramsci's earlier years, published too late to be used here, is Giuseppe Fiori, *Vita di Antonio Gramsci* (Bari: Laterza, 1966).
5. G to Tatiana, 13.i.30, *Lettere* [1], p. 86.
6. G to Tatiana, 28.xii.31, Ferrata and Gallo [12], II, 310. See also G to his mother, 25.iv.27, *Lettere* [2], p. 80.
7. G to Tatiana, 7.ix.31, *Lettere* [1], p. 136.
8. See the oblique reference in G to Julca, 16.i.33, *ibid.*, p. 19.
9. G to Grazietta, 31.x.32, *Lettere* [2], p. 686 and note.
10. Gramsci's older sister, Emma, died of pernicious malaria in December 1920. See Preface to *Lettere* [2], p. vii. See also G to mother, 24.viii.31, *Lettere* [1], p. 134.
11. S. F. Romano, pp. 13–14.
12. G to Grazietta, 29.xii.30, *Lettere* [1], p. 108.
13. G to Giulia, 18.viii.24, Ferrata and Gallo [12], II, 55.
14. G to mother, 28.ii.27, *Lettere* [2], p. 53.
15. G to mother, 15.vi.31, *Lettere* [1], p. 128.
16. G to Grazietta, 29.xii.30, *ibid.*, p. 109.
17. G to Teresina, 17.xi.30, *ibid.*, p. 105.
18. S. F. Romano, p. 17.

19. In 1900, Italian public education consisted of 5 years of elementary school and 8 years of secondary school, the latter period divided into the 5 years of the *ginnasio* (students from 10 or 11 to 15 or 16 years of age) and the 3 years of the *liceo* (students from 15 or 16 to 18 or 19 years of age). See Villari, pp. 237–56, for a thoroughly negative evaluation of Italian education in this period.

20. G to Tatiana, 2.i.28, *Lettere* [1], p. 52.

21. "La luce che si è spenta" (20.xi.15), in *Scritti giovanili* [9], p. 10.

22. G to mother, 12.ix.32, *Lettere* [1], p. 206. Emilio Salgari (1863–1910) was a popular writer of tales of adventure for boys.

23. See the collection of these stories in Gramsci's *L'Albero del riccio* [14]. The work also contains stories by other authors which Gramsci refers to in his letters.

24. Répaci, p. 41.

25. See G to Delio, 22.ii.32, *Lettere* [1], pp. 167–68. See also S. F. Romano, pp. 21–23, which contains some fine passages on Gramsci's love of the animal world.

26. G to Tatiana, 9.iv.28, *Lettere* [1], p. 61.

27. See S. F. Romano, p. 49, for a photographic copy of Gramsci's certificate of completion of the examinations.

28. *Ibid.*, pp. 26–27.

29. G to Tatiana, 3.x.32, *Lettere* [1], p. 207. At the time of Gramsci's schooling there were only ten ginnasi and three licei in all Sardinia. (Thomas Ashby, "Sardinia," in *Encyclopedia Britannica*, 11th ed., 1910.)

30. G to Julca, 16.i.33, *Lettere* [1], p. 220.

31. G to Tatiana, 3.x.32, *ibid.*, p. 208.

32. G to Tatiana, 30.i.33, *ibid.*, p. 221.

33. For this episode, see G to Tania, 12.ix.32, *ibid.*, p. 206.

34. G to Tatiana, 5.iii.28, *ibid.*, p. 59.

35. G to Giulia, 13.ii.23, Ferrata and Gallo [12], p. 23.

36. G to Giulia, 6.iii.24, *ibid.*, p. 33.

37. See S. F. Romano, p. 33, and "Cronologia della vita di Antonio Gramsci," in *Lettere* [2], p. xxi.

38. G to Tatiana, 12.ix.32, *Lettere* [1], p. 206.

39. See the story of his encounter with a band of brigands. G to Tania, 26.xii.27, *ibid.*, pp. 49–50.

40. G to Tatiana, 12.ix.32, *ibid.*, p. 206.

41. G to Tatiana, 9.iv.28, *ibid.*, p. 61.

42. "Oppressi ed oppressori," Ferrata and Gallo [12], pp. 13–15.

43. *Ibid.*, p. 15. Emphasis mine.

44. King and Okey, p. 112: "Nowhere in Italy is the gap so great between rich and poor [as it is in the Mezzogiorno]. . . . The educated Neapolitan rarely talks dialect like the Piedmontese or Lombard or Sicilian." The long and still very strong separatist tradition in Sicily accounts for the widespread use of the dialect there.

45. G to Teresina, 26.iii.27, Ferrata and Gallo [12], p. 114. See also Togliatti, "Gramsci sardo," p. 1088.

46. G to Giulia, 6.iii.24, Ferrata and Gallo [12], p. 33.

47. See Gramsci, "Gli scopritori" (24.v.16), in *Sotto la mole* [11], pp. 148–50. In this piece Gramsci viciously satirizes Pietro Mascagni's rather patronizing impressions of a recent trip to Sardinia.

48. As quoted in S. F. Romano, p. 46.

49. See Gramsci, "Lettere al 'Grido' " (4.iii.16), in *Scritti giovanili* [9], p. 28. For a description of *Il Viandante,* see Spriano, *Torino operaia,* p. 20.

50. G to Giulia, 6.iii.24, Ferrata and Gallo [12], p. 32.

51. Gramsci, *Intellettuali* [4], p. 52.

52. *Annuario statistico italiano* (1912), II, 96.

53. *Ibid.,* p. 114.

54. *Ibid.,* p. 222. The Chamber of Labor is a local institution somewhat like the English "Trade Council" but with wider powers and of greater relative importance. See Rigola, pp. 157–62, and Spriano, *Socialismo e classe operaia,* p. 40. See also pp. 21–22 in Chapter 2 of this work.

55. Michels, p. 174. As late as 1904, there were only 127 members of Socialist organizations on the entire island. This is a smaller figure, even on a per capita basis, than for any other region of Italy.

56. Corsi, p. 39. Until 1914, the miners' union (Associazione Generale degli Operai delle Miniere di Sardegna) was a part of the Chamber of Labor at Cagliari (*ibid.,* p. 232), so Gramsci was probably very well informed of its activities in this early period.

57. *Ibid.,* p. 227. This work also contains a facsimile of Gramsci's letter, which carries the letterhead of the Turin edition of *Avanti!*

58. *Passato e presente* [8], p. 3.

59. G to Giulia, . . . 1923, Ferrata and Gallo [12], p. 24.

60. G to Giulia, 5.iii.24, *ibid.,* p. 32. See also pp. 23, 24, 546, and *Lettere* [1], p. 43.

61. G to Giulia, 13.ii.23, Ferrata and Gallo [12], p. 23. See also p. 24.

62. G to Giulia, 6.iii.24, *ibid.,* p. 32.

63. G to Carlo, 12.ix.27, *Lettere* [2], p. 126.

64. G to Tatiana, 3.x.32, *Lettere* [1], p. 207.

65. Gramsci discerned a parallel between this particular activity of Machiavelli and that of the French Jacobins, who created a national militia including the peasants for the defense of France against military invasion. See pp. 209–12 for a discussion of Gramsci and Machiavelli.

66. See Garosci, "Totalitarismo," pp. 194–95. Gramsci himself has obliquely alluded to the influence of Sardinia on his character: "In Italian literature it has been written that if Sardinia is an island, then every Sardinian is an island within an island. I remember a very comical article by a writer for the *Giornale d'Italia* who in 1920 attempted to explain my intellectual and political tendencies in these terms. But perhaps there is a little truth in it." G to Julca, 5.i.37, *Lettere* [1], p. 241.

Chapter Two

1. Salomone, *Italian Democracy,* pp. 95–97; Croce, *Storia d'Italia,* pp. 236–42; and King and Okey, pp. 371–74. According to King and Okey (p. 371), "The expansion since 1900 is almost without parallel in the history of nations." Many writers have expressed similar enthusiasm regarding Italian economic expansion in the late 1950's and early 1960's.

2. "L'Esposizione internazionale," p. 494.

3. For a discussion of the ideas of the nationalists and a description of their founding Congress in Florence (December 3–5, 1910), see Salomone, *Italian Democracy,* pp. 89–94. See also Croce's eloquent and ironical discussion of nationalism in *Storia d'Italia,* pp. 259–63. According to Franz Neumann, Enrico Corradini, the ideologist of Italian nationalism, was the first "to utilize the forces making for class struggle to develop an imperialistic Socialism." See his *Behemoth,* p. 162.

4. As quoted in Salomone, *Italian Democracy,* p. 42.

5. Cf. Giolitti's statement to the Chamber on December 15, 1913: "I undertook it [the Libyan War] ... after having carefully calculated on the one hand the great advantage of possessing a vast colony in the Mediterranean, and, on the other, the disaster to which we should have exposed ourselves had we not undertaken it." As quoted in *ibid.,* p. 103.

6. Rodolfo Morandi, p. 179.

7. For a fine summary of Italian culture from 1871 to 1915, see Croce, *Storia d'Italia,* chaps. 5, 6, 10. An excellent guide to developments in literature, including historiography and scholarship in general, is provided in Vittorio Rossi, III, 218–339. For a brief discussion from a Marxist point of view of Italian literature in this period, see Salinari, *Storia popolare,* III, 217–85.

8. As quoted in Spriano, *Torino operaia,* p. 32.

9. Garosci, "Totalitarismo," p. 196.

10. Engels, III, 28–32.

11. Garosci, "Totalitarismo," p. 196.

12. Togliatti, *Gramsci* (1955), p. 73.

13. Spriano, *Socialismo e classe operaia,* p. 60.

14. Norberto Bobbio, Preface to Mautino, p. x.

15. See Ferrara and Ferrara, p. 73; Garosci, "Totalitarismo," p. 195; Gioele Solari, "Aldo Mautino nella tradizione culturale torinese da Gobetti alla resistenza," in Mautino, p. 53.

16. *Gramsci* (1955), p. 77.

17. The lira was worth 19.6 cents in 1911. An automobile worker in Turin, by way of comparison, received from 30 to 70 centesimi an hour depending upon his experience and qualifications. See Montagnana, p. 13.

18. Zucaro, "Gramsci all'Università," pp. 1092–93. Ferrara and Ferrara, p. 9, state that Gramsci placed seventh in the examination, and Bellini and Galli, p. 22, give him sixth place. Zucaro, however, offers the only documenta-

tion: the results of the examination as published in the *Gazzetta del popolo* of October 29, 1911.

19. Gramsci's university curriculum and the results of his examinations are given in Russo, p. 238n. It is a wonder that Gramsci even passed the examinations. At the end of his last year at the liceo, as we have seen, he was in a state of severe malnutrition, and he was able to devote only a month to preparation. "I don't know how I was able to get through the examinations, because I fainted two or three times." Cf. G to Carlo, 12.ix.27, *Lettere* [2].

20. See Platone, "Opere di Gramsci."

21. G to Tatiana, 19.iii.27, *Lettere* [1], p. 27.

22. De Felice, pp. 219–21.

23. Togliatti, *Gramsci* (1955), p. 74.

24. Ferrara and Ferrara, pp. 34–35.

25. G to Julca, 5.i.37, *Lettere* [1], p. 241.

26. Gramsci, *Il Materialismo storico* [3], p. 199. Still, Professor Garin has pointed out the greater importance for Gramsci, even in these years, of De Sanctis, Labriola, and Renato Serra. See his "Gramsci nella cultura italiana," in *Studi gramsciani*, pp. 398–99. See also Gramsci's moving tribute to Serra's memory: "La Luce che si è spenta" (20.xi.15) in *Scritti giovanili* [9], pp. 10–12.

27. Gramsci (5.xi.20), *L'Ordine nuovo* [10], pp. 362–63.

28. Lombardo Radice and Carbone, p. 25.

29. G to Grazietta [1916], Ferrata and Gallo [12], p. 19. Some years before publication of the entire letter, this passage had already been quoted in Togliatti, *Gramsci* (1955), p. 81.

30. See the report of the administrative council of the Collegio delle Province, as reproduced in Zucaro, "Gramsci all'Università," p. 1100. The report noted Gramsci's critical state of health but held back his stipend until the examinations were completed in March-April 1914.

31. The dates and grades of these examinations are given in Russo, p. 238n. In his more recent article, Zucaro adds that Gramsci took his last examination—in Italian literature—on April 12, 1915 ("Gramsci all'Università," p. 1110).

32. Zucaro, Review of Lombardo Radice and Carbone, p. 702.

33. As quoted in Zucaro, "Gramsci all'Università," p. 1109.

34. Zucaro, Review of Lombardo Radice and Carbone, p. 702.

35. Levi, pp. 1039–50.

36. Prato, p. 5. As early as 1898, there was some awareness of this problem among Turin Socialists. See Spriano, *Socialismo e classe operaia*, p. 77.

37. Prato, pp. 8, 166.

38. *Ibid.*, p. 216.

39. *Ibid.*, p. 60.

40. Levi, p. 1041.

41. *Ibid.*; see also Prato, pp. 59, 108.

42. Gobetti, p. 111.

43. Garosci, "Totalitarismo," p. 197. The Radical and Republican Parties—the "advanced parties," as Paolo Spriano calls them, of the petty bourgeoisie—did not have "an electoral base, an efficient organization, or any influence on the people" of Turin. See his *Socialismo e classe operaia*, p. 43. In the provincial elections of November 6, 1904, the "Monarchic" parties received 48,579 votes and the PSI 14,511; the Radicals attracted only 3,005 votes! (*Ibid.*, p. 139.) Ezio Avigdor also mentions the sharp division between the working class and the bourgeoisie of Turin. See his "Il Movimento operaio torinese durante la prima guerra mondiale," in *La Città futura*, p. 88, n. 16.

44. Garosci, "Totalitarismo," p. 197.

45. For an informative survey of the Italian working class and its economic institutions at this time, see Procacci, "La Classe operaia," pp. 3–76.

46. 63.2% in England, 46% in Belgium, 43.6% in Germany. *Ibid.*, p. 3, n. 2.

47. *Ibid.*, pp. 5–6.

48. *Ibid.*, p. 14.

49. So it seemed to Samuel Gompers, whom Procacci quotes to this effect (*ibid.*, p. 35).

50. *Ibid.*, pp. 26, 64. Seventeen of the twenty national trade unions active in 1904 were founded after the turn of the century.

51. In 1891, the Turin Chamber of Labor received 5,000 lire from the city government (Spriano, *Socialismo e classe operaia*, p. 41).

52. *Ibid.*

53. Procacci, "La Classe operaia," p. 56.

54. Rigola, pp. 224–25.

55. Procacci, "La Classe operaia," pp. 61–62.

56. *Ibid.*, p. 62.

57. Candeloro, *Il Movimento sindacale*, p. 58.

58. Procacci, "La Classe operaia," pp. 70–73.

59. *Ibid.*, p. 68.

60. Spriano, *Socialismo e classe operaia*, p. 34.

61. Spriano (*ibid.*, p. 19) lists the following: Ansaldi (enlarged in 1895), makers of machine tools, farm machinery, and artillery: Employed about 400. The Ferrieri Piemontese (1899), railroad equipment. The Nebbiolo type foundary: From 1890 also produced printing equipment. Savigliano (1899), electric motors and equipment. Fiat (1899), automobiles: Employed only 50 workers in that year. Tedeschi Bros. (1888), electric cables: Employed 250 in 1898.

62. As quoted in *ibid.*, p. 39. The date of this issue is August 14, 1892, but the situation, as will be seen, was not markedly different in 1900. Before the turn of the century, only the printers and construction workers (in 1872 and 1886) had carried out really notable strikes in Turin.

63. Procacci, "La Classe operaia," pp. 56–57. In 1902, the Milan Chamber had 43,192 members. In 1904, the Naples Chamber had 12,727 members and the Rome Chamber 10,834. The Turin Chamber in 1902 had only 8,083 members. Spriano, from a different source, asserts that the Genoa Chamber had 28,000 members in 1902.

64. Spriano, *Socialismo e classe operaia*, p. 197.

65. *Ibid.*, p. 252.

66. *Ibid.*, p. 54, n. 6.

67. *Ibid.*, p. 36. The AGO established its first retail cooperative in 1854.

68. *Ibid.*, p. 76.

69. *Ibid.*, p. 75. At this time, Turin's first Socialist deputies, Quirino Nofri and Oddino Morgari, were sent to the Chamber.

70. Michels, p. 74. By 1904, the region even had more Socialist members than any other.

71. Procacci, "La Classe operaia," p. 68.

72. As quoted in Spriano, *Socialismo e classe operaia*, p. 253.

73. *Ibid.*, p. 105.

74. Tasca, "La Storia e la preistoria" (in "I Primi Dieci Anni"), p. 3. This work is hereafter cited as "La Storia."

75. Garosci, "Totalitarismo," p. 198.

76. As quoted in Spriano, *Socialismo e classe operaia*, p. 196.

77. Prato, p. 63.

78. Rodolfo Morandi, pp. 210–11.

79. Spriano, *Socialismo e classe operaia*, pp. 154–55.

80. Prato, pp. 63–64. Spriano adds that in 1907 the total investment in the auto industry was 90 million lire, of which the Turin industry had 38 million (*Socialismo e classe operaia*, p. 154).

81. Spriano, *Socialismo e classe operaia*, p. 156.

82. Terracini, "Gramsci e gli operai," p. 1035. Cf. Spriano, *Socialismo e classe operaia*, pp. 274, 285 (n. 25).

83. Spriano, *Socialismo e classe operaia*, pp. 160–61.

84. According to Procacci ("La Classe operaia," p. 75), the first demands for "internal committees" were made almost simultaneously at Milan, Florence, and Turin (in the foundryworkers' strike of December 1900). The Turin demand seems to have been the earliest. The workers at the Pirelli plant in Milan (spring 1902) were the first to actually achieve recognition of such a committee, albeit for only a short time.

85. Spriano, *Socialismo e classe operaia*, pp. 64–69.

86. *Ibid.*, pp. 171–74.

87. *Ibid.*, p. 191, n. 55.

88. *Ibid.*, p. 200.

89. *Ibid.*, pp. 182–83.

90. *Ibid.*, p. 212.

91. Spriano (*ibid.*, p. 209) estimates that the average Italian auto cost

about 15,000 lire and required 10,000 lire annually for upkeep. Thus no more than 7,000 persons in Italy could afford one.

92. *Ibid.,* pp. 214–16.

93. *Ibid.,* pp. 222–23. The most important Turinese additions to the new organization were the textile industrialists of Biella, Val Sessana, Val Stroma, and Valsesia, and the cement-makers of Casale.

94. *Ibid.,* pp. 245–46.

95. *Ibid.,* pp. 247, 257 (n. 33).

96. *Ibid.,* p. 224.

97. *Ibid.,* p. 268, and Prato, p. 7. There were 93,640 industrial workers in Turin at this time according to *Annuario statistico italiano* (1912), p. 112.

98. Spriano, *Socialismo e classe operaia,* pp. 209, 272.

99. Prato, pp. 72–74. Prato concludes from his analysis of wages in the principal industries of Turin that the metalworkers constituted a "privileged category."

100. The standard account of the two strikes is, of course, Spriano's *Socialismo e classe operaia,* pp. 270–305. Mario Montagnana vividly recalls them in his memoirs (pp. 11–13), and their importance is emphasized by Tasca, "La Storia," p. 3, and Leonetti, *Mouvements ouvriers et socialistes,* pp. 113, 116.

101. In Turin, 16,800 workers were employed in metalworking and mechanical industries not directly connected with the manufacture of automobiles. The "vehicle" factories employed 14,607, of which about 6,500 were directly engaged in producing cars, trucks, and buses in the great auto plants. See Spriano, *Socialismo e classe operaia,* p. 268.

102. *Ibid.,* p. 276.

103. From a speech of February 3, 1912, as quoted in *ibid.,* p. 279.

104. *L'Ordine nuovo* [10], p. 179.

105. Spriano, *Socialismo e classe operaia,* p. 299.

106. *Ibid.,* p. 300.

107. Gramsci, "Il Movimento torinese," in *L'Ordine nuovo* [10], p. 178.

108. See Spriano, *Torino operaia,* p. 34, on the activities of the young "ciclisti rossi."

109. *Ibid.,* p. 47; Tasca, "La Storia," p. 3.

110. Montagnana, p. 24.

111. Togliatti, as quoted in Lombardo Radice and Carbone, p. 25.

112. In 1931 Gramsci said, "We participated, completely or in part, in the movement for intellectual and moral reform promoted in Italy by Benedetto Croce." (G to Tatiana, 17.viii.31, *Lettere* [1], p. 132.) Togliatti has similarly declared his debt to idealism: "We arrived the same way as Karl Marx, that is, beginning from the philosophy of Hegel." (As quoted in Garosci, "Totalitarismo," p. 198.)

113. Tasca, "La Storia," p. 3. At Turin, the Socialists elected three out of five deputies and received 44 per cent of the vote. According to Gramsci's later recollection, the Sardinian peasants in 1913 had a "mystical conviction

that everything would be changed after the vote." *Risorgimento* [5], p. 113, n. 1.

114. Tasca, "La Storia," p. 3. In these early years—according to Lombardo Radice and Carbone (p. 29)—Gramsci also helped organize welfare institutions for Turin's workers, notably arrangements for maternal care, children's aid, and assistance to invalids and the aged. This judgment, however, seems to rest on the mistaken belief that Gramsci wrote a series of articles signed "a.g." on these subjects for *Il Grido del popolo*. The dates of the pieces, all written in 1912, are given in Ottino, p. 16, n. 9. More recently, however, Zucaro has shown that they were written by Adolfo Giusti, then Secretary of the AGO ("Gramsci all'Università," pp. 1096–98).

115. Gramsci, *Scritti giovanili* [9], pp. 21–22. Gramsci's editors note that the "leader" he referred to was G. M. Serrati, but Aldo Romano asserts that it was Mussolini! See his "Gramsci tra la guerra," p. 413.

116. Gramsci was the first to write of this episode ("Alcuni temi" [35], pp. 12–13). However, some details of his account have been corrected: see Salvemini, *Questione meridionale*, pp. xxiii–xxvi; Zucaro, "Gramsci all'Università," pp. 1103–4; Tasca, "La Storia," p. 3; and Spriano, *Torino operaia*, pp. 58–60, which is based on a letter of June 16, 1958, from Ottavio Pastore. Tasca states that he and Pastore originally thought of offering the candidacy to Salvemini, though he implies that Gramsci was first to stress the importance of the problem to the Party.

Chapter Three

1. Malatesta, p. 20. Malatesta and Ambrosoli (*Nè aderire nè sabotare*) are the standard works on Italian Socialism during the war. There are many interesting anecdotes in Montagnana and Germanetto.

2. Malatesta, p. 19.

3. Lenin, *Movimento italiano*, p. 88. See also Aldo Romano, pp. 436–37: "Among all the Socialist parties of Europe, the PSI was the one that displayed the most logical and consistent conduct, within the limits of the possibilities offered by the grave situation." Bukharin referred to the PSI as "one of the rare Socialist parties that remained faithful to the International amid the madness of belligerency, a healthy, sane party in the aggressive tradition of the communism of Marx and Engels." As quoted from his message to the 16th Congress of the PSI in *Il Partito socialista*, p. 54.

4. Ambrosoli, *Nè aderire*, p. 64.

5. Spriano, *Torino operaia*, p. 92.

6. *Ibid.*, pp. 101–2.

7. Montagnana, p. 51.

8. *Ibid.*, pp. 51–52. The text of the declaration of the Party directorate is in Ambrosoli, *Nè aderire*, pp. 340–41.

9. Malatesta, pp. 32–36.

10. As quoted by Aldo Romano, pp. 418–19.

11. Now in *Scritti giovanili* [9], pp. 3–7. See Spriano, *Torino operaia*, pp. 84–91, for a discussion of the debate.

12. "Neutralità . . . ," *Scritti giovanili* [9], p. 4, and "La Commemorazione di Miss Clavell" (17.i.16), *ibid.*, pp. 17–19.

13. *Scritti giovanili* [9], p. 6.

14. Ferrara and Ferrara, p. 36.

15. Tasca, "La Storia," p. 4; Bellini and Galli, p. 26. As Aldo Romano has shown (p. 424), the theory of World War I as an imperialist war was not exclusively Lenin's, though he did give the idea a strong base in economic theory. Even the idea of the transformation of war into civil war was held by many Socialists before 1914. In 1905, Juarès advocated insurrection in case of war (see Joll, p. 133), as did the Unione Sindacale Italiana in the summer of 1914.

16. The entire series of Gramsci's drama reviews have been collected and reprinted as an appendix to *Letteratura e vita nazionale* [7]. Eric Bentley, the American drama critic, has stated that Gramsci's reviews contain some of the "keenest theater criticism I know of in Italy" ("Italian Theater," p. 19). Gramsci's local news chronicles, mostly written between 1916 and 1918, now appear in *Sotto la Mole* [11].

17. See Spriano, *Torino operaia*, pp. 116–36, for a succinct description of events in Turin through late 1916.

18. *Ibid.*, p. 123.

19. Cf. Gramsci, "I Ricordi delle storie e le vicende delle cotoniere" (9.xii.16), *Scritti giovanili* [9], pp. 48–53.

20. As quoted in Spriano, *Torino operaia*, p. 124.

21. Spriano (*ibid.*, p. 127) describes the subscription for civilian assistance to the war effort as "paltry." As of March 1916, only 1.7 million lire were collected in Turin as compared to 10 million in Milan.

22. As quoted in Ambrosoli, *Nè aderire*, p. 102.

23. An important work on the Zimmerwald Conference is Alfred Rosmer, *De l'Union Sacrée*, pp. 368–419, 554–57. The manifesto and other related documents are reproduced in Rosmer's book (pp. 374–83, 554–57) and in Ambrosoli, *Nè aderire*, pp. 370–83.

24. See Malatesta, pp. 86–87. Malatesta was at that time a reporter for *Avanti!*

25. Spriano, *Torino operaia*, p. 129.

26. Montagnana, p. 55.

27. "Dopo il Congresso socialista spagnuolo" (13.xi.15), *Scritti giovanili* [9], p. 7.

28. On the Kienthal Conference and its background, see Rosmer, *De Zimmerwald*, pp. 70–97. See also Ambrosoli, *Nè aderire*, pp. 124–39, 384–94.

29. "La Matrice" (23.vi.16), *Sotto la Mole* [11], p. 181.

30. "Il Compagno G. M. Serrati e le generazioni del socialismo italiano," Ferrata and Gallo [12], p. 770.

31. As quoted in Spriano, *Torino operaia*, p. 164.

32. *Ibid.*, p. 167.

33. G to Tatiana, 7.ix.31, *Lettere* [1], p. 137.

34. *Scritti giovanili* [9], pp. 22–26.

35. It seems more important to emphasize Gramsci's dialectical approach to theory and practice than his so-called "operaismo," or adulation of the workers, as the following points in the text show. See Paris, "Una Revisione," pp. 165–66.

36. *Scritti giovanili* [9], p. 24.

37. *Ibid.*, p. 25.

38. "L'Università populare" (29.xii.16), *Scritti giovanili* [9], pp. 61–64.

39. "Uomini o macchine?" (24.xii.16), *Scritti giovanili* [9], pp. 57–59.

40. "I Ricordi delle storie e le vicende delle cotoniere," *Scritti giovanili* [9], pp. 48–49. Several passages in this article recall the scenes of Mario Monicelli's recent film *The Organizer* (*I Compagni*), which does in fact deal with the first textile strike in Turin, though not on a strictly historical basis.

41. "Carlo Péguy ed Ernesto Psichari" (6.v.16), *Scritti giovanili* [9], pp. 33–34.

42. "Il Mezzogiorno e la guerra" (1.iv.16), *Scritti giovanili* [9], pp. 30–32. Labriola, who was born in Naples in 1875, was a revolutionary syndicalist who supported intervention. Giolitti chose him as Minister of Labor in his last government of 1920–21, where Labriola played an important part in the negotiations regarding the occupation of the factories.

43. *La Città futura* [22], p. 4.

44. *Scritti giovanili* [9], pp. 73–78.

45. Togliatti concedes in *Gramsci* (1955), p. 77, that in *La Città futura* "elements of the idealistic dialectic still prevail."

46. *Scritti giovanili* [9], pp. 78–80.

47. "Disciplina e libertà," *Scritti giovanili* [9], p. 82.

48. "Margini, 6," *Scritti giovanili* [9], pp. 84–85.

49. *Ibid.*, p. 85.

50. *La Città futura* [22], p. 4. In 1933, Gramsci described his attitude toward Croce during the period of *La Città futura*: "In February of 1917, in a brief note preceding the reprinting of Croce's article 'Religione e serenità,' ... I wrote that just as Hegelianism had been the premise of [Marxism] in the nineteenth century ... so Crocean philosophy could be the premise of a renewal of [Marxism] in our day." Actually, Gramsci's memory seems to be at fault on this point, for the only mention of Croce in the preface to Croce's article in *La Città futura* is the remark quoted in the text; however, the observation of 1933 does help us to understand why Gramsci reprinted Croce's article. Felice Platone made the following judgment of *La Città futura*: "It is interesting to observe that the influence of idealistic culture is not manifested in [theory of knowledge, etc.], but in the appreciation and acceptance of its demand for seriousness and coherence of thought and character, in its rejection of the improvisations and banalities of so-called positivistic thought. There was no influence of idealistic culture in the judgment of historical facts." Platone, "L'Ordine nuovo," p. 36.

51. "Il Movimento operaio torinese," *L'Ordine nuovo* [10], p. 179.

52. This term was first used in reference to the Turin gas workers' strike of 1902. See Spriano, *Socialismo e classe operaia,* p. 109.

53. Monticone, "Il Socialismo torinese"; "Il Movimento operaio," in *La Città futura* (Milan, 1959), pp. 41–90; Spriano, *Torino operaia,* pp. 170–269; Zucaro, "La Rivolta di Torino"; Ambrosoli, *Nè aderire,* pp. 196–237. Other accounts of some value are to be found in Montagnana, pp. 68–74; Germanetto, pp. 122–27; Kirova; Castagno, *Bruno Buozzi,* pp. 33–36; and "Cronaca dei 'fatti di agosto'." In his article, Zucaro published for the first time the "Sentence" of the Territorial Military Court, which contains a detailed account of all the events, from May 1915 on, that contributed—in the judgment of the Court—to the uprising. Since censorship prevented the newspapers from publishing news of most of these events, and since the facts were "ascertained with due control over the various sources on the part of the magistrates themselves," Zucaro ("La Rivolta," p. 439) considers this document the basic primary source for the August uprising. Ambrosoli is not so sure. He points out (*Nè aderire,* p. 200, n. 7) that police reports tend to distort, and that "historical truth is not always identical with legal truth." Monticone was the first to use the material contained in the files of the Ministry of the Interior, now in the Archivio Centrale in Rome. He has constructed a good narrative of the August insurrection; however, as Zucaro says ("La Rivolta," p. 439), he did not place the events of August within the framework of the whole history of the Turin labor movement. Had he done so, it is unlikely that he would have judged the Turin workers as "particularly excited by an extremist and revolutionary minority," since Spriano and others have shown that the Turin labor movement as a whole had become "extremist" long before the August uprising. On the other hand, Zucaro goes too far (p. 440) when he states that it was the "Turinese proletariat that brought Italian Socialism out of its national limitations and onto a new and European level for the first time." The vast majority of the PSI took a "European" position on the war.

54. Zucaro, "La Rivolta," p. 445.

55. A flyer in the Archivio Centrale dello Stato, dated November 13, 1916, as quoted in Spriano, *Torino operaia,* p. 172. Cf. a similar manifesto in Zucaro, "La Rivolta," pp. 445–46.

56. Zucaro, "La Rivolta," p. 446.

57. Spriano, *Torino operaia,* p. 175.

58. Zucaro, "La Rivolta," p. 447.

59. Spriano, *Torino operaia,* pp. 178–79. The Director's information was evidently based on a confidential letter he received from Senator Frassati, the editor of *La Stampa.*

60. *Ibid.,* pp. 188–93. Fossati, for example, argues that in the war years "the purchasing power of real wages had descended to levels equal to less than one-fourth of the real wages of 1913."

61. Prato, p. 117. Prato (p. 94) asserts that wages lagged behind prices in

Turin, except among the metalworkers, who had high piecework premiums and overtime rates.

62. As quoted in Spriano, *Torino operaia*, p. 196.

63. "Bolscevismo intellettuale" (16.v.18), *Scritti giovanili* [9], p. 227.

64. "Note sulla rivoluzione russa" (29.iv.17), *Scritti giovanili* [9], p. 105.

65. Spriano, *Torino operaia*, p. 211; Zucaro, "La Rivolta," pp. 448–49. The Russian Revolution was cited in the "Sentence" for the first time in connection with this incident.

66. As quoted in Spriano, *Torino operaia*, p. 218.

67. Zucaro, "La Rivolta," p. 451.

68. Spriano, *Torino operaia*, p. 215.

69. *Ibid.*, p. 216.

70. *Ibid.*, pp. 220–22. The text of the "Manifesto della frazione intransigente rivoluzionaria" is in Ambrosoli, *Nè aderire*, pp. 357–59.

71. As quoted in Spriano, *Torino operaia*, p. 219.

72. *Ibid.*, p. 219.

73. Ambrosoli, *Nè aderire*, p. 221.

74. Accounts of this event may be found in the following works: Zucaro, "La Rivolta," pp. 454–57; Spriano, *Torino operaia*, pp. 225–28; Ambrosoli, *Nè aderire*, pp. 223–27; Montagnana, p. 65; Kirova, pp. 79–80; Monticone, pp. 70–73.

75. Kirova, p. 79. *Avanti!* (14.viii.17) estimated 30,000-40,000. According to Montagnana (p. 65) and Spriano (p. 227) the crowd numbered 40,000. Ambrosoli (p. 225) says "several thousand," but the "Sentence" published by Zucaro (p. 454) gives the figure of "seven or eight thousand."

76. "I Massimalisti russi" (28.vii.17), *Scritti giovanili* [9], p. 124.

77. Zucaro, "La Rivolta," p. 455.

78. *Ibid.*, p. 456.

79. *Torino operaia*, p. 228. Ambrosoli refers to it as a "proof of the strength of the Turin labor movement" (p. 227).

80. Zucaro, "La Rivolta," p. 457.

81. As quoted in *ibid.*, p. 459.

82. Montagnana, p. 69.

83. For a description of these barricades, see "Cronaca dei 'fatti di agosto'," p. 660.

84. See Zucaro, "La Rivolta," p. 447, n. 16, and Ambrosoli, *Nè aderire*, pp. 205–6, n. 18, for some information on the wartime propaganda of the PSI among the soldiers. It does not seem to have had much effect.

85. "Cronaca dei 'fatti di agosto'," p. 661.

86. *Bruno Buozzi*, p. 34.

87. See "Cronaca dei 'fatti di agosto'," p. 660: "In 1920 we heard from anarchists who were in contact with the Ordine Nuovo group that in 1917 the group at the Barriera di Milano was technically preparing for the uprising. Certainly a people's revolt cannot last several days, as was the case in Turin, without creating centers of leadership, which, in the event of victory, will

become centers of power. And the nucleus of these centers is always held by those who are 'prepared' to fight. The Communists must keep this truth in mind." Judging by their superb contribution to the Resistance movement of 1943–45, the Communists did "keep this truth in mind"!

88. Montagnana, p. 72.

89. Castagno, p. 34.

90. Text in Zucaro, "La Rivolta," p. 459.

91. Text of the statement in *ibid.*, p. 460.

92. Perhaps these figures are based on the article of 1927 in *Lo Stato operaio*, p. 665, which states: "With regard to the dead, the officially given figure was 42. It is far short of the true figure. Outside of Turin and at the front, they spoke of thousands of deaths. However, precise figures are not to be had even by going to the cemetery. There were probably about 500 dead. The wounded were undoubtedly several thousands."

93. Monticone, p. 86, n. 3.

94. Spriano, *Torino operaia*, p. 256.

95. The "Sentence" is in Zucaro, "La Rivolta." Those on trial were G. M. Serrati, Francesco Barberis, Pietro Rabezzana, Maria Giudice, Giuseppe Pianezza, Zaverio D'Alberto, Virginio Boccignoni, Anselmo Acutis, Leopoldo Cavallo, Elvira Zocchi, Ettore Ercole, Luigi Faggiano, and Luigi Chignoli.

96. *Torino operaia*, p. 257.

97. Cf. Ambrosoli, *Nè aderire*, p. 232, n. 21, and p. 236, n. 26, on this point.

98. *Torino operaia*, p. 259.

99. Lenin, *Movimento operaio*, p. 102.

100. "Cronaca dei 'fatti di agosto'," p. 655.

101. *Passato e presente* [8], pp. 45, 51–52.

102. Monticone, pp. 92–94; Spriano, *Torino operaia*, p. 257, and p. 279, nn. 11–12.

103. Spriano, *Torino operaia*, p. 256.

104. Page, pp. 303–4, 307–8.

105. Grieco, "Le Ripercussioni," p. 990.

106. Pieri, "La Leggenda di Caporetto." See Ambrosoli, *Nè aderire*, pp. 205–6, n. 18, for a reference to this article.

107. Gramsci, "Il Grido del popolo" (19.x.18), *Scritti giovanili* [9], p. 325.

108. *Ibid.*

109. Spriano, *Torino operaia*, p. 271.

110. Gramsci, "Il movimento operaio," *L'Ordine nuovo* [10], p. 183; Spriano, *Torino operaia*, pp. 272–73.

111. Text of the manifesto in Ambrosoli, *Nè aderire*, pp. 357–59.

112. Spriano, *Torino operaia*, p. 284.

113. As quoted in Germanetto, p. 135.

114. Text of the manifesto in Malatesta, p. 272.

115. Bellini and Galli, p. 29.

116. Germanetto, p. 135. Aldo Romano agrees that during the war Bordiga was "the outstanding figure of Italian Socialism" (p. 433). However, it seems

to me, on the basis of Romano's own documentation, that he has exaggerated Bordiga's virtues.

The above description of the Florence Conference has been drawn mainly from Germanetto's book, the only detailed source of that event known to me. It is essential to use either the Paris edition (1930) in Italian, or the English edition of 1935, since many of Germanetto's remarks on Bordiga were deleted in later editions. Spriano's account of the meeting (*Torino operaia*, pp. 281–87) adds some important information based on his archival research.

117. *Il Materialismo storico* [3], p. 20. Of course, this delegate may have been a maximalist; but he could not have been a reformist, since that group was not represented at the meeting.

118. *Passato e presente* [8], p. 59.

119. See Arfè, *Storia dell'Avanti!*, pp. 156–57; Tasca, "La Storia," p. 4.

120. Arfè, *Storia dell'Avanti!*, pp. 156–57.

121. Gobetti, p. 117.

122. Soave, p. 2. See the recent memoirs by Max Eastman: "In reporting Russian developments with theoretic understanding, . . . [the *Liberator*] was alone, almost, in the Western world. I was told later by Antonio Gramsci, then secretary of the Italian Communist Party, that even in Italy the first inkling of what was really going on in Russia came through a translation from the *Liberator* of my essay on Lenin. So tight and bristly was the blockade around the Soviets." (Eastman, p. 138.) In a letter of September 4, 1965, to this writer, Mr. Eastman says that his "meeting with Gramsci took place during the Fourth Congress of the International, in November 1922, in Moscow. I have a feeling that we met on the street outside the Congress rather than in the corridor of the Congress itself, but I am not absolutely sure about that. It was a brief meeting and a brief conversation."

123. Togliatti, "Il Leninismo nel pensiero e nell'azione di Antonio Gramsci (appunti)," in *Studi gramsciani*, p. 20.

124. "Il Nostro Marx" (4.v.18), *Scritti giovanili* [9], pp. 217–21.

125. "La Critica critica" (12.i.18), *Scritti giovanili* [9], pp. 153–55.

126. "Un Anno di storia" (16.iii.18), *Scritti giovanili* [9], p. 195.

127. "I Massimalisti russi" (28.vii.17), *Scritti giovanili* [9], pp. 122–24.

128. "La Rivoluzione contro il *Capitale*" (5.i.18), *Scritti giovanili* [9], pp. 149–53.

129. "L'Opera di Lenin" (14.ix.18), *Scritti giovanili* [9], p. 312.

130. "Per conoscere la rivoluzione russa" (22.vi.18), *Scritti giovanili* [9], pp. 263–69.

Chapter Four

1. Tasca, *Nascita*, p. 15. Villari says that "The knowledge of these losses created a deep impression in Italy, but it was felt that they were not adequately appreciated in Allied countries" ("Italy," *Encyclopedia Brittanica*, 13th ed., Vol. 30, p. 561).

2. See Chabod, *Italie contemporaine*, p. 17, for the figures on the deficit.

The figures on the cost of living are drawn from Riccardo Bachi's index, as quoted in Prato, p. 137, n. 2.

3. Bonomi, p. 30.

4. As quoted in Tasca, *Nascita,* p. 16.

5. Nenni, p. 6.

6. Tasca, *Nascita,* p. 18.

7. Leonetti, *Mouvements ouvriers,* p. 133.

8. Arfè, *Storia dell'Avanti!,* p. 158.

9. The meeting of the CGL directors in Bologna at the end of January 1919 is a good example of their tendency to arrive at positions intermediate to those of the other two Socialist institutions. The CGL proposed a democratic republic without qualification, but rejected the dictatorship of the proletariat. (Nenni, p. 14.)

10. Arfè, *Storia dell'Avanti!,* p. 158.

11. Gramsci, "Il Partito comunista, II" (9.x.21), *L'Ordine nuovo* [10], p. 161.

12. *Il Partito,* III, 49.

13. The directing committee of the CGL telegraphed Orlando on June 14, 1919, to protest Italian recognition of the Kolchak "White" government. Gramsci wrote at least six articles in this period aimed at arousing opinion against Allied intervention in Russia.

14. Tasca, *Nascita,* p. 35, n. 43. The *Liberator,* a strongly pro-Bolshevik American periodical, had a correspondent in Italy during the General Strike. He was so impressed with the event that he declared Italy to be on the verge of revolution.

15. Bonomi, p. 34.

16. As quoted in Tasca, *Nascita,* p. 36, n. 44. Pietro Nenni (p. 34) traced the first postwar illusions of Italian workers to this strike.

17. In Turin, the Socialist victory was even more striking. The PSI elected eleven deputies, and all other parties together only seven.

18. For a summary of the Congress, see *Il Partito,* III, 45–103. Brief accounts of the Congress may be found in Nenni, pp. 40–46; Arfè, *Storia dell'Avanti!,* pp. 162–64; Tasca, *Nascita,* pp. 89–90; and Bellini and Galli, pp. 35–38.

19. Arfè, *Storia dell'Avanti!,* p. 164.

20. Spriano, ed., *L'Ordine nuovo,* p. 44, n. 1.

21. Gramsci, "Due Rivoluzioni" (3.vii.20), *L'Ordine nuovo* [10], p. 137.

22. Gramsci, "I Rivoluzionari e le elezioni" (15.xi.19), *L'Ordine nuovo* [10], p. 307.

23. Gramsci, "I Risultati che attendiamo" (17.vii.19), *L'Ordine nuovo* [10], p. 309.

24. Gramsci (4.x.19), *L'Ordine nuovo* [10], p. 458.

25. Gramsci, "Salveminiana" (June 28–July 5, 1919), *L'Ordine nuovo* [10], p. 258.

26. His judgment of the General Strike in July, for example, was far too

optimistic. See "Italiani e cinesi" (18.vii.19), *L'Ordine nuovo* [10], p. 262.

27. Communism as a "national" force was one of Gramsci's favorite themes. Variations on it appear in many of his articles written in 1919, including: "Cronache dell'Ordine Nuovo, VII" (9.vii.19), *L'Ordine nuovo* [10], p. 450; "L'Unità nazionale" (4.x.19), *ibid.*, p. 278; "Industriali, operai, produzione" (21.xi.19), *ibid.*, p. 50.

28. Gramsci, "Nel Paese di Pulcinella" (2.x.20), *L'Ordine nuovo* [10], p. 415.

29. Tasca, *Nascita*, p. 87.

30. Gramsci, "Cos'è la reazione?" (24.xi.20), *L'Ordine nuovo* [10], pp. 365–66.

31. Nenni, p. 22, n. 1. In this footnote, Nenni also criticizes the program of *Ordine nuovo*. It must be remembered that the future leader of the PSI was a bitter political enemy of Gramsci's in the later years of the *primo dopoguerra*.

32. "20–21 luglio" (19.vii.19), *L'Ordine nuovo* [10], p. 267.

33. "Il Programma dell'*Ordine nuovo*, I" (14.viii.20), *L'Ordine nuovo* [10], p. 146.

34. See Ferrara and Ferrara, p. 44, as an example.

35. Soave, "Appunti sulle origine teoriche e pratiche dei Consigli di fabbrica a Torino."

36. From "Evoluzione delle Trade Unions inglesi," *Il Grido del popolo* (27.iv.18), as quoted in Soave, pp. 3–4.

37. "Nella Organizzazione sindacale tedesca," *Il Grido del popolo* (9.iii.18), as quoted in Soave, p. 4.

38. Cole and Postgate, p. 519.

39. Soave, p. 5.

40. Richard Müller, "Comment naquirent les Conseils Révolutionnaires d'Usine," *Spartacus* (1.vii.21), as quoted by Soave, pp. 5–6.

41. Gramsci, "Il Patto d'alleanza" (12.x.18), *Scritti giovanili* [9], pp. 321–22.

42. "Il dovere di essere forti" (25.xi.18), *Scritti giovanili* [9], pp. 337–40. See also Soave, p. 7, who perhaps reads too much of Gramsci's future thought into this article.

43. See Boero's letter to *Avanti!* (13.iii.19), entitled "Grido d'allarme," now in Caracciolo, pp. 17–18. Most of this letter is merely a diatribe against electioneering.

44. "All'alba dell'Ordine Nuovo," *Avanguardia* (March 1919), as quoted in Soave, p. 14.

45. See Spriano, *Torino operaia*, pp. 298–301, and Soave, pp. 10–12, for information on the internal committees in 1918.

46. Spriano, ed., *L'Ordine nuovo*, p. 41.

47. Arturo Jacchia, "Vita operaia" (12.vii.19), in Spriano, ed., *L'Ordine nuovo*, p. 181. See also: excerpts from a speech on the factory councils by Enea Matta, then a worker in the Lancia body plant, delivered to the Con-

gress of the Unione Sindacale Italiana, as quoted in Soave, p. 12; and Terracini, "I Consigli di fabbrica: vicende e problemi, dall'Inghilterra alla Russia, dalla Germania a Torino," in *L'Almanacco socialista* (1920).

48. Gramsci, "Il Programma dell'*Ordine nuovo*, I," *L'Ordine nuovo* [10], p. 147.

49. Gramsci, "Il Programma dell'*Ordine nuovo*, I," *L'Ordine nuovo* [10], p. 148. See also Gobetti, p. 118.

50. A summary of Gramsci's speech was published in *Avanti!* (25.vi.19) and has been reprinted in Caracciolo, pp. 18–19.

51. Spriano, ed., *L'Ordine nuovo*, p. 45.

52. Gramsci (1.xi.19), *L'Ordine nuovo* [10], p. 464.

53. Gobetti, p. 122. This figure, if correct, probably refers to the *province* of Turin, which had a population more than twice as large as the city itself. Gramsci, too, asserted that the movement for councils in Turin "embraced a whole mass of 150,000 workers." "Soviet e consigli di fabbrica" (3–10.iv.20) in Spriano, ed., *L'Ordine nuovo*, p. 477.

54. Spriano, ed., *L'Ordine nuovo*, pp. 68–69, nn. 3–4.

55. Text of the resolution in Caracciolo, p. 20.

56. Gramsci, "Democrazia operaia" (21.vi.19), *L'Ordine nuovo* [10], p. 10.

57. *Ibid.*, p. 11.

58. Gramsci, "Azione positiva" (6–13.xii.19), *L'Ordine nuovo* [10], p.315.

59. Gramsci, "Lo Strumento del lavoro" (14.ii.20), *L'Ordine nuovo* [10], p. 79.

60. Gramsci, "Due Rivoluzioni," *L'Ordine nuovo* [10], pp. 136–37.

61. Gramsci, "Partito di governo e classe di governo" (February 28–March 6, 1920), *L'Ordine nuovo* [10], pp. 92–93.

62. Gramsci, "Lo Strumento del lavoro," *L'Ordine nuovo* [10], p. 82.

63. *Ibid.*, pp. 82–83.

64. Gramsci, "L'Operaio di fabbrica" (21.ii.20), *L'Ordine nuovo* [10], pp. 325–26.

65. Gramsci, "La Relazione Tasca e il Congresso camerale di Torino" (5.vi.20), *L'Ordine nuovo* [10], p. 129. A number of articles contributed by other writers to *Ordine nuovo* may also be regarded as sources for the "Programma." Cf. for example Ottavio Pastore, "Il Problema delle commissioni interne" (16.vii.19), in Spriano, ed., *L'Ordine nuovo*, pp. 244–48.

66. "Il Programma dei commissari di reparto" (8.xi.19), *L'Ordine nuovo* [10], p. 194.

67. *Ibid.*, p. 195.

68. "Il Programma," *L'Ordine nuovo* [10], p. 195.

69. *Ibid.*, p. 193.

70. Montagnana, p. 118.

71. *Ibid.*, p. 117.

72. "Il Programma," *L'Ordine nuovo* [10], p. 198.

73. *Ibid.*, p. 196.

74. Spriano, ed., *L'Ordine nuovo*, p. 37, n. 1. Also Togliatti, "Creare una scuola" (15.xi.19), *ibid.*, pp. 358–62.

75. See, for example, Togliatti's "A Un Rivoluzionario vinto d'Europa" (12.vii.19), in Spriano, ed., *L'Ordine nuovo*, pp. 183–84.

76. *L'Ordine nuovo* [10], p. 447. In December 1919 *Avanguardia*, organ of the FGS, published the program of the School of Culture and Socialist Propaganda, thus giving it national publicity. Even prior to that, Gramsci had received many letters from workers and students outside of Turin that expressed great interest in the program of studies followed in the school (*ibid.*, pp. 467–68).

A principal source for Gramsci's view of culture in the revolution was Anatole Lunacharsky and his proletarian cultural movement. On June 1, 1918, Gramsci published in *Il Grido* an article by the Russian intellectual, which maintained that the cultural movement must be regarded with the same seriousness as the other three branches of the labor movement—the political, economic, and cooperative. With great satisfaction, Gramsci noted that the Turin Socialist movement had also taken this position; hence, Lunacharsky's article provided still another proof "of the great similarity which exists between the moral and intellectual conditions of the two proletariats, the Italian and the Russian." See Spriano, ed., *L'Ordine nuovo*, p. 26, for a discussion of this point.

77. "Il Programma," *L'Ordine nuovo* [10], p. 198. See also p. 33.

78. Gramsci, "Sindacalismo e consigli" (8.xi.19), *L'Ordine nuovo* [10], p. 46.

79. "Controllo di classe" (3.i.20), in Spriano, ed., *L'Ordine nuovo*, pp. 414–17. See Ottino, pp. 23–24, for development of the idea of the council as a revolutionary tool.

80. Gramsci, "Sindacati e consigli" (11.x.19), *L'Ordine nuovo* [10], p. 37.

81. "Il Programma," *L'Ordine nuovo* [10], p. 195.

82. This statement and preceding quotations in the same paragraph are from "La Conquista dello Stato" (12.vii.19), *L'Ordine nuovo* [10], pp. 14–15.

83. *Ibid.*, p. 15.

84. Paraphrased from "Sindacalismo e consigli," *L'Ordine nuovo* [10], pp. 45–46.

85. *Ibid.*, p. 46.

86. Paraphrased from Gramsci, "I Sindacati e la dittatura" (25.x.19), *L'Ordine nuovo* [10], p. 41.

87. The question of "industrial legality" is discussed in "Sindacati e consigli" (12.vi.20), *L'Ordine nuovo* [10], pp. 131–33.

88. *Ibid.*, p. 133.

89. Gramsci, "L'Unità proletaria" (February 28–March 6, 1920), *L'Ordine nuovo* [10], p. 98. See also his "I Gruppi comunisti" (17.vii.20), *ibid.*, p. 140.

A possible source for Gramsci's ideas on the nature of the Socialist party under capitalism is Daniel De Leon's *Socialist Reconstruction of Society*, a speech delivered at Minneapolis in July 1905. De Leon says, for example, "Socialism is the outgrowth of the higher development from capitalism. As such, the methods of the Socialist movement on its march toward Socialist society are perforce primarily dictated by the capitalist shell from which Socialism is hatching." (p. 39.) And again, "The reason for a political party, we have seen, is to contend with capitalism on its own special field—the field that determines the fate of political power. It follows that the structure of a political party must be determined by the capitalist governmental system of territorial demarcations." (p. 46.)

90. This quality separates Gramsci from many Marxist thinkers, for he was far more relentless than most of them in his attempts to reduce all ideas and institutions solely to their historical context. Few Marxists, for example, have explored the idea that even a Socialist party, because of its origin in a capitalist society, is actually a form of that society. The following is another good example of Gramsci's historicism: "The Marxist criticism of liberal economics is a criticism of the idea of perpetuity of human economic and political institutions. It is the reduction to historicity and contingency of every fact. It is a lesson in realism to abstract pseudo-scientists, defenders of strongboxes." "La Sovranità della legge" (1.vi.19), *L'Ordine nuovo* [10], p. 4.

91. See especially "Il Partito e la rivoluzione" (27.xii.19), *L'Ordine nuovo* [10], pp. 67–71.

92. "Il Problema del potere" (29.xi.19), *L'Ordine nuovo* [10], pp. 59–60. Gramsci's general position on working-class democracy was that all political persuasions expressed by the proletariat should enjoy complete freedom of activity. His views on this question were no different from those expressed by the Bolsheviks at this time. As late as February 1920, there were 40 Mensheviks elected to the Moscow Soviet. According to Livio Maitan, a Trotskyite, the prohibition of non-Bolshevik political activities came only after the attempted assassination of Lenin, the assassination of the Bolsheviks Volodarsk and Uritsky, an attempted coup d'etat, and, above all, the attitude taken by the Mensheviks and Social Revolutionaries during the Civil War. Trotsky himself explained: "The prohibition of other Soviet parties was not at all derived from any Bolshevik theory. It was a defense measure of the dictatorship in a backward and exhausted country surrounded by enemies on every side. . . . If the revolution had won, even in Germany alone, the necessity to prohibit other Soviet parties would not have arisen." Maitan, *Attualità*, p. 22, n. 11.

According to *Ordine nuovo* (daily) of February 25, 1921, Lenin strongly defended working-class democracy in the trade unions: "We must make use of these formidable professional organizations in order to defend ourselves against our own State, that is against all its shortcomings, against the bureaucratism of the state organs where many bourgeois elements and employees of the old regime have penetrated." See Tamburrano, p. 82, n. 31, for the reference to this point.

93. These distinctions are presented in the following articles by Gramsci, all in *L'Ordine nuovo* [10]: "Il Programma dell'*Ordine nuovo*, II" (28.viii. 20), p. 150; "Il Partito e la rivoluzione," p. 67; and "Il Consiglio di fabbrica" (5.vi.20), p. 124. Gramsci also described the trade union as a "voluntary" organization.

94. This problem, implicit in many of Gramsci's articles of this period, is explicitly discussed in the following, all in *L'Ordine nuovo* [10]: "Il Partito e la rivoluzione," pp. 67–71; "Il Consiglio di fabbrica," pp. 123–27; and "Due Rivoluzioni," pp. 135–40.

95. To "predictions," Gramsci characteristically added "within the limits of historical probability," thus protecting himself from charges of metaphysical dogmatism. See "Il Consiglio di fabbrica," *L'Ordine nuovo* [10], p. 123.

96. "Il Partito e la rivoluzione" [10], p. 68.

97. "Due Rivoluzioni" [10], p. 135.

98. "Il Consiglio di fabbrica" [10], p. 127.

99. Leonetti, *Mouvements ouvriers*, p. 130. Previously the so-called "Piedmontese edition" of *Avanti!* had been the same as the Milan edition with an added page devoted to the local news of Turin.

100. Arfè, *Storia dell'Avanti!*, p. 70.

101. Ferrara and Ferrara, p. 59.

102. Gramsci, "*L'Ordine nuovo* e battaglie sindacali" (6–13.xii.19), *L'Ordine nuovo* [10], p. 386.

103. This letter may be seen in Lenin, *Movimento italiano*, pp. 164–65. The last quotation from this letter was censored in *Avanti!*, but the entire letter did appear in the *Corriere della sera* of December 8, as well as in other newspapers: see Salvemini, *Scritti sul fascismo*, I, p. 494, n. 6.

104. Gramsci, "Il Rivoluzionario qualificato" (20.xii.19), *L'Ordine nuovo* [10], pp. 387–88.

105. As far back as 1916, Lenin had urged the expulsion of at least the "social-chauvinist" group of reformists from the PSI. In that year he wrote to the Italian Socialists: "The representatives of our party have worked together with yours at Zimmerwald and Kienthal. Our only serious disagreement concerned the inevitability and necessity of rupture with the Socialists in words but chauvinists in deeds, and precisely with all those who directly or indirectly supported their 'own' government, their 'own' bourgeoisie, in this reactionary and mercenary war made for the partition of colonies and for domination of the world." (Lenin, *Movimento italiano*, p. 110.)

106. Caracciolo, "Serrati, Bordiga, e la polemica gramsciana contro il 'blanquismo' o settarismo di partito," in *La Città futura* (Milan, 1959), p. 94.

107. Nor, according to Caracciolo (*ibid.*, p. 94), was Serrati's position anything like Lenin's view of the revolution. The Russian leader was influenced to a certain extent by blanquismo, but the whole corpus of his thought on the revolution was "much more complex and 'democratic.'" But see Stanley Moore's *Three Tactics*. In this fascinating little book, Moore shows that the

doctrine of "minority revolution" (or of "permanent revolution") was one of three patterns for the transition from capitalism to Socialism continually recurring in Marxist thought.

108. As quoted in Nenni, p. 71, n. 1.

109. Terracini, "Il Consiglio nazionale di Firenze" (24–31.i.20), in Spriano, ed., *L'Ordine nuovo*, p. 437. Togliatti, in two articles on the Bombacci project, also attacked its legalism: "Marx taught us that law is only a superstructure; Bombacci is contented with the superstructure." See his "La Costituzione dei Soviet in Italia, I" (14.ii.20), *ibid.*, p. 446.

110. Serrati later declared that the councils were "defended by extremists of the right and of the left from Rigola to Gramsci, and were fought by extremists of the right and left from Buozzi to Bordiga." Serrati, "Documentazione unitaria," p. 540.

111. *Ibid.*, p. 540. In the same article (p. 541), Serrati charged the Turin Socialists with being "more inspired by the English syndicalists of the shop-steward movement than by the Russian example [of Soviets]."

112. Serrati in *Avanti!* (14.iii.20), as quoted in Nenni, p. 71, n. 2.

113. According to Spriano (*L'Ordine nuovo*, p. 71), Bordiga's displeasure was in direct proportion to the degree of collaboration of his followers in Turin with the program of *Ordine nuovo*. The leading abstentionists in Turin were Giovanni Boero and Giovanni Parodi.

114. Bordiga, "Per la costituzione dei Consigli operai in Italia," *Il Soviet* (4.i.20), as quoted in Spriano, ed., *L'Ordine nuovo*.

115. Bordiga, "Lo Sciopero," pp. 57–58.

116. Gramsci, "Primo: rinnovare il Partito" (24–31.i.20), *L'Ordine nuovo* [10], p. 391.

117. *Ibid.*, p. 391.

118. *Ibid.*, p. 393.

119. Gramsci, "Programma d'azione della sezione socialista torinese" (24–31.i.20), *L'Ordine nuovo* [10], p. 393. "The Turinese Socialist section must assume the role of goading the Socialist Party into promoting in all Italy the creation of workers' and peasants' Councils."

120. *Ibid.*, p. 395.

121. Tasca, "L'Ordine Nuovo" ("I Primi Dieci Anni, 2"), p. 5.

122. See Chapter VI of this work for an analysis of these essays.

123. A letter of March 27, 1924, from Gramsci to Togliatti. See Togliatti's *La Formazione*, p. 257.

124. Gramsci, "La Funzione storica delle città" (17.i.20), *L'Ordine nuovo* [10], p. 320. Gramsci, in his intense desire for historical justification, saw Turin's present role as no more than a completion of its role during the Risorgimento. In the nineteenth century, Milan represented the "fulcrum" of Italian economic wealth; but it had required the "disciplined" energy of the Turin bourgeoisie to unify Italy. In 1920 Milan remained the fulcrum of the national economy and the Socialist Party, but only the Turin proletariat, with its superior discipline, could carry out the revolution.

Chapter Five

1. Chabod, *L'Italie contemporaine*, p. 19. The value of the lira, 13.07 lire to the dollar in December 1919, declined to 22.94 in April 1920, and 28.57 in December 1920 (*ibid.*, p. 18).

2. Bachi, p. 236. Bachi asserts that figures on unemployment in this period are very unreliable, since they were gathered by local authorities according to widely varying criteria of measurement.

3. Tasca, *Nascita*, p. 125, n. 1.

4. *Ibid.*, p. 26, n. 4, and Salvatorelli and Mira, p. 71, give several examples of this *scioperomania*. One such is the strike at the Ferriere Piemontese in Turin, where the workers struck because of a rumor that "the brother of a worker had applied to join the Royal Guards."

5. Nenni, p. 76.

6. Tasca, *Nascita*, p. 95. Salvatorelli and Mira (p. 71) merely assert that the victims were numerous. According to Nenni (p. 85), May Day of 1920 alone saw 12 workers killed: 5 at Turin, 2 at Pola, 3 at Paola, and 2 in the province of Padua. *Avanti!* claimed on May 1, 1920, that between April 1919 and April 1920 there were 145 deaths and 444 woundings of workers and peasants.

7. Technically, the Confindustria was merely being reestablished, since a Confederazione Italiana dell'Industria had already been founded at Turin in May 1910. However, this association was really limited to firms in Piedmont, Lombardy, and Liguria, and it did not survive the war. See Spriano, *Socialismo e classe operaia*, p. 247 and p. 257, n. 33.

8. Tasca, *Nascita*, p. 113. The text of the manifesto voted by the industrialists is in Nenni, p. 69.

9. Gramsci, "Superstizione e realtà" (8.v.20), *L'Ordine nuovo* [10], p. 109. The text of Olivetti's report, "L'Opinione degli industriali sui Consigli di fabbrica," was reprinted in *Ordine nuovo*, II, 2 (15.v.20).

10. "Per un rinnovamento del Partito socialista" (8.v.20), *L'Ordine nuovo* [10], p. 117. Actually, Gramsci had indicated his fear of a reactionary dictatorship as early as January 1920: "We hold that the bourgeoisie cannot avoid the destiny that awaits it without a reactionary and military dictatorship, to which it will sooner or later resort" ("Programma d'azione della sezione socialista torinese," *L'Ordine nuovo* [10], p. 396). Errico Malatesta, dean of Italian anarchists, was another rare spirit who saw the danger of catastrophe to the labor movement. In January 1920 he declared: "If we let this favorable moment pass we shall later pay with tears of blood for the fear we have instilled in the bourgeoisie." As quoted in Sforza, p. 264.

11. Tasca, *Nascita*, p. 110. See also Luigi Einaudi, p. 323; Salvatorelli and Mira, p. 72; and Ferrara and Ferrara, p. 67.

12. Montagnana, p. 119.

13. *Ibid.*, pp. 119–20.

14. Evidently, as a first step, management demanded that the members of the "internal commission" be removed and declared ineligible for election

for one year. See Gramsci, "Superstizione e realtà," *L'Ordine nuovo* [10], p. 110.

15. *Ibid.*, pp. 109–10. On April 3 Gramsci declared that Turin was a "garrisoned fortress" containing 50,000 soldiers, with artillery emplacements on the surrounding hills. See "Torino e l'Italia" (3.iv.20), *L'Ordine nuovo* [10], p. 106. Spriano (*L'Ordine nuovo*, p. 78) has shown that as early as March 20 the industrialists had informed the Prefect of Turin that they intended to make use of a general lockout "within a very short time."

16. Gramsci, "Superstizione e realtà," *L'Ordine nuovo* [10], p. 110.

17. Tasca, *Nascita*, p. 126, n. 5.

18. *Ibid.*

19. "Superstizione e realtà," *L'Ordine nuovo* [10], p. 111.

20. "Il Movimento torinese dei consigli di fabbrica," *L'Ordine nuovo* [10], p. 177.

21. Tasca, *Nascita*, p. 126, n. 5.

22. Bachi, p. 343. This judgment agrees closely with that of Montagnana (p. 121): "For eleven days the life of the city and province remained completely paralyzed. Tramways, railroads, public services, and many commercial businesses ceased functioning, in addition to the whole of industry. There were absolutely no scabs. The workers' movement was soon coordinated with a strike of the agricultural workers in nearby provinces."

23. Gramsci, "Il Movimento torinese," *L'Ordine nuovo* [10], p. 177.

24. Nenni, p. 77.

25. As quoted in Tasca, *Nascita*, p. 127, n. 5. This document is also to be found in Caracciolo, "Il Movimento torinese," pp. 21–22.

26. Bachi, as quoted in Luigi Einaudi, p. 324, and Montagnana, p. 123. According to Bachi, meetings of commissars with workers during working hours would no longer be permitted.

27. Togliatti, *Gramsci* (1955), p. 28.

28. Montagnana, p. 122.

29. Genoa seems to have been the only other city that gave extensive support to the Turin workers. See Spriano, ed., *L'Ordine nuovo*, p. 82, n. 1.

30. Gramsci, "Il Movimento torinese," *L'Ordine nuovo* [10], p. 186.

31. *Ibid.*

32. Serrati later remarked that the Turin motion was rejected "not through aversion to the principles declared in it," but "in order not to appear to authorize similar procedures contrary to Party discipline and the interests of the proletariat" ("Documentazione, I," p. 543).

33. Cf. p. 91 of this work.

34. As quoted in Nenni, p. 81, n. 1.

35. "Il Movimento torinese," *L'Ordine nuovo* [10], p. 186.

36. As quoted in Nenni, p. 77. It is interesting to note that even a "Communist" member of the Party Directorate like Egidio Gennari criticized the general strike as an irresponsible and undisciplined act. Gennari so defined it in his report to the Congress of Livorno (Jan. 1921), reprinted in Serrati,

"Documentazione, I," pp. 541–42. This clearly indicates the almost complete isolation of the Turin Socialists.

37. The entire text of the article is reproduced in Nenni, p. 78.

38. Gobetti, p. 123.

39. "Per un rinnovamento del Partito socialista," *L'Ordine nuovo* [10], pp. 116–23.

40. Lombardo Radice and Carbone, p. 90. For the history of this document, see Gramsci, "Cronache dell'Ordine nuovo, XXXII" (21.viii.20), *L'Ordine nuovo* [10], p. 484.

41. "Per un rinnovamento," *L'Ordine nuovo* [10], p. 118.

42. *Ibid.,* p. 119.

43. *Ibid.,* p. 121.

44. Tasca, "Comunismo e fascismo" ("I Primi Dieci Anni, 3"), p. 9. Gramsci said the report "was known only by the readers of *Ordine nuovo* and by the few readers of the pamphlet 'Per un rinnovamento del Partito socialista italiano.' It was not taken into consideration by the central and responsible organisms of the Party." See "Cronache dell'Ordine nuovo, XXXII," *L'Ordine nuovo* [10], p. 484.

45. Bellini and Galli, p. 39.

46. Lenin, *The Communist International,* p. 200.

47. Lenin, " 'Left-wing' Communism, an Infantile Disorder," in *ibid.,* p. 155.

48. Lenin, "Speech on Parliamentarianism," in *ibid.,* pp. 246–48.

49. According to Bellini and Galli (p. 41), Bordiga explained somewhat lamely that his attitude "was nothing but a tactical difference, which in no way involved questions of theory and principle."

50. From the "Conditions of Admission to the Communist International Approved by the Second Comintern Congress," in Degras, ed., *The Communist International,* I, 166–72. The Twenty-One Points were published by *Ordine nuovo* in its issue of September 4.

51. From "Serrati's Speech to the 7th Meeting of the 2nd Congress of the Communist International," in the appendix to Lenin, *Movimento italiano,* p. 282.

52. Lenin, "Theses on the Fundamental Tasks of the Second International,"*The Communist International,* p. 177. See also Zinoviev's strong attack on Turati during the 6th Meeting of the 2nd Congress in the appendix to Lenin, *Movimento italiano,* pp. 276–77.

53. *The Communist International,*p. 212, and *Movimento italiano,*p. 196.

54. Gramsci, *L'Ordine nuovo* [10], p. 484.

55. Bordiga's article (from *Il Soviet* of October 3, 1920) was reprinted by Gramsci, along with his own remarks, in "Cronache dell'Ordine nuovo, XXXV" (9.x.20), *L'Ordine nuovo* [10], pp. 488–89.

56. Togliatti, *Gramsci* (1955), p. 32. See also Platone, "L'Ordine Nuovo," p. 40: "I believe this [weakness] was due in great part to the extreme seriousness of Gramsci, who hesitated to take his place as national director of the

labor movement." Gobetti, too, refers to Gramsci's "reticence and timidity." See his "Storia dei comunisti torinesi scritta da un liberale," in Valeri, ed., *Antologia*, p. 218.

57. Togliatti, *Gramsci* (1955), p. 32.

58. Two examples of such control are given in Ferrara and Ferrara, p. 69, and Tasca, "L'Ordine Nuovo" ("I Primi Dieci Anni, 2"), p. 5.

59. G to Ferri (Alfonso Leonetti), Vienna (28.i.24), in Togliatti, *La Formazione*, p. 183. Gramsci similarly confessed to Togliatti on January 27 that "We committed a serious error in 1919 and 1920 in not attacking the Socialist leadership more resolutely, and even in not running the risk of an expulsion" (*ibid.*, p. 180).

60. Bordiga declared to Lenin that *Ordine nuovo*, "besides being contrary to the directives of the Congress on the union question and on the constitution of Soviets, had been a proponent of Party unity until shortly before the Convention of Florence [January 1920]." This quotation is from *Il Soviet* of October 3, 1920, as reprinted by Gramsci in "Cronache dell'Ordine nuovo, XXXV," *L'Ordine nuovo* [10], p. 488.

61. Gramsci warned, for example (in "Due Rivoluzioni," *L'Ordine nuovo* [10], p. 138), that the Party must not be sidetracked by narrow problems like electoral abstentionism or the constitution of a "truly" Communist Party, but must create conditions in the masses in which all these problems would be resolved as organic problems of the Communist revolution's development:

"In fact, can a Communist Party exist as a party of action (and not an academy of doctrinaire purists and politicians who think 'well' and express themselves 'well' on Communist matters), if the masses do not have the spirit of historical initiative and desire for industrial autonomy that must be reflected and synthesized in the Communist Party? The rise of real historical forces and the formation of parties that reflect them does not come suddenly out of nothing, but develops from a dialectical process: therefore, should not the chief task of the Communist forces be to organize and instruct the essentially Communist productive power that must be developed and expanded as an economic base for any political power the proletariat may possess?"

62. As quoted in Spriano, ed., *L'Ordine nuovo*, p. 86, n. 1. Gramsci's statement is from *Il Soviet* of May 16.

63. The speech was reprinted in *Ordine nuovo*, II, 3 (29.v.20).

64. Tasca, "Comunismo e fascismo" ("I Primi Dieci Anni, 3"), p. 9. See also his editorial "Cercando la verità," *Ordine nuovo*, II, 5 (12.vi.20). In "Comunismo e fascismo," Tasca declares that Gramsci "changed his mind during his years in prison, since he denounced an attempt at Bologna to substitute a council for the Chamber." Tasca refers to an episode mentioned in *Passato e presente* [8], p. 59, in which Gramsci characterizes as "stupid and trivial formalistic voluntarism" the "1920 project of constituting an urban council at Bologna with its sole elements being the organizations [i.e., the trade unions, etc.]. That is, of creating a useless duplication, of replacing an

historical organism rooted in the masses, like the Chamber of Labor, with a purely abstract and bookish organism." Here Tasca fails to see that a council "formed with its sole elements being the organizations" would not be a council at all in Gramsci's sense of the term.

65. Gramsci, "La Relazione Tasca e il congresso camerale di Torino," *L'Ordine nuovo* [10], pp. 127–31. See also "Il Programma dell'*Ordine nuovo*," *ibid.*, pp. 146–54. Tasca's reply to Gramsci's attack is contained in a series of articles entitled "Polemiche sul programma dell'*Ordine nuovo*," reprinted in Spriano, ed., *L'Ordine nuovo*, pp. 518–30, 534–41.

66. Tasca, "Comunismo e fascismo," p. 9. Togliatti and Terracini also had differences of opinion with Gramsci in the summer of 1920. Felice Platone, one of the younger members of the Ordine Nuovo group, wrote in 1951 that Togliatti "was willing to descend to contacts and agreements that would isolate the reformists, the Serratians, and Tasca; Gramsci was more fastidious about this, preferring a tacit alliance with the extreme left, that is, the abstentionists." See Platone, "L'Ordine Nuovo," p. 39. Of course, one is tempted to ask with whom Togliatti sought agreements, besides the extreme left, if he wanted to isolate "the reformists, the Serratians, and Tasca." See also Ferrara and Ferrara, p. 85, and Ferri, "Consiglio di fabbrica," p. 466. Ferri says that Gramsci tended to adopt a "minority" position in considering the Party's "renewal," trying to defeat the reformists on theoretical grounds without going to the mass of the Party for support.

These early examples only hinted at the conflicts between Gramsci and other Ordinovisti: recent publications have made the positions of the Turin Socialist leaders in 1920 much clearer. See Ferri, "La Situazione," and Togliatti, *La Formazione*. Ferri's article includes programs drawn up by the various Communist groups in the Turin section during the election of a new executive committee for the section. They were first published in the Piedmontese edition of *Avanti!* for August 12, 1920.

67. For details and quotations in this and the next two paragraphs, see Ferri, "La Situazione."

68. "Il Partito comunista, I" (4.ix.20), *L'Ordine nuovo* [10], p. 158.

69. "Il Partito comunista, II" (9.x.20), *L'Ordine nuovo* [10], p. 161.

70. In 1920 Scoccimarro was the secretary of the Friuli Provincial Federation of the PSI.

71. G to Togliatti (18.v.23) in Togliatti, *La Formazione*, p. 65.

72. Gramsci to Scoccimarro (5.i.24) in *ibid.*, pp. 151–52. We owe the preservation of this letter to Angelo Tasca, who in fact published the above quotation as early as 1953.

73. Ferrara and Ferrara, pp. 74–75.

74. In September 1920, the CGL and the Confederazione Italiana del Lavoro (the Catholic labor organization) had nearly two million members apiece, although four-fifths of the Catholics were agricultural workers. The Unione Sindacale Italiana, an anarcho-syndicalist group, had more than 300,000. The Unione Italiana del Lavoro, the "Republican" or Mazzinian

group, had less than 200,000, nearly all concentrated in Emilia-Romagna and Latium. See Spriano, *L'Occupazione,* pp. 17–18.

75. This statement seems to have been correct. In 1925, however, AMMA itself admitted that the statistics of Riccardo Bachi were generally recognized as more authoritative. As compared with 1913, the Milan index stood at 441 in 1920 and the Bachi index at 624. Cf. Prato, p. 137, n. 2. See also Spriano, *L'Occupazione,* pp. 35–46, for more details on the economic background of the occupation.

76. As quoted in Spriano, *L'Occupazione,* p. 42, from the "Relazione del Comitato centrale della Fiom sull'agitazione dei metallurgici italiani" (Turin, 1921), p. 20.

77. Prato, p. 150.

78. Prouteau, p. 54.

79. As quoted in Luigi Einaudi, pp. 327–28.

80. Tasca, *Nascita,* p. 119. Italian precedents for an occupation of the factories probably convinced the Fiom leaders that such a movement was not necessarily revolutionary. In March 1917 the interventionists, led by a certain Nosengo, had occupied a plant at Dalmine (Bergamo). Mussolini applauded this action "as a creative strike that does not interrupt production" (Prouteau, p. 37). In March 1920 some metalworking plants near Genoa were similarly occupied, but the movement was quickly ended by police intervention. See Togliatti, "Rapporto sui fatti di Sestri." On these early occupations, see the recent work by Spriano (*L'Occupazione,* pp. 25–26). Spriano says that the CGL viewed these occupations with great suspicion, partly because it thought that the anarcho-syndicalists were behind them.

81. As quoted in Prouteau, p. 54. Just how far Bruno Buozzi, the leader of the Fiom in this period, was from regarding the trade union as a revolutionary body may be seen from the following quotation: "One must admit that during this period a dangerous tendency developed among certain leaders of the workers' associations, and especially among the leaders of the Socialist Party: a tendency to employ the economic strike for political ends." (As quoted in *ibid.,* pp. 48–49.) Yet Buozzi was generally considered to have stood rather to the left among the reformists.

82. Spriano (*L'Occupazione,* pp. 60–61) lists 59 cities where plants were occupied in the first few days of the movement. By September 8, many smaller towns were also affected (*ibid.,* p. 90).

83. See Spriano (*ibid.,* pp. 63–69) for much interesting material on events in Turin during the occupation. See also Giovanni Parodi, "L'Occupazione delle fabbriche," in *Fascismo e antifascismo,* I, 88–92. Parodi managed the Fiat-Centro plant during the occupation.

84. This editorial may be found in Caracciolo, ed., "Il Movimento torinese," p. 24.

85. Montagnana, pp. 139–40.

86. As quoted in Spriano's introduction to Gobetti's *Opere complete,* p. xxvi.

87. Montagnana, pp. 139–40. See also Ferrara and Ferrara, pp. 75–76.

88. Gramsci, "Domenica rossa" (5.ix.20), *L'Ordine nuovo* [10], p. 164.

89. *Ibid.*

90. Luigi Einaudi, p. 328.

91. With regard to the participation of clerks and technicians in the occupation, Spriano (*L'Occupazione*, pp. 64–65) says the "workers' sources are very unreliable," but "in fact, desertions were very extensive and tended to grow rapidly." In some cases, the owners themselves may have encouraged a few of the engineers to remain in the plants to watch over the equipment.

92. Prato, p. 152.

93. Ferrara and Ferrara, p. 77.

94. Montagnana, p. 137.

95. Spriano, *L'Occupazione*, p. 66, n. 2. Spriano adds that during the period of the slowdown in late August, only 27 cars a day were produced.

96. Trevisani, ed., *Enciclopedia*, I, 501. According to Germanetto (p. 207), most of the technicians and clerks in the Savigliano plant remained at their posts, which undoubtedly contributed to the high level of production there.

97. According to Ugo Camurri, an engineer in the Ferriere Piemontese plant in Avigliano, steel production was more than 60% of normal during the occupation. See Spriano, *L'Occupazione,* p. 138, n. 3 and p. 140, n. 5.

98. Luigi Einaudi, p. 329. Labriola stated that "in this controversy the government has always sought to maintain a position of perfect neutrality, and has done and will do everything possible to return the struggle to the level of legality through a reopening of negotiations. But every time that there have been attempts by either side to use arbitrary or violent means, we see that the State is constrained to intervene in favor of private rights or the threatened juridical order." Labriola was not popular with the Left, but it would not be long before such liberal views would be regarded with nostalgia!

99. As described in Sforza, p. 282. Count Sforza was the Foreign Minister in this, the last of Giolitti's cabinets.

100. "From the outset I had a firm and clear conviction that experience would teach the workers that they could not attain their objectives. . . . As I saw it, the episode was repeating, in a way and in different conditions, the analogous situation of the general strike of 1904, which had roused such fear and then revealed itself as inept. I was absolutely convinced that our government's conduct ought to imitate the government then in power [also Giolitti's government]. Accordingly, I let the experiment develop up to a certain point, in order to convince the workers that it was impossible for them to succeed and to prevent the agitators from blaming others for their failures" (Giolitti, p. 598). According to Bonomi (p. 36), Giolitti's method was "not meditated, but imposed by the organic weakness of the forces of the State."

101. This motion is contained in full in Nenni, pp. 100–101.

102. In fact, it was incongruent to threaten a virtual revolution because

the immediate economic demands of the workers were not being satisfied. See Spriano, *L'Occupazione*, pp. 78–79.

103. *Ibid.*, pp. 80–81.

104. The manifesto appeared on p. 1 of *Avanti!* in all its editions on September 6, and is here quoted from Spriano, *ibid.*, p. 81.

105. Tasca, *Nascita*, p. 121.

106. As quoted in Spriano, *L'Occupazione*, pp. 96–97.

107. The most detailed account of this meeting is to be found in *ibid.*, pp. 101–6. See also Nenni, pp. 101–3, which includes the motion calling for socialization. The figure indicating the number of votes held by the Fiom is taken from Spriano and from Luigi Einaudi, p. 332. Einaudi is wrong, however, in reckoning the vote at 591 to 245. He undoubtedly misinterpreted the meaning of the *591,245* votes obtained by the CGL.

108. As quoted in Tasca, *Nascita*, p. 122.

109. See "Extracts from an ECCI letter to the Italian proletariat," in Degras, *The Communist International*, I, 192–93.

110. *L'Occupazione*, p. 107.

111. "Extracts from an ECCI letter to the Italian Socialist Party," in Degras, *The Communist International*, I, 188–91.

112. See Spriano, *L'Occupazione*, pp. 119–24, for details of the negotiations. See also Luigi Einaudi, p. 333 and Montagnana, p. 149.

113. Trevisani, *Enciclopedia*, p. 502. Spriano (*L'Occupazione*, p. 144) merely says that "only the anarchists who led the Turin section of the Federation, Ferrero and Garino, expressed sharply critical observations."

114. Only at Turin was the vote even close—18,740 to 16,909, with 1,024 abstentions. According to Spriano (*L'Occupazione*, p. 145), the total vote was 127,904 to 44,531. These figures show that only a small number of the workers involved in the occupation took the trouble to vote.

115. For a detailed account of the ultimate fate of this bill, see Tasca, *Nascita*, pp. 190–91, n. 2, and Spriano, *L'Occupazione*, p. 155. In 1921, wages were reduced by at least 15% according to figures of the General Confederation of Industry. (Salvatorelli and Mira, p. 92.)

116. Luigi Einaudi, p. 336.

117. See an editorial by Ottavio Pastore in *Avanti!*, Piedmont ed., XXIV, 241 (22.ix.20), as quoted in Tasca, *Nascita*, p. 134, n. 40:
"There isn't a single industrialist who isn't so excited and furious that he conceives the craziest propositions: openly refusing to accept the agreements; sabotaging their practical applications; striking down the hated government in Parliament or on the streets.... The President of the Turin Industrial League has resigned. Other resignations have been announced, and the whole capitalist class is planning revenge and reconquest."
Salvatorelli and Mira (p. 89) also state that "the bourgeoisie felt they had been in great danger, from which the government had not defended them."

118. Tasca, *Nascita*, p. 123. For a detailed discussion of the results of the

occupation, from the points of view of both contemporaries and historians, see Spriano, *L'Occupazione,* pp. 151-64.

In his comments on the impending reaction, Gramsci was already beginning to formulate some interesting ideas on the nature of Fascism. On October 17 he declared: "It is certain that the Italian reaction is strengthening and will soon attempt to impose itself violently. . . . Terrorism wants to move from the private field to the public field. It is no longer content with immunity from the State; it wishes to become the State." "La Reazione" (17.x.20), *L'Ordine nuovo* [10], p. 351. As early as November 24, 1920, he was beginning to see Fascism as an international movement and as a new phase in the general history of the class struggle: "The phenomenon of 'fascism' is not only Italian, just as the formation of the Communist Party is not only Italian. 'Fascism' is the preparatory phase of the restoration of the State, that is . . . of a harshening of the capitalist struggle against the outstanding men of the proletarian class. . . . Fascism assassinates the militants of the working class: the State restored will send them to prison 'legally'." ("Cos'è la reazione?," *L'Ordine nuovo* [10], p. 366.)

119. Gramsci (2.x.20), *L'Ordine nuovo* [10], p. 487. Arfè *(Storia dell'Avanti!,* p. 173) states that the Turin edition of *Avanti!* greeted the settlement as a victory. It is possible that some of the *Avanti!* reporters were so persuaded, but nobody on the staff of *Ordine nuovo* was optimistic. C. N. [Niccolini], for example, in his article "Il Movimento dei metallurgici," *Ordine nuovo,* II, 16 (2.x.20), stated that "it would be a lack of frankness and sincerity to deny that our revolutionary movement has received a powerful blow." Niccolini, while also blaming the CGL for the defeat, absolved the Chambers of Labor within it from this charge. The Chambers, unlike the Federations (trade unions), usually voted with the Party and the Left.

120. Gramsci, "Capacità politica" (24.ix.20), *L'Ordine nuovo* [10], p. 170.

Chapter Six

1. Gramsci (21.ii.20), *L'Ordine nuovo* [10], pp. 471-72.

2. As quoted in Prouteau, p. 41. Tasca *(Nascita,* p. 128, n. 5) notes that the reasons for the adherence of the anarchists to the movement are given in an article in *Volontà* (Ancona, 1.vi.20).

3. Borghi, p. 206.

4. Petri, whose real name was Pietro Mosso (1893-1945), was a student of engineering and of experimental logic. For a time, he was Professor Annibale Pastore's assistant at the University of Turin, where Gramsci probably met him. See Masini, *Gramsci e l'Ordine Nuovo,* pp. 22-23, n. 8. Petri wrote many articles for *Ordine nuovo,* most of them dealing with either "anarchic Communism" or "Taylorism."

5. Gramsci, "La Relazione Tasca e il congresso camerale di Torino," *L'Ordine nuovo* [10], p. 130. See also Maurizio Garino's speech on the "Consigli di fabbrica e d'azienda" to the Congress of the Unione Anarchica

Italiana held in Bologna in July 1920, in Masini, *Anarchici,* pp. 26–31. Garino made a special point of distinguishing the councils from "soviets."

6. As quoted by Gramsci in *L'Ordine nuovo* [10], p. 460. Sorel's article, "Sindacati e Soviet," was reprinted in *Ordine nuovo,* I, 26 (15.xi.19). In it the French syndicalist attempted to reconcile his former attachment to trade unions with his present interest in factory councils. This reconciliation was not difficult to accomplish, granted Sorel's insistence on direct action by the workers. "Today," he said, "the *soviet* is the only form of organization in which [the workers] believe."

7. All quotations in this paragraph are from *L'Ordine nuovo* [10], pp. 460–61. See also "Il Partito comunista, I," *ibid.,* p. 154. Here Gramsci stated that "Sorel is in no way responsible for the spiritual meanness and crudity of his Italian admirers, just as Karl Marx was not responsible for the absurd ideological pretensions of the 'Marxists.' Sorel is, in the field of historical research, an 'inventor.' He cannot be imitated. He does not place at the service of his aspiring disciples a method that can be applied mechanically, always and by everyone, and result in intelligent discoveries."

8. Cf. "Per un rinnovamento del PSI," *L'Ordine nuovo* [10], p. 119, and "Dove va il Partito socialista?" (10.vii.20), *L'Ordine nuovo* [10], p. 403. Masini (*Gramsci e l'Ordine Nuovo,* p. 11) emphasizes Gramsci's fear of anarchist advances.

9. Gramsci, "Lo Stato e il socialismo" (June 28–July 5, 1919), *L'Ordine nuovo* [10], p. 379. See also "L'Operaio di fabbrica," *ibid.,* p. 326, in which Gramsci asserts that the "General Confederation of Labor is formed of more 'revolutionary' working masses than the masses organized in the Italian Syndical Union [the trade-union organization of the anarcho-syndicalists], because the Confederation embraces the workers of those industries which are 'more revolutionary' and in the vanguard, whereas the Syndical Union is a makeshift that has not pulled out of a gelatinous and indistinct stage, the stage of world-view proper to petty bourgeois who have not become capitalists, proper to artisans or peasants who have not become proletarians."

10. Gramsci, "Che Cosa intendiamo per demagogia?" (29.vii.20), *L'Ordine nuovo* [10], pp. 410–11.

11. Paraphrased from "Lo Stato e il socialismo," *L'Ordine nuovo* [10], p. 378. Cf. Gramsci's contrast of political and civil society in Chapter IX of this work.

12. *Ibid.,* pp. 378–79.

13. *Ibid.,* pp. 381–82. In these passages, Gramsci's debt to Lenin's *State and Revolution* is obvious.

14. Gramsci (3–10.iv.20), *L'Ordine nuovo* [10], p. 477.

15. *Ibid.* Again, compare Gramsci's more mature discussion of "spontaneity" in Chapter IX of this work.

16. Gramsci, "Discorso agli anarchici" (3–10.iv.20), *L'Ordine nuovo* [10], p. 397.

17. Gramsci, "Che Cosa intendiamo?," *L'Ordine nuovo* [10], pp. 411–12.

18. "Lo Stato e il socialismo," *L'Ordine nuovo* [10], p. 379.

19. Gramsci, "Discorso agli anarchici," *L'Ordine nuovo* [10], p. 398.
20. *Ibid.*
21. A facsimile of Mussolini's telegram is in *Exposition de la Presse*, p. 47.
22. Valeri, *Giolitti a Mussolini*, p. 214.
23. *Ibid.*
24. *Ibid.*, p. 221.
25. Gramsci, "Alcuni Temi," *L'Ordine nuovo* [10], p. 25.
26. *Ibid.*
27. *Ibid.*
28. Gramsci, "Il Saccheggio" (21.vi.19), *L'Ordine nuovo* [10], p. 245.
29. 1.xi.19, in *L'Ordine nuovo* [10], pp. 284–86.
30. For a critical view of this article, see Maitan, *Attualità*, p. 47. Maitan views this thesis as an example of the "impressionism and exaggeration" that he alleges occasionally appear in Gramsci's work. But the immense power of Christian Democracy in Italy today suggests that Gramsci's statement was not hyperbolic.

Gramsci's later views on Catholic politics and the problems of Church and State in Italy may be found in an interesting compilation of passages from the Quaderni del Carcere: *Il Vaticano e l'Italia*, Elsa Fubini, ed. (Rome, 1961).

31. Gramsci's arguments are contained in *L'Ordino nuovo* [10], pp. 475–76.
32. Montagnana, p. 98. In 1920 the Federazione had 889,085 members, most of them wage-earning agricultural workers. The "White" or Catholic Federation had 944,812 members, only 94,961 of whom were wage earners. Of its total, 741,262 were sharecroppers or tenant farmers (*mezzadri* and *piccoli affittuari*) and 108,589 were small proprietors. These figures are from A. Serpieri, *La Guerra e le classi rurali italiane* (Bari, 1933), pp. 290–92, as quoted in Tasca, *Nascita*, p. 103, n. 5.
33. Tasca, *Nascita*, p. 126, n. 3.
34. Serrati, "Documentazione, I," p. 549. To Serrati, this peasant movement deserved no support because its aim was the "private possession of land," whereas in Socialist peasant organizations the aim must be "collective property and labor in common." See Serrati, "Risposta," p. 252.
35. Gramsci wrote several articles directed against these attempts: "Il Rivoluzionario e la mosca cocchiera" (25.xi.19), pp. 51–53; "Fuori del dilemma" (29.xi.19), pp. 53–56; and "Cos'è la reazione?," pp. 365–67. See also his long analysis of Giolittianism: "Dietro lo scenario del giolittismo" (5–8.xi.19), *L'Ordine nuovo* [10], pp. 287–303.
36. Gramsci, "La Rivoluzione e la mosca cocchiera," *L'Ordine nuovo* [10], p. 51.
37. Gramsci, "Operai e contadini" (3.i.20), *L'Ordine nuovo* [10], pp. 316–18, and "Un programma di governo" (30.iv.20), *ibid.*, p. 335.
38. "Operai e contadini," *L'Ordine nuovo* [10], p. 90.
39. Gramsci, "Programma d'azione della sezione Socialista torinese," *L'Ordine nuovo* [10], p. 396.

40. In the Milan edition of *Avanti!*, according to Arfè, *Storia dell'Avanti!*, p. 174.

41. Lenin, "False Speeches about freedom," in *The Communist International*, p. 253. Terracini, Gennari, Rogent, Tuntar, Casucci, Marxiale, and Belloni voted with the International, and Serrati, Baratono, Zanarini, Bacci, and Giacomini were opposed.

42. A good source for some of the material of this polemic is Partito Socialista Italiano, *Lettere e polemiche*.

43. Lenin, "A Letter to the German and French workers," in *The Communist International*, p. 250.

44. Serrati, "Di alcuni nostre ragioni," p. 306.

45. Serrati made these points respectively in: "Risposta," p. 250; "Di alcune nostre ragioni," pp. 307–9; *ibid.*, p. 310.

46. Gennari, p. 76.

47. Nenni, pp. 111–12. Lenin, in answer to Serrati's arguments that the cooperation of the reformists was necessary to avoid disaster, suggested a plan that would have avoided this dilemma: "Separate yourselves from Turati's faction, and then make an alliance with it." Serrati could only reply that, given the Italian character, a separation would cause so much bitterness that an alliance would be impossible (Serrati, "Documentazione, II," p. 599).

48. Serrati, "Documentazione, I," pp. 536–50 *passim*.

49. Valiani, *Histoire,* p. 136.

50. Bordiga in *Il Soviet,* 3.x.20, as quoted by Gramsci in *L'Ordine nuovo* [10], p. 488. It is true that *Ordine nuovo* had published an editorial on October 18, 1919, called "L'Unità del Partito," which urged a unity of all elements in the Party and claimed that the Congress of Bologna had proved all could work together.

51. Serrati, "Risposta," p. 254.

52. Arfè, *Storia dell'Avanti!*, p. 175.

53. Gramsci, "La Disciplina internazionale" (16–23.x.20), *L'Ordine nuovo* [10], pp. 353–55.

54. Gramsci, "Nota comunista" (16.xii.20), *L'Ordine nuovo* [10], p. 433.

55. From the deliberations of the reformist Congress at Reggio Emilia, October 10–11, 1920, as quoted in Tasca, *Nascita,* p. 144.

56. The program-manifesto was published in *Ordine nuovo,* II, 19 (30.x.20), and also, along with Serrati's comments, in *Comunismo,* II, 4 (15–30.xi.20), 185–89. Angelo Tasca claimed ("Comunismo e fascismo," p. 9) that the Imola Manifesto had "no trace of Gramsci's influence or ideas." Perhaps not. I could find, however, nothing in the manifesto discordant with Gramsci's thought.

57. There is a good analysis of these elections in Salvatorelli and Mira, pp. 93–95. See also Serrati's comments in *Comunismo,* II, 2–3 (October 15–November 15, 1920), 173–74.

58. Ferrara and Ferrara, pp. 86–87. Gramsci was particularly furious with the Giolittians for aligning themselves with the Catholics. Despite its pre-

tense of secularity, the Turinese Liberal Party, said Gramsci, had never hesitated to make such an alliance if it was necessary to defeat Socialism. The liberals were "cowards" and the Catholics were "blackmailers." See "Tra Vigliacchi e ricattatori" (28.x.20), *L'Ordine nuovo* [10], pp. 359–61.

Spriano (*L'Ordine nuovo*, p. 105) says that the Socialists had a majority after the first count of the votes; but a recount the next day gave the majority to the "Constitutional" bloc by "a few dozen votes." The Socialists charged fraud, touching off a heated debate. Among other things, the Socialists charged that the ballots of an entire electoral district had been seized and replaced with new ones by a group of "Fiumean legionnaires."

59. Arfè, *Storia dell'Avanti!*, pp. 176–77.

60. Gramsci, *L'Ordine nuovo* [10], p. 495.

61. *Ibid.*, p. 493.

62. *L'Humanité*'s comments are quoted by Gramsci in *ibid.*, p. 469.

63. Valiani, *Histoire*, p. 132; Ferrara and Ferrara, p. 96; A. Mezio, "Lettere di Gobetti a Croce," *Il Mondo*, 3.x.62. Gramsci later wrote: "In November 1920, Giuseppe Prezzolini persuaded me to let his firm publish a collection of [my] articles that really were written according to a single plan, but in January 1921 I decided to pay the expenses for the work already done and withdraw the manuscript." (G to Tatiana, 7.ix.31, in *Lettere* [1], p. 137.) Gramsci invited Prezzolini to lecture to the Turin workers. The theme of the lecture, which was given on February 27, 1921, was "Intellectuals and workers." Thereafter, Prezzolini wrote that "Gramsci is one of the most notable men of Italy. His *Ordine* has an original theme. And he personally has faith and energy, and does not work for the moment." See Prezzolini, p. 193. For the content of his lecture to the workers, see p. 189.

64. "Pacificazione," pp. 290–91.

65. The first non-Italian, non-leftist reference to Gramsci known to me occurs in Lémonon, p. 200. With reference to the leaders of the occupation of the factories, Lémonon said: "One of the most violent was Enea Matta, vice-secretary of the Turin Chamber of Labor. Beside [these leaders] stood a great number of intellectuals grouped around the Communist newspaper *L'Ordine nuovo*, which had replaced [sic] *Avanti!*, alleged to be too moderate. The leader of this group was citizen Gramcci [sic], a little, hunchbacked dreamer and a dangerous idealist."

Chapter Seven

1. The Comintern offered its heartiest congratulations and hopes for success to the new journal. See "Dalla Internazionale Comunista alla Sezione Socialista Torinese e alla redazione dell'*Ordine nuovo* quotidiano," *Ordine nuovo* (daily), I, 1 (1.i.21).

2. The five provisional motions, accompanied by Serrati's comments, are contained in "Preparando il Congresso," *Comunismo*, II, 4 (15–30.xi.20), 177–89.

3. *Ibid.*, pp. 177, 182. The International reserved the term "centrist" for Serrati himself.

4. On the eve of the Congress, Gramsci wrote a scathing editorial on the "Report of the Party Directorate," which had just been made public. Although the Report was written by Gennari, Gramsci characterized it as "truly worthy, in its arid bureaucratic schematism, of what has been the life of the Party in these months." See "Forza e prestigio," *Ordine nuovo* (daily), I, 14 (14.i.21).

5. "La Sezione Socialista e il Congresso," *Ordine nuovo* (daily), I, 5 (5.i.21).

6. "La Parola della Terza Internazionale," *Ordine nuovo* (daily), I, 13 (13.i.21).

7. "Vigilia di Congresso," *Ordine nuovo* (daily), I, 14 (14.i.21), and "Mentre si apre il Congresso Socialista," *Ordine nuovo* (daily), I, 15 (15.i.21).

8. *Resoconto*, p. 16. This work and the reports in *Ordine nuovo* (daily) are the main primary documents used in writing this chapter.

Togliatti, who was publishing the paper in Gramsci's absence, had Levi's statement put in bold letters in the upper-right-hand corner (the *manchette*) of the first page of *Ordine nuovo* for January 16, 1921.

9. *Resoconto*, p. 67.

10. The proceedings of January 16 are in *Ordine nuovo* (daily), I, 17 (17.i.21).

11. Matyas Rakosi, the Hungarian Communist leader, was the only other Comintern delegate. His name appears as "Rakowski" in the *Resoconto* and in other literature on the Congress. Georgi Dimitrov, the Bulgarian Communist, also attended the Congress, though not in an official capacity. See his letters containing impressions of the Congress in "Inediti."

12. "Due Discorsi," *Ordine nuovo* (daily), I, 17 (17.i.21). Dimitrov felt (p. 9) that "Khristo carried out his work as representative of the Communist International excellently, despite the devilish screams and whistles of the reformists and centrists."

13. *Resoconto*, p. 113.

14. "La Situazione," *Ordine nuovo* (daily), I, 17 (17.i.21).

15. *Resoconto*, pp. 146–47, 149.

16. Terracini's speech (*Resoconto*, pp. 165–206) was recently reprinted in *Rinascita*, XIX, 25–26 (Oct. 27, Nov. 3, 1962). *Rinascita* states that the speech is still of great value in understanding the "historical reasons for the constitution of the Communist Party."

17. *Resoconto*, p. 201.

18. "La Mozione unitaria," *Ordine nuovo* (daily), I, 18 (18.i.21).

19. *Resoconto*, p. 238. Bellini and Galli speculate (p. 45) that this act of Bombacci's was "typically Romagnole." In reality, it was Terracini who handed the pistol to Bombacci, evidently feeling that the latter might really need it for protection! See "Note al Congresso di Livorno: La giornata di

Stenterello," *Ordine nuovo* (daily), I, 19 (19.i.21). This article was probably written by Gramsci.

20. See *Ordine nuovo* (daily), I, 20 (20.i.21).

21. Bordiga first stated that there had been two kinds of opposition to the war: one for merely humanitarian purposes, the other aimed at transforming it into civil war. At that point a voice from the gallery accused Gramsci of being a "War Socialist," thereby raising the hoary question of the attitude of Italian Socialism toward World War I. The unitarians had celebrated the non-collaboration of the Italian reformists during the war as an example of revolutionary fervor. Actually, the intransigence of the PSI toward various parties and groups during the war was a principal reason for its inability to forge alliances with the veterans' organizations and the Left peasant groups. Bordiga laid the issue to rest, for the first time, in the following words: "I am not a War Socialist, nor are there many among the Communists; however, to one who was silent during the war ["Neither support nor sabotage of the war"] and who now shouts that he was against the war, I prefer those young men who through the experience of sacrifice learned in the war have returned with new faith in their hearts."

22. See *Ordine nuovo* (daily), I, 20 (20.i.21), and *Resoconto*, p. 294.

23. With respect to this last point, Serrati had already made the following remarks ("Preparando il Congresso," *Comunismo*, II, 4, p. 185): "If the unitarians are not all of one piece and one color, the secessionists are certainly not either. Since they claim to follow pure orthodoxy and to be the champions of maximum centralization and the strictest discipline, they really ought to display more homogeneity. Instead, we are confronted with the most beautiful rainbow. Voluntarist and spiritualist Bergsonians like Seassaro in the company of pure materialist Marxists like Bordiga; pragmatists like Tasca; *quarantottisti* like Bombacci; *'realizzatori'* like Pastore; idealists like Fortichiari; defenders of the work of the past directorate like ... Gennari, and its relentless critics like Gramsci; electionists like Caroti or Bellini, and abstentionists like Boero."

24. *Resoconto*, p. 317.

25. *Ibid.*, pp. 332–33, and *Ordine nuovo* (daily), I, 20.

26. *Resoconto*, p. 346.

27. Gennari did not explain why, with a Communist majority in the directorate, Serrati was permitted to use the daily organ of the Party to propound his minority view that the reformists should be retained in the PSI.

28. Said *Ordine nuovo*: "Its task had been to deliver a couple of tearful speeches."

29. *Resoconto*, pp. 396–97.

30. See *ibid.*, pp. 441–46, for the final motions of the three factions. Although the results are not strictly comparable, it is interesting to note the progress of the extreme Left since the Congress of Bologna. There the vote was: Left, 3,417; Center, 48,411; Right, 14,480.

31. See "Le Cifre," p. 444.

32. The proceedings of Friday, January 21, for both the Socialist and Communist Congresses are in *Ordine nuovo* (daily), I, 22 (22.i.21). A résumé of the proceedings and several documents of the first Congress of the PCI are in *Resoconto,* pp. 449–77.

33. *Resoconto,* p. 411.

34. From 1921 to 1943 the official name of the Party was Partito Comunista d'Italia, Sezione Italiana della III Internazionale. Since May 24, 1943, when the Communist International was dissolved, the official name has been Partito Comunista Italiano. See Bellini and Galli, p. 51, n. 1.

35. Bellini and Galli (p. 49) do not include the names Ambrogio Belloni and Cesare Sessa in the central committee; but they are in the list given in *Ordine nuovo* (daily), I, 22 (22.i.21), and in *Resoconto,* p. 451.

36. "Deliberati del nuovo Partito," *Ordine nuovo* (daily), I, 23 (23.i.21).

37. Interestingly enough, this final statement by the abstentionist faction still insisted on the theoretical value of its criticisms of the "parliamentary tactic," although it grudgingly admitted that the problem had been "resolved in the field of action by the deliberations of the Second Congress of the Communist International." It was there that Lenin had mercilessly criticized Bordiga's abstentionism. See *ibid.* and *Resoconto,* p. 451.

38. See Davidson, "The Russian Revolution and the Formation of the Italian Communist Party," for a defense of the Communist position at Livorno.

39. Nenni, p. 125.

40. Gramsci's name was included in the original list of speakers. "Figure del Congresso," *Ordine nuovo* (daily), I, 16 (16.i.21). The article is a sketch of Gramsci and Bordiga, the leaders of the two groups constituting the "core" of the Communist faction at Livorno.

41. Pastore had previously edited the Piedmontese edition of *Avanti!* The plan to establish an official biweekly, *Il Comunista,* at Milan never came to much; instead, the three dailies mentioned were all made official organs of the PCI.

Chapter Eight

1. The explanation for the publication of this correspondence is most interesting. In 1928, Angelo Tasca, who had earlier led the right-wing "minority" in the PCI, was sent to Moscow as Party representative to the Executive Committee of the Comintern. There he discovered that copies of these letters, as well as other documents, were in the archives of the Italian section of the International. Tasca made copies of this material, which he kept even after his expulsion from the party in 1929. A few years before his death, in 1960, Tasca gave his entire collection to the Istituto Giangiacomo Feltrinelli in Milan. About the same time, some of this material was published by Giorgio Galli in the periodical *Corrispondenza socialista,* whereupon Palmiro Togliatti turned necessity into virtue by publishing the entire lot, plus other letters and documents from the Party archives and personal papers of

several Party leaders. See Tasca, "L'Ordine Nuovo" ("I Primi Dieci Anni, 2"), p. 5; and Togliatti, *La Formazione*, p. 43.

2. G to Giulia, Vienna, 6.iii.24, in Ferrata and Gallo [12], II, 33–34.

3. Ferrata and Gallo [12], I, 531–831. Giansiro Ferrata's long preface (pp. 9–145), despite occasional obscure passages, is learned and perceptive.

4. Stefano Merli, one of the editors of this periodical, has also contributed an excellent bibliography of sources for the early history of the PCI: "Il Partito comunista d'Italia, 1921–1926."

5. Ferrata and Gallo [12], I, 534.

6. "Uomini di carne e ossa" (8.v.21), Ferrata and Gallo [12], I, 582–84.

7. "Fiume" (11.i.21), Ferrata and Gallo [12], I, 554–56.

8. See Caprioglio, p. 269. Nino Danieli was the author of this passage.

9. Ferrata and Gallo [12], I, 535. See pp. 534–38 for an interesting discussion of Gramsci's views on the PSI and Fascism in 1921–22.

10. In the revolutionary climate of the early 1920's, Giolitti saw the Marxist and Popular (Catholic) parties, the two traditional enemies of the liberal State, as especially strong and dangerous. Fascism seemed made to order for Giolitti, as a counter to these "subversive" forces; he tacitly supported it, especially in 1921, and saw it as a youthful and exuberant wing of the "traditional political class." Fascist violence, to Giolitti, was all the more necessary because the system of electoral proportioning then in use was favorable to the Socialist and Popular parties. See Carocci, *Giolitti*, pp. 181–82.

11. See "Cronologia," *Lettere* [2], p. xxxii. On September 8, 1922, at Trotsky's request, Gramsci wrote a short essay on Italian futurism, which Trotsky published in 1923 as an appendix to his *Literature and Revolution*. The essay is now available in Ferrata and Gallo [12], I, 633–35.

12. *La Formazione*, p. 59.

13. Letter of March 1, 1924, *La Formazione*, p. 228. It is interesting that in these remarks Gramsci and his friends do not specifically refer to Bordiga's "intellectual" ability.

14. As quoted by Terracini in a letter of April 18, 1924, *La Formazione*, p. 280.

15. Carr, p. 501, n. 1. Carr states that Bordiga was the outstanding representative of the Left at the Sixth Plenum.

16. *Ibid.*

17. Letter of March 27, 1924, *La Formazione*, pp. 254–55.

18. The first lengthy and scholarly analysis of "Bordighismo" by an Italian Communist has recently been published. See Santarelli, *La Revisione*, pp. 235–92.

19. See Garosci, "The PCI," p. 160, and Silone, pp. 55–56.

20. Degras, *The Communist International*, I, 306–16. In its Italian application, the policy can even be traced back to Lenin's admonition to the Italians at the Second Congress: "Separate yourselves from Turati, and then make an alliance with him."

21. Even after the Livorno Congress, the PSI was a member of the Comintern until November 2, 1921. *Il PSI,* III, 276.

22. Zinoviev, as quoted in Degras, *The Communist International,* I, 308.

23. "Lettera ai comunisti tedeschi," *Movimento italiano,* p. 233.

24. Degras, *The Communist International,* I, 308.

25. Bordiga, as quoted in Bellini and Galli, p. 65.

26. Letter of February 9, 1924, in Togliatti, *La Formazione,* p. 199. Articles 51 and 52 had previously categorically excluded the possibility of a dictatorship of the extreme right. After modification, they indicated that the present reaction in Italy would "probably" not take the "formal" character of such a dictatorship. See Ferrata and Gallo [12], II, 544.

27. Letter of February 9, 1924, in Togliatti, *La Formazione,* pp. 192–93.

28. *Ibid.,* pp. 193–94.

29. *Ibid.,* p. 71.

30. Letter of March 1, 1924, *ibid.,* p. 228. Professor Giuseppe Berti has recently informed me that Chiarini's real name was Chaim Heller, and that he died in Moscow in 1933 or 1934.

31. *Ibid.*

32. *Ibid.*

33. For biographical details on the Schucht family, see *Lettere* [2], pp. vii–viii.

34. See S. F. Romano, pp. 469–91, for a long essay on the effects of this experience on Gramsci's life.

35. "Extracts from the Theses on Tactics adopted by the Fourth Comintern Congress," Degras, *The Communist International,* I, 425–26.

36. Togliatti in *La Formazione,* pp. 45–46.

37. Letter of March 1, 1924, *ibid.,* p. 229.

38. As quoted in Merli, "Le Origini," p. 608. At the end of 1923, Togliatti lamented that if Gramsci had been more effective at the Fourth Congress, the " 'Center' of which you [Gramsci] speak would now have been built." See *La Formazione,* p. 142.

39. Letter of March 1, 1924, in Togliatti, *La Formazione,* p. 228.

40. *Ibid.,* p. 229.

41. See Terracini's letter, 8.iii.23, in *ibid.,* pp. 45–50.

42. *La Formazione,* p. 51.

43. The manifesto is in Merli, ed., "Nuova Documentazione," pp. 515–20.

44. Gramsci, 18.v.23, in Togliatti, *La Formazione,* pp. 63–70.

45. "Lettera" [27], pp. 115–16.

46. For new information on Gramsci's activities in Vienna, see Zamis.

47. See G to Giulia, 15.iii.24, Ferrata and Gallo [12], II, 36.

48. Togliatti, *La Formazione,* p. 165. Cf. the quotation on p. 166 of the present work.

49. Letter of January 2, 1924, in Togliatti, *La Formazione,* p. 146. "Masci" was Gramsci's pen name in this period.

50. G to Terracini, 13.i.24, *ibid.,* p. 183.

51. Letter of May 18, 1923, *ibid.*, p. 65.

52. Letter of February 9, 1924, *ibid.*, pp. 196–97.

53. On this occasion he expressed this idea with some irony: "If the International is a world Party, even understood with many grains of salt . . ." (*ibid.*, p. 196).

54. G to Terracini, 27.iii.24, in *ibid.*, p. 261.

55. *Ibid.*, pp. 261–63.

56. *Ibid.*, p. 200.

57. See Gramsci, "Les élections italiennes" (17.iv.24), *International Press Correspondence* (French edition), reprinted in *Rivista storica del socialismo*, IV, 3–4 (May–Dec. 1961), 641–44.

58. "Alcuni Temi della quistione meridionale," *Stato operaio*, IV, I (1930), 9–26. This essay has been reprinted many times.

59. Ferrara and Ferrara, p. 152. Velio Spano says the text was "written by Togliatti in strict collaboration with Gramsci." See Spano, p. 235.

60. S. F. Romano, p. 536.

61. *Il Partito*, p. 60. In an older Communist work, Montagnana (p. 274), Togliatti's brother-in-law, wrote that the Theses were "prepared by Gramsci or under his immediate guidance."

62. S. F. Romano, p. 536.

63. Spano, p. 238.

64. *Il Partito*, p. 60.

65. Garosci, "Totalitarismo," p. 212.

66. S. F. Romano, p. 536.

67. Spano, p. 239.

68. See Degras, *The Communist International*, II, 188–205 for extracts from the "Theses on the Bolshevization of Communist Parties adopted at the Fifth ECCI Plenum," and extracts from the theses on the "peasant question." They were originally published in *International Press Correspondence* (German ed.) on May 11, 1925.

69. Thesis I, Alatri, *L'Antifascismo*, p. 415. Most of the text of the Theses is to be found on pp. 415–46 of this useful and accessible anthology. They were first published in "Tesi" [31]. Whenever necessary, I have made reference to this edition. See also Gramsci's report on the Congress, "La Relazione" [32].

70. Thesis 28, Alatri, *L'Antifascismo*, p. 440.

71. Thesis 25, *ibid.*, p. 435.

72. Thesis 31, "Tesi" [31], pp. 494–95.

73. Cf. Gramsci's views on the nature of political parties as discussed in Chapter IX of this work.

74. "La Relazione" [32], p. 519.

75. Thesis 29, "Tesi" [31], pp. 493–94.

76. Thesis 36, Alatri, *L'Antifascismo*, p. 441.

77. *Ibid.*

78. In April 1926 the Rocco law gave a monopoly of representation to

the Fascist trade unions. On January 4, 1927, the CGL proclaimed its own dissolution.

79. "La Relazione" [32], p. 522.

80. Alatri, *L'Antifascismo*, p. 442.

81. "Work in the existing social-democratic and other (yellow, National-Socialist, confessional, and Fascist) trade unions is a most important and integral part of bolshevization." See Degras, *The Communist International*, II, 192.

82. "La Relazione" [32], pp. 521 and 522.

83. Thesis 38, Alatri, *L'Antifascismo*, p. 442. Thesis XXI, F4, of the Fifth Plenum, which deals specifically with the PCI, demanded that the party "begin systematic work to create, consolidate, and capture the factory committees." See Degras, *The Communist International*, II, p. 196.

84. Thesis 30, "Tesi" [31], p. 494.

85. Thesis 19, Alatri, *L'Antifascismo*, p. 431.

86. There is a more detailed analysis of the several peasant groups in "La Relazione" [32], p. 523.

87. See Thesis XII of the Fifth Plenum decisions in Degras, *The Communist International*, II, 193.

88. Thesis 39, Alatri, *L'Antifascismo*, p. 443.

89. Thesis 40, *ibid.*, p. 445.

90. Thesis XII of the resolutions of the Fifth Plenum, in Degras, *The Communist International*, II, 193.

91. Thesis 20, Alatri, *L'Antifascismo*, p. 432.

92. *Ibid.*, p. 435.

93. Thesis 39, *ibid.*, pp. 443, 445.

94. Spano, p. 39.

95. Theses 4 to 7, Alatri, *L'Antifascismo*, pp. 418–20.

96. Thesis 8, *ibid.*, pp. 420–21.

97. "La Relazione" [32], p. 523.

98. Lin Piao, p. 24. Cf. on the same page: "The peasants constitute the main force of the national-democratic revolution." Cf. also the "Program of the Communist International" (September 1, 1928), which at one point employs terminology similar to Gramsci's: "In the transition period colonies and semi-colonies are also important because they represent the village on a world scale vis-à-vis the industrial countries, which represent the town in the context of world economy." (In Degras, ed., *The Communist International*, II, 508.)

99. Thesis 9, Alatri, *L'Antifascismo*, p. 421.

100. *Ibid.* Here, Gramsci points to a similarity of conditions in Italy and the Russia of 1917. Elsewhere, he emphasized differences. This is not, to my mind, a contradiction. Both countries possessed a weak industrialist class that had to make compromises with other ruling groups. This is the problem dealt with here. Elsewhere, Gramsci points out that Italy is similar to

the rest of Western Europe, and different from the Russia of 1917, in possessing a strong and complex civil society.

101. *Ibid.,* pp. 421–25. A summary of Gramsci's ideas on the role of the Church in recent Italian history: From 1870 to 1890, the Vatican continued its struggle against the bourgeois State on the one hand—a factor that contributed to the weakness of that State—and on the other hand worked to enroll the peasantry in a "reserve army" against the advance of the proletariat. In 1891, the Church took a programmatic stand against Socialism with Leo XIII's encyclical *Rerum novarum,* at the same time laying the basis for its own social program. The latter was implemented in the next period, 1900–1914, by the Catholic Action movement. Meanwhile, under the pressure of the growing Socialist movement, the Church finally came to an agreement with the ruling classes to give the State a more secure base. It abolished the "non expedit," or prohibition to participate in the work of the State, and, by the Gentiloni pact of 1913, agreed to support liberal parliamentary candidates under certain conditions. During the postwar period, in response to the massive growth of the Left, the Vatican established its own political party, the Partito Popolare Italiano, to hold the peasant masses within the framework of the bourgeois state.

102. Thesis 15, *ibid.,* p. 426.

103. *Ibid.*

104. Thesis 16, *ibid.,* p. 427. Emphasis mine.

105. Thesis 16, *ibid.,* pp. 428–29.

106. See "Carbonarismo" [29], p. 15.

107. *Ibid.,* p. 16.

108. See "Gramsci al CC" [34]. Less than three months before Togliatti's death, this letter, Togliatti's reply, and an introduction by him were published in *Rinascita,* causing considerable comment in many countries. Few seemed to realize that the letter had already been published by Angelo Tasca in April 1938, in *Problemi della Rivoluzione italiana,* an Italian-language publication of Marseilles. In 1953, Tasca again published salient passages of the letter in "Ordinovisti e bordighisti" ("I Primi Dieci Anni del PCI, 4"). These previous publications are ignored by Isaac Deutscher (*The Prophet Outcast*) and K. S. Karol. Nor does either author make it clear that Gramsci was not trying to defend Trotsky politically. Indeed, he regarded the "opposition" as mainly responsible for the crisis in the Russian Party. Finally, Deutscher is inaccurate in his assertion that Gramsci's memory was consigned to oblivion during the Stalin era.

109. "Gramsci al CC" [34], pp. 18–19.

110. *Ibid.,* p. 19.

111. "Discussione politica con Gramsci in carcere." A few weeks after the publication of this document, the historian Paolo Spriano urged other former political prisoners who knew Gramsci at Turi to come forth with their testimonials. So far, Lay and Trombetti have responded. See Spriano,

"Sul rapporto"; Lay, "Colloqui"; and Trombetti, "Piantone." Trombetti concludes his article with a wonderful "cazzotto nell'occhio" (punch in the eye) for all those inns in which George Washington slept. After World War II, Gramsci's cell was set aside and consecrated to his memory. According to Trombetti, who visited Turi shortly thereafter, not only are the bunk and the table in the cell spurious, but the cell itself is not the one where Gramsci was confined!

112. Ferri, "Valore," p. 19. See also Lay, p. 21. Lay adds several other names to the group, but he apparently did not consider Piacentini and Ceresia to be anarchists.

113. Lisa, p. 20.

114. Lay, p. 22.

115. *Ibid.* Scucchia was later expelled from the party for Trotskyist deviations. Some time later, an even more violent attack on Gramsci—and on other imprisoned Communist leaders—was launched by Ezio Taddei, an anarchist formerly at Turi (see his "Di ritorno"). Mussolini quoted this article with great relish in *Il Popolo d'Italia* of December 31, 1937 ("Gramsci's figure has been liquidated by these revelations."). See "Alterini." Some years later, Taddei evidently changed his opinion of Gramsci and other Communists. In a letter of November 19, 1965, to this writer, Luca Pavolini, Vicedirector of *Rinascita,* stated that "after World War II, when I personally knew him, Taddei was close to the Communists and often contributed to *L'Unità* and other publications of ours."

116. Lay, p. 21. This did not mean, said Lay, that Gramsci "could not tolerate disagreement with his ideas. Athos Lisa was not in agreement with Gramsci's theses ... nevertheless, Gramsci esteemed and valued him."

117. Trombetti, "Piantone," p. 32.

118. *Ibid.,* pp. 31–32.

119. Ferri, "Valore," p. 20.

120. Lisa, p. 18. It must be kept in mind that the precise language of these statements may be Lisa's; but there is no doubt that the ideas themselves are Gramsci's.

121. Gramsci had already raised the question of agitation against the Monarchy in the Lyons Theses (Thesis 39 *bis,* in Alatri, *L'Antifascismo,* p. 445), but in a much more guarded way, his primary purpose being to "unmask some of the self-styled anti-Fascist groups" in the Aventine.

122. The Lisa report (p. 19) merely says 6,000 active members. But Lay (p. 22) asserts that Gramsci explicitly stated in one of his conversations that he was referring only to the party cadres, and not to the total membership.

123. Lisa, p. 20.

124. Ferri, "Valore," p. 19.

125. Cf. also a "transitional" article from the *Bollettino del Partito comunista d'Italia* of April 1933 entitled "Fronte unico di lotta per infrangere l'offensiva del capitale e del fascismo." This article has been reprinted in

Alatri's very useful anthology *L'Antifascismo*, II, 265–72. Ferri ("Valore," p. 21) says "The political line of the Communist Party was already being corrected in the direction of Gramsci's observations from the beginning of 1931, in practice and in political formulations—as is shown by Party documents, speeches by Togliatti and Grieco, and programs of action of the Communists." An investigation of this problem would be most interesting.

126. Cortesi, p. 166.

Chapter Nine

1. G to Tatiana, 19.iii.27, *Lettere* [1], p. 27.

2. "Gramsci e la cultura italiana," *Studi gramsciani*, p. 400. In his recent testimonial on Gramsci's imprisonment, Gustavo Trombetti ("Piantone," p. 31) wrote of Gramsci's views on the future value of his notebooks: "He believed that (these are his words) if he got out of prison alive, which he doubted very much, there would be abundant material to develop; if not, however, they would not even be of much use to others, on account of—he said—the form and the terms used so as not to give the prison censors an excuse to confiscate them."

3. "Stato attuale," p. 307.

4. Russo, pp. 248, 252.

5. *Note* [6], p. 34.

6. One of Gramsci's most interesting and comprehensive philosophical essays is "Note critiche su un tentativo di 'Saggio Popolare' di sociologia," in *Il Materialismo storico* [3], pp. 117–168. A translation of most of this essay is in *The Modern Prince* [17], pp. 90–117. See also the very fine article by Aldo Zanardo, "Il 'Manuale' di Bukharin visto dai comunisti tedeschi e da Gramsci," in *Studi gramsciani*, pp. 337–68. Zanardo says that Gramsci's imprisonment, in addition to his long experience with a real labor movement, permitted him to resist the "theoretical reorganization" (!) of world Communism that began about 1931. It is significant that Gramsci regarded even Plekhanov as sometimes guilty of "vulgar" materialism. See *Il Materialismo storico* [3], p. 80.

7. *Il Materialismo storico* [3], p. 199.

8. *Ibid.*, p. 68.

9. *Ibid.*, p. 49.

10. *Ibid.*, p. 12.

11. See, for example, his statement that the idealist claim of reality as a creation of the human spirit corresponds to the Marxist idea of structure and superstructure; but the former retains a strong element of the metaphysical, whereas the latter is "concrete" and "historical" (*ibid.*, p. 139).

12. See Morpurgo Tagliabue, pp. 429–38, and Garosci, "Totalitarismo," pp. 193–257.

13. *Il Materialismo storico* [3], p. 91.

14. *Ibid.*, pp. 138–45.

15. "Il Leninismo," p. 15.

16. *Note* [6], p. 17.

17. *Ibid.*, p. 81.

18. Cf. *Passato e presente* [8], p. 158.

19. Political parties are to the modern world what the "Prince" was to Machiavelli's world: "The modern Prince, the myth-Prince, cannot be a real person, a concrete individual; he can only be an organization. . . . This organization is already obvious from historical development, and it is the political party." *Note* [6], p. 5.

20. *Ibid.*, p. 20.

21. *Ibid.*, p. 21.

22. *Ibid.*

23. See "Il Discorso" [30], a speech to the Chamber of Deputies in 1925, for an earlier statement of this idea.

24. *Note* [6], pp. 21–22. In these observations Gramsci probably had the National Fascist Party in mind, but he was well aware that Communist parties were also capable of such degeneration.

25. *Passato e presente* [8], pp. 68–69.

26. *Ibid.*, p. 65.

27. *Ibid.*

28. *Ibid.*

29. *Note* [6], p. 19. This "sense of historical continuity" is very different, says Gramsci, from a tendentious "cult of tradition"—implying a conscious *choice* and a determined end—which is a matter of "ideology."

30. *Ibid.*, pp. 23–24.

31. *Ibid.*

32. *Ibid.*, p. 42. Emphasis mine.

33. *Ibid.*, p. 48. After having read Mathiez' account of the causes of the French Revolution, Gramsci asserted that revolution did not occur for "mechanical" economic reasons, but because of "conflicts superior to the immediate economic world, connected to class 'prestige' (future economic interests) and to a stimulation of the feelings of independence, autonomy, and power." On this point, cf. Lisa, p. 20.

34. See, for example, *Il Materialismo storico* [3], p. 199. Probably the most important works of Lenin dealing with the "new" political party are: *What is to be Done?* (1902), against economism and spontaneity and stressing the role of theory; *One Step Forward, Two Steps Back* (1904), on the principles of organization of the party; *What the "Friends of the People" Are and How They Fight the Social-Democrats* (1894), against the Narodniks and for the defense of Marxian dialectics; *The State and Revolution* (1917), on the nature of the bourgeois and socialist states; and *"Left-Wing" Communism, an Infantile Disorder* (1920), an exposition of the nature and work of the Party in the form of a critique of Bordiga and other "Left" Communists.

35. *Note* [6], p. 80. As noted before, Gramsci, like many Western intel-

lectuals of this century, regarded science, or at least "scientism," much more critically than most Russians.

36. *Ibid.*, p. 294.

37. *Ibid.*, p. 38.

38. *Ibid.*

39. *Ibid.*, p. 39.

40. *Ibid.*, p. 28.

41. *Passato e presente* [8], p. 59.

42. *Ibid.*

43. *Ibid.*, p. 60.

44. *Ibid.*, p. 55.

45. *Ibid.* This point leads one to consider the game American newspapers have played in attempts to determine whether certain demonstrations on civil rights or American foreign policy are "spontaneous" or "organized." From the tone of such articles, one might conclude that the less human intelligence and "foresight" is applied to demonstrations, the more "authentic" they are!

46. *Ibid.*, p. 57.

47. *Note* [6], p. 36.

48. *Ibid.*, p. 37.

49. *Passato e presente* [8], pp. 70–71.

50. *Note* [6], p. 23.

51. *Passato e presente* [8], p. 7.

52. *Ibid.* Gramsci mentions another common shortcoming of the sectarian point of view, closely related to "belittling the adversary." This is a tendency to pick only second-rate opponents for ideological polemics. See *Il Materialismo storico* [3], pp. 130–31.

53. *Note* [6], pp. 36–37.

Chapter Ten

1. *Intellettuali* [4], pp. 6–7.

2. See G to Tatiana, 7.ix.31, *Lettere* [1], p. 137. "I extend the term 'intellectuals' very broadly, and do not limit myself to the current usage, which refers only to the great intellectuals."

3. *Intellettuali* [4], p. 3.

4. In Athos Lisa's report (p. 18) on Gramsci's views in 1930 there is still another Gramscian classification of intellectuals. But this one is similar to the distinction between "technical" and "directive" intellectuals: in 1930 Gramsci evidently used the terms "semi-intellectuals" and "intellectuals."

5. *Intellettuali* [4], p. 4.

6. *Ibid.*, p. 5.

7. *Ibid.*, p. 9.

8. *Ibid.*, p. 3.

9. *Ibid.*

10. *Ibid.*, p. 8.

11. *Risorgimento* [5], pp. 71–72.

12. *Intellettuali* [4], p. 8.

13. According to the *Cambridge Italian Dictionary* (1962), Volume I, "paglietta" is a derogatory term for an astute lawyer, taken from the black straw hats formerly worn by Neapolitan lawyers.

14. *Risorgimento* [5], p. 97.

15. *Intellettuali* [4], p. 7.

16. *Ibid.*, p. 9. See also *Passato e presente* [8], pp. 164–65.

17. *Intellettuali* [4], p. 10.

18. G to Tatiana, 7.ix.31, *Lettere* [1], p. 137.

19. Williams, p. 587.

20. *Intellettuali* [4], p. 9.

21. See Crisafulli, p. 593.

22. *Note* [6], pp. 45–46.

23. See *Risorgimento* [5], p. 70. See also Serafino Cambareri, "Il Concetto di egemonia nel pensiero di A. Gramsci," *Studi gramsciani*, p. 91, and Williams, p. 594.

24. *Il Materialismo storico* [3], p. 75.

25. See *Studi gramsciani*, p. 91, and Tamburrano, p. 245ff. But see the review of the latter by Robert Paris, "Una Revisione 'nenniana' di Antonio Gramsci."

26. *Il Materialismo storico* [3], pp. 201, 189, 32, 39.

27. Most Communist writers have tended to identify the views of Gramsci and Lenin on hegemony, whereas non-Communist writers have tended to emphasize Gramsci's originality. For the first group, see Sereni, p. 28, and Togliatti, "Il Leninismo," in *Studi gramsciani*, p. 34. For the second group, see Matteucci, *Gramsci e la filosofia*, p. 76, and the cited works by Williams and Tamburrano.

28. *Il Materialismo storico* [3], p. 194.

29. *Note* [6], p. 68.

30. *Ibid.*, p. 68. Cf. also, in this connection, Gramsci's note on "State-idolatry": "For some social groups, which before their rise to an autonomous State life did not have a long period of independent cultural and moral development . . . a period of State-idolatry is necessary and even opportune. . . . However, this 'State-idolatry' should not be left to itself. Especially, it should not become theoretical fanaticism and be conceived as 'perpetual.'" (*Passato e presente* [8], pp. 165–66.)

31. This view is not contradictory to the fact that some Italian intellectuals have been extremely chauvinistic. Chauvinism flourishes where there is a lack of national sentiment based on real political and economic conditions. See *Passato e presente* [8], pp. 15–16.

32. *Intellettuali* [4], p. 49.

33. *Ibid.*, p. 22.

34. The revival of Roman law, insofar as it was characterized by abstract universalism, also reinforced Italian cosmopolitanism (*ibid.*, pp. 25–27). It is significant that the Italians were much the earliest in establishing special schools for the study of this universal law.

35. *Ibid.*, p. 34. See also G to Tatiana, 7.ix.31, *Lettere* [1], p. 138.

36. In the language of Francesco Guicciardini, to one's own *particolare.* Cf. *Note* [6], p. 81.

37. Giuseppe Toffanin, *Che Cosa fu l'umanesimo?* (Florence, 1929). But it seems that Gramsci arrived at his conclusions prior to his reading of Toffanin: "These ideas of Toffanin often coincide with the notes that I have already made elsewhere." (*Intellettuali* [4], p. 38.)

38. *Intellettuali* [4], p. 38.

39. *Ibid.*, p. 40.

40. *Note* [6], p. 7.

41. On Gramsci's view of the French Jacobins, cf. *Risorgimento* [5], pp. 75–86.

42. G to Tatiana, 7.ix.31, *Lettere* [1], p. 138.

43. *Note* [6], p. 15.

44. *Ibid.*, p. 117.

45. *Ibid.*, p. 3.

46. *Ibid.*, pp. 39–40.

47. *Ibid.*, pp. 3–4.

48. See Gilbert, "The Concept of Nationalism in Machiavelli's *Prince*," a very interesting and important article.

49. Chapter XX of the *Prince*. See also Chapter VIII: "above all, a prince must live with his subjects in such a way that no accident of good or evil fortune can deflect him from his course"; and Chapter XIX: "One of the most potent remedies that a prince has against conspiracies is that of not being hated by the mass of the people."

50. Even Robespierre's famous distinction between a "Revolutionary government and a constitutional government" finds an equivalent in Machiavelli: "And if Princes show themselves superior in making laws, and in forming civil institutions and new statutes and ordinances, the people are superior in maintaining those institutions, laws, and ordinances." (*Discourses*, I, 58.)

51. G to Delio, no date, *Lettere* [1], p. 255.

Appendix

1. The articles later appeared as a book with the title *Risorgimento e capitalismo* (Bari, 1959).

2. *Ibid.*, p. 96.

3. For Gramsci's ideas on the unification movement in Italy, see *Risorgimento* [5], *passim*; but especially "Il Problema della direzione politica nella formazione e nello sviluppo della Nazione e dello Stato moderno in Italia,"

pp. 69–95, and "Il Rapporto città-campagna nel Risorgimento e nella struttura nazionale italiana," pp. 95–104.

4. Cf. *Risorgimento* [5], pp. 150, 88.

5. *Ibid.*, p. 55.

6. "La Nascita," p. 445.

7. Cf. Gastone Manacorda in *Studi gramsciani*, p. 504.

8. See the "Catechism of the Third Degree Carbonaro" in Francovich, pp. 140–44. Francovich also reproduces the "Catechism of the Three Degrees of the *Adelfia*," another secret society widely diffused in north Italy during the Restoration. This document contains the phrase "Mishaps, vices, and crimes came from the foolish division of land. Then peaceful equality disappeared, and greed for gold and power entered" (pp. 145–46).

9. As quoted in Candeloro, *Storia,* II, 157.

10. Della Peruta, and Berti.

11. Mack Smith, p. 96.

12. Manacorda, p. 508.

13. *Ibid.,* p. 509.

14. Candeloro, in *Studi gramsciani*, p. 521.

15. *Risorgimento* [5], p. 75: "Ferrari was unable to 'translate' French into Italian."

16. *La Pensée,* 95 (Jan.–Feb., 1961), pp. 63–73.

17. Talamo, p. 698. Apparently the question of land distribution—or appropriation—was rather important in the Kingdom of Naples in 1848!

18. "If a Jacobin party was not formed in Italy, the reasons are to be sought in the economic field—that is, in the relative weakness of the Italian bourgeoisie and in the changed historical climate of Europe after 1815" (*Risorgimento* [5], p. 87). "The moderates represented a relatively homogeneous social group" (*Risorgimento,* pp. 69–70), which permitted them to gradually "absorb elites from enemy groups." One example: "The liberal movement succeeded in arousing a Catholic-liberal force and arranging matters so that Pius IX himself, however temporarily, would take a stand for liberalism (which was enough to disintegrate the ideologico-political apparatus of Catholicism, and destroy its faith in itself). This was the political masterpiece of the Risorgimento" (p. 50).

19. *Ibid.,* p. 88. Cf. Zangheri, in *Studi gramsciani,* p. 371.

20. *Risorgimento* [5], p. 151.

21. *Ibid.*

22. *Ibid.,* p. 108.

23. *Ibid.,* pp. 94–95.

24. Berselli, pp. 497–98.

25. "The *Risorgimento* between Ideology and History: The Political Myth of *rivoluzione mancata*," pp. 46–49.

26. Macchioro, p. 512.

27. As quoted in Berti, pp. 784–85.

28. Romeo, *Risorgimento,* p. 49.
29. *Ibid.,* p. 47.
30. *Ibid.*
31. Cafagna, "Intorno," p. 1033.
32. *Risorgimento* [5], p. 210. Even Alexander Gerschenkron, in some ways sympathetic to Romeo, is annoyed by Romeo's tendency to justify every development in the Italian economy before 1890. See Gerschenkron, p. 584.
33. For details on the fourth point of Romeo's critique, see my article "Two Recent Polemics on the Character of the Italian Risorgimento."

Bibliography

The Bibliography is in two parts, *Gramsci's Writings* and *Other Works Consulted*. Gramsci's writings, in three subclassifications, are numbered for convenience of reference in the Notes.

Gramsci's Writings

A. Collected Works [Opere di Antonio Gramsci (Turin: Einaudi, 1947–)]

[1] Vol. I. Lettere dal carcere. 1947.
[2] ———. Rev. ed., 1965. This work, edited by Sergio Caprioglio and Elsa Fubini, completely supersedes the earlier edition of Lettere. I have been able to use it only for occasional indispensable references.
[3] Vol. II. Il Materialismo storico e la filosofia di Benedetto Croce. 1948.
[4] Vol. III. Gli Intellettuali e l'organizzazione della cultura. 1949.
[5] Vol. IV. Il Risorgimento. 1949.
[6] Vol. V. Note sul Machiavelli, sulla politica, e sullo stato moderno. 1949.
[7] Vol. VI. Letteratura e vita nazionale. 1950.
[8] Vol. VII. Passato e presente. 1951.
[9] Vol. VIII. Scritti giovanili, 1914–1918. 1958.
[10] Vol. IX. L'Ordine nuovo, 1919–1920. 1954.
[11] Vol. X. Sotto la Mole, 1916–1920. 1960.

(Volume XI, containing Gramsci's writings of 1921–22, will soon appear. Another volume made up of his work from 1923 to 1926 will complete the *Opere,* except for letters written before Gramsci's imprisonment. Most of these may be found in the anthology by Ferrata and Gallo and in Togliatti's *La Formazione del gruppo dirigente del PCI.* A number of other writings have recently been identified, which must be included in later editions of Volumes VIII and IX.)

B. Other Collections and Anthologies of Gramsci's Work

[12] Ferrata, Giansiro, and Niccolò Gallo, eds. 2000 Pagine di Gramsci. Volume I, Nel tempo della lotta (1914–1926); Volume II, Lettere edite e inedite (1912–1937). Milan: Il Saggiatore, 1964. Volume I has an in-

formative introduction by Ferrata and includes nearly three hundred pages of Gramsci's writings between 1921 and 1926. Volume II includes 64 letters written between November 1912, and November 1926; many of these were previously unpublished.

[13] Salinari, Carlo, and Mario Spinelli, eds. *Antonio Gramsci, antologia degli scritti*. Rome: Editori Riuniti, 1963. 2 vols. Volume I contains a number of articles of 1921 that have not yet appeared in the collected works and are not included in the anthology by Ferrata and Gallo.

[14] *L'Albero del riccio*. Milan: Milano—Sera editrice, 1948. An illustrated edition of the children's stories contained in the *Lettere* and stories written by others to whom Gramsci referred.

[15] *Americanismo e fordismo*. Edited by Felice Platone. Milan: Universale economica, 1950. A compilation from *Note sul Machiavelli* and from the *Lettere*.

[16] *Elementi di politica*. Edited and presented by Mario Spinelli. Rome: Editori Riuniti, 1964. Selections for the most part from Volumes III, V, and VII of Gramsci's *Opere*.

[17] *The Modern Prince and Other Writings*. Translated with an introduction by Louis Marks. New York: International Publishers, 1959. First published in London by Lawrence and Wishart in 1957. Contains selections mainly from Volumes II, III, and V of Gramsci's *Opere*, in addition to the 1926 essay on the "Southern Question." Selections from this translation are included in Albert Fried and Ronald Sanders, *Socialist Thought: A Documentary History*. Garden City, N. Y.: Doubleday Anchor Books, 1964, pp. 513–26. Gramsci is introduced (p. 512) as "one of the few creative Marxists of our time."

[18] *The Open Marxism of Antonio Gramsci*. Translated and annotated by Carl Marzani. New York: Cameron Associates, 1957. A short selection from *Il Materialismo storico* with many notes aimed at relating the material to "American problems."

[19] *La Questione meridionale*. Third edition. Rome: Editori Riuniti, 1957. First compiled in 1951, this work is made up of the essay "Alcuni Temi della quistione meridionale" and selections from *Il Risorgimento*.

[20] *Sul Risorgimento*. Edited by Elsa Fubini, with a Preface by Giorgio Candeloro. Rome: Editori Riuniti, 1959. Consists mostly of selections from *Il Risorgimento*.

[21] *Il Vaticano e l'Italia*. Edited by Elsa Fubini, with a Preface by Alberto Cecchi. Rome: Editori Riuniti, 1961. Selections mainly from Volumes II, IV, and V of Gramsci's *Opere*.

C. Other Works by Gramsci (in chronological order of original composition)

[22] *La Città futura* ("Numero Unico Pubblicato dalla Federaz. Giovanile Socialista Piemontese"). Turin, February 11, 1917. A photographic reproduction of *La Città futura* was published at Turin by the Casa

editrice Viglongo in 1952. The issue is now contained in *Scritti Giovanili*, pp. 73–89. However, the following items were not included: the preface on p. 2 to the articles by Croce and Carlini entitled "Due Inviti alla meditazione," the article on p. 4 entitled "Modello e realtà," and the general postscript on p. 4 in which Gramsci called for a rebirth of the "tradizione mazziniana rivissuta dai socialisti."

[23] "Nuovi Contributi agli scritti giovanili di Gramsci," *Rivista storica del socialismo*, III, 10 (May–Aug. 1960), 545–50. Edited by Luigi Ambrosoli. Two comments on Esperanto, written in January 1918.

[24] "Una Lettera inedita del 1918 a Giuseppe Lombardo Radice: Una iniziativa di Gramsci," *Rinascita*, XXI, 10 (7.iii.64), 28.

[25] "Gli Editoriali di Gramsci nei tre giorni che precedettero il Congresso di Livorno," *Rinascita*, XXI, 3 (18.i.64), 17–19.

[26] "Note sulla situazione italiana 1922–1924 (a cura di Aldo Romano)," *Rivista storica del socialismo*, IV, 13–14 (May–Dec. 1961), 625–44. Includes the following articles that Gramsci contributed to *La Correspondance Internationale*: "Les Origines du cabinet Mussolini" (20.xi.22); "Le Parlementarisme et le fascisme en Italie" (28.xii.23); "L'Échec du syndicalisme fasciste" (3.i.24); "Italie et Yougoslavie" (30.i.24); "Le Vatican" (12.iii.24); "Les Élections italiennes" (17.iv.24).

[27] "Lettera inedita per la fondazione de 'L'Unità,'" *Rivista storica del socialismo*, VI, 18 (Jan.–Apr. 1963), 115–23. A letter of September 12, 1923. The same letter was published in *Rinascita*, XXI, 6 (8.ii.64), 25.

[28] "1924: Al professore Zino Zini, collaboratore dell'Ordine Nuovo: Due lettere inedite di Gramsci," *Rinascita*, XXI, 17 (25.iv.64), 32. Introduction by p. t. (Palmiro Togliatti).

[29] "1925: In una lettera all'Esecutivo dell'Internazionale comunista Gramsci respinge le critiche del compagno Manuilski: 'Legalismo' e 'Carbonarismo' nel Partito comunista d'Italia," *Rinascita*, XX, 34 (31.viii.63), 15–16.

[30] "Il Discorso al parlamento italiano nel maggio, 1925," *Rinascita*, XIX, 6 (9.vi.62), 17–21. With an introduction by Togliatti.

[31] "Tesi sulla situazione italiana e sui compiti del PCI, approvate dal III Congresso nazionale nel gennaio 1926," *Stato operaio*, II, 6–7 (June–July 1928), 390–400 and 490–501. Written with Togliatti.

[32] "La Relazione di Antonio Gramsci sul III Congresso (Lione) del PCI," *Rinascita*, XII, 10 (Oct. 1956), 516–24. The only extensive report on the Congress now available. First published in *L'Unità* on February 24, 1926.

[33] "Come si determinano le nostre prospettive e i nostri compiti," in *Lo Stato operaio*. Rome: Editori Riuniti, 1964, Volume I, pp. 144–53. Gramsci's report to the central committee of the PCI in August 1926.

[34] "Gramsci al CC del PC(b); Togliatti a Gramsci," *Rinascita*, XXI, 22 (30.v.64), 17–20. Gramsci's letter of October 14, 1926, to the Russian Party. Includes Togliatti's reply to Gramsci and an introduction by Togliatti.

[35] "Alcuni Temi della quistione meridionale," *Stato operaio*, IV, 1 (Jan. 1930), 9–26. Written in 1926, but first published here.

[36] "Notes on anti-semitism," *The Promethean Review*, I, 4 (Oct.–Nov. 1959), 39–42. From letters to his sister-in-law, written in 1931. Translated by Hamish Henderson.

[37] "Benedetto Croce and his Concept of Liberty," *Science and Society*, X (Summer 1946), 283–92. From letters to his sister-in-law, written in 1932. Translated by Samuel Putnam.

[38] "In Search of the Educational Principle," *New Left Review*, 32 (July–Aug. 1965), 53–62. Translation with an introduction by Quintin Hoare. A translation of "Per la ricerca del principio educativo," in *Gli Intellettuali e l'organizzazione della cultura*, pp. 108–17.

Other Works Consulted

A.L. "Giacinto Menotti Serrati," *Ordine nuovo* (daily), I, 10 (10.i.21). Probably by Alfonso Leonetti.

Alatri, Paolo, ed. L'Antifascismo italiano. Rome: Ed. Riuniti, 1961. 2 vols. A most useful collection of documents.

———. *Le Origini del fascismo*. Rome: Ed. Riuniti, 1956.

———. "Recenti studi sul fascismo," *Studi storici*, III, 4 (Oct.–Dec. 1962), 757–836. An extended bibliographical discussion.

Albergamo, Francesco, Armando Borelli, and Omero Bianca, with a reply by Massimo Aloisi. "Scienza, natura e storia in Gramsci," *Società*, VII (Mar. 1951), 95–114.

Alderisio, Felice. "Ripresa machiavelliana. Considerazioni critiche sulle idee di A. Gramsci, di B. Croce, e di L. Russo intorno a Machiavelli," *Annali dell'Istituto universitario di magistero di Salerno*, 1949–50, I, 205–66.

Alicata, Mario. "Gramsci e l'Ordine Nuovo," *Società*, XI, 2 (1955), 197–204. Asserts a complete continuity between the Gramsci of the Ordine Nuovo period and the Gramsci of the Quaderni.

———. "Il Risorgimento, Gramsci e noi," *Rinascita*, XVI, 6 (June 1959), 421–23.

Almanacco socialista. Milan: Avanti!, 1917–25.

Aloisi, Massimo. "Gramsci, la scienza e la natura come storia," *Società*, VI (Sept. 1950), 385–410.

Ambrosoli, Luigi. "Interpretazioni e studi sul movimento cattolico italiano," *Movimento operaio*, VII (Jan.–Feb. 1955), 135–50.

———. Nè aderire, nè sabotare, 1915–1918. Milan: Avanti!, 1961.

Annuario statistico italiano, 2nd series, volume II, 1912.

"Appello ai giovani comunisti italiani," *Ordine nuovo* (daily), I, 15 (15.i.21). An appeal from the Executive Committee of the Communist Youth International to support the Communist faction in the PSI.

"Appunti per una critica del bordighismo," pp. 372–79, in Lo Stato operaio. Volume I. Rome: Ed. Riuniti, 1964.

Arfè, Gaetano. "Le Origini del movimento giovanile socialista," *Mondo operaio*, X, 4 (Apr. 1957), 33–37; 5 (May 1957), 24–26; 6 (June 1957), 30–34.

——. "La Rivoluzione liberale di Piero Gobetti," *Rivista storica italiana*, LXXIV, 2 (June 1962), 313–23.

——. Storia dell'Avanti!, 1896–1926. Milan: Avanti!, 1956.

Ashby, Thomas. "Sardinia," *Encyclopedia Britannica* (11th ed.), XXIV, 210–17. Statistics and information on the island during Gramsci's youth.

Autodifese di militanti operai e democratici italiani davanti ai tribunali (1875–1937). Edited by Stefano Merli, with a Preface by Piero Caleffi. Milan: Avanti!, 1958. See especially the statements by Serrati, Malatesta, Bordiga, Terracini, and Gramsci.

Bachi, Riccardo. L'Italia economica, 1920. Annuario della vita commerciale, industriale, agraria, bancaria, finanziaria e della politica economica, Anno XII. Città di Castello: Casa Tipografica—Editrice S. Lapi, 1921.

Baratono, Adelchi. "L'Azione del PSI nei rapporti con la IIIᵃ Internazionale: Relazione della tendenza Unitaria al XVIIº Congresso nazionale," *Comunismo*, II, 7 (1–15.i.21), 369–78.

Basso, Lelio. Il Partito socialista italiano. Milan: Nuova Accademia editr., 1958.

Bellini, Fulvio, and Giorgio Galli. Storia del Partito comunista italiano. Milan: Schwarz, 1953. Cf. the review by Togliatti in *Rinascita*, X, 7 (July 1953), 447–48.

Bentley, Eric. "The Italian Theater," *The New Republic*, CXXIX, 10 (5.x.53), 18–20. A reference to Gramsci's theater criticism.

Berselli, Aldo. "Risorgimento e capitalismo," *Il Mulino*, 92 (1959), 494–508.

Berti, Giuseppe. I democratici e l'iniziativa meridionale nel Risorgimento. Milan: Feltrinelli, 1962.

Bianchi Bandinelli, Ranuccio. "Antonio Gramsci nella cultura italiana," pp. 231–48 in *Dal diario di un borghese e altri scritti*. Milan: Il Saggiatore, 1962. First published in 1947.

Bibliografia della stampa periodica operaia e socialista italiana (1860–1926). I periodici di Milano. Bibliografia e storia. Milan: Feltrinelli, 1956–60. 2 vols.

Bonomi, Ivanoe. Dal socialismo al fascismo. La sconfitta del socialismo. 2nd edition. Rome: Cernusco sul Naviglio, 1946. First published in 1924.

Bordiga, Amadeo. "Lo Sciopero di Torino," *Rinascita*, XVIII, 1 (Jan. 1961), 57–58. Reprint of an article from *Il Soviet* of May 2, 1920.

——. "Tesi sulla tattica del Partito comunista d'Italia che saranno presentate e discusse al prossimo Congresso," *Il Comunista*, I (31.xii.21), pp. 3–4. The "Rome Theses."

Borghi, Armando. Mezzo secolo di anarchia, 1898–1945. Naples: ESI, 1954. Preface by Gaetano Salvemini.

Borkenau, Franz. World Communism: A History of the Communist International. Ann Arbor: The University of Michigan Press, 1960. New introduction by Raymond Aron. First published in 1939.

Cachin, Marcel. "Soyons dignes de Gramsci!," pp. 165–67 in *Ecrits et Portraits*. Edited by Marcelle Hertzog-Cachin. Paris: Les Éditeurs Français Réunis, 1964. A commemorative article of April 30, 1937.

Cafagna, Luciano. "Intorno al 'revisionismo risorgimentale,' " *Società*, XII, 6 (Dec. 1956), 1015–34.

———. "Il Saggio di R. Romeo su 'Risorgimento e capitalismo,' " *Cultura moderna*, 40 (Apr. 1959), 6–10.

Califano, E., and G. Bollino. "Articoli e pubblicazioni sui trent'anni del Partito comunista italiano," *Movimento operaio*, IV, 6 (Nov.–Dec. 1952), 979–1023. A bibliography of articles appearing between the end of 1950 and the end of 1951 from Italian national and local periodicals.

Calosso, Umberto. "Gobetti tra Gramsci e Einaudi," *Il Mondo*, I, 13 (14.v.49), 7.

———. "Gramsci e l'Ordine Nuovo," in *Quaderni di Giustizia e Libertà*, 8 (Aug. 1933), 71–79.

Camera del Lavoro di Torino e Provincia. Sindacato e consigli di fabbrica. Ragioni che giustificano la trasformazione del Sindacato sulla base dei consigli di fabbrica. Turin: Tip. Alleanza coop. torinese, [1920?].

Cammett, John M. "Italy," and "The Vatican," pp. 520–39 in *Soviet Foreign Relations and World Communism: A Selected, Annotated Bibliography of 7,000 Books in 30 Languages*. Thomas T. Hammond, ed. Princeton, N.J.: Princeton University Press, 1965.

———. "Two Recent Polemics on the Character of the Italian Risorgimento," *Science and Society*, XXVII 4 (Fall 1963), 433–57. The second "polemic" deals with the controversy between Rosario Romeo and Italian Marxist historians.

Candeloro, Giorgio. Il Movimento sindacale in Italia. Rome: Ed. di Cultura sociale, 1950.

———. "La Nascita dello stato unitario," *Studi storici*, I, 3 (1959–60), 445–71.

———. Storia dell'Italia moderna. Milan: Feltrinelli, 1956–64. 4 vols. This work, which is still in progress, deals with the years from 1700 to 1860 and is inspired by a Gramscian point of view.

Cappa, Arturo. "Scissione inevitabile," *Ordine nuovo* (daily), I, 8 (8.i.21).

Caprioglio, Sergio. "Un Mancato incontro Gramsci-D'Annunzio a Gardone nell'aprile 1921 (con una testimonianza di Palmiro Togliatti)," *Rivista storica del socialismo*, V, 15–16 (Jan.–Aug. 1962), 263–73.

Caracciolo, Alberto, ed. "Il Movimento torinese dei Consigli di fabbrica," *Mondo operaio*, XI, 2 (Feb. 1958), 16–26. A collection of 12 documents.

Carbone, Giuseppe. "I Libri del carcere di Antonio Gramsci," *Movimento operaio*, IV (July–Aug. 1952), 640–89. A bibliography of works used by Gramsci in prison and an essay on his use of them.

———. "Su alcuni commenti delle opere di Antonio Gramsci," *Società*, VII (Mar. 1951), 131–58. A bibliography of works on Gramsci, including reviews.

Carocci, Giampiero. Giolitti e l'età giolittiana. Turin: Einaudi, 1961. A work based on the documents of the *Archivio Giolitti.*

————. Giovanni Amendola nella crisi dello Stato italiano, 1911–1925. Milan: Feltrinelli, 1956.

————. "Gramsci fra Croce e Lenin," *Belfagor,* III, 4 (31.vii.48), 435–45.

Carr, Edward H. Socialism in One Country, 1924–1926. Vol. III. London: Macmillan, 1964.

Castagno, Gino. Bruno Buozzi. Milan: Avanti!, 1955. Preface by Fernando Santi. For details on the Turin labor movement.

————. 1854, Centenario ACT: Storia di una cooperativa. Turin: Alleanza coop. torinese, 1954.

Casucci, Costanzo, ed. Il Fascismo: Antologia di scritti critici. Bologna: Il Mulino, 1961. An anthology of interpretations of Fascism.

Catalano, Franco. Dall'unità al fascismo. Milan: Istituto editoriale Cisalpino, 1961. pp. 293–340 on Gramsci.

Chabod, Federico. "L'Età del Rinascimento," in *Cinquant'anni di vita intellettuale italiana, 1896–1946.* Naples: ESI, 1950.

————. L'Italie contemporaine. Conférences données à l'Institut d'Etudes Politiques de l'Université de Paris. Paris: Editions Domat-Montchrestien, 1950. There is now an English translation of this work: A History of Italian Fascism. London: Weidenfeld & Nicolson, 1963.

Ciasca, Raffaele. "Sardegna," *Enciclopedia italiana* (1936), XXX, pp. 836–67.

"Le Cifre ufficiali della votazione," *Comunismo,* II, 8–9 (Jan. 15–Feb. 15, 1921), 444. The results of the vote at Livorno by provincial federations.

La Città futura: Saggi sulla figura e il pensiero di Antonio Gramsci. Edited by Alberto Caracciolo and Gianni Scalia. Milan: Feltrinelli, 1959. See especially the following essays: Carlo Cicerchia, "Rapporto col leninismo e il problema della rivoluzione italiana"; Ezio Avigdor, "Il Movimento operaio torinese durante la prima guerra mondiale"; Alberto Caracciolo, "Serrati, Bordiga e la polemica gramsciana contro il 'blanquismo' o settarismo di partito"; Giuseppe Tamburrano, "Fasi di sviluppo del pensiero politico di Gramsci."

Clough, Shepherd B. The Economic History of Modern Italy. New York: Columbia University Press, 1965.

C. N. "Il Centrismo nel movimento socialista italiano," *Ordine nuovo* (daily), I (4.i.21). C. Niccolini was probably the author.

————. "Il Movimento dei metallurgici," *Ordine nuovo,* II, 16 (2.x.20).

Cole, G. D. H., and Raymond Postgate. *The British Common People, 1746–1946.* New York: Barnes and Noble, 1961.

La Confederazione generale del lavoro negli atti, nei documenti, nei congressi, 1906–1926. Edited by Luciana Marchetti. Milan: Avanti!, 1962.

"Il Congresso di Livorno," *Comunismo,* II, 8–9 (Jan. 15–Feb. 15, 1921), 433–42. Analysis of the Congress from the unitarian point of view. Probably written by Serrati.

"Il Congresso di Livorno," *Ordine nuovo* (daily), I, 13 (13.i.21). Probably written by Gramsci.

"Controllo di classe," *Ordine nuovo*, I, 32 (3.i.20). Probably written by Togliatti.

Corsi, Angelo. L'Azione socialista tra i minatori della Sardegna, 1898–1922. Contributo allo studio del movimento operaio italiano. Milan: Edizioni di Comunità, 1959.

Cortesi, Luigi. "Alcuni Problemi della storia del PCI," *Rivista storica del socialismo*, VIII, 24 (Jan.–Apr. 1965), 143–72.

"Cosa dicono i nostri nemici," *Ordine nuovo* (daily), I, 22 (22.i.21). The reaction of the bourgeois press to the founding of the PCI.

Crisafulli, Vezio. "Stato e società nel pensiero di Gramsci," *Società*, VII (Dec. 1951), 583–609.

Croce, Benedetto. "De Sanctis–Gramsci," *Lo Spettatore italiano*, V, 7 (July 1952), 294–96.

———. "Un Gioco che ormai dura troppo," *Quaderni della Critica*, 17–18 (Nov. 1950), 231–32.

———. Review of *Lettere dal carcere*, in *Quaderni della Critica*, III, 8 (July 1947), 86–88.

———. Review of *Il Materialismo storico e la filosofia di Benedetto Croce*, in *Quaderni della Critica*, IV, 10 (Mar. 1948), 78–79.

———. Storia d'Italia dal 1871 al 1915. 9th edition. Bari: Laterza, 1947.

———. Teoria e storia della storiografia. 7th edition. Bari: Laterza, 1954.

"Cronaca dei 'fatti di agosto,'" *Stato operaio*, I, 6 (Aug. 1927), 651–66.

"Cronologia della vita di Antonio Gramsci," pp. xxi–xlvi in *Lettere dal carcere*. Edited by Sergio Caprioglio and Elsa Fubini. Turin: Einaudi, 1965. An indispensable tool of research.

"Dalla Internazionale comunista alla Sezione socialista torinese e alla redazione dell''Ordine Nuovo' quotidiano," *Ordine nuovo* (daily), I, 1 (1.i.21).

Davidson, Alastair. "The Russian Revolution and the Formation of the Italian Communist Party," *The Australian Journal of Politics and History*, X, 3 (Dec. 1964), 355–70. Supports the views of the Communist faction at the Congress of Livorno.

"La Decomposizione del bordighismo," pp. 380–95 in *Lo Stato operaio*, I, 380–95. Rome: Ed. Riuniti, 1964.

De Felice, Renzo. "Un Corso di glottologia di Matteo Bartoli negli appunti di Antonio Gramsci," *Rivista storica del socialismo*, VII, 21 (Jan.–Apr. 1964), 219–21.

Degras, Jane, ed. The Communist International, 1919–1943. London: Oxford University Press, 1956–60. 2 vols. Volume I covers 1919–22 and Volume II, 1923–28.

———. "United Front Tactics in the Comintern, 1921–1928," pp. 9–22 in *International Communism* ("St. Antony's Papers—Number 9"). Edited by David Footman. London: Chatto & Windus, 1960.

De Leon, Daniel. Socialist Reconstruction of Society: The Industrial Vote. New York: New York Labor News Company, 1930. A speech delivered at Minneapolis in July 1905.

"Deliberati del nuovo Partito," *Ordine nuovo* (daily), I, 23 (23.i.21). Lists the members of the PCI's central and executive committees.

Della Peruta, Franco. I democratici e la rivoluzione italiana. Dibattiti ideali e contrasti politici all'indomani del 1848. Milan: Feltrinelli, 1958.

Delzell, Charles F. "Benito Mussolini: A Guide to the Biographical Literature," *Journal of Modern History*, XXXV, 4 (Dec. 1963), 339–53.

————. "Italian Historical Scholarship: A Decade of Recovery and Development, 1945–1955," *Journal of Modern History*, XXVIII, 4 (Dec. 1956), 374–88.

————. Mussolini's Enemies: The Italian Anti-Fascist Resistance. Princeton, N.J.: Princeton University Press, 1961.

Desanti, Jean T. "Antonio Gramsci militant et philosophe," *Cahiers Internationaux*, 93 (Feb. 1958), 39–46.

Deutscher, Isaac. The Prophet Unarmed, Trotsky: 1921–1929. London: Oxford University Press, 1959.

————. The Prophet Outcast, Trotsky: 1929–1940. London: Oxford University Press, 1963.

"Dibattiti su Gramsci," *Rinascita*, VIII, 5 (May 1951), 248–49.

Dimitrov, George. "Inediti di Dimitrov sul Congresso di Livorno del '21 e sul VII Congresso del Comintern," *Rinascita*, XIX, 9 (30.vi.62), 9–10.

"Discorsi e contrasti sulla proposta comunista di un 'blocco di unità proletaria' per le elezioni del 1924," *Rinascita*, XX, 4 (26.i.63), 17–20.

Dore, Giampietro. 10 Anni di lotta politica (1915–1925). Rome: Il Solco, 1947.

"I Due Congressi," *Ordine nuovo* (daily), I, 22 (22.i.21). An editorial describing the founding of the PCI.

Eastman, Max. Love and Revolution: My Journey Through an Epoch. New York: Random House, 1964.

Einaudi, Luigi. La Condotta economica e gli effetti sociali della guerra italiana. ("Pubblicazioni della Fondazione Carnegie per la Pace Internazionale. Sezione di Storia ed Economia. Storia economica e sociale della guerra mondiale. Serie italiana.") Bari: Laterza, 1933.

Einaudi, Mario. "Western European Communism, a Profile," *American Political Science Review*, VL (Mar. 1951), 185–208.

Enciclopedia italiana. Appendice II. Rome: Istituto dell'Enciclopedia italiana, 1948–49. 2 vols.

Engels, Friedrich. Preface to Karl Marx, *Capital*, Vol. III. Chicago: Kerr, 1909.

Ente per la Storia del Socialismo e del Movimento Operaio Italiano. Bibliografia del socialismo e del movimento operaio italiano. Vol. I: Periodici, tratti dalle raccolte della Biblioteca Nazionale di Firenze, Two books. Vol. II: Libri, opuscoli, articoli, almanacchi, numeri unici. Book 1 (A–DU). Rome–Turin: Edizioni ESMOI, 1956–62. A detailed description of nearly all Italian publications on these subjects from 1848 to 1950.

"L'Esposizione internazionale di Torino nel 1911," *Almanacco italiano,* XVI (1911), 494.

Exposition de la Presse Antifasciste italienne, Cologne—10 juin, 1928. Paris: Union des Journalistes Antifascistes Italiens "Giovanni Amendola," 1928.

Faenza, Liliano. "Antonio Gramsci tra l'agiografia e la critica." *Il Mulino,* 94 (Apr. 1960), 323–64.

Falqui, Enrico. Novecento letterario (Fifth series). Florence: Vallechi, 1957.

Fascismo e Antifascismo (1918–1948). Milan: Feltrinelli, 1962. 2 vols. In Vol. I, see especially Lelio Basso, "Le Origini del fascismo"; Paolo Alatri, "La Crisi della classe dirigente e le lotte sociali del primo dopoguerra"; Giovanni Parodi, "L'Occupazione delle fabbriche"; Nino Valeri, "La Marcia su Roma"; Franco Catalano, "Il Movimento operaio tra il 1920 e il 1924"; Luigi Salvatorelli, "Il Delitto Matteotti e la crisi del 1924–26."

Ferrara, Marcella and Maurizio. Conversando con Togliatti. Milan: Edizioni di Cultura sociale, 1953.

Ferretti, Giancarlo. "I Corsivi di *Sotto la Mole,*" Società, XVI, 5 (Sept.–Oct. 1960), 824–36.

———. "Gli *Scritti giovanili* nella formazione di Antonio Gramsci," *Società,* XV, 2 (Jan.–Feb. 1959), 308–24.

———. "Sulle cronache teatrali di Gramsci," *Società,* XIV, 2 (Mar. 1958), 263–94.

Ferri, Franco. "Consiglio di fabbrica e partito nel pensiero di Gramsci," *Rinascita,* XIV, 9 (Sept. 1957), 461–67.

———. "Questione meridionale e unità nazionale in Gramsci," *Rinascita,* IX, 1 (Jan. 1952), 6–10.

———. "La Rivoluzione d'ottobre e le sue ripercussioni nel movimento operaio italiano," *Società,* XIV, 1 (Jan. 1958), 73–100.

———. "La Situazione interna della sezione socialista torinese nell'estate del 1920," *Rinascita,* XV, 4 (Apr. 1958), 259–65.

———. "Valore e senso del documento," *Rinascita,* XXI, 49 (12.xii.64), 17–21. The introduction to Athos Lisa's report.

"Figure del Congresso," *Ordine nuovo* (daily), I, 16 (16.i.21). Sketches in word and pencil of Gramsci and Bordiga.

Fiori, Giuseppe. Vita di Antonio Gramsci. Bari: Laterza, 1966. The most important book for the facts of Gramsci's life, especially for the early years. Published too recently to be used here.

Francovich, Carlo. Idee sociali e organizzazione operaia nella prima metà dell'800. Milan: Avanti!, 1959.

Frassati, Alfredo. Giolitti. Florence: Parenti, 1959.

Galli, Giorgio. Storia del Partito comunista italiano. Milan: Schwarz, 1958.

Garin, Eugenio. Cronache di filosofia italiana (1900–1943). Bari: Laterza, 1955.

Garosci, Aldo. "The Italian Communist Party," in *Communism in Western*

Europe. Edited by Mario Einaudi. Ithaca, N.Y.: Cornell University Press, 1951.

———. "Totalitarismo e storicismo nel pensiero di Antonio Gramsci," in his *Pensiero politico e storiografia moderna.* Pisa: Nistri-Lischi, 1954, pp. 193–260.

Gennari, Egidio. "Alla Commissione esecutiva della III* Internazionale," *Comunismo,* II, 2–3 (Oct. 15–Nov. 15, 1920), 75–77.

Gentile, Panfilo. 50 Anni di socialismo in Italia. Milan: Longanesi, 1948.

Germanetto, Giovanni. Memoirs of a Barber. New York: International Publishers, 1935.

Gerratana, Valentino. "De Sanctis–Croce o De Sanctis–Gramsci?" *Società,* VIII, 13 (Sept. 1952), 497–512.

Gerschenkron, Alexander. "Rosario Romeo e l'accumulazione primitiva del capitale," *Rivista storica italiana,* LXXI, 4 (1960), 557–86.

Ghezzi, Raoul. Comunisti, industriali e fascisti a Torino, 1920–1923. Turin: Ditta eredi Botta, 1923. The industrialists' point of view.

Gilbert, Felix. "The Concept of Nationalism in Machiavelli's Prince," *Studies in the Renaissance,* I (1954), 38–48.

Giolitti, Giovanni. Memorie della mia vita. Third edition. Monza: Garzanti, 1945.

"I Giovani Socialisti aderiscono al Partito Comunista," *Ordine nuovo* (daily), I, 32 (1.ii.22).

Giusti, Ugo. Le Correnti politiche italiane attraverso due riforme elettorali, dal 1909 al 1921. Florence: Alfani & Venturi, 1922.

Gobetti, Piero. Opere complete. Vol. I. Turin: Einaudi, 1960. Edited with an introduction by Paolo Spriano.

———. La Rivoluzione liberale; saggio sulla lotta politica in Italia. Turin: Einaudi, 1948. First published in 1924.

Grieco, Ruggiero. "Grieco a Togliatti sull'arresto di Gramsci," *Rinascita,* XXII, 30 (24.vii.65), 20–21.

———. "Le Ripercussioni della rivoluzione russa in Italia," *Stato operaio,* I, 9–10 (Nov.–Dec. 1927), 985–94.

Grilli, Giovanni. Due Generazioni: Dalla settimana rossa alla guerra di liberazione. Rome: Ed. Rinascita, 1953.

Gruppi, Luciano. "The Legacy of Gramsci," *World Marxist Review,* II, 12 (Dec. 1959), 81–84. A review of *Studi gramsciani.*

Hallett, Fred. "Antonio Gramsci," *Political Affairs,* XXXVI, 4 (Apr. 1958), 55–59.

Hilton-Young, W. The Italian Left: A Short History of Political Socialism in Italy. London and New York: Longmans, Green, 1949.

Hoare, Quintin. "What is Fascism?" *New Left Review,* 20 (Summer 1963), 99–111. An interpretation inspired by a reading of Gramsci.

Hughes, H. Stuart. "Gramsci and Marxist Humanism," pp. 96–104 of his *Consciousness and Society: The Reorientation of European Social Thought, 1890–1930.* New York: Alfred A. Knopf, 1958.

Hulse, James W. The Forming of the Communist International. Stanford, Calif.: Stanford University Press, 1964.

"L'Imminente Congresso socialista: La preparazione a Livorno," *Ordine nuovo* (daily), I, 11 (11.i.21).

Imperatori, Ugo E. Dizionario di italiani all'estero (dal secolo XIII sino ad oggi). Genoa: L'Emigrante, 1956.

International Labor Office, Geneva. The Dispute in the Metal Industry in Italy. Studies and Reports. Series A. No. 2 (24.ix.20) and No. 11 (5.xi.20). The latter includes the texts of the final agreements ending the occupation of the factories.

———. The Bill to Establish Workers' Control in Italy. Studies and Reports. Series B. No. 7 (1921). Nos. 6 and 8 deal with workers' control in Germany and France.

"Intervista con U. Terracini sul Congresso di Livorno," *Ordine nuovo* (daily), I, 25 (25.i.21).

Istituto Giangiacomo Feltrinelli. Annali, 1958–64. Milan: Feltrinelli, 1959–1965. 7 vols. Important articles and bibliography on the theory and practice of labor and Socialist movements in Italy and the rest of the world.

Joll, James. The Second International, 1889–1914. New York: Praeger, 1956.

Kabakchiev, Khristo S. *Die Gründung der Kommunistischen Partei Italiens.* Hamburg: Verlag der Kommunistischen Internationale, 1921.

Karol, K. S. "Togliatti Resurrects Trotsky," *New Statesman*, LXVII, 1736 (19.vi.64), 938–40.

King, Bolton, and Thomas Okey. Italy Today. London: James Nisbet & Co., 1909.

Kirova, K. E. "Massovoe dvizhenie v Italii protiv imperialisticheskoi voiny letom 1917 goda," *Voprosy istorii*, IX, 6 (June 1953), 68–85.

Kula, Witold. "Secteurs et régions arrières dans l'èconomie du capitalisme naissant," *Studi storici*, I, 3 (Apr.–June 1960), 569–85.

Lay, Giovanni. "Colloqui con Gramsci nel carcere di Turi," *Rinascita*, XXII, 8 (20.ii.65), 21–22.

Lazzari, Costantino. "Per l'unità socialista proletaria e rivoluzionaria: Proposta di conclusione per l'art. 6 dell'o.d.g. al Congresso nazionale," *Ordine nuovo* (daily), I, 7 (7.i.21).

Lazzeri, Gerolamo. La Scissione socialista. Milan: Modernissima, 1921.

Lémonon, Ernest. L'Italie d'après Guerre, 1914–1921. Paris: Librairie Félix Alcan, 1922.

Lenin, V. I. Selected Works, Volume X: The Communist International. 2d edition. London: Lawrence & Wishart, 1946.

———. Sul movimento operaio italiano. Rome: Ed. Riuniti, 1962. New edition with an introduction by Paolo Spriano.

Leonetti, Alfonso. "Gramsci al 'Quisisana,'" *Rinascita*, XXII, 45 (13.xi.65), 26. Asserts that (1) Gramsci's death was due solely to the conditions of his imprisonment and not to earlier infirmities; and (2) he was under 24-hour surveillance by the police right up to April of 1937.

————. Mouvement ouvriers et socialistes (chronologie et bibliographie). L'Italie (dès origines à 1922). Paris: Editions Ouvrières, 1952.

————. "Propositi," *Ordine nuovo* (daily), I, 24 (24.i.21).

Lepre, Aurelio. "La Questione meridionale nella lettera di Antonio Gramsci per la fondazione dell'*Unità*," *Rinascita*, XXI, 6 (8.ii.64), 25–27.

Levi, Riccardo. "Spirito dell'industria piemontese," *Il Ponte*, V, 7–8 (Aug.–Sept. 1949), 1039–44.

Li Causi, Girolamo. "Un Giornale di massa," *Rinascita*, XXI, 6 (8.ii.64), 32. An article on the situation when *L'Unità* was first published.

Lichtheim, George. Marxism: An Historical and Critical Study. New York: Praeger, 1961. Pages 368–70 are on Gramsci.

Liebknecht, Helmut. "Testimonianza su Francesco Misiano," *Rivista storica del socialismo*, VI, 18 (Jan.–Apr. 1963), 199–207. A defense of Misiano, who was allegedly slurred by Gramsci.

Lin Piao, "Long Live the Victory of a People's War!," *Peking Review*, VIII, 30 (3.ix.65), 9–30.

Lisa, Athos. "Discussione politica con Gramsci in carcere," *Rinascita*, XXI, 49 (12.xii.64), 17–21.

Lombardo Radice, Lucio. "Spunti di educazione nuova nelle *Lettere* di Antonio Gramsci," *Rinascita*, IV, 8 (Aug. 1947), 229–30.

————, and Giuseppe Carbone. Vita di Antonio Gramsci. Third edition. Rome: Edizioni di Cultura sociale, 1952. Now hopelessly out-of-date.

Longo, Luigi. "I Social-unitari," *Ordine nuovo* (daily), I, 9 (9.i.21).

Lovecchio, Antonio. Il Marxismo in Italia. Milan: Bocca, 1952.

Macchioro, Aurelio. "Risorgimento, capitalismo e metodo storico," *Rivista storica del socialismo*, II, 7–8 (July–Dec. 1959), 673–709. An attack on Romeo's interpretation of Gramsci's *Il Risorgimento*.

Mack Smith, Denis. Garibaldi. London: Hutchinson, 1957.

Maitan, Livio. Attualità di Gramsci e politica comunista. Milan: Schwarz, 1955. A Trotskyist interpretation.

————. Teoria e politica comunista nel dopoguerra. Milan: Schwarz, 1959.

Malatesta, Alberto. I Socialisti italiani durante la guerra. Milan: Mondadori, 1926. Reproduces many official documents.

Manacorda, Gastone. "A Proposito dei 'Quaderni' di Gramsci: Filologia e anticomunismo," *Rinascita*, XIX, 33 (22.xii.62), 7. A reply to the charges of Maturi and Marcelli that the texts of the *Quaderni* had been altered.

Marcelli, Umberto. "Interpretazioni del Risorgimento," *Convivium*, XXVII, 4–5 (1959), 385–407, 513–32.

Marino, Gaetano. "Dalle memorie di un comunista napoletano," *Movimento operaio*, VI, 5 (Sept.–Oct. 1954), 731–49.

Marks, Louis. "Antonio Gramsci," *The Marxist Quarterly*, III, 4 (Oct. 1956), 225–38.

"Marxism and Culture in Italy," *Times Literary Supplement*, XLVII (28.viii.48), 492.

Masini, Pier Carlo. *Anarchici e comunisti nel movimento dei consigli a*

Torino (primo dopoguerra rosso 1919–1920). Turin: a cura del Gruppo "Barriera di Milano," 1951.

———. Antonio Gramsci e l'Ordine Nuovo visti da un libertario. Vercelli: Ed. "L'Impulso," 1956.

Matteucci, Nicola. Antonio Gramsci e la filosofia della prassi. Milan: Giuffre, 1951.

———. "Interpretazioni del Risorgimento: Un nuovo revisionismo cattolico," *Il Mulino*, X, 3 (Mar. 1961), 151–57.

———. "Partito e consiglio di fabbrica nel pensiero di Gramsci," *Il Mulino*, IV, 4 (Apr. 1955), 350–59.

Maturi, Walter. Interpretazioni del Risorgimento: Lezioni di storia della storiografia. Turin: Einaudi, 1962. See especially pp. 617–41 on Gramsci and Marxist historiography.

———. "Gli Studi di storia moderna e contemporanea," *Cinquant'anni di vita intellettuale in Italia*. Naples: ESI, 1950. See Vol. I, p. 273 for a discussion of Gramsci's views on Jacobinism.

Mautino, Aldo. La formazione della filosofia politica di Benedetto Croce. Edited by Norberto Bobbio, with a study of the author and the Turinese cultural tradition from Gobetti to the Resistance by G. Solari. Bari: Laterza, 1953. The "study" deals with that "tradition of political intransigence and militant culture characteristic of the University of Turin, which was the heritage of Gobetti and Gramsci."

McInnes, Neil. "Antonio Gramsci," *Survey: A Journal of Soviet and East European Studies*, 53 (Oct. 1964), 3–15. A general article on Gramsci's thought, perhaps best characterized as sympathetic criticism.

McKenzie, Kermit E. "The Communist International (Comintern)," pp. 942–77 in *Soviet Foreign Relations and World Communism*. Thomas T. Hammond, editor. Princeton, N.J.: Princeton University Press, 1965. An extensive annotated bibliography.

"Mentre si apre il Congresso Socialista," *Ordine nuovo* (daily), I, 15 (15.i.21). A report on the political maneuvers immediately before the opening of the Congress of Livorno.

Merli, Stefano, ed. "Nuova Documentazione sulla 'svolta' nella direzione del PCd'I nel 1923–24 (Scritti inediti o non noti di A. Bordiga, U. Terracini, P. Tresso, A. Gramsci, P. Togliatti)," *Rivista storica del socialismo*, VII, 23 (Sept.–Dec. 1964), 513–40. See especially Amadeo Bordiga, "Manifesto ai compagni del PCd'I"; Gramsci, "Il Problema di Milano"; and Palmiro Togliatti et al, "Verbale della riunione del Comitato centrale del 18 aprile 1924."

———. "Le Origini della direzione centrista nel Partito comunista d'Italia," *Rivista storica del socialismo*, VII, 23 (Sept.–Dec. 1964), 605–25.

———. "Il Partito comunista italiano, 1921–1926 (Contributi bibliografici)," *Annali Feltrinelli*, III (1960), pp. 656–739. An excellent bibliography of sources for the early history of the PCI.

Michels, Roberto. Il Proletariato e la borghesia nel movimento socialista italiano. Turin: Fratelli Bocca, 1908.

Mondolfo, Rodolfo. Intorno a Gramsci e alla filosofia della prassi. Milan: Ed. "Critica Sociale," 1955. Preface by Enrico Bassi.

Montagnana, Mario. Ricordi di un operaio torinese. Rome: Edizioni Rinascita, 1952.

Monticone, Alberto. "Il Socialismo torinese ed i fatti dell'agosto 1917," *Rassegna storica del Risorgimento italiano*, XLV, 1 (Jan.–Mar. 1958), 57–96.

Moore, Stanley. Three Tactics: The Background in Marx. New York: Monthly Review Press, 1963.

Morandi, Carlo. "Per una storia degli italiani fuori d'Italia (A proposito di alcune note di Antonio Gramsci)," *Rivista storica italiana*, LXI, 3 (Sept. 1949), 379–84.

Morandi, Rodolfo. Storia della grande industria in Italia. Bari: Laterza, 1931.

"More about Gramsci," *Times Literary Supplement*, LI (5.xii.52), 796.

Morpurgo Tagliabue, Guido. "Gramsci tra Croce e Marx," *Il Ponte*, IV, 5 (May 1948), 429–38.

———. "Il Pensiero di Gramsci e il marxismo sovietico," *Rassegna d'Italia*, III (July–Aug. 1948), 779–85 and 879–86.

Muratori, Giulio. Review of Gramsci's *Works*, vols. I and II in *Science and Society*, XIII (Winter 1948–49), 79–81.

Mussolini, Benito. "Altarini," pp. 44–45 in *Opera omnia di Benito Mussolini*, *XXIX*. Florence: La Fenice, 1959. A reference to the article by Ezio Taddei (q.v.).

———. "Per la vera pacificazione," pp. 290–91 in *Opera omnia di Benito Mussolini*, *XVII*. Florence: La Fenice, 1955.

"Nel X° anniversario dei 'fatti di agosto,'" *Stato operaio*, I, 8 (1927), 635–40.

"Nel X° anniversario dell'occupazione delle fabbriche," *Stato operaio*, IV (1930), 635–55, 717–38.

Nenni, Pietro. Storia di quattro anni. Rome: Einaudi, 1946. Second edition. A history of the years after World War I, containing many valuable documents.

Neufeld, Maurice F. Italy: School for Awakening Countries; The Italian Labor Movement in Its Political, Social, and Economic Setting from 1800 to 1960. Ithaca, N.Y.: N. Y. School of Industrial and Labor Relations, 1961.

———. Labor Unions and National Politics in Italian Industrial Plants (Cornell International Industrial and Labor Relations Reports, no. 1). Ithaca, N.Y.: Cornell University Press, 1954. Contains some material on Gramsci and the factory councils.

Neumann, Franz. Behemoth: The Structure and Practice of National Socialism. London: Victor Gollancz, 1943.

Niccolini, G. "L'Intransigenza di Serrati (A proposito del III° Congresso dell'Internazionale comunista)," *Ordine nuovo*, II, 16 & 19 (2,30.x.20).

Noaro, Jean. "La Vie, la mort et le triomphe d'Antoine Gramsci," *La Pensée*, n.v., 50 (Sept.–Oct. 1953), 74–87.

Noether, Emiliana Pasca. "Italy Reviews Its Fascist Past: A Bibliographical Essay," *American Historical Review*, LXI, 4 (July 1956), 877–99.

Nolte, Ernst. Three Faces of Fascism: Action Française, Italian Fascism, National Socialism. Translated from the German by Leila Vennewitz. New York: Holt, Rinehart, and Winston, 1966. See p. 166, on the influence of liberalism on Gramsci.

Onofri, Fabrizio. "La Via sovietica (leninista) alla conquista del potere e la via italiana, aperta da Gramsci," in his *Classe operaia e partito*. Bari: Laterza, 1957.

"L'Origine e l'organizzazione del Partito comunista," *Ordine nuovo* (daily), I, 25 (25.i.21). Directions for organizing the Party sections.

Ottino, Carlo L. Concetti fondamentali nella teoria politica di Antonio Gramsci. Milan: Feltrinelli, 1956.

Page, Thomas Nelson. Italy and the World War. New York: Scribner's, 1920.

"La Parola della Terza Internazionale," *Ordine nuovo* (daily), I, 13 (13.i.21). The Comintern telegram to the Italian Communists condemning the unitarian position.

Paris, Robert. Histoire du fascisme en Italie. I: Dès origines à la prise du pouvoir. Paris: François Maspero, 1962.

―――. "Una Revisione 'nenniana' di Antonio Gramsci," *Rivista storica del socialismo*, VII, 21 (Jan.–Apr. 1964), 1–20.

Partito Socialista Italiano. Lettere e polemiche fra l'Internazionale comunista, il Partito socialista e la Confederazione generale del lavoro d'Italia. Milan: Società editrice Avanti!, 1921.

Il Partito socialista italiano nei suoi congressi. Volume II: *1902–1917*. Volume III: *1917–1926*. Milan: Avanti!, 1961–63.

Peck, George T. "Giovanni Giolitti and the Fall of Italian Democracy, 1919–1922." Unpublished Ph.D. dissertation, University of Chicago, 1945.

Pedrazzi, Orazio. La Sardegna e i suoi problemi. Milan: Treves, 1922.

Petri, Carlo. "Comunismo anarchico e comunismo critico," *Ordine nuovo*, I, 43 (3–10.iv.20).

Pieri, Piero. "La Leggenda di Caporetto," *Il Ponte*, VII, 11 (Nov. 1951), 1450–56.

Pischel, Giuliano. Review of Gramsci's *Opere, IX*, in *Il Ponte*, XI, 6 (June 1955), 916–20.

Platone, Felice. "Opere di Gramsci," *Dizionario letterario Bompiano*, vol. V, pp. 234–36. Milan: Bompiani, 1948.

―――. "L'Ordine Nuovo," in *Trenta Anni di storia e di lotta del PCI*, pp. 35–40. Rome: Rinascita, 1951.

―――. "Relazione sui Quaderni del carcere," *Rinascita*, III, 4 (Apr. 1946).

Prato, Giuseppe. Il Piemonte e gli effetti della guerra sulla sua vita economica e sociale. ("Pubblicazioni della Fondazione Carnegie per la Pace Internazionale"). Bari: Laterza, 1925.

"Preparando il Congresso," *Comunismo*, II, 4 (15–30.xi.20), 177–89. Contains preliminary motions of all the factions later present at Livorno. Commentary on the motions was undoubtedly written by Serrati.

Prezzolini, Giuseppe. L'Italiano inutile: Memorie letterarie di Francia, Italia e America. Milan: Longanesi, 1953.

Procacci, Giuliano. "La Classe operaia italiana agli inizi del secolo XX," *Studi storici*, III, 1 (Jan.–Mar. 1962), 3–76.

———. "L'Internazionale comunista dal I al VII Congresso, 1919–1935," *Annali Feltrinelli, 1958*, pp. 283–313. A bibliography.

Proceedings of the Congress of Livorno, in *Ordine nuovo* (daily), I, 16–22 (16–22.i.21).

"Progetto di programma per il Partito comunista," *Ordine nuovo* (daily), I, 14 (14.i.21). A statement of the principles upon which the new Party would be built.

Prouteau, Henri. Les Occupations d'usines en Italie et en France (Thèse pour le doctorat en droit). Paris: Librairie Technique et Economique, 1937.

Pugliese, Guido. Il Bolscevismo in Italia. Florence: Bemporad, 1920. Includes the Gennari-Regent-Baldesi motion on the constitution of "Soviety."

"Quindici Mesi di attività del PSI," *Ordine nuovo* (daily), I, 14 (14.i.21). A summary of the report of the Party directorate to the Congress of Livorno.

Rassegna enciclopedica Labor 1935–1951. Milan: Edizioni Labor, 1951.

Ravera, Camilla. "La Lettera di Camilla Ravera a Ercoli (Togliatti)," *Rinascita*, XXI, 48 (5.xii.64), 21–25. A description of Gramsci's arrest and the situation of the Party at that time.

———. "Torino, 1914–1917: Pane e pace," *Rinascita*, XVIII, 3 (Mar. 1961), 238–44.

Répaci, Leonida. Ricordo di Gramsci. Rome: Macchia, 1948.

Resoconto stenografico del XVII Congresso nazionale del Partito socialista italiano, Livorno 15–20 gennaio 1921. Con l'aggiunta dei documenti sulla fondazione del Partito comunista d'Italia. Milan: Avanti!, 1962.

Richet, Denis. "Gramsci et l'histoire de France," *La Pensée*, n.s., 55 (1954), 61–78.

Rigola, Rinaldo. Storia del movimento operaio italiano. Milan: Domus, 1947.

Rizzo, Franco. Nazionalismo e democrazia. Manduria-Bari-Perugia: Lacaita, 1960. See especially the essays "Storiografia marxista sulle origini del fascismo," "Antonio Gramsci e la critica desanctisiana," and "Le 'Lettere dal carcere' di Antonio Gramsci."

Rolland, Romain. "For those Dying in Mussolini's Jails. Antonio Gramsci," pp. 307–13 in *I Will Not Rest*. New York: Liveright Publishing Company, n.d. A translation from *Antonio Gramsci. Ceux Qui Meurent dans les Prisons de Mussolini*. Paris: Les Editeurs du S.R.I., 1934.

Romano, Aldo. "Antonio Gramsci tra la guerra e la rivoluzione," *Rivista storica del socialismo*, I, 1 (1958), 405–42.

Romano, Salvatore Francesco. Antonio Gramsci. Turin: UTET, 1965. This work appeared too late for extensive use by the present writer except in Chapter One, which does take account of Romano's interesting material on Gramsci's childhood and youth in Sardinia.

Romeo, Rosario. "Capitalismo e disonestà scientifica: ovvero del senatore Emilio Sereni," *Nord e Sud,* VI, 59 (1959), 70–85.

———. Risorgimento e capitalismo. Bari: Laterza, 1959.

Rosmer, Alfred. Le Mouvement ouvrier pendant la Guerre. Volume I: De l'Union Sacrée à Zimmerwald. Paris: Librairie du Travail, 1936.

———. Le Mouvement ouvrier pendant la Première Guerre Mondiale. Volume II. De Zimmerwald à la Révolution Russe. Paris: Mouton, 1959.

Rossi, Cesare. Il Tribunale speciale. Milan: Ceschina, 1952.

Rossi, Vittorio. Storia della letteratura italiana. Volume III. 15th edition. Milan: Vallardi, 1946.

Rossi-Doria, Manlio. "The Land Tenure System and Class in Southern Italy," *American Historical Review,* LXIV, 1 (Oct. 1958), 46–53.

"Russia e Internazionale," *Ordine nuovo* (daily), I, 9 (9.i.21). An editorial probably written by Gramsci.

Russo, Luigi. "Gramsci e l'educazione democratica," in *De vera religione.* Turin: Einaudi, 1949.

Salinari, Carlo. "Letteratura e vita nazionale nel pensiero di Gramsci," *Rinascita,* VIII, 2 (Feb. 1951), 85–88.

———. Storia popolare della letteratura italiana. Volume III. Rome: Ed. Riuniti, 1962.

Salomone, A. William. Italian Democracy in the Making: The Political Scene in the Giolittian Era, 1900–1914. Philadelphia: University of Pennsylvania Press, 1945. Second edition, with an additional section "Giolittian Italy Revisited," entitled: Italy in the Giolittian Era: Italian Democracy in the Making, 1900–1914. Philadelphia: University of Pennsylvania Press, 1960.

———. "The *Risorgimento* between Ideology and History: The Political Myth of *rivoluzione mancata,*" *American Historical Review,* LXVIII, 1 (Oct. 1962), 38–56.

Salvatorelli, Luigi, and Giovanni Mira. Storia del Fascismo: L'Italia dal 1919 al 1945. Rome: Edizioni Novissimi, 1952. New Edition: Storia d'Italia nel periodo fascista. Turin: Einaudi, 1957. A standard work.

Salvemini, Gaetano. Scritti sul fascismo. Volume I. Milan: Feltrinelli, 1961.

———. Scritti sulla questione meridionale. Turin: Einaudi, 1955.

Santarelli, Enzo. "Regioni e regionalismo nel pensiero di Gramsci," *Rinascita,* XIV, 6 (June 1957), 304–7.

———. La Revisione del marxismo in Italia. Milan: Feltrinelli, 1964. See especially the chapters on Sorel and Bordiga.

———. Il Socialismo anarchico in Italia. Milan: Feltrinelli, 1959.

Santhià, Battista. Con Gramsci all'Ordine Nuovo. Rome: Ed. Riuniti, 1956. See the review of this work by Antonino Repaci in *Movimento di liberazione in Italia,* 43 (July 1956), 59–61.

Santoli, Vittorio. "Antonio Gramsci, scrittore," *Il Ponte*, III, 8–9 (Aug.–Sept. 1947), 788–800. A general work despite the title.

———. "Tre Osservazioni su Gramsci e il folclore," *Società*, VII (Sept. 1951), 389–97.

Scalia, Gianni. "Il Giovane Gramsci," *Passato e presente*, 9 (May–June 1959), 1132–70.

Schneider, Herbert W. Making the Fascist State. New York: Oxford University Press, 1928. Still a useful work, especially for its many documents of early Fascism.

Seassaro, Cesare. "I Dibattiti sul Congresso: I sistemi polemici di G. M. Serrati," *Ordine nuovo* (daily), I, 13 (13.i.21).

Secchia, Pietro. "Giacinto Menotti Serrati (Ricerche e ricordi)," *Movimento operaio*, VI, 4 (July–Aug. 1954), 590–628.

The Second Congress of the Communist International as Reported and Interpreted by the Official Newspapers of Soviet Russia, Petrograd-Moscow July 19–August 7, 1920. Washington: Government Printing Office, 1920.

Sereni, Emilio. "Antonio Gramsci e la scienza d'avanguardia," *Società*, IV (Jan.–Mar. 1948), 3–30.

———. "Mercato nazionale e accumulazione capitalistica nella unità italiana," *Studi storici*, I, 3 (Apr.–June 1960), 513–68.

Serge, Victor. Memoirs of a Revolutionary, 1901–1941. Translated and edited by Peter Sedgwick. London: Oxford University Press, 1963. See especially the portrait of Gramsci on pp. 186–87.

Serrati, Giacinto Menotti. "Di alcune nostre ragioni," *Comunismo*, II, 6 (15–31.xii.20), 305–11.

———. "Documentazione unitaria," *Comunismo*, II, 10 and 11 (Feb. 15–28 and Mar. 1–15, 1921), 536–50, 598–604.

———. "Il Dovere dell'ora presente," *Comunismo*, II, 1 (1–15.x.20), 1–4.

———. "La Quindicina politica," *Comunismo*, II, 2–3 (Oct. 15–Nov. 15, 1920), 172–76.

———. "Risposta di un comunista unitario al compagno Lenin," *Comunismo*, II, 5 (1–15.xii.20), 249–56.

Seton-Watson, Hugh. From Lenin to Khrushchev: The History of World Communism. New York: Praeger, 1960.

"La Sezione socialista e il Congresso: tre rappresentanti comunisti ed uno unitario," *Ordine nuovo* (daily), I, 5 (5.i.21). On the selection of representatives from the Turin section to the Congress of Livorno.

Sforza, Count Carlo. Contemporary Italy: Its Intellectual and Moral Origins. Translated by Drake and Denise De Kay. New York: Dutton, 1944.

Silone, Ignazio. Der Faschismus, seine Entstehung und seine Entwicklung. Zurich: Europa Verlag, 1934.

Soave, Emilio. "Appunti sulle origini teoriche e pratiche dei Consigli di fabbrica a Torino," *Rivista storica del socialismo*, VII, 21 (Jan.–Apr. 1964), 1–20.

Soboul, Albert. "Risorgimento et Révolution bourgeoise," *La Pensée*, 95 (Jan.-Feb. 1961), 63-73.

Sorel, Georges. "Sindacati e soviet," *Ordine nuovo*, I, 26 (15.xi.20).

Spano, Velio. "Il Congresso di Lione. Per la storia del PCI," *Rinascita*, XII, 4 (Apr. 1956), 235-40.

Spinelli, Mario. "Nuovi Dati per lo studio di Gramsci," *Società*, XVI, 3 (May-June 1960), 487-92.

Spriano, Paolo. "A proposito della lettera di Antonio Gramsci a Giuseppe Lombardo Radice," *Rinascita*, XXI, 13 (28.iii.64), 28.

———. "I Consigli di fabbrica," *Rinascita*, XX, 3 (19.i.63), 3-5.

———. "Il Dibattito tra il 'Soviet' e 'L'Ordine Nuovo.'" *Rinascita*, XVIII, 1 (Jan. 1961), 41-51.

———. L'Occupazione delle fabbriche, settembre, 1920. Turin: Einaudi, 1964.

———, ed. "L'Ordine Nuovo," 1919-1920 ("La Cultura italiana attraverso le riviste, VI"). Turin: Einaudi, 1963. An anthology of articles from the Turinese weekly, mainly by authors other than Gramsci. Spriano's long introduction is very informative.

———. Socialismo e classe operaia a Torino dal 1892 al 1913. Turin: Einaudi, 1958.

———. "Sul rapporto di Athos Lisa: Il cazzotto nell'occhio," *Rinascita*, XXII, 3 (16.i.65), 31.

———. Torino operaia nella grande guerra (1914-1918). Turin: Einaudi, 1960.

Sprigge, Cecil. Benedetto Croce: Man and Thinker. New Haven, Conn.: Yale University Press, 1952. On pp. 52-53, Sprigge refers to Gramsci's work as "the most impressive study of Croce as an historical figure."

"Stato attuale dell'edizione degli scritti di Gramsci," *Rinascita*, XIV, 6 (June 1957), 307.

"Statuto del Partito comunista d'Italia," *Ordine nuovo* (daily), I, 41 (10.-ii.21). The Constitution of the PCI.

Studi gramsciani: Atti del convegno tenuto a Roma nei giorni 11-13 gennaio 1958. Compiled by the Istituto Antonio Gramsci. Rome: Ed. Riuniti, 1958. See especially the following studies: Serafino Cambereri, "Il Concetto di egemonia nel pensiero di Gramsci"; Alberto Caracciolo, "A Proposito di Gramsci, la Russia e il movimento bolscevico"; Giuseppe Tamburrano, "Gramsci e l'egemonia del proletariato"; Aldo Zanardo, "Il 'Manuale' di Bukharin visto dai comunisti tedeschi e da Gramsci"; Renato Zangheri, "La Mancata Rivoluzione agraria nel Risorgimento e i problemi economici dell'unità"; Eugenio Garin, "Gramsci nella cultura italiana"; Palmiro Togliatti, "Gramsci e il leninismo"; and the "Interventi" of Gastone Manacorda and Giorgio Candeloro.

"Sulla strada di Gramsci," *Vie nuove*, XII, 3 (19.i.57), 4-11. An article containing many interesting photographs, as well as two previously unpublished letters by Gramsci, written to his parents in 1909 or 1910.

Sworakowski, Witold S. The Communist International and Its Front Orga-
nizations: A Research Guide and Checklist of Holdings in American
and European Libraries. Stanford, Calif.: The Hoover Institution on
War, Revolution, and Peace, 1965.
Taddei, Ezio. "Di ritorno," L'Adunata dei Refrattari (New York), XVI, 48
(4.xii.37). Taddei, an anarchist, was imprisoned for a time at Turi.
He was most unfavorably impressed with Gramsci.
Talamo, Giuseppe. "La Prima Guerra d'indipendenza," in the Storia d'Ita-
lia. Volume III. Turin: UTET, 1959.
Tamburrano, Giuseppe. Antonio Gramsci. Manduria-Bari-Perugia: Lacaita,
1963.
Tasca, Angelo. "Cercando la verità," Ordine nuovo, II, 5 (12.vi.20).
————. I Consigli di fabbrica e la rivoluzione mondiale: Relazione letta
all'assemblea della sezione socialista la sera del 13 aprile, 1920. Turin:
Alleanza coop. torinese, 1921.
————. Nascita e avvento del fascismo: Italia dal 1918 al 1922. Florence:
La Nuova Italia, 1950. A standard work.
————. "Polemiche sul programma dell'Ordine nuovo," Ordine nuovo, II,
5 and 6 (12, 19.vi.20), and II, 8 (3.vii.20).
————. "I Primi Dieci Anni del Partito comunista italiano," Il Mondo, V,
33–38 (Aug. 18–Sept. 22, 1953). The titles of the separate articles are:
"La Storia e la preistoria," 33 (18.viii), 3–4; "L'Ordine Nuovo," 34
(25.viii), 5; "Comunismo e fascismo," 35 (1.ix), 9–10; "Ordinovisti e
bordighisti," 36 (8.ix), 9–10; "La Direzione clandestina," 37 (15.ix),
9–10; "La Nuova politica," 38 (22.ix), 9–10.
————. "I Valori politici e sindacali dei Consigli di fabbrica," Ordine
nuovo, II, 3 (29.v.20).
"La Tattica del fronte unico di lotta contro il fascismo in una iniziativa
del Partito comunista d'Italia: Le elezioni truffa dell'aprile 1924, e la
proposta comunista di un blocco di unità proletaria," Rinascita, XX,
3 (19.i.63), 17–19.
"La Tattica del fronte unico di lotta contro il fascismo . . . : Le elezioni del
1924," Rinascita, XX, 5 (2.ii.63), 17–20.
Terracini, Umberto. "Antonio Gramsci e gli operai torinesi," Il Ponte, V,
7–8 (Aug.–Sept. 1949), 1033–38.
————. "Il Consiglio nazionale di Firenze," Ordine nuovo, I, 35 (24–
31.i.20).
————. "Il Discorso di Umberto Terracini al Congresso di Livorno del PSI
(gennaio 1921)," Rinascita, XIX, 25–26 (Oct. 27, Nov. 3, 1962), 17–20,
17–20.
————. "Gramsci e i consigli di fabbrica," Calendario del popolo, XI, 125
(Feb. 1955), 1931.
————. "Gramsci e l'Ordine Nuovo nel tempestoso biennio '19–'21: Matura
lo scontro decisivo nel caos dell'immediato dopoguerra," Calendario
del popolo, XI, 124 (Jan. 1955), 1906.

———. "Perchè è sorto il Partito comunista," *Ordine nuovo* (daily), I, 51 (21.ii.21).

"La III³ Internazionale al Partito comunista d'Italia," *Ordine nuovo* (daily), I, 33 (2.ii.21). Contains a telegram from the International recognizing the PCI as the sole representative of the Italian proletariat in the International.

Togliatti, Palmiro. "Alcuni Problemi della storia dell'Internazionale comunista," *Rinascita*, XVI, 7–8 (July–Aug. 1959), 467–81.

———. "A Proposito dello scambio di lettere tra Gramsci e Togliatti," *Rinascita*, XXI, 24 (13.vi.64), 24.

———. "Che Avverrà?" *Ordine nuovo* (daily), I, 22 (22.i.21). This commentary on the founding of the PCI, though unsigned, was written by Togliatti according to Ferrara and Ferrara, *Conversando con Togliatti*, p. 88.

———. "Il Discorso di Ercole al VI Congresso Internazionale: Classe operaia e fascismo nell'Europa del 1928," *Rinascita*, XXI, 28 (11.vii.64), 15–20.

———. "Fascisti e popolari nel 1922–1923," *Rinascita*, XX, 12 (23.iii.63), 17–19. A republication of three articles written in 1922–23.

———. La Formazione del gruppo dirigente del PCI nel 1923–1924. Rome: Ed. Riuniti, 1962. See p. 260, n. 1 for information on this book.

———, et al. Gramsci. Rome: Edizioni Rinascita, 1948. A collection of commemorative articles by many of Gramsci's former comrades.

———. Gramsci. Florence: Parenti, 1955. A collection of his articles and addresses on Gramsci.

———. "Gramsci sardo," *Il Ponte*, VII, 9–10 (Sept.–Oct. 1951), 1085–88.

———. "Il Leninismo nel pensiero e nell'azione di Antonio Gramsci (Appunti per la relazione al convegno di studi gramsciani)," *Rinascita*, XV, 2 (Feb. 1958), 109–16. The speech itself is in *Studi gramsciani*, pp. 418–44 and in *Rinascita*, XV, 3 (Mar. 1958), 181–90.

———. Momenti della storia d'Italia. Rome: Ed. Riuniti, 1963. A collection of articles and speeches. For the purposes of this book, the most important items are: "Serrati," "Discorso su Giolitti," "Appunti e schema per una storia del Partito comunista italiano," and "L'Antifascismo di Antonio Gramsci." The last essay is also in Togliatti's *Gramsci* (1955), listed above.

———. "Parassiti della cultura (a proposito di *Energie nuove*)," *Ordine nuovo*, I, 2 (15.v.19).

———. Il Partito comunista italiano. Milan: Nuova Accademia, 1958.

———. "Rapporto sul fascismo per il IV Congresso dell'Internazionale (1922)," *Rinascita*, XIX, 30–31 (1, 8.xii.62), 17–20, 17–20.

———. "Rapporto sui fatti di Sestri," *Ordine nuovo*, I, 40 (13.iii.20). Probably written with Andrea Viglongo.

———, ed. Trenta Anni di vita e di lotte del PCI ("Quaderni di Rinascita, 2"). Rome: Ed. Rinascita, 1952. The most extensive history of the PCI.

Tosi, Dario. "Sulle forme iniziali di sviluppo economico e i loro effetti nel lungo periodo: l'agricoltura italiana e l'accumulazione capitalistica," *Annali Feltrinelli*, IV (1961), 199–222.

Trent'Anni di storia italiana (1915–1945). Lezioni con testimonianze presentate da Franco Antonicelli. Turin: Einaudi, 1961. See especially the main addresses by Paolo Alatri and Lelio Basso and the "testimonials" by Giovanni Parodi, Maurizio Garino, Gino Castagno, Umberto Terracini, Franco Antonicelli, Ottavio Pastore, Barbara Allason, Mauro Scoccimarro, and Camilla Ravera.

Trent'Anni di storia politica italiana (1915–1945). Turin: ERI Edizioni della RAI, 1962. See especially the speeches by Gino Luzzatto, Augusto Monti, and Gaetano Arfè.

Trevisani, Giulio, ed. Piccola Enciclopedia del socialismo e del comunismo. 4th edition. Milan: Soc. ed. de "Il Calendario del popolo," 1958–62. 2 vols. Despite its excessive dogmatism, this is a useful work.

———. "La Stampa comunista anteriore all'avvento del fascismo," *Movimento operaio*, II (Feb.–Mar. 1950), 180.

Trombetti, Gustavo. "In cella con la matricola 7047 (detenuto politico A. Gramsci)," *Rinascita*, III, 9 (Sept. 1946), 233–35.

———. " 'Piantone' di Gramsci nel carcere di Turi," *Rinascita*, XXII, 18 (1.v.65), 31.

"L'Unità del Partito," *Ordine nuovo*, I, 22 (18.x.19). A demand for the unity of all groups in the PSI. Probably written by Angelo Tasca.

Valeri, Nino, ed. Antologia della "Rivoluzione Liberale." Turin: Francesco De Silva, 1948. A selection of articles from Piero Gobetti's Turinese weekly.

———. Da Giolitti a Mussolini: Momenti della crisi del liberalismo. Florence: Parenti, 1956.

———. "Gramsci, 1919–1920," *Il Mondo*, VI, 45 (9.xi.54), 1–2.

Valiani, Leo. Histoire du Socialisme au XXᵉ Siècle. Paris: Editions Nagel, 1948.

———. "La Storia del movimento socialista in Italia dalle origini al 1921; studi e ricerche nel decennio 1945–1955," *Rivista storica italiana*, LXVIII, 3–4 (1956), 447–510, 620–69. A large analytical bibliography.

"Vigilia di Congresso," *Ordine nuovo* (daily), I, 14 (14.i.21). Written from Livorno on the political situation just before the Congress.

Vigorelli, Giancarlo. "Gramsci e Togliatti," *Rassegna di politica e di storia*, I, 10 (Aug. 1955), 27–32.

Villari, Luigi. Italian Life in Town and Country. New York: Putnam, 1902.

Violante, Cinzio. "Storia ed economia dell'Italia medioevale," *Rivista storica italiana*, LXXIII, 3 (1961), 513–35. On Gramsci's idea of the role of Italians abroad, which influenced Morandi, Procacci, Cantimori, Verlinden, and Melis.

Vita di un italiano. 60° compleanno di Palmiro Togliatti. Edited by S. Scuderi. Rome: Ed. di Cultura sociale, 1953. A volume of photographs depicting Togliatti's life. Many of the photographs pertain to the Ordine Nuovo period and the first years of Italian Communism.

Webster, Richard A. The Cross and the Fasces. Stanford, Calif.: Stanford University Press, 1960. A history of Christian Democracy in Italy from 1860 to 1960.

——. "From Insurrection to Intervention: The Italian Crisis of 1914," *Italian Quarterly*, V–VI, 20–21 (Winter 1961–Spring 1962), 27–50.

——. "Autarchy, Expansion, and the Underlying Continuity of the Italian State," *Italian Quarterly*, VIII, 32 (Winter 1964), 3–27.

Williams, Gwynn A. "Gramsci's Concept of *Egemonia*," *Journal of the History of Ideas*, XXI, 4 (Oct.–Dec. 1960), 586–99.

Zamis, Guido. "Gramsci a Vienna nel 1924," *Rinascita*, XXI, 47 (28.xi.64), 22–23.

Zibordi, Giovanni. Storia del Partito socialista italiano attraverso i suoi congressi. Reggio Emilia: La Giustizia, n.d. By a reformist.

Zucaro, Domenico. "Antonio Gramsci all'Università di Torino, 1911–1915," *Società*, XIII, 6 (Dec. 1957), 1091–1111.

——. Il Processone. Rome: Ed. Riuniti, 1961. Gramsci's trial by the Special Tribunal.

——. Review of Lombardo Radice and Carbone, *Vita di Antonio Gramsci*, in *Movimento operaio*, IV (July–Aug. 1952), 702–5. This review disclosed new information concerning Gramsci's earlier years in Turin.

——. "La Rivolta di Torino del 1917 nella sentenza del Tribunale militare territoriale," *Rivista storica del socialismo*, III, 10 (May–Aug. 1960), 437–69.

——. Vita del carcere di Antonio Gramsci. Milan: Avanti!, 1954. With an appendix of 15 documents.

Index